Multimedia Applications

Even if you're not a gamer, there's still plenty for you here. The chapters in Part III show how to use the CD-ROM's Multimedia and Switch OCX controls to work with a variety of multimedia devices.

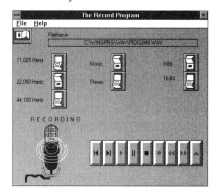

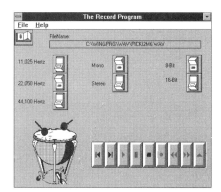

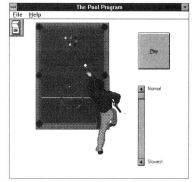

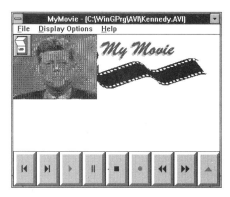

The WAVInfo program lets you play WAV files and see their recording characteristics; the Record program lets you record and save your own WAV files; the Pool program lets you play MIDI files (as a background to an animation clip) and control their tempo; MyMovie lets you play AVI movie files; and the MyCD program lets you play audio CDs.

The WinG Bible:
For Visual Basic 4
Programmers

Nathan Gurewich
and
Ori Gurewich

SYBEX®

San Francisco • Paris • Düsseldorf • Soest

Acquisitions Manager: Kristine Plachy
Developmental Editor: Jane Reh
Editor: James A. Compton
Technical Editor: Ricardo Birmele
Book Designer: Suzanne Albertson
Technical Artist: Cuong Le
Desktop Publishers: Stephanie Hollier and Deborah A. Bevilacqua
Proofreader/Production Assistant: Renée Avalos
Indexer: Matthew Spence
Cover Designer: Design Site
Cover Illustrator: Mike Miller

Library of Congress Card Number: 9569362
ISBN: 0-7821-1727-9

Manufactured in the United States of America

10 9 8 7 6 5 4 3 2 1

Warranty

SYBEX warrants the enclosed CD-ROM to be free of physical defects for a period of ninety (90) days after purchase. If you discover a defect in the CD during this warranty period, you can obtain a replacement CD at no charge by sending the defective CD, postage prepaid, with proof of purchase to:

SYBEX Inc.
Customer Service Department
2021 Challenger Drive
Alameda, CA 94501
(800)227-2346
Fax: (510) 523-2373

After the 90-day period, you can obtain a replacement CD by sending us the defective CD, proof of purchase, and a check or money order for $10, payable to SYBEX.

Disclaimer

SYBEX makes no warranty or representation, either express or implied, with respect to this medium or its contents, its quality, performance, merchantability, or fitness for a particular purpose. In no event will SYBEX, its distributors, or dealers be liable for direct, indirect, special, incidental, or consequential damages arising out of the use of or inability to use the software even if advised of the possibility of such damage.

The exclusion of implied warranties is not permitted by some states. Therefore, the above exclusion may not apply to you. This warranty provides you with specific legal rights; there may be other rights that you may have that vary from state to state.

Copy Protection

None of the programs on the CD is copy-protected. However, in all cases, reselling or making copies of these programs without authorization is expressly forbidden.

Acknowledgments

At Sybex, we would first like to thank Gary Masters, who asked us to write this book.

We would also like to thank Jim Compton at Sybex, the editor of this book, for his superior work and especially for the suggestions he made throughout the evolution of the book.

We would also like to thank Jane Reh at Sybex, who was the developmental editor of this book, and helped us define the book's content and direction.

The following people at Sybex also helped to bring this book to life: Cuong Le rendered the technical illustrations; Stephanie Hollier and Debi Bevilacqua handled the desktop publishing; and Renée Avalos did the proofreading.

We would also like to thank Ricardo Birmele, the technical editor, who executed all the book's programs to verify that they work properly, and also made a number of useful suggestions.

We would also like to thank various companies and people in the software industry who supplied us with beta programs and with technical information regarding Visual Basic, OCX technology, and the use of OCX from within programming languages such as Visual Basic, Visual C++, Borland C++, and others:

- Thanks to the people at TegoSoft Inc., who supplied us with various powerful OCX controls and sample applications.
- Thanks to the people at Microsoft Corporation, who supplied us with a variety of technical information regarding Visual Basic, Windows, and OCX technology. In particular, thanks to Sumeet Shrivastava, Mike Clark, and Steve MacKenzie.
- Thanks to Borland International, Inc., and particularly Nan Borreson, for supplying us with technical information.

CONTENTS AT A GLANCE

TABLE OF CONTENTS

Part III   Multimedia

9 Determining the Multimedia Capabilities of Your PC   143

10 Executing the WinGMult Program   153

35 Creating Your Own World 663

36 Modifying the 3D Floor during Runtime 675

Introduction

In the last decade, PC technology has advanced tremendously. Both the hardware and the software of personal computers are more powerful than ever.

On the hardware side, the CPU of the PC has evolved from the 8086 to the 80286, and then to the 80386, 80486, and now the Pentium.

In terms of software, PC users can use Windows as a graphical operating system (instead of the text-based DOS). Windows itself had been upgraded from a 16-bit to a 32-bit operating system (Windows '95 and Windows NT). Also, visual programming languages such as Visual Basic have been introduced to let programmers develop Windows applications with great ease.

So putting it all together, the PC has become more powerful, and people now expect more from it. As a programmer, you now have all the tools to supply your users with sophisticated and powerful Windows programs. Among the features your users expect are multimedia capability, animation, and 3D virtual reality programs. Until recently, however, the PC could not perform fast graphics operations under Windows. Why? Because Windows was designed to display only static graphics, such as pushbuttons. It could not display 3D pictures and let the user "move" within the 3D environment at a speed that users find acceptable. This is why some of the most sophisticated games programs are available only for DOS and not for Windows.

To overcome this limitation of Windows, Microsoft has released the WinG library, a toolkit that enhances the graphics capabilities of Windows.

In this book you'll learn how to incorporate multimedia technology, animation technology, and graphics technology into your Windows programs. Thanks to the use of WinG technology, the Windows/WinG programs that you'll write will perform very fast.

You'll write the programs using the Visual Basic for Windows programming language (version 4.0 or above). Why was Visual Basic selected for writing these programs? Because as you'll see during the course of this book, you'll be able to write some very powerful and sophisticated programs in a very short time. The Visual

Basic programs that you'll write in this book will perform as fast as programs written in other programming languages (for example, Visual C++ or Borland C++), because these Visual Basic programs use OCX technology (provided on the companion CD-ROM). The OCX controls you'll incorporate into the programs were written with programming languages such as Visual C++. So the bottom line is that the Visual Basic programs that you write will perform as well as if they were written with Visual C++, for example. But it takes much less time to implement Visual Basic programs than to write the same programs with other programming languages.

The book's companion CD-ROM contains all the software that you'll need during the course of this book—all the WAV, MIDI, BMP, and Movie AVI files, as well as various software such as OCX files, WinG files, and others. All you need is a PC with Windows installed (Windows 3.1x, Windows '95 or Windows NT), and Visual Basic for Windows version 4.0 or above. If you have a sound card, you'll also be able to hear the programs. The CD-ROM also includes the book's EXE programs, so that you can immediately execute the programs and gain a better understanding of what they are supposed to do. And it includes the program source code, so that you can compare your work with the finished programs.

Make sure to read the ReadMe.TXT file, in the CD-ROM's root directory. This file shows you exactly how to install the CD software on your hard drive and provides important copyright information.

WinG, multimedia, animation, and 3D virtual reality are a lot of fun! As you read this book, many new ideas will no doubt come to mind for adding new features, enhancing the features, and writing your own programs. Don't forget to write down these ideas. When you're finished studying a particular project in this book, go ahead and try out your ideas.

PART I

WinG and Visual Basic

ONE

WinG—What Is It
and Who Needs It?

This chapter explains what WinG is all about and why it is a *must* for programmers developing games, multimedia, and other Windows applications that use the monitor extensively.

Programming in Windows vs. DOS

WinG is a software technology that you use in the development of Windows applications. Before going any further, let's examine the reasons why most people are using Windows and not DOS. (In the following discussion, the term *Windows* refers to any of the Windows operating systems: Windows 3.1, Windows for Workgroups 3.11, Windows '95 (Chicago), or Windows NT.)

Device Independence

When writing DOS programs, the programmer must always consider the type of peripheral equipment the application's user will work with. For example, suppose you are developing a DOS program that sends data to the printer.

In this case, your program must accommodate the particular printer in your user's system. If your user has an IBM printer, then your program must send commands to the printer, and these commands must match the technical requirements of this particular printer. Of course IBM markets many printer models, each with specific printer commands; and IBM is not the only manufacturer of printers. The user may have an Epson printer, a Hewlett-Packard printer, or whatever. As a programmer, you must take into account that your user may have any of hundreds of printer models.

In DOS programs the printer problem is typically solved by simply asking the user some questions during installation. That is, your program asks the user to select the name of the printer used; it then "knows" which commands should be sent to the printer during execution.

1

As you can imagine, accommodating many types of printers is a lot of work. The programmer must study many types of printers, poring through their manuals, and then write a lot of code that accommodates all these printers. And guess what? When you are done, you'll probably get calls from a few users, telling you that their printers are not listed in your application's Install program!

When writing Windows applications, however, you do not have to worry at all about the type of printer your application's user will have. When installing Windows on a PC, the user also installs the printer. This printer installation process requires the user to select a printer from a list of printers. Windows also requires a special file called a *driver* for the printer. Each printer has its own unique driver file, supplied on a diskette. At the time of installation, the user inserts this diskette into the A: drive, and Windows copies this file onto the Windows System directory on the hard drive. In many cases, the user does not have to use the disk that comes with the printer, because the driver files are already included with Windows. (That is, the printer manufacturer has supplied the driver file to Microsoft, which includes it on the Windows installation disks or CD-ROM.)

From your point of view, the user simply has a printer, which your program treats like any other printer. The printer commands within your application are the same for *all* printers. It is the responsibility of Windows to translate the commands of your application to the commands of specific printers. What if the driver does not work? It's not your problem. Your application assumes that your user has a good printer and a good driver. If for some reason the driver is not doing its job, Windows should have rejected the driver.

As you can see, using Windows saves the programmer a lot of time. The same principle of device independence applies to other peripherals such as monitors, keyboards, sound cards, joysticks, scanners, mouse devices, CD-ROM drives, and so on. That is, as long as Windows has accepted the device, you can use the device from within your programs, without worrying about its specific requirements.

The Common User Interface

Another major reason for the popularity of Windows—with users as well as programmers—is that all Windows applications have a similar user interface mechanism, known as the Common User Interface (CUA). You can expect your user to know what kind of information an About dialog box contains, how to select a menu, how to check a check box, how to select an option button, how to use a scroll bar, and so on. This means that you don't have to waste time explaining to your user about these CUA mechanisms. Theoretically, even the most complex and complicated Windows application can be shipped without any documentation. Your user should be able to operate the program by "knowing" Windows.

Your User Already Has the Code...

Another reason for the popularity of Windows is that your user already has more than half of your application before you write even a single line of code. For example, your application uses the mouse, but you don't have to supply the corresponding mouse code, because with Windows installed, your user already has all the DLLs and other software that operate the mouse. In a similar way, your code will display menus. But the DLLs that enable Windows to display and operate menus already reside on your user's hard disk, because they are an integral part of Windows.

To summarize, then, when you write a Windows application, you can concentrate on *your* application. Windows has been designed so that you do not have to write code that is already written!

So Why Are So Many Games Written for DOS?

From the above discussion one might conclude that only a masochist would want to write DOS applications when a powerful operating system such as Windows is readily available. So why are *Doom, Wolfenstein 3D,* and so many popular game and multimedia programs written for DOS and not for Windows?

Well, Windows is very good, but until lately, it lacked a very important feature; it does not have the ability to move graphic objects on the screen efficiently. As you know, Windows is sometimes referred to as a graphical operating system. This means that it displays graphic objects such as pushbuttons, check boxes, and so on. But when it comes to moving graphic objects on the screen, Windows is very slow.

As discussed, Windows is designed so that it can use a monitor from within an application in such a way that the programmer does not have to care about the monitor's specific requirements. As long as Windows has accepted the monitor, the monitor is good! But the tradeoff is that operations related to the monitor are *slow*. When you issue drawing commands to the monitor from within your Windows programs, you let Windows translate your commands to the particular monitor that is being used. But this "translation" takes time, and the end result is that Windows displays things on the monitor very slowly. Using Windows for applications such as word processors, spreadsheets, and so on, you will not notice this lack of speed. You may not notice it even with graphic applications that let the user display two-dimensional (2D) and three-dimensional (3D) static graphs and pictures.

The problem arises with applications that must display many pictures in real time. For example, suppose your application has to display animation, which progresses according to user input. It may show a person walking inside a room; and according to the mouse movement, the person walks into different parts of the room. As you can imagine, your application must move the person from one place to another in real time. As the person moves, you also have to display the area of the screen that the person left. For example, suppose the person is sitting on a chair and then gets up. Your application has to show the person standing up, and also show an empty chair. Typically, you want to display the person's actions at a realistic speed. This means that in a very short amount of time you want to:

1. Display the person in a new position.
2. Display the empty chair.

As it turns out, when the pictures of the person, the chair, and other objects in the room are highly detailed (with the resolution you see in a photograph), Windows is too slow to perform these operations. So at this point, you have two choices:

- You can still use Windows, but your end product will look like a movie in a slow motion.
- You can forget about Windows and write the application in an operating system that enables you to move graphic objects on the screen quickly (such as DOS).

DOS is an operating system that lets you move objects on the screen very quickly because your program can directly access the memory that is responsible for displaying pixels on the monitor. So the moment you change a byte in the memory area that corresponds to the monitor, you immediately see the corresponding change on the monitor. You can't perform monitor operations faster than this!

In Windows, you do not have access to the memory that corresponds to the monitor. Your program is very "far" from the actual hardware of the monitor. When you issue a command to change pixels on the screen, Windows goes through various layers of software, and eventually changes the memory that corresponds to the monitor. But this process takes time, and the end result is that you can't display pictures fast enough.

Of course, the applications that most need to display pictures in rapid succession are typically 3D virtual reality (programs that let the user travel inside a 3D picture according to user's actions), games, and multimedia. Many other types of applications require fast monitor operations, but with these applications, speed is particularly critical.

This is why until the introduction of WinG, popular games such as *DOOM* and *Wolfenstein 3D* were written for DOS and not for Windows. (By the way, in this book you'll learn how to write 3D virtual reality programs yourself. As you'll see, you'll write these programs for Windows.)

WinG to the Rescue

As games and multimedia have become more popular, Microsoft realized this limitation of Windows regarding monitor operations. In response, they released a set of libraries known as WinG. As you might have guessed, this software lets you write Windows applications that perform fast monitor operations. (As you'll see in subsequent chapters, the book's CD includes all the software that enables you to use WinG technology.)

So here is the bottom line: thanks to WinG technology, Windows is now capable of performing fast monitor operations, and you can now write 3D virtual reality programs for Windows. That's what this book is all about.

Visual Basic

1

You'll implement the programs of this book using the Visual Basic package. This book assumes that version 4.0 or higher of Visual Basic is used and that you already have the Visual Basic package installed on your PC.

You can install Visual Basic as a 16-bit or a 32-bit system. If you are using 16-bit Windows such as Windows 3.1 or Windows for Workgroups 3.11, you have to install the 16-bit Visual Basic. If you are using a 32-bit Windows such as Windows '95 or Windows NT, then install the 32-bit Visual Basic. This book is applicable to both 16-bit and 32-bit Visual Basic. No matter which version of Visual Basic you are using, the way you write applications is identical. Naturally, there are some minor differences between the 16-bit and 32-bit versions of Visual Basic. For example, the border and the titles of the windows look a little bit different. Also, the dialog boxes that let you select a file are a little different. However, as stated, you can use this book with either version. Naturally, programs generated with the 32-bit Visual Basic are much faster than those generated with the 16-bit version.

The Companion CD-ROM

This book's companion CD-ROM contains the EXE files of the book's programs, so that you can immediately execute the programs and gain a better understanding of what they are supposed to do.

The CD-ROM also contains the source code of the programs. We recommend that you implement the programs by entering this code yourself. However, if you make an error entering the code, you'll be able to compare your work with the source code supplied on the book's CD-ROM.

The CD-ROM also contains various files that are needed for the execution of the programs—BMP picture files, WAV sound files, MIDI synthesized sound files, movie AVI files, and so on. Before attempting to execute the book's programs from the CD-ROM, read the ReadMe.TXT file (discussed under "Installing the CD-ROM" below).

The OCX Controls

One of the main advantages of using Visual Basic for developing Windows applications is that it enables you to use third-party OCX controls. That is, for a reasonable price, you can purchase controls that will save you a lot of programming time. So instead of spending your time writing software that has already been written by others and is readily available, you can concentrate on your own programs by using third-party OCX controls. This is the trend in modern object-oriented programming when you are developing powerful state-of-the-art Windows applications. In this book you'll use various OCX controls that are supplied on the CD-ROM.

For the price of this book, you've bought a powerful set of programming tools that you'll use over and over again in your own multimedia applications.

Installing the CD-ROM

The root directory of the CD-ROM includes a file named ReadMe.TXT, which tells you how to install the CD. It is essential that you read the ReadMe.TXT file, because it contains important information regarding the execution of the book's programs. The CD-ROM also includes a directory called License; make sure to read the software license agreements in this directory.

Developing Games, Multimedia, and WinG Programs Is Fun...

The programs that you'll develop during the course of this book are multimedia, games, 3D virtual reality, animation, and so on. In other words, these are fun programs. As with any programming language, the only way to master the language is by experimenting with it. This is particularly true when you are developing games, 3D virtual reality, and multimedia applications. In other words, don't be afraid to experiment with the programs. As you develop the book's programs, try doing things differently. Instead of simply asking yourself "what would happen if I change this statement to…," actually perform the experiment and observe the results. Don't forget that you are developing fun programs, and any new ideas that you have may make your programs more interesting and fun.

So relax and prepare yourself for a very pleasant journey.

CHAPTER

TWO

2

WinG, Seeing Is Believing

In this chapter, you'll learn about important topics you should understand before diving into the exciting world of WinG games, 3D virtual reality, and multimedia applications for Windows. You'll also see how this book is organized, and get a taste of things to come.

Windows—Which One?

Nowadays, when somebody mentions the term "Windows," you need to ask "Which Windows?" There are several Windows operating systems, and they fall into two categories:

1. 16-bit Windows

2. 32-bit Windows

For example, Windows version 3.11 is a 16-bit Windows. Windows for Workgroups version 3.11 is another 16-bit Windows.

Windows NT is an example of a 32-bit Windows. Windows is also a 32-bit Windows.

The Evolution of the Intel 80x86 and Windows

A little history will help explain why Windows is available in both 16-bit and 32-bit versions.

IBM designed its first PC with Intel's 8086 chip as the CPU. Thanks to the popularity of the 8086-based PC, Intel upgraded the chip, and released the 80286 chip. IBM (and many other PC makers) started to build their PCs with a 80286 CPU. Because there were so many 8086-based PCs in the market, Intel designed the 80286 chip so that all the software that ran on the old 8086 could also run on the 80286. In other words, Intel designed the 80286 chip to be *backward compatible*.

And the same goes for the operating system. The same DOS that runs on the 8086 PC still runs on the 80286.

2

Business was good for everybody (Intel, Microsoft, PC vendors, software vendors), and there was enough market to justify the upgrading of the 80286 to the 80386, the 80386 to the 80486, and finally (as of now) to the Pentium.

Throughout the upgrading, each major vendor (Intel, Microsoft, and the software vendors) designed their software to work on as many types of PCs as possible. That is, ideally, a Windows application should work fine on an 80286-based PC, an 80386-based PC, and so on.

The fact that Windows has been designed so that you can run it (and its applications) on both older and newer CPUs is both good and bad. It is good in the sense that no matter what PC the user has, your software will be able to run on it.

However, maintaining backward compatibility has its drawbacks. To enable the new software to run on old CPU technology, the designer of the software has to keep in mind the "lowest common denominator." That is, the newer CPUs can perform tasks faster, because they can use the 32-bit bus (transferring 32 bits simultaneously). By contrast, the older PCs are only capable of transferring 16 bits at a time.

So the bottom line is that a program designed to work on both 16-bit and 32-bit PCs must be written as 16-bit software, because if it were written as 32-bit software, 16-bit CPUs would not be able to execute it. This penalizes the users of 32-bit PCs, who have to use 16-bit software even though their hardware can run 32-bit software.

Well, enough is enough! Microsoft has decided to release a 32-bit Windows operating system that will work only on hardware capable of executing 32-bit software.

As previously stated, Windows 3.11 is an example of 16-bit software. Thus, you can execute Windows 3.11 on 80386-based PCs. Naturally, you can also use Windows 3.11 on 32-bit hardware such as a Pentium PC.

However, Windows NT and Windows '95 are true 32-bit software. As such, these Windows can only be executed on hardware that is capable of executing 32-bit software.

Software Development Tools

Now that you understand the difference between a 16-bit Windows and a 32-bit Windows, the question is: which development tools should you use for your Windows applications?

If your application is intended for 16-bit Windows, then your development tools must generate 16-bit applications. For example, Visual Basic 4.0 and above comes in two versions; a 16-bit version and a 32-bit version. If you intend to develop 16-bit Windows applications, use the 16-bit version of Visual Basic. And if your application is intended for a 32-bit Windows, use the 32-bit Visual Basic.

VBX Controls, OCX Controls, DLLs—Which One?

Visual Basic uses visual controls. For example, a file such as the Grid.VBX file is an example of a visual control. You can use a VBX control from within your Visual Basic programs, but you have to consider that a VBX control is a 16-bit control. There is no such thing as a 32-bit VBX control.

Microsoft has designed the protocol of another type of visual control, called OCX controls. These are very similar to VBX controls, and you can use them from within your Visual Basic programs.

OCX controls can be 16-bit controls, executable on 16-bit as well as 32-bit Windows versions, or 32-bit controls, executable only on a 32-bit Windows.

As you probably know, DLLs are often used from within Visual Basic programs. And yes, there are 16-bit DLLs and 32-bit DLLs. As you might expect, a 16-bit DLL can be executed on both 16-bit and 32-bit Windows. However, a 32-bit DLL can only be executed on a 32-bit Windows.

Table 2.1 summarizes the 16-bit and 32-bit compatibility issues.

TABLE 2.1: 16-Bit and 32-Bit Software Compatibility

Software	Use with 16-Bit Windows?	Use with 32-Bit Windows?
16-bit application	Yes	Yes
16-bit VBX control	Yes	Yes
16-bit OCX control	Yes	Yes
16-bit DLL	Yes	Yes
16-bit Visual Basic	Yes	Yes
32-bit application	No	Yes
32-bit VBX control*	N/A	N/A
32-bit OCX control	No	Yes
32-bit DLL	No	Yes
32-bit Visual Basic	No	Yes

*No such thing.

About CD-ROM Drives

CD-ROM drives are becoming very popular, and many PCs now come with a CD-ROM drive already installed. Typically, CD-ROM drives are used to read data from a data CD (like the one that accompanies this book). Used in this way, a CD-ROM drive is just like your hard-disk drive, except that you can read data from the CD, but you cannot write data to it.

A CD-ROM drive can also typically serve as a CD audio player. That is, you purchase an audio CD in a music store and then use your PC to play the music on that disk. You cannot write into an audio CD, and you cannot read data from it.

CD-ROM Drives and Windows NT Version 3.5

When purchasing a CD-ROM drive, be careful if you plan to use it with Windows NT version 3.5. This operating system requires that the CD-ROM drive use a SCSI interface to connect to your PC. So even if your CD-ROM drive works fine with Windows version 3.11 and Windows '95, if the CD-ROM drive is not a SCSI drive, your Windows NT version 3.5 will tell you that your PC does not have a CD-ROM drive installed.

Using Visual Basic as the Development Tool

This book is for Visual Basic programmers. You'll implement the programs here by using Visual Basic 4.0 or higher. Writing Windows applications with Visual Basic is very easy. But what about speed? There is a rumor floating around that applications written with Visual Basic are slow! As you'll soon see, thanks to some very sophisticated OCX controls, Visual Basic programs can be just as fast as Visual C++ programs.

When performing sophisticated 3D WinG/Virtual reality and advanced multimedia applications, speed is of prime importance. You cannot write, for example, a virtual reality 3D program using "pure" Visual Basic code. However, thanks to the introduction of OCX controls, your Visual Basic program can be as fast as any Windows program.

Note that when you click a button during the execution of a Visual C++ program, the program will probably respond faster than a Visual Basic program would. But this time difference will not be noticeable to the user; you'll need an oscilloscope to measure it. The time difference becomes very important with tasks such as displaying graphic objects, rotating 3D objects, and performing complex mathematical calculations. But as you'll see in this book, it does not matter whether you use Visual C++ or Visual Basic. Why? Because these operations are performed by the OCX control (which was designed and written using Visual C++).

The bottom line is that you use Visual Basic for the user interface mechanism, and hence your user will not notice any performance differences.

How This Book Is Organized

This book has six parts. There is a lot of material in this book, so in the future, you can refer to this section to locate a particular topic in this book.

2

Part I: WinG and Visual Basic

Part I of this book (Chapters 1 and 2) is what you're reading now—an introduction to the main topics we'll be covering.

Part II: The Principles of WinG

Part II of this book consists of Chapters 3 through 8. In Chapter 3 you'll execute your first WinG program, VBWinG.EXE, which demonstrates that when you perform intensive monitor operations without using WinG technology, flickering occurs. Yet when you perform the same operation using WinG, the flickering disappears.

In Chapter 4 you'll implement the VBWinG program without WinG technology. In Chapter 5 you'll write WinG code that performs the same monitor operations as the code you wrote in Chapter 4. Thus, you'll be able to see WinG code in action. As stated, the VBWinG program uses the WinG OCX control. You'll learn how to place this control inside the toolbox window of Visual Basic (see Figure 2.1), and then use the WinG control from within your Visual Basic programs.

FIGURE 2.1:

The WinG control inside the Visual Basic toolbox

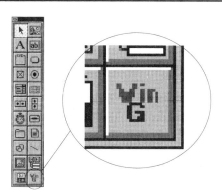

In Chapter 6 you'll practice with WinG by slightly modifying the program that you wrote in the previous two chapters. You'll see that thanks to the speed of WinG, Windows is capable of keeping up with the mouse movement.

In Chapter 7 you'll execute the VBBmp.EXE program, which loads a BMP file from the hard drive and then uses WinG technology to display the file. As you can imagine, loading BMP picture files during runtime is very important in games and multimedia programs. In Chapter 7 you'll also learn about solid colors, composite colors, and other important related topics.

In Chapter 8 you'll write the code of the VBBmp program by using Visual Basic/WinG.

Part III: Multimedia

Part III of this book (Chapters 9 through 21) deals with the popular topic of multimedia.

In Chapter 9 you'll learn how to examine the multimedia capabilities of your PC. You'll learn how to determine whether your PC is capable of working with WAV files, MIDI files, CD audio, and AVI files.

In Chapter 10 you'll execute a program called WinGMult.EXE that demonstrates how to incorporate WinG and Multimedia WAV technology so that you can perform animation with background music. In particular, you'll implement a program that displays an animation sequence showing two planets colliding with each other, with sound in the background. The same program will enable your user to run a different animation show (a man playing a string bass). In Chapter 11 you'll learn how to design and write the WinGMult program yourself.

In Chapter 12 you'll execute the WAVInfo application, which demonstrates how the Multimedia control can read recording parameters such as sampling rate, Mono/Stereo recording, and 8-bit/16-bit recording. In Chapter 13 you'll write the WAVInfo application yourself.

In Chapter 14 you'll execute the Record program, which demonstrates how to record WAV files. As you'll see, the Record program also includes two animation sequences. During the recording of a WAV file the user sees a microphone animation (Figure 2.2), and during the playback, the user sees a drum animation. In Chapter 15 you'll write the Record program by yourself.

2

FIGURE 2.2:

The Record program. During recording, the user sees a visual indication that recording is in progress.

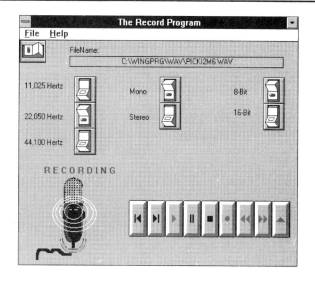

In Chapter 16 you'll execute the Pool program, which displays a pool table and a player. Once the player hits the cue ball, it proceeds to hit the rest of the balls into the pockets. The topic of the Pool program is MIDI files. As you'll see, while the Pool program is in progress, the user can play background MIDI music. This program also demonstrates how the tempo (playback speed) can be modified. In Chapter 17 you'll write the Pool program yourself.

In Chapter 18 you'll execute MyMovie, a program that plays movie files. As you'll see, the user has the option to display the movies either in the application window or in a separate window. In Chapter 19 you'll write the MyMovie program yourself.

In Chapter 20 you'll execute the MyCD program, which lets your user play audio CDs. In Chapter 21 you'll implement the MyCD program.

Part IV: Sprites and Animation

Part IV consists of Chapters 21 through 26. Here you'll learn about the powerful Sprite/WinG OCX control that lets you perform sophisticated animation with great ease.

In Chapter 22 you'll learn about sprites—graphic objects that you can move around a screen without worrying about redrawing the background—and how you can create them.

In Chapter 23 you'll execute a program that uses sprites for animation. In particular, you'll create the MySprite program, which has a background picture as shown in Figure 2.3.

FIGURE 2.3:

The background picture

The MySprite program includes a Control Panel window, which lets the user moves a tank around the screen. Thus, your user will be able to move the tank forward, from left to right, from right to left, and backward. Figures 2.4 shows a snapshot of the tank's movement. The thing to note is that as the tank moves, the background picture is redrawn automatically.

In Chapters 24 and 25 you'll implement the MySprite program. Finally, in Chapter 26 you'll add sound effects to the program.

Part V: Creating Windows 3D Virtual Reality Games

Part V (Chapters 27–38) takes you into the world of 3D virtual reality games programming. In Chapter 27 you'll learn what 3D virtual reality programs are and some of the issues involved in creating them.

In Chapter 28 you'll learn how to generate the 2D drawings that form the basis of the 3D virtual reality programs that you'll write in subsequent chapters.

FIGURE 2.4:

The tank moves forward (toward the user)

In Chapter 29 you'll load several floor files (2D drawings of floors and rooms), you'll convert the 2D drawings to 3D pictures, and then you'll travel around the 3D pictures! As you move inside the 3D picture, you see 3D views as would have been seen in a real room that corresponds to the 2D drawing (hence the name virtual reality). In Chapter 30 you'll implement the 3D virtual reality program that you executed in Chapter 29.

In Chapter 31 you'll add an ASCII view feature to the program that you implemented in Chapter 30. That is, while moving within the 3D picture, users may want to see a 2D map that shows their current location and any obstacles. In this chapter you'll implement this mechanism.

In Chapter 32 you'll implement code that lets the user work with the mouse in this program. In particular, you'll implement a Mouse Control Panel that lets the user control the speed at which movement inside the 3D picture is performed.

In Chapter 33 you'll execute the MyWalls program, which lets the user set and display the precise direction while moving inside 3D pictures (see Figure 2.5). The My-Walls program also lets the user paint the walls of the 3D picture, the ceiling, the strips on the walls, and the floor of the rooms and halls (see Figure 2.6). In Chapter 34 you'll implement the MyWalls program.

FIGURE 2.5:

A Control Panel window that lets the
user set and display the precise
direction while moving inside the
3D picture

FIGURE 2.6:

Letting the user paint the walls,
stripes, ceiling and floor

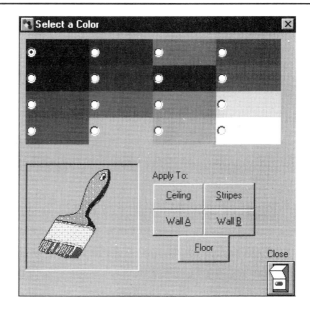

In Chapter 35 you'll execute the MyWorld program, which lets you create your own
3D virtual reality world. That is, you'll create a 2D drawing, and the MyWorld program will display it as a 3D drawing. Your user will be able to travel inside the 3D

2

picture, and while traveling into rooms and halls, will see various objects (sprites) walking around. Figure 2.7 shows how you implement a lamp in the 3D pictures.

FIGURE 2.7:

Implementing lamps in the rooms of the 3D pictures

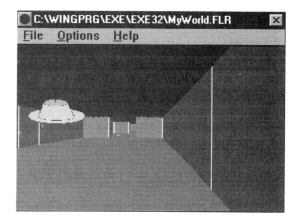

Figure 2.8 shows a man with a sword. As you'll see, this man runs across the halls of the 3D picture while the user moves within the picture.

FIGURE 2.8:

A man with a sword, seen as the user moves around the 3D picture

It is your own world, so you can place whatever you want in it! For example, Figure 2.9 shows president Lincoln standing in one of the rooms, and Figure 2.10

FIGURE 2.9:

Placing president Lincoln in one of the rooms

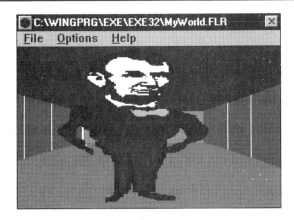

FIGURE 2.10:

Placing president Kennedy in one of the rooms

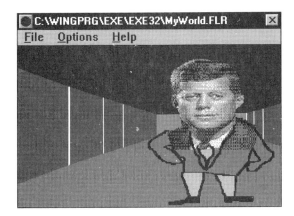

shows president Kennedy standing in another room. You can even have historical figures from different eras such as presidents Lincoln and Kennedy meet in the same room, as shown in Figure 2.11.

And of course, you can place other sprites, like those shown in Figures 2.12 and 2.13. As you enter the room shown in Figure 2.13, the man plays the flute, and the snake dances.

In Chapter 36 you'll start implementing the MyWorld program.

FIGURE 2.11:

Placing Lincoln and Kennedy in the same room

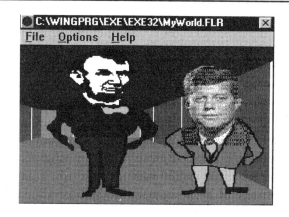

FIGURE 2.12:

Placing other sprites inside the different rooms of the 3D floor

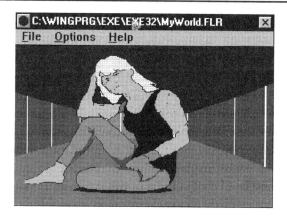

In Chapter 37 you'll learn how to place static sprites inside the room and halls of the 3D picture.

In Chapter 38 you'll learn how to animate sprites inside the 3D picture. You'll also add sound effects to the MyWorld program. So for example, when you enter the room where president Kennedy is located, your sound card will automatically start playing a famous speech by Kennedy.

FIGURE 2.13:

Performing an animation show
inside the 3D picture

Part VI: WinG Drawing

Part VI of this book is located on the companion CD-ROM. It contains information about drawing operations with WinG and Visual Basic.

This part of the book further extends the VBWinG program that you developed in Chapter 3. You'll see how you can draw various graphic shapes and perform other drawing tasks by using WinG and the Windows API drawing functions from within your Visual Basic programs.

PART II

The Principles of WinG

CHAPTER

THREE

3

Executing Visual Basic/WinG Programs

In this chapter you'll execute the VBWinG.EXE program. This Visual Basic program illustrates that a screen operation performed using WinG technology is by far faster—and therefore apparently smoother—than the same monitor operation performed without using WinG technology.

In this brief chapter you'll only execute the VBWinG.EXE program. In subsequent chapters you'll learn how to write the program by yourself.

Executing the VBWinG.EXE Program

The VBWinG.EXE program resides in the \EXE directory of this book's CD-ROM.

- Execute the VBWinG.EXE program.

The window shown in Figure 3.1 appears.

FIGURE 3.1:

The window displayed by the VBWinG.EXE program

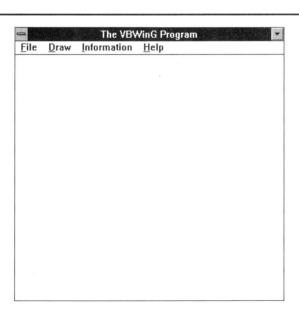

As you can see, the VBWinG.EXE program presents four menus: File, Draw, Information, and Help. The Help menu is shown in Figure 3.2.

FIGURE 3.2:

The Help menu of the
VBWinG.EXE program

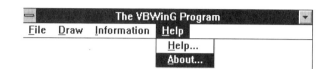

• Select the About item from the Help menu.

VBWinG.EXE responds by displaying the About dialog box (see Figure 3.3).

FIGURE 3.3:

The About dialog box of the
VBWinG.EXE program

• Click the OK button of the About dialog box.

VBWinG.EXE responds by closing the About dialog box.

- Click the Help item of the Help menu.

VBWinG.EXE responds by displaying the Help window (see Figure 3.4).

FIGURE 3.4:

The Help window of the VBWinG.EXE program

- Click the OK button of the Help window.

VBWinG.EXE responds by closing the Help window.

The Draw Menu of the VBWinG Program

The Draw menu contains two items: Do It with WinG and Do It without WinG (see Figure 3.5).

Let's first see how the VBWinG.EXE program performs monitor operations without using WinG:

- Select Do It without WinG from the Draw menu.

FIGURE 3.5:

The Draw menu of the
VBWinG.EXE program

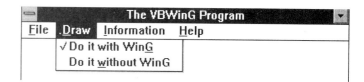

- Place the mouse cursor inside the VBWinG window, press down the left mouse button, and while holding down the button move the mouse.

As you move the mouse, VBWinG draws red rectangles inside the application window. You can see on your screen, however, that there is a lot of flickering as the mouse moves! Why? Because there are a lot of screen operations during the process of moving the mouse. The entire application window must be filled with a white rectangle, and then a red rectangle is drawn. This process of painting and repainting, known as *refreshing* the screen, is repeated many times as you move the mouse. When it uses WinG technology, the VBWinG.EXE program is capable of performing the task without any flickering.

- Select Do It with WinG from the Draw menu.

- Place the mouse cursor inside the VBWinG window, press down the left mouse button, and while holding down the button move the mouse.

As you move the mouse, VBWinG draws red rectangles inside the application's window. However, now there is no flickering.

Figure 3.6 shows the icon of the VBWinG.EXE program. You'll need to design similar icons for your own Visual Basic programs.

FIGURE 3.6:

The icon of the
VBWinG.EXE program

The VBWinG.EXE program also presents the Information menu, shown in Figure 3.7.

FIGURE 3.7:

The Information menu of the
VBWinG.EXE program

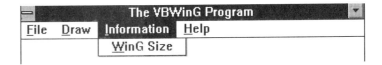

When you select the WinG Size item from the Information menu, the WinG
Information dialog box is displayed (Figure 3.8).

FIGURE 3.8:

The WinG Information dialog box

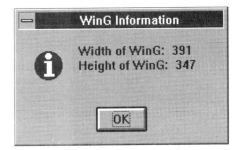

The Information dialog box reports the size of a window named WinG. It provides
this information for the sake of illustrating an important WinG concept—namely,
the use of *virtual windows*. The WinG window exists only in memory; you can't see
it on the screen. In Chapter 5, as you write the VBWinG.EXE program yourself,
you'll learn more about virtual windows and the advantages they provide.

- Experiment with the VBWinG.EXE program. Run it a few times with and
  without WinG to see the difference this technology makes, and try out the
  other menu options. When you are ready to terminate the program, select
  the Exit item from the File menu.

Summary

In this chapter you executed the VBWinG.EXE program, an application that was written with Visual Basic '95. In subsequent chapters you'll write the VBWinG.EXE program by yourself. The main thing to note about the VBWinG program is that when WinG technology is used, no flickering occurs.

3

CHAPTER

FOUR

Designing a Visual Basic/WinG Program: The VBWinG Program

4

In this chapter you'll start writing the VBWinG program, the Visual Basic program you ran in the last chapter, which demonstrates the advantages of WinG technology. You'll begin by creating a project for the program and then write the code for its non-WinG drawing operations.

Creating the VBWinG Project

You'll now create the project file for the VBWinG program.

- Start the Visual Basic program.

- From the File menu, select New Project and then save the new project files as follows:

    - Save the new form as VBWinG.FRM in the C:\WinGPrg\CH03 directory.

    - Save the new project file as VBWinG.MAK in the C:\WinGPrg\CH03 directory.

Adding the TegWinG3.OCX (or TegWinG1.OCX) Visual Control to Your Project

The VBWinG program uses the TegWinG?.OCX control, which enables you to write WinG-based programs with great ease.

If you are using a 32-bit Windows, then the program uses the TegWinG3.OCX control. If you are using a 16-bit Windows, then the program uses the TegWinG1.OCX control. Note that the character 3 in the filename TegWinG3.OCX indicates that this OCX control was designed for 32-bit Windows, and the character 1 in the TegWinG1.OCX name indicates that this OCX control was designed for 16-bit Windows. So remember: 3 stands for 32-bit Windows, and 1 stands for 16-bit Windows.

This OCX file resides in the \WinGPrg\OCX directory of the accompanying CD-ROM, and the CD's Install program should have copied it to your Windows system directory. Take a moment now to make sure it's there. If it's not, you'll need to copy it manually from the CD-ROM to your Windows directory.

You now have to add the TegWinG3.OCX (or TegWinG1.OCX) control to the VBWinG.MAK project. Here is how you do that:

- Select Custom Controls from the Tools menu.

Visual Basic responds by displaying the Custom Controls dialog box (see Figure 4.1).

4

FIGURE 4.1:

The Custom Controls dialog box of Visual Basic

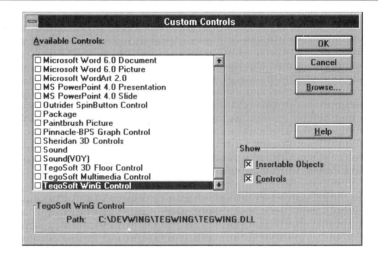

- Click the Browse button and select the TegoSoft WinG OCX control (TegWinG3.OCX or TegWinG1.OCX) from the Windows system directory.

- Close the Custom Control dialog box by clicking its OK button.

Visual Basic responds by adding the icon of the WinG OCX control to the Tools window.

Figure 4.2 shows the icon of the TegWinG?.OCX control inside the Tools window of Visual Basic.

Now the Tools window contains the icon of the TegWinG1.OCX control.

FIGURE 4.2:

The icon of the TegWinG3.OCX
(or TegWinG1.OCX) control inside
the Tools window

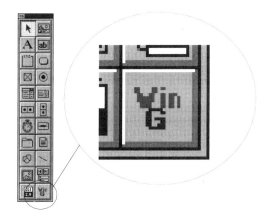

Naming OCX Files

The software industry is still trying to evolve a consistent file-naming convention for OCX files. As with all DOS filnames, only eight characters are available to identify the individual file. The last two characters usually indicate whether the file is a 16-bit version of the OCX control or a 32-bit version. For example, a 16-bit control could be named ??????16.OCX. The same OCX control in its 32-bit version would be named ??????32.OCX. So the vendor has only six characters to play with.

Typically, the vendor of the OCX control wants to associate their own name with the filename. For example, OCX files from Microsoft typically start with the characters MS. So in the case of the Microsoft OCX controls, a 16-bit control will typically have a name like MS????16.OCX, and the same control in its 32-bit version will typically have a name like MS????32.OCX. As you can see, there are only four characters left to describe the control.

Occasionally, an OCX control vendor will use three characters at the beginning of the OCX filename to identify themselves. This leaves only three characters to identify the control. In such cases, the vendor will use 1 as the last character in the filename to identify the OCX as a 16-bit control, and 3 as the last character to identify the OCX as a 32-bit control.

Naming OCX Files (continued)

For example, TegoSoft Inc. produces the TegWinG1.OCX control. The subject of the control is WinG, and because the last character of the control is 1, you know that the control is a 16-bit OCX control.

Likewise, the TegWinG3.OCX control is the 32-bit version of TegoSoft's WinG OCX control.

Generally speaking, there are no rules regarding the filename convention for OCX controls (and there is no Windows requirement regarding the names of the OCX files). So occasionally, you'll encounter an OCX control that does not follow the naming conventions just described.

4

Placing the WinG Control in the Form

You'll now place the WinG OCX control in the new form of the VBWinG.MAK project.

- Double-click the icon of the WinG OCX control in the Tools window.

Visual Basic responds by placing the control inside the form, as shown in Figure 4.3.

FIGURE 4.3:

Placing the WinG OCX control inside the form

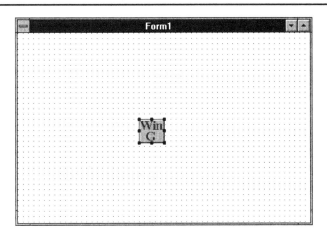

NOTE   Although Visual Basic allows you to change the size of some controls, such as forms, labels, buttons, and so on, you cannot resize the WinG control. That's because this control is always invisible during runtime, and so it makes no sense to resize it. (The same is true for the Timer control, for example.)

The default name that Visual Basic assigned to the WinG OCX control is Tegwing1. You can verify this by inspecting the control's Properties window (shown in Figure 4.4). Make sure the WinG OCX control is selected in the form, and press F4 to display the Properties window of the control.

FIGURE 4.4:
The Properties window of the Tegwing1 control

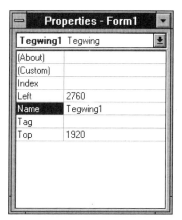

Implementing the frmVBWinG Form of the VBWinG Program

You'll now complete implementing the form of the VBWinG program.

- Set the Name property of the form to frmVBWinG.

- Complete the design of the frmVBWinG form according to Table 4.1. When you're finished, the frmVBWinG form should look as shown in Figure 4.5.

4

TABLE 4.1: The Properties of the frmVBWinG Form

Object: Form
Object Name: frmVBWinG

Property	Value
BackColor	(light gray)
BorderStyle	'Fixed Single
Caption	"The VBWinG Program"
Height	5880
Icon	C:\WinGPrg\Icons\VBWinG.ICO
Left	1035
MaxButton	0 'False
ScaleMode	3 'Pixel
Top	1170
Width	5970

Object: Shape control
Object Name: shpRedRectangle

Property	Value
BackColor	Red
BackStyle	1 'Opaque
Height	495
Left	240
Top	1920
Visible	0 'False
Width	615

TABLE 4.1: The Properties of the frmVBWinG Form(continued)

Object: Shape control
Object Name: shpWhiteRectangle

Property	Value
BackColor	White
BackStyle	1 'Opaque
BorderColor	Black
Height	495
Left	240
Top	2520
Visible	0 'False
Width	1215

Object: TegoSoft WinG OCX Control
Object Name: Tegwing1

Property	Value
Left	240
Top	3360

FIGURE 4.5:

The frmVBWinG form in
design mode

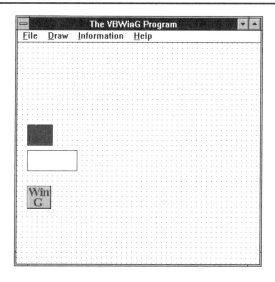

Implementing the Menu of the frmVBWinG Form

You'll now implement the menu of the frmVBWinG form.

- Select Menu Editor from the Tools menu of Visual Basic, and implement the menu of the frmVBWinG form with the properties listed in Table 4.2. When you complete implementing the menu, it should look as shown in Figures 4.6, 4.7, 4.8, and 4.9.

TABLE 4.2: The Menu of the frmVBWinG Form

Caption	Name	Other Settings
&File	mnuFile	
...E&xit	mnuExit	
&Draw	mnuDraw	
...Do it with Win&G	mnuWithWinG	Checked = -1 'True
...Do it &without WinG	mnuWithoutWinG	
&Information	mnuInformation	
...&WinG Size	mnuWinGSize	
&Help	mnuHelp	
...&Help	mnuHelpMe	
...&About	mnuAbout	

The Code of the General Declarations Section of the frmVBWinG Form

You'll now write the code of the General Declarations section of the frmVBWinG form.

- Enter the following code inside the General Declarations section of the frmVBWinG form:

```
Option Explicit
```

FIGURE 4.6:
The File menu of the frm VBWinG form

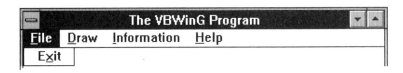

FIGURE 4.7:
The Draw menu of the frm VBWinG form

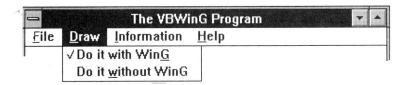

FIGURE 4.8:
The Information menu of the frmVBWinG form

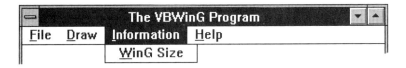

FIGURE 4.9:
The Help menu of the frm VBWinG form

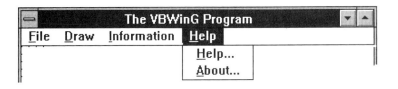

This instruction forces you to declare all variables. That is, if you do not declare a variable with the Dim statement, as in

```
Dim MyVariable
```

when Visual Basic encounters the variable in your program, it will refuse to use the variable and will prompt you with an error message.

The Code Executed upon Starting the frmVBWinG Program

When you start the VBWinG program, it loads the frmVBWinG form and the Form_Load( ) procedure is executed. The code that you'll now enter for this procedure does various initializations.

- Enter the following code inside the Form_Load( ) procedure of the frmVBWinG form:

```
Private Sub Form_Load()

    Me.ScaleMode = 3 'Pixels

    ' Tell the TegoSoft WinG control
    ' in which window to draw
    Tegwing1.hWndDisplay = Me.hWnd

    ' Open a WinG session
    Tegwing1.OpenWinG

End Sub
```

The statement

```
  Me.ScaleMode = 3 'Pixels
```

sets the ScaleMode property of the frmVBWinG to 3, which means that the units used to describe various dimensions are in pixels.

In the Properties window, you already set the ScaleMode property of the form to 3 (which represents pixels). So you really don't need to set this property again in the Form_Load() procedure. However, we included this setting inside the Form_Load() procedure simply to emphasize the fact that the ScaleMode is in pixels. As you'll see, it is easier to work with pixels as the units of the form, because the WinG OCX control can only accept dimensions in units of pixels, and the code that you'll write will pass various dimensions from Visual Basic to the WinG control.

The next statement in Form_Load( ) sets the hWndDisplay property of the WinG control to the hWnd property of the frmVBWinG form:

```
' Tell the TegoSoft WinG control
' in which window to draw
Tegwing1.hWndDisplay = Me.hWnd
```

The WinG control is capable of drawing very fast. But in which window will the WinG control draw? The WinG control will draw inside the window whose handle is equal to the value of the hWndDisplay property. In the preceding code you set the hWndDisplay property of the WinG control to the hWnd property of the frmVBWinG form. Thus, the WinG control will draw inside the frmVBWinG form.

The next statement inside the Form_Load( ) procedure uses the OpenWinG method:

```
' Open a WinG session
Tegwing1.OpenWinG
```

So from now on, the WinG control is ready to work for you. In particular, it will draw inside the frmVBWinG form.

The Code of the Exit Menu Item

You'll now write the code that is executed whenever the user selects Exit from the File menu.

- Enter the following code inside the mnuExit_Click( ) procedure of the frmVBWinG form:

```
Private Sub mnuExit_Click( )

    Unload Me

End Sub
```

This code unloads the frmVBWinG form (which causes the program to execute the Form_Unload( ) procedure).

Closing the WinG Session

The code you placed inside the mnuExit_Click( ) procedure instructs Visual Basic to execute the Form_Unload( ) procedure whenever the user selects Exit from the File menu.

Also, if the user clicks the control-menu box (in the upper-left corner of the window) and then selects Close from the system popup menu, the Form_Unload( ) procedure is executed. The form is then unloaded and the program terminates.

So to summarize, the Form_Unload( ) procedure is a focal point in the program where you write code that is executed whenever the user terminates the program. Here is your chance to write clean-up code.

- Enter the following code inside the Form_Unload( ) procedure of the frmVBWinG form:

```
Private Sub Form_Unload(Cancel As Integer)

    ' Close the WinG session
    Tegwing1.CloseWinG
```

```
End Sub
```

This code closes the WinG session by applying the CloseWinG method.

The Draw Menu

The Draw menu has two items: Do It with WinG and Do It without WinG. When you start the program, Do It with WinG is checked, because you set its Checked property when you designed the menu in the Menu Editor window.

While the program is running, the user can select either of these menu items. The selected item is marked with a check mark. If the selection changes, the check mark disappears from the old item and appears next to the new one. You'll now implement this feature:

- Enter the following code inside the mnuWithWinG_Click( ) procedure of the frmVBWinG form:

```
Private Sub mnuWithWinG_Click( )

        mnuWithoutWinG.Checked = False
        mnuWithWinG.Checked = True

End Sub
```

These statements uncheck the Do it without WinG item and check the Do it with WinG item.

- Enter the following code inside the mnuWithoutWinG_Click( ) procedure:

```
Private Sub mnuWithoutWinG_Click( )

        mnuWithoutWinG.Checked = True
        mnuWithWinG.Checked = False

End Sub
```

These statements check the Do It without WinG item and then uncheck the Do It with WinG item.

Drawing the Rectangles (without WinG)

You'll now write the code that is executed whenever the user presses the left mouse button inside the form. Recall that when the user presses the mouse button, the program draws a white rectangle over the entire window of the application and then draws a red rectangle inside the window.

How does the program draw the white and red rectangles? It depends on the current setting of the Draw menu. Let's start by drawing the rectangles using regular Visual Basic code (that is, without using WinG). In the next chapter we'll write the code that uses WinG to draw the rectangles.

4

- Enter the following code inside the Form_MouseDown( ) procedure of the frmVBWinG form:

```
Private Sub Form_MouseDown(Button As Integer, _
    Shift As Integer, X As Single, Y As Single)

Dim Width, Height

If mnuWithWinG.Checked = True Then

  ' To be implemented in the next chapter

End If

If mnuWithoutWinG.Checked = True Then

  ' Draw the white rectangle
  shpWhiteRectangle.Top = 0
  shpWhiteRectangle.Height = frmVBWinG.ScaleHeight
  shpWhiteRectangle.Left = 0
  shpWhiteRectangle.Width = frmVBWinG.ScaleWidth
  shpWhiteRectangle.Visible = True

  ' Draw the red rectangle
  shpRedRectangle.Top = Y
  shpRedRectangle.Height = DRAWING_WIDTH
  shpRedRectangle.Left = X
  shpRedRectangle.Width = DRAWING_HEIGHT
  shpRedRectangle.Visible = True
```

```
    End If

  End Sub
```

The first If statement checks the status of the Checked property of the Do It with WinG menu item:

```
If mnuWithWinG.Checked = True Then

  ' To be implemented in the next chapter

End If
```

Drawing the White Rectangle

The second If statement checks the status of the Do It without WinG menu item. If this menu item is checked, the code under the If statement draws a white rectangle over the entire area of the application's windows and then draws a red rectangle:

```
If mnuWithoutWinG.Checked = True Then

  ' Draw the white rectangle
  shpWhiteRectangle.Top = 0
  shpWhiteRectangle.Height = frmVBWinG.ScaleHeight
  shpWhiteRectangle.Left = 0
  shpWhiteRectangle.Width = frmVBWinG.ScaleWidth
  shpWhiteRectangle.Visible = True

  ' Draw the red rectangle
  shpRedRectangle.Top = Y
  shpRedRectangle.Height = DRAWING_WIDTH
  shpRedRectangle.Left = X
  shpRedRectangle.Width = DRAWING_HEIGHT
  shpRedRectangle.Visible = True

End If
```

Recall that in the design stage you placed the shpWhiteRectangle shape control inside the form. The code that you just entered sets the size of this white rectangle so that it will have the size of the entire application's window, as follows:

```
shpWhiteRectangle.Top = 0
shpWhiteRectangle.Height = frmVBWinG.ScaleHeight
```

```
shpWhiteRectangle.Left = O
shpWhiteRectangle.Width = frmVBWinG.ScaleWidth
```

In the design stage, you set the Visible property of the white rectangle to False. Now the code under the If statement sets the Visible property of the white rectangle to True:

```
shpWhiteRectangle.Visible = True
```

The application's window now contains a white rectangle that covers the entire area of the window.

Drawing the Red Rectangle

The Form_MouseDown( ) procedure has the parameters X and Y, representing the x and y coordinates of the mouse cursor at the time the left mouse button was pressed. You want to draw the red rectangle so that its upper-left corner is at the (x,y) coordinates. Here is how you accomplish that:

```
' Draw the red rectangle
shpRedRectangle.Top = Y
shpRedRectangle.Height = DRAWING_WIDTH
shpRedRectangle.Left = X
shpRedRectangle.Width = DRAWING_HEIGHT
```

The Height and Width of the red rectangle are set to DRAWING_WIDTH and DRAWING_HEIGHT. You'll declare the DRAWING_WIDTH and DRAWING _HEIGHT constants later in this chapter. Figure 4.10 shows the various coordinates of the red rectangle.

Finally, you set the Visible property of the red rectangle to True:

```
shpRedRectangle.Visible = True
```

FIGURE 4.10:

Drawing the red rectangle

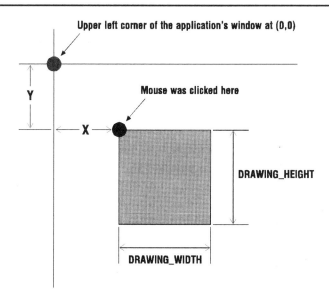

Drawing Red Rectangles as the Mouse Moves (without WinG)

You'll now write the code that draws red rectangles as the mouse moves.

- Enter the following code inside the Form_MouseMove( ) procedure:

```
Private Sub Form_MouseMove(Button As Integer, _
    Shift As Integer, X As Single, Y As Single)

Dim Width, Height

If mnuWithWinG.Checked = True And Button <> 0 Then

   ' You'll write the WinG code
   ' in the next chapter

End If

If mnuWithoutWinG.Checked = True And Button <> 0 Then
```

```
' Draw the white rectangle
shpWhiteRectangle.Top = 0
shpWhiteRectangle.Height = frmVBWinG.ScaleHeight
shpWhiteRectangle.Left = 0
shpWhiteRectangle.Width = frmVBWinG.ScaleWidth

' Draw the red rectangle
shpRedRectangle.Top = Y
shpRedRectangle.Height = DRAWING_WIDTH
shpRedRectangle.Left = X
shpRedRectangle.Width = DRAWING_HEIGHT

End If

End Sub
```

An If statement is used to determine the status of the Do It with WinG menu item. If this menu item has a check mark, then the code under the If statement is executed:

```
If mnuWithWinG.Checked = True And Button <> 0 Then

    ' You'll write the WinG code
    ' in the next chapter

End If
```

As you can see, you'll write the WinG code in the next chapter.

A second If statement is used to determine whether the Do It without WinG menu item has a check mark:

```
If mnuWithoutWinG.Checked = True And Button <> 0 Then

    ' Draw the white rectangle
    shpWhiteRectangle.Top = 0
    shpWhiteRectangle.Height = frmVBWinG.ScaleHeight
    shpWhiteRectangle.Left = 0
    shpWhiteRectangle.Width = frmVBWinG.ScaleWidth

    ' Draw the red rectangle
    shpRedRectangle.Top = Y
    shpRedRectangle.Height = DRAWING_WIDTH
    shpRedRectangle.Left = X
    shpRedRectangle.Width = DRAWING_HEIGHT
```

```
End If
```

So if the mouse is moved and the left button of the mouse is down, the code under the If statement is executed.

> **NOTE**
>
> The code under the If statement will also be executed if, for example, the right mouse button is down. This is because the If statement simply verifies that Button is not equal to 0; it does not further investigate which button is down. A program that uses only one of the mouse buttons would, of course, need to make this further test.

The code under the If statement is identical to the code inside the Form_Mouse-Down( ) procedure. In other words, every time the user moves the mouse (while one of the mouse buttons is down), the Form_MouseMove( ) procedure fills the entire window with a white rectangle, and then draws a small red rectangle.

> **NOTE**
>
> You may correctly argue that instead of filling the entire application's window with a white rectangle each time the mouse position changes, it would be more efficient simply to fill the previous red rectangle with a white color, and then draw the new red rectangle in its new position. This would be more efficient, but the point of this exercise is to demonstrate the superior ability of WinG over conventional Visual Basic code. So we deliberately made this program use as many screen operations as possible. As you'll see when you'll write the WinG code, you'll use the same technique when applying the WinG code. That is, you'll first fill the entire window with a white rectangle, and then draw a small red rectangle. Thus, the comparison between the non-WinG code and the WinG code is fair.

Restoring the Original Window

Once the user releases the mouse button, the application's original window is restored. This is accomplished inside the Form_MouseUp( ) procedure of the frmVBWinG form.

- Enter the following code inside the Form_MouseUp( ) procedure of the frmVBWinG form:

```
Private Sub Form_MouseUp(Button As Integer, _
    Shift As Integer, X As Single, Y As Single)

        shpWhiteRectangle.Visible = False
        shpRedRectangle.Visible = False
        Cls

End Sub
```

The first two lines set the Visible property of the white and red rectangles to False, and then the Cls statement clears the contents of the frmVBWinG form.

- Select Save from Visual Basic's File menu to save the frmVBWinG form.

Creating a Module for Global Variables and Constants

As you saw, the red rectangle has a width equal to DRAWING_WIDTH and a height equal to DRAWING_HEIGHT. You'll now declare these constants.

You can declare the constants inside the General Declarations section of the frmVBWinG form, or you can create a new BAS module that serves as a module for holding global variables and constants that are accessible from every procedure of any form of the application.

Here is how you create a new module:

- Select Insert Module from the Insert menu of Visual Basic.

Visual Basic responds by inserting a new BAS module into the VBWinG.MAK project. It names the module Module1.BAS.

- Display the Project window, and make sure the new BAS module that you added is selected. Select Save As from the File menu, and save the new module as VBWinG.BAS in the C:\WinGPrg\CH03 directory.

- Make sure that the new BAS module that you added is selected inside the Project window, and then click the View Code button.

Visual Basic responds by displaying the VBWinG.BAS module ready for you to edit.

- Enter the following code inside the General Declarations section of the VBWinG.BAS module:

```
Option Explicit

' The size of the red rectangle
Public Const DRAWING_WIDTH = 150
Public Const DRAWING_HEIGHT = 150

Public Const PS_SOLID = 0
Public Const PS_DASH = 1
Public Const PS_DOT = 2
Public Const PS_DASHDOT = 3
Public Const PS_DASHDOTDOT = 4
Public Const PS_NULL = 5
Public Const PS_INSIDEFRAME = 6
```

As you can see, the DRAWING_WIDTH and DRAWING_HEIGHT are declared as 150 pixels each. This means that the red rectangle is 150 pixels wide and 150 pixels high.

You also typed a set of other constants (which start with the letters PS_). These constants are needed for the WinG code that you'll write in the next chapter.

- Select Save from the File menu to save the VBWinG.BAS file.

Executing and Testing the VBWinG program

You've completed writing the code that draws without using WinG technology.

- Execute the VBWinG program.

- Select Do It without WinG from the Draw menu.

- Press the left mouse button inside the application's window, and drag the mouse. As you move the mouse, a red rectangle is drawn, moving with the mouse.

4

Notice that there is a lot of flickering going on! In fact, there is so much flickering that a program written this way would be totally unacceptable to your users; you could not release it.

Summary

In this chapter you created the VBWinG project file and wrote the code that draws without using WinG technology. As you saw, the resulting program performance is totally unacceptable.

Fortunately, Microsoft realized this graphic limitation of Windows, and introduced WinG. As you'll see in the next chapter, the same monitor operation can be accomplished without flickering by utilizing WinG technology.

Note that in this chapter you prepared WinG. That is, you opened a WinG session (in the Form_Load( ) procedure), and you closed the WinG session (in the Form_Unload( ) procedure).

Drawing with WinG in Visual Basic Programs

In the previous chapter you implemented the VBWinG program's drawing operations by using conventional Visual Basic code. As you saw, a lot of flickering occurred (because you did not use WinG technology). In this chapter you'll continue to develop the VBWinG.EXE program, using WinG technology to perform the same monitor operation that you performed without WinG.

In particular, you will write code that sends WinG commands to the Tegwing1 WinG control, which you placed inside the form. These WinG commands cause the control to draw a white rectangle over the entire area of the frmVBWinG form, and then to draw the red rectangle with its upper-left corner at the location of the mouse cursor, so that the rectangle moves along with the mouse.

When you use the WinG control, the drawing will be performed without flickering.

The WinG Concept

As you'll soon see, the code that instructs WinG to draw the white and red rectangles is similar to the code you wrote to draw the rectangles without the use of WinG. To understand the difference between the two approaches, you need to know something about the concept underlying WinG. Here it is in a nutshell.

When using WinG, you are creating a *virtual window* in memory. This virtual window is just like a regular window—you can set its size and you can draw into it. However, this window exists only in memory, not on the screen. So you can't see the contents of the WinG window.

Once you've completed drawing into the virtual WinG window (which from now on will be simply referred to as WinG), you transfer ("slam") the contents of WinG into the real window you are drawing into. In this case we want to draw into the frmVBWinG form.

At first glance, it looks as if this approach would slow things down. That is, you are adding an extra step. But in reality, the transfer of the WinG contents into the application's window is accomplished very fast. (That's why in this book we refer to this transfer as "slamming" the WinG contents into the application's window.)

How is the slamming of WinG into the application's window accomplished so fast? WinG is designed in a special way that takes into account the way monitors and monitor cards work. In particular, one of the reasons that flickering occurs when you do not use WinG is that there is no correlation between the monitor operation and the drawing functions.

The monitor works in the following manner: A beam scans across the horizontal lines of the monitor. Depending on certain values in the memory of the monitor card, the intensity of the beam changes, which causes the beam to generate different colors on the screen. First the beam extracts a value for the pixel at location (0,0) from the memory of the monitor card. Based on the value, the intensity of the beam is set to certain values. This causes the pixel at point (0,0) of the screen to appear as a pixel with a color that corresponds to the value in memory. Then the beam extracts the value of the next location in the monitor card memory. Based on this value, the beam intensity changes, the beam position moves to the second pixel (1,0), and this second pixel therefore appears as dictated by its corresponding memory. This process continues until the beam scans the entire screen.

Once the beam completes scanning the entire screen, the whole process starts all over again. The process of scanning the screen is called refreshing, because the screen is being updated (refreshed) with the values from memory.

Refreshing the Screen

Consider the situation of the pixel at location (0,0) on the screen. The beam touched this point with a certain intensity, and this caused the point to appear on the screen with a certain color and brightness. The beam then goes on to take care of the next pixel. But while the beam is busy taking care of the next pixel, the pixel at point (0,0) is still glowing. Why? Because the inner surface of the monitor is made of a special material that continues to glow for a certain time after the beam moves on.

How long will the pixel (0,0) remain glowing? Not for long! The beam has to work very fast scanning all the pixels of the screen. After a short time, the beam will return to pixel (0,0) and will refresh it. If the value of pixel (0,0) was changed by the program during the time the beam was scanning the screen, then the beam intensity will be according to the new value when it touches pixel (0,0) again. In either case, whether pixel (0,0) has to appear exactly as before or with a new value, the refreshing must occur.

The software that you write changes the values of the memory locations of the monitor card that correspond to pixel locations on the screen. During the refreshing, the new values will be realized on the screen.

What happens when values in the monitor card's memory change while the beam is scanning the monitor? As it turns out, this is what causes flickering. So in essence, two things need to be done to prevent the flickering. There must be some type of synchronization between the refreshing process and the time the memory of the monitor card is updated with new values. And also, the process of updating the memory of the monitor card must be accomplished very fast. WinG accomplishes both of these tasks.

To begin with, while you are drawing into WinG, you are not disturbing the monitor card's memory, because when you are drawing into WinG, you are drawing into a regular memory area of the PC. And when it is time to slam the contents of WinG into the screen, WinG knows when to slam it without causing flickering. Figure 5.1 shows this process in our VBWinG program. The right window in Figure 5.1 represents the WinG virtual window. You draw into the WinG window the white and red rectangles as follows: the white rectangle has its upper-left corner at location (0,0); and the red rectangle, whose upper-left corner is defined as the current mouse position is at location (x,y). The WinG virtual window holds this information until the SlamIt method (which will be discussed shortly) transfers the updated information from the WinG virtual window into the frmVBWinG form.

FIGURE 5.1:

Drawing into WinG and then slamming the WinG contents into the screen.

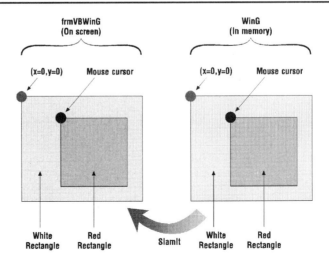

The WinG concept is actually an old concept, frequently used in DOS applications. It is basically the old double-buffering trick. You buffer the new picture that you want to draw, and when everything is ready for displaying, you slam the contents of the buffer into the screen.

In DOS you can access practically any memory area you like (including the memory area that corresponds to the screen), because DOS is not a protected-mode operating system. Windows, however, works in the so-called protected mode, which means there are various memory areas that your application cannot touch. This is why, before the introduction of WinG, your application could not refresh the screen quickly. Now, with the introduction of WinG, your Windows application still cannot touch screen memory directly (that is, the protected-mode feature of Windows is still valid), but WinG does the work for you. WinG works with the memory that corresponds to the screen in a very effective way.

OK, enough talking. Let's write the code that draws the white and red rectangles by using WinG technology.

Adding WinG Code to the Form_MouseDown( ) Procedure

At this point, the Form_MouseDown( ) procedure contains two If statements. One If statement is executed when the Do It with WinG item of the Draw menu is selected, the other when Do It without WinG is selected. In the previous chapter you wrote the code for the If statement that is executed when Do It without WinG is selected. You'll now write the code that is executed when the Do It with WinG menu item is selected.

- Modify the Form_MouseDown( ) procedure so that it looks as follows:

```
Private Sub Form_MouseDown(Button As Integer, _
        Shift As Integer, X As Single, Y As Single)

Dim Width, Height
```

```
If mnuWithWinG.Checked = True Then

    ' Draw the white rectangle inside WinG
    Tegwing1.SetPen PS_SOLID, 1, RGB(255, 255, 255)
    Tegwing1.SetSolidBrush RGB(255, 255, 255)
    Width = Tegwing1.WinGWidth
    Height = Tegwing1.WinGHeight
    Tegwing1.DrawRectangle 0, 0, Width - 1, Height - 1

    ' Draw the red rectangle inside WinG
    Tegwing1.SetSolidBrush RGB(255, 0, 0)
    Tegwing1.DrawRectangle X, _
        Y, _
        X + DRAWING_WIDTH - 1, _
        Y + DRAWING_HEIGHT - 1

    Tegwing1.SlamIt

End If

If mnuWithoutWinG.Checked = True Then

    ' Draw the white rectangle
    shpWhiteRectangle.Top = 0
    shpWhiteRectangle.Height = frmVBWinG.ScaleHeight
    shpWhiteRectangle.Left = 0
    shpWhiteRectangle.Width = frmVBWinG.ScaleWidth
    shpWhiteRectangle.Visible = True

    ' Draw the red rectangle
    shpRedRectangle.Top = Y
    shpRedRectangle.Height = DRAWING_WIDTH
    shpRedRectangle.Left = X
    shpRedRectangle.Width = DRAWING_HEIGHT
    shpRedRectangle.Visible = True

End If

End Sub
```

As you can see, the Form_MouseDown( ) procedure contains two If statements. We're interested in the first of these, executed when the Do It with
WinG menu item is selected. (The second If statement contains the code we
wrote in Chapter 4, which is executed when Do It without WinG is selected.)

The first line in the If statement uses the SetPen method of the WinG control to set a pen for WinG:

```
Tegwing1.SetPen PS_SOLID, 1, RGB(255, 255, 255)
```

Setting a pen for WinG means defining the characteristics of the pen that draws inside this virtual window—its line style, its width, and its color.

The first parameter of the SetPen method is PS_SOLID, which instructs the WinG control to use a solid line for the pen. Recall that in the previous chapter you entered the following constants in the General Declarations section of the VBWinG.BAS module:

```
Public Const PS_SOLID = 0
Public Const PS_DASH = 1
Public Const PS_DOT = 2
Public Const PS_DASHDOT = 3
Public Const PS_DASHDOTDOT = 4
Public Const PS_NULL = 5
Public Const PS_INSIDEFRAME = 6
```

5

So for example, if you want to select a pen that draws solid lines, supply 0 (PS_SOLID) as the first parameter of the SetPen method. If you want the pen to draw dashed lines, then supply 1 (PS_DASH) as the first parameter of the SetPen method, and so on.

The second parameter of the SetPen method is 1. This means that the width of the pen is 1 pixel.

The third parameter of the SetPen method is RGB(255,255,255). In the RGB screen technology, setting all three component colors (red, green, and blue) to their maximum value produces a white color. So to summarize, you set the characteristics of the pen with the SetPen method of the WinG control. This pen draws solid lines, 1 pixel wide, in the color white. It will draw the sides of the rectangle. We also need to define the brush that will paint the interior of the rectangle.

The next statement executes the SetSolidBrush method of the WinG control:

```
Tegwing1.SetSolidBrush RGB(255, 255, 255)
```

A solid brush needs only its color defined, so the only parameter here is RGB (255, 255, 255). This defines the brush color as white. So putting it all together, if you now draw a rectangle inside the WinG virtual window, it will be filled with white.

The next statement extracts the width of the WinG window:

```
Width = Tegwing1.WinGWidth
```

and the following statement extracts the height of the WinG window:

```
Height = Tegwing1.WinGHeight
```

Recall that you created the WinG window (in the Form_Load( ) procedure of the frmVBWinG form) with the OpenWinG method as follows:

```
Tegwing1.OpenWinG
```

This statement created a WinG window. But what is the size of the WinG window? Well, inside the Form_Load( ) procedure you set the hWndDisplay property of the WinG control as follows:

```
Tegwing1.hWndDisplay = Me.hWnd
```

This means that later, when you slam the contents of WinG to the screen, the contents will be transferred to the window whose handle is equal to hWnd. In other words, the WinG contents will be slammed into the frmVBWinG form. Also, the size of the WinG window is the same as the size of the frmVBWinG form.

You extracted the width and height of WinG by setting the value of the Width variable to the WinGWidth property of the WinG control:

```
Width = Tegwing1.WinGWidth
```

and you set the value of the Height variable to the WinGHeight property of the WinG control:

```
Height = Tegwing1.WinGHeight
```

Again, the WinGWidth and WinGHeight properties of the WinG control are the width and height of the frmVBWinG form.

The next statement draws a white rectangle over the entire WinG window:

```
Tegwing1.DrawRectangle 0, 0, Width - 1, Height - 1
```

The DrawRectangle method of the WinG control draws a rectangle inside WinG. The sides of the rectangle will be drawn with the pen that you set with the SetPen method. And the rectangle is filled with the brush that you set with the SetSolidBrush method.

BWinG form. The code
nG form as follows:

that fills the entire form,
int where the left mouse

e( ) procedure of the
If statements—one exe-
and the other executed
er you entered the code
e first If statement.

frmVBWinG form so

gle method is the x-coordinate of the upper-
drawn inside WinG, and the second parame-
pplied (0,0) as the first two parameters of the
hat the upper-left corner of the rectangle is
VinG window.

ngle method is the x-coordinate of the lower-
ou want the white rectangle to fill the entire
1) as this parameter.

ectangle method is the y-coordinate of the
ecause you want the white rectangle to fill
d (Height − 1) as this parameter.

ctangle over the entire WinG window.

brush with a red brush:

), 0)

ewly defined brush:


```
JG_WIDTH - 1, _
JG_HEIGHT - 1
```

per-left corner at the point where the mouse
e button was pressed. That is, the upper-left
X,Y). (Recall that X and Y are the parameters
e, so that (X,Y) represents the coordinate po-
ne the Form_MouseDown( ) procedure is

VING_WIDTH and the height of the red rec-
u declared these constants inside the
chapter.)

at this point, you would see a window that
indow. Also, the entire window is filled with
ed rectangle with its upper-left corner at the

5

The WinG window is ready to be slammed into the frm▼ that you typed slams the WinG contents into the frmVBW

```
Tegwing1.SlamIt
```

Inside the frmVBWinG form you now see a white rectangle and a small red rectangle with its upper-left corner at the po button was pressed.

Adding WinG Code to the Form_MouseMove( ) Procedure

You'll now add WinG code to the Form_MouseMov frmVBWinG form. Recall that this procedure contains two cuted when the Do It with WinG menu item is selected, when Do It without WinG is selected. In the previous chap of the second If statement. Now you'll enter the code of th

- Add code to the Form_MouseMove( ) procedure of th that it looks as follows:

```
Private Sub Form_MouseMove(Button As Integer, _
    Shift As Integer, X As Single, Y As Single)

Dim Width, Height

If mnuWithWinG.Checked = True And Button <> 0 The

    ' Draw the white rectangle inside WinG
    Tegwing1.SetPen PS_SOLID, 1, RGB(255, 255, 255
    Tegwing1.SetSolidBrush RGB(255, 255, 255)
    Width = Tegwing1.WinGWidth
    Height = Tegwing1.WinGHeight
    Tegwing1.DrawRectangle 0, _
                           0, _
                           Width - 1, _
                           Height - 1

    ' Draw the red rectangle inside WinG
    Tegwing1.SetSolidBrush RGB(255, 0, 0)
```

```
        Tegwing1.DrawRectangle X, _
                               Y, _
                               X + DRAWING_WIDTH - 1, _
                               Y + DRAWING_HEIGHT - 1

     Tegwing1.SlamIt

  End If

  If mnuWithoutWinG.Checked = True And Button <> 0 Then

     ' Draw the white rectangle
     shpWhiteRectangle.Top = 0
     shpWhiteRectangle.Height = frmVBWinG.ScaleHeight
     shpWhiteRectangle.Left = 0
     shpWhiteRectangle.Width = frmVBWinG.ScaleWidth

     ' Draw the red rectangle
     shpRedRectangle.Top = Y
     shpRedRectangle.Height = DRAWING_WIDTH
     shpRedRectangle.Left = X
     shpRedRectangle.Width = DRAWING_HEIGHT

  End If

End Sub
```

This code is identical to the code you entered in the first If statement of the Form_MouseMove( ) procedure. That is, a white rectangle fills the entire WinG window, and then a red rectangle is drawn with its upper-left corner at the (X,Y) point (the mouse cursor's coordinate position at the time the mouse was moved).

And finally, the contents of WinG are slammed into the form.

Executing and Testing the WinG Operation

Now you can execute the VBWinG program and verify that indeed WinG produces no flickering.

- Select Save from the File menu of Visual Basic.

- Execute the VBWinG program.

- Make sure that the Do It with WinG menu item of the Draw menu is selected, place the mouse cursor inside the application's window, press the left mouse button, and drag the mouse.

As you can see, the entire area of the application's window is white, and when you move the mouse, a red rectangle is drawn with its upper-left corner at the coordinate of the mouse cursor.

Extracting the Size of the WinG Window

In the Form_MouseDown( ) and Form_MouseMove( ) procedures you extracted the width and height of the WinG window as follows:

```
Width = Tegwing1.WinGWidth
Height = Tegwing1.WinGHeight
```

The Information menu lets the user view the values of WinG's width and height.

- Enter the following code in the mnuWinGSize_Click( ) procedure:

```
Private Sub mnuWinGSize_Click( )

    Dim Message As String
    Dim LFCR

    LFCR = Chr(10) + Chr(13)

    Message = "Width of WinG: "
    Message = Message + Str(Tegwing1.WinGWidth)
    Message = Message + LFCR

    Message = Message + "Height of WinG: "
    Message = Message + Str(Tegwing1.WinGHeight)
    Message = Message + LFCR

    MsgBox Message, vbInformation, "WinG Information"

End Sub
```

First, the local variables are declared:

```
Dim Message As String
Dim LFCR
```

The LFCR variable is assigned with the linefeed carriage return characters:

```
LFCR = Chr(10) + Chr(13)
```

And then the Message variable is constructed:

```
Message = "Width of WinG: "
Message = Message + Str(Tegwing1.WinGWidth)
Message = Message + LFCR

Message = Message + "Height of WinG: "
Message = Message + Str(Tegwing1.WinGHeight)
Message = Message + LFCR
```

Finally, the MsgBox statement is used to display the contents of the Message variable:

```
MsgBox Message, vbInformation, "WinG Information"
```

Note that Tegwing1.WinGWidth is the width of the WinG window, and Tegwing1.WinGHeight is the height of the WinG window (these are also the width and height of the frmVBWinG form).

- Select Save from the File menu of Visual Basic.

You can now execute the VBWinG program:

- Execute the VBWinG program.

- Select the WinG Size item from the Information menu.

The VBWinG program responds by displaying the message box, as shown in Figure 5.2.

You displayed the size of the WinG virtual window for the sake of illustrating the WinGWidth and WinGHeight properties of the WinG control. As you can see, the width and height of the virtual WinG window are the same as the width and height of the frmVBWinG form.

- Experiment with the VBWinG program's options and then select Exit from the File menu to terminate the program.

FIGURE 5.2:

Displaying the size of WinG

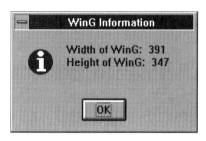

Implementing the Help Menu of VBWinG Program

Recall from Chapter 3 that the VBWinG program's Help menu has two options, About and Help. In this section you'll write the code that implements both of these options.

Implementing the About Option

Here is how you implement the functionality of the About menu item:

- Add the following code inside the mnuAbout_Click( ) procedure of the frmVBWinG form:

```
Private Sub mnuAbout_Click( )

    frmAbout.Show 1

End Sub
```

This instructs Visual Basic to display the frmAbout form as a modal form. (That is, the user must close the frmAbout form before returning to the frmVBWinG form.)

You implement the frmAbout form as follows:

- Select Form from the Insert menu of Visual Basic.

Visual Basic responds by adding a new form to the VBWinG.MAK project.

- Save the new form as About.FRM inside the C:\WinGPrg\CH03 directory.

- Implement the frmAbout form with the Properties settings listed in Table 5.1. When you complete implementing the form, it should look as shown in Figure 5.3.

TABLE 5.1: The Properties of the frmAbout Form

Object: Form
Name: frmAbout

Property	Value
BorderStyle	1 'Fixed Single
Caption	"About"
Height	5910
Left	1095
MaxButton	0 'False
MinButton	0 'False
Picture	C:\VBProg\CH03\About01.BMP
Top	660
Width	5985

Object: Command Button
Name: cmdOK

Property	Value
Caption	"&OK"
Height	495
Left	4320
Top	3480
Width	735

5

FIGURE 5.3:

The frmAbout form in
design mode

> **NOTE** The file About01. BMP, which contains the picture used in the About
> window, was created in Paintbrush.

Unloading the About Form

When you select About from the Help menu, the About dialog box (the frmAbout
form) is displayed. You can then click the OK button to close the About dialog box.
You'll now write the code that closes this form.

- Enter the following code inside the cmdOK_Click( ) procedure of the
  frmAbout form:

```
Private Sub cmdOK_Click( )

    Unload Me

End Sub
```

This instruction unloads (closes) the frmAbout dialog box.

- Select Save from the File menu to save your work.

Implementing the Help Option

Here is how you implement the functionality of the Help menu's Help item:

- Add the following code inside the mnuHelpMe_Click( ) procedure of the frmVBWinG form:

```
Private Sub mnuHelpMe_Click( )

    frmHelp.Show 1

End Sub
```

This code displays the frmHelp form as a modal form. (That is, the user must close the frmHelp form before returning to the frmVBWinG form.)

You can implement the frmHelp form as follows:

- Select Form from the Insert menu of Visual Basic.
  Visual Basic responds by adding a new form to the VBWinG.MAK project.

- Save the new form as Help.FRM inside the C:\WinGPrg\CH03 directory.

- Implement the frmHelp form with the settings listed in Table 5.2. When you complete implementing the form, it should look as shown in Figure 5.4.

NOTE The file Help01. BMP, which contains the picture used in the Help window, was created in Paintbrush.

Unloading the Help Form

When you select the Help item from the Help menu, the Help dialog box (the frmHelp form) is displayed. You can then click the OK button of this dialog box to close it. You'll now write the code that closes this form.

- Enter the following code inside the cmdOK_Click( ) procedure of the frmAbout form:

```
Private Sub cmdOK_Click( )
    Unload Me
End Sub
```

The code that you typed unloads (closes) the frmHelp dialog box.

- Select Save from the File menu to save your work.
- Execute the VBWinG program and verify that the About and Help menus are working correctly.

TABLE 5.2: The Properties of the frmHelp Form

Object: Form
Name: frmHelp

Property	Value
BorderStyle	3 'Fixed Double
Caption	"Help"
Height	5850
Left	990
MaxButton	'False
MinButton	0 'False
Picture	C:\WinGPrg\CH03\Help01.BMP
Top	630
Width	6255

Object: Command Button
Name: cmdOK

Property	Value
Caption	"&OK"
Height	495
Left	5280
Top	4800
Width	495

FIGURE 5.4:

The frmHelp form in design mode

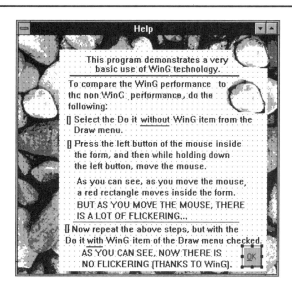

Closing the WinG Session

Don't forget to close the WinG session as follows:

```
Private Sub Form_Unload(Cancel As Integer)
    ' Close the WinG session
    Tegwing1.CloseWinG
End Sub
```

Summary

In this chapter you implemented the parts of the VBWinG program that draw by using WinG technology. As you saw, when you draw with WinG, the flickering disappears. Here is a summary of the essential steps you took in implementing the WinG portion of the VBWinG program:

1. You created a WinG window (inside the Form_Load( ) procedure) as follows:

```
Private Sub Form_Load( )
```

```
Me.ScaleMode = 3 'Pixels
    ' Tell the TegoSoft WinG control
    ' in which window to draw
    Tegwing1.hWndDisplay = Me.hWnd
    ' Open a WinG session
    Tegwing1.OpenWinG

End Sub
```

Don't forget to close the WinG session as follows:

```
Private Sub Form_Unload(Cancel As Integer)

    ' Close the WinG session
    Tegwing1.CloseWinG

End Sub
```

2. You then drew into the WinG window by using the various drawing functions of the WinG control. But before you could do this, you had to set the pen and the brush used for the drawing:

```
Tegwing1.SetPen PS_SOLID, 1, RGB(255, 255, 255)
Tegwing1.SetSolidBrush RGB(255, 255, 255)
```

3. Also, to draw inside WinG you used drawing functions such as the DrawRectangle method to draw a rectangle:

```
Width = Tegwing1.WinGWidth
Height = Tegwing1.WinGHeight
Tegwing1.DrawRectangle 0, 0, Width - 1, Height - 1
```

4. You were then ready to draw inside the WinG window. For example, in this program you drew a white rectangle over the entire WinG window, and then you drew a small red rectangle inside the WinG window.

5. Finally, when you completed drawing inside the WinG virtual window, the contents of the WinG window were slammed into the screen as follows:

```
Tegwing1.SlamIt
```

CHAPTER

SIX

Practice with Visual Basic/WinG

6

In the previous chapter you used Visual Basic/WinG to draw inside a window. In this chapter you'll slightly modify the VBWinG program that you wrote in the previous chapter, just to get some practice working with WinG.

Executing the VBWinG2.EXE Program

Before modifying the VBWinG program, let's execute a copy of the modified version of the program; it resides in the \WinGPrg\EXE\ directory of the book's CD-ROM. The modified version of the program is called VBWinG2.EXE.

- Execute the VBWinG2.EXE program that resides on the book's CD-ROM. The main window of the application appears as shown in Figure 6.1.

FIGURE 6.1:
The VBWinG2.EXE program windows

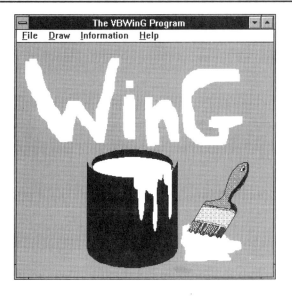

As you can see, the modified version of the program has a picture inside its main application window.

- Make sure that the Do It with WinG menu item is selected, place the mouse cursor inside the application's window, press the left mouse button, and drag the mouse.

The VBWinG2.EXE program responds by drawing red rectangles in accordance with the mouse movements (see Figure 6.2).

FIGURE 6.2:

Drawing red rectangles according to the mouse movements

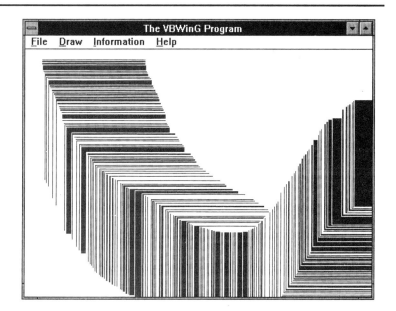

Unlike the VBWinG.EXE program, VBWinG2.EXE lets you change the size of the window during runtime.

- Drag the sides of the window, and practice with the VBWinG2.EXE program.
- When you're finished experimenting, select Exit from the File menu to terminate the VBWinG2.EXE program.

Sizing the Window of the Application

Currently, you cannot maximize the size of the application's window during runtime because the MaxButton property of the frmVBWinG form was set to False. Also, when designing the form, you set its BorderSize property to 1=Fixed Single. This means that the user cannot size the application's window. You'll now add code that enables the user to do this. First you need to make some changes in the Properties window:

- Set the BorderSize property of the frmVBWinG form to 2= Sizable.

- Set the MaxButton property to True.

- Set the Picture property of the frmVBWinG form to \WinGPrg\CH03\Brush.BMP (or any other BMP picture that you'd like to use). The Brush.BMP picture is shown in Figure 6.3.

- Set the BackColor property of the frmVBWinG form to light gray.

FIGURE 6.3:
The Brush.BMP picture that is used as the background picture of the frmVBWinG form.

You'll now add code that enables the user to size the WinG window. You have to add code that takes into consideration the fact that the user may change the size of the application's window while running the program, and you need to make sure that the WinG virtual window changes along with the application window.

Recall that whenever the Form_Load( ) procedure of the frmVBWinG form is executed (upon executing the program), the following statements are executed:

```
Tegwing1.hWndDisplay = Me.hWnd
Tegwing1.OpenWinG
```

That is, you want to open a WinG session, and the size of the WinG window is the same as the size of the frmWinG form.

When the user changes the size of the frmVBWinG form, the Form_Resize( ) procedure is automatically executed.

- Add the following code within the Form_Resize( ) procedure of the frmVBWinG form:

```
Private Sub Form_Resize( )

    ' Close the WinG session
    Tegwing1.CloseWinG

    ' Tell the TegoSoft WinG control
    ' in which window to draw
    Tegwing1.hWndDisplay = Me.hWnd

    ' Open a WinG session
    Tegwing1.OpenWinG

End Sub
```

This code closes the current WinG session with the CloseWinG method:

```
Tegwing1.CloseWinG
```

and then opens a new WinG session:

```
Tegwing1.hWndDisplay = Me.hWnd
Tegwing1.OpenWinG
```

6

To summarize, we've opened a new WinG session. The size of the WinG window is the same as the new size of the frmVBWinG form. Each time the application window size changes, the old WinG session is closed and a new session opened, with its size the same as that of the application window.

Modifying the WinG Code of the Form_MouseMove( ) Procedure

Currently, the Form_MouseMove( ) procedure includes WinG code that:

1. Draws a white rectangle.

2. Draws a red rectangle according to the mouse movements.

In other words, before drawing the red rectangle, the program fills the entire WinG window with a white rectangle.

To make the VBWinG2.EXE program behave as you saw when you executed it at the beginning of this chapter, you have to comment out the statements that draw the white rectangle.

- Comment out the statements that draw a white rectangle inside the WinG window. When you're finished, the Form_MouseMove( ) procedure of the frmVBWinG form should look as follows:

```
Private Sub Form_MouseMove(Button As Integer, _
        Shift As Integer, X As Single, Y As Single)

Dim Width, Height

If mnuWithWinG.Checked = True And Button <> 0 Then

' Draw the white rectangle inside WinG
'''Tegwing1.SetPen PS_SOLID, 1, RGB(255, 255, 255)
'''Tegwing1.SetSolidBrush RGB(255, 255, 255)
'''Width = Tegwing1.WinGWidth
'''Height = Tegwing1.WinGHeight
'''Tegwing1.DrawRectangle 0, 0, Width - 1, Height - 1
```

```
' Draw the red rectangle inside WinG
Tegwing1.SetSolidBrush RGB(255, 0, 0)

Tegwing1.DrawRectangle X, _
                       Y, _
                       X + DRAWING_WIDTH - 1, _
                       Y + DRAWING_HEIGHT - 1

Tegwing1.SlamIt

End If

If mnuWithoutWinG.Checked = True And Button <> 0 Then

shpWhiteRectangle.Top = 0
shpWhiteRectangle.Height = frmVBWinG.ScaleHeight
shpWhiteRectangle.Left = 0
shpWhiteRectangle.Width = frmVBWinG.ScaleWidth
shpRedRectangle.Top = Y
shpRedRectangle.Height = DRAWING_WIDTH
shpRedRectangle.Left = X
shpRedRectangle.Width = DRAWING_HEIGHT
End If
End Sub
```

- Select Save from the File menu of Visual Basic to save your work.

- Execute the program and verify its proper operation.

NOTE

> Basically, you've learned how to draw rectangles using WinG technology. But how do you draw circles, ellipses, and other shapes in WinG? As it turns out, you draw these shapes inside the WinG virtual window in the same manner that you draw inside a "regular" window. The WinG Bible, located on the accompanying CD-ROM, shows how this is accomplished.

6

Summary

In this chapter you learned how to write WinG code inside the Form_Resize( ) procedure (executed whenever the user changes the size of the form). This code closes the current WinG session and opens a new one, with a window the same size as the application window. By including these statements, you've made sure that the WinG virtual window remains the same size as the application window whenever the user resizes the application window.

You also modified the code inside the Form_MouseMove( ) procedure so that instead of filling the WinG window with a white rectangle for each mouse movement, the procedure only draws red rectangles. This means that as the user moves the mouse, additional red rectangles appear inside the window. (As you saw in Figure 6.2, some interesting special effects can be produced this way.)

CHAPTER

SEVEN

Loading and Displaying Bitmaps with Visual Basic/WinG

7

In this chapter you'll execute the VBBMP.EXE program, for which you'll write the code in Chapter 8. This program illustrates how to load BMP (bitmap) files from the hard drive and display them using WinG technology. Along the way, you'll see that it's important to save your bitmap files in 256-color format, and you'll also see a problem that can arise with composite (nonsolid) colors.

Executing the VBBMP.EXE Program

The VBBMP.EXE program resides in the \WinGPrg\EXE\ directory of the book's CD-ROM.

- Execute the VBBMP.EXE program. The blank window shown in Figure 7.1 appears.

FIGURE 7.1:

The window of the VBBMP.EXE program

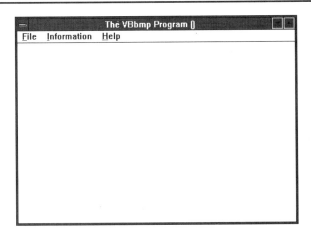

As shown in Figure 7.1, the title bar of the window initially reads "The VBbmp Program( )." As usual in Windows applications, the parentheses will contain the name of a data file you've loaded (in this case, a BMP file) but they are empty now, because you have not yet loaded a BMP file.

The VBBMP program presents three menus: File, Information, and Help. These menus are shown in Figures 7.2 through 7.4.

FIGURE 7.2:

The File menu of the VBBMP.EXE program

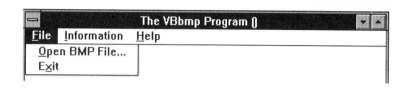

FIGURE 7.3:

The Information menu of the VBBMP.EXE program

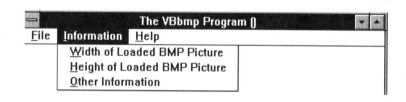

FIGURE 7.4:

The Help menu of the VBBMP.EXE program

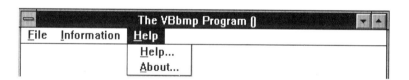

The Information menu is included in this program so that the user will be able to determine the size in pixels of the displayed BMP pictures, and the color format of the BMP picture.

To see the Help menu in action:

- Select Help from the Help menu. You'll see the Help window, as shown in Figure 7.5.

- Click the OK button to close the Help window.

FIGURE 7.5:

The Help window of the VBBMP program

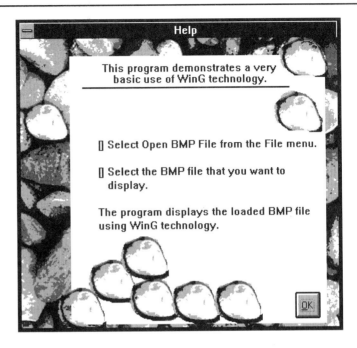

To see the About menu in action, select About from the Help menu. You'll see the About window, as shown in Figure 7.6.

- Click the OK button to close the About window.

Loading and Displaying BMP Files with the VBBMP Program

You'll now load and display a BMP file with the VBBMP program.

- Select Open BMP File from the File menu. You'll see the Open dialog box, as shown in Figure 7.7.

- Select the file named Bucket.BMP, which resides on the book's CD-ROM in the \WinGPrg\BMP directory.

FIGURE 7.6:

The About window of the VBBMP program

FIGURE 7.7:

The Open dialog box

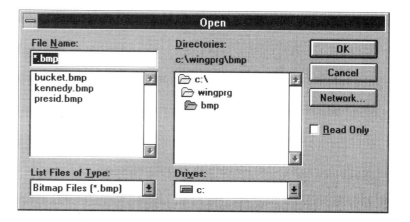

VBBMP responds by loading the Bucket.BMP file, and displaying it as shown in Figure 7.8. As you can see, the window's title bar now indicates that the Bucket.BMP file is loaded.

FIGURE 7.8:

Loading the Bucket.BMP file from the \WinGPrg\BMP directory of the book's CD-ROM

- Drag the borders of the window to change its size.

As you resize the window, the Bucket.BMP picture is stretched or compressed so that it fills the entire area of the window. Figures 7.9 through 7.11 show the window of the VBBMP program with various window sizes.

- Experiment with the VBBMP program by loading other BMP files. (They must be 256-color BMP files. You'll learn more about 256-color BMP files in the next section of this chapter.)

FIGURE 7.9:

The VBBMP program window with the Bucket.BMP picture in it (enlarged).

FIGURE 7.10:

The window of the VBBMP program with the Bucket.BMP picture in it (reduced).

Figure 7.12 shows the program window with the Presid.BMP file from the CD-ROM's \WinPrg\BMP directory. In Figure 7.13, the image (the presidential seal) has been stretched and distorted to fit the window's size and shape. Figure 7.14

FIGURE 7.11:

The VBBMP program window with the Bucket.BMP picture (reduced further).

FIGURE 7.12:

The VBBMP program window with the Presid.BMP picture at the window's default size

shows a reduced version of the image; the window has been resized so that the image appears in its correct proportions. You can experiment with the Kennedy.BMP file (a portrait of John F. Kennedy), also from the \WinGprg\BMP directory, to get the same effects.

• Select Exit from the File menu to terminate the program.

FIGURE 7.13:

The window of the VBBMP program with the Presid.BMP picture in it. The window size was enlarged, and the picture was stretched accordingly.

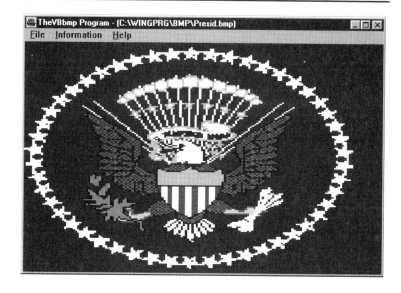

7

FIGURE 7.14:

The VBBMP program window with the Presid.BMP picture resized to the image's correct proportions

256-Color BMP Files

When you save a BMP file with a drawing program such as Paintbrush, you can save it as either a 16-color BMP file or a 256-color BMP file.

- From the Program Manager in Windows, start Paintbrush (usually in the Accessories group).

- Draw something, and then select Save As from the File menu of Paintbrush.

Stretching BMP Pictures Proportionally

As you can see from the illustrations of the presidential seal and Kennedy, it is important to stretch the BMP pictures in a proportional manner.

Of course, if you let your user stretch the BMP pictures (as is the case in the VBBmp program), you have no control how your user resizes the window. But if you are resizing the window from within your code, then you'd better resize the window in a proportional manner. For example, if the "natural" size of the BMP picture is 50 pixels wide by 100 pixels high (50 by 100), then resize the window so that its new width and height are enlarged/reduced by the same amount. For example, the enlarged version of the 50 by 100 BMP picture can be 50*1.5 pixels wide and 100*1.5 pixels high. And the reduced size of the 50 by 100 BMP pictures can be 50*0.5 pixels wide by 100*0.5 pixels high.

To force your user to enlarge/reduce the BMP pictures in a proportional manner, set the BorderStyle property of the window that holds the BMP picture to Fixed. Your program should then include a Zoom menu that enlarges/reduces the window size according to the user's selection from the Zoom menu.

Paintbrush responds by displaying the Save As dialog box (see Figure 7.15).

FIGURE 7.15:

Saving a BMP file as a 16-color BMP file with Paintbrush

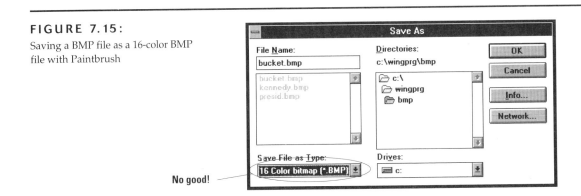

As you can see, the default setting of Paintbrush (in our configuration) is to save a BMP file in 16-color format. Note that depending on the particular setting of your Windows, your Paintbrush may suggest a different default format for saving the BMP file. However, the VBBMP program expects a 256-color BMP. So when generating a BMP file with Paintbrush, you need to save it as a 256-color BMP file (see Figure 7.16).

FIGURE 7.16:

Saving a BMP file as a 256-color BMP file with Paintbrush

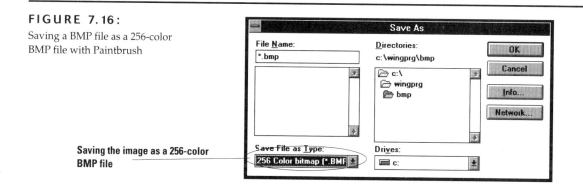

Saving the image as a 256-color BMP file

Solid and Composite Colors in Bitmaps

Figure 7.17 shows the default color palette in Paintbrush. To see the colors, of course, you'll need to look at Paintbrush on your own screen.

Some of the colors in the palette are solid colors, and some are composite colors, created by mixing several solid colors together.

To verify this, perform the following steps:

- Draw several squares inside the desktop of Paintbrush and then fill the squares with colors as shown in Figure 7.18.

The leftmost square in Figure 7.18 was filled with a solid black color. The rightmost square was filled with a composite color. To verify that the color is a composite:

- Select Zoom In from the View menu of Paintbrush.

Paintbrush responds by displaying a small square as the mouse cursor.

FIGURE 7.17:
The default available colors (palette) of Paintbrush

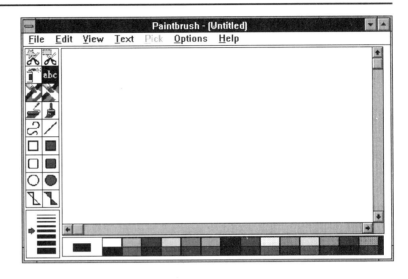

FIGURE 7.18:
Filling squares with colors.

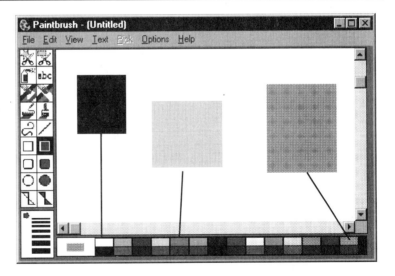

- Click the mouse inside the rightmost square.

Paintbrush responds by zooming into the section that you clicked (see Figure 7.19). As you can see, what appeared to be a solid color is actually composed of more than one color. The alternating pixels create the illusion of a solid color.

FIGURE 7.19:

Zooming in on a composite color

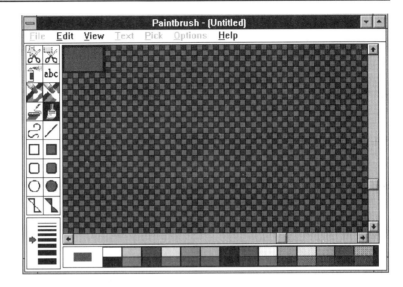

- Select Zoom Out from the View menu to return to a normal view in Paintbrush.

In the next section you'll see a problem that can arise when bitmap images containing composite colors are stretched.

Stretching BMP Pictures

During the course of this book, you'll display BMP files, and you'll stretch them. That is, just as in the VBBMP program, you'll copy the contents of the BMP files into areas on the screen that may or may not match the image's correct proportions.

The problem with composite colors is that the composite color will only look good if the pixels of the filled color are arranged in a certain alternating order. For example, a certain composite color may be a result of mixing the green and blue colors. Let's assume that the combined color has 50% green in it and 50% blue in it. Thus, the composite color should have the pixels arranged in the following order:

```
green blue green blue green blue
green blue green blue green blue
```

```
green blue green blue green blue
green blue green blue green blue
green blue green blue green blue
green blue green blue green blue
```

...and so on

If the green-blue order is changed, it will result in a different color! When you stretch an area that is filled with a composite color, the area is enlarged or shrinked, and if you enlarge the area by a value that's not an exact integer multiple of the original size, the original order of the green-blue arrangement will not be maintained. To see this in action, perform the following experiment:

- Start a new drawing with Paintbrush.

- Draw a square and fill it with a composite color.

- Click the Pick tool (the right tool on the first row of the Tools window of Paintbrush), place the mouse cursor inside the square, press the left mouse button and drag the mouse. As you drag, a rectangle is drawn.

- Release the left mouse button.

As you can see, an area is enclosed by a rectangle. This area is referred to as the *source area*.

- Select Shrink + Grow from the Pick menu of Paintbrush, then place the mouse cursor inside a free area on the desktop of Paintbrush, and while the left button is still held down, move the mouse. As you drag the mouse, a rectangle is drawn. This area is called the *destination* or *target area*.

- Release the left mouse button.

Paintbrush responds by drawing, inside the destination area, the contents of the source area. Because the size of the source area is not equal to that of the destination area, Paintbrush will stretch the area that is copied from the source to the destination. Furthermore, because the destination area is almost certainly not an integer multiple of the source area, it will have a different color than the original source area. For example, if the width and height of the source area are 100 pixels by 50 pixels and the width and height of the destination area are 135 pixels by 172 pixels, the color filled in the destination area will be different than the original composite color that existed in the source area.

Figure 7.20 show several destination areas that were generated by using the Shrink + Grow item of the Pick menu. Even in black-and-white you can see that some of the squares have distracting stripes or patterns in them. Again, the reason for this is that the composite colors are not arranged in the same order as in the original source area. (Paintbrush does its best to arrange the pixels so as to avoid this problem, but because the contents of the source area have been enlarged or shrunken, the order of the pixels will be changed.)

FIGURE 7.20:

When you shrink or grow an area filled with a composite color, the result may be a different color than the original.

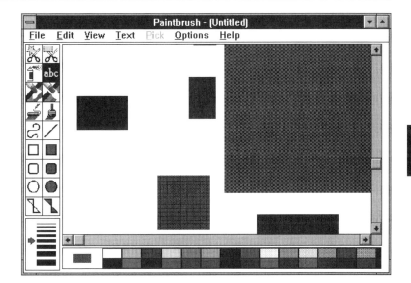

Figure 7.21 shows a picture that was enlarged. The shirt of the man in this picture changed colors, because the original shirt was painted with a composite color.

FIGURE 7.21:

After enlarging the picture of the man, the shirt changed colors.

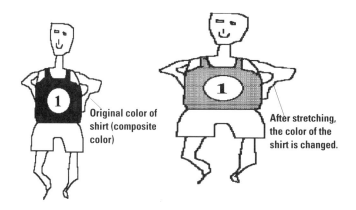

Original color of shirt (composite color)

After stretching, the color of the shirt is changed.

NOTE

The distorting effect of stretching areas with composite colors can affect your program's performance in potentially embarrassing ways. For example, you can design a program for children that illustrates a story about a little girl with a little red hat. But if your user enlarges the pictures, the little girl's hat may not appear as red. Even worse, an international crisis might occur if your program draws flags of countries, and because you did not use solid colors, the enlarged flag appears with stripes and wrong colors. In writing any Windows program, you must assume that users will be free to resize your application window. So to avoid these problems (and thus achieve world peace) make sure your bitmap illustrations use only solid colors.

Summary

In this chapter you executed the VBBMP.EXE program. In the next chapter you'll write the code for this program by using Visual Basic/WinG.

As you saw in this chapter, the VBBMP program loads a BMP file and then displays the BMP file. The window of the VBBMP program can be sized, and the BMP picture is stretched accordingly.

You also learned in this chapter how to use Paintbrush for saving BMP files in 256-color BMP format, and you also learned that it is better to avoid using composite colors if your program allows the user to stretch a window containing bitmapped colors. As stated in this chapter, you can zoom into an area in Paintbrush to examine whether the color is solid or composite.

7

CHAPTER

EIGHT

The WinG Code of the VBBMP Program

In this chapter you'll write the code of the VBBMP program, which you executed in the previous chapter. This program loads and displays BMP files available on your disk.

Creating the VBBMP Project

As usual, the first step is to create the project of the VBBMP program.

- Start the Visual Basic program.

- Select New Project from the File menu and save the new project files as follows: Save the new form as VBBMP.FRM in the C:\WinGPrg\CH07 directory. Save the new project file as VBBMP.MAK in the same directory.

Implementing the frmVBBMP Form

You'll now implement the frm VBBMP form.

- To add the TegoSoft WinG control to the project, select Custom Controls from the Tools menu and select the TegoSoft WinG control.

- Implement the frmVBBMP form with the Properties settings shown in Table 8.1. When you're finished, the form should look as shown in Figure 8.1.

Two controls appear in the frmVBBMP form. One is the familiar icon of the TegoSoft WinG control. The other control is the common dialog box control that comes with Visual Basic. The icon of the WinG control inside the Tools window is shown in Figure 8.2, and once you place the WinG control inside the form, the control appears inside the form as shown in Figure 8.3.

TABLE 8.1: The Properties of the frmVBBMP Form

Object: Form
Object Name: frmVBBMP

Property	Value
Caption	"The VBbmp Program ()"
Height	4920
Left	035
Top	1185
Width	6840

Object: CommonDialog
Object Name: CommonDialog1

Property	Value
Left	360
Top	2160
cancelerror	'True

Object: TegoSoft WinG Control
Object Name: Tegwing1

Property	Value
Left	360
Top	2880

8

Creating the Menu of the frmVBBMP Form

You'll now create the menu of the frmVBBMP form.

FIGURE 8.1:

The frmVBBMP form of the VBBMP
program in design mode

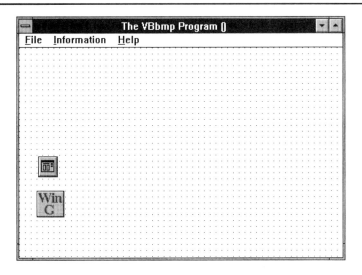

FIGURE 8.2:

The icon of the WinG control inside
the Tools window of Visual Basic

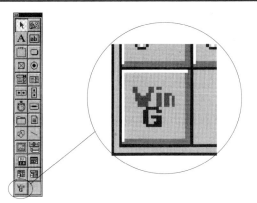

FIGURE 8.3:

The WinG control inside the form

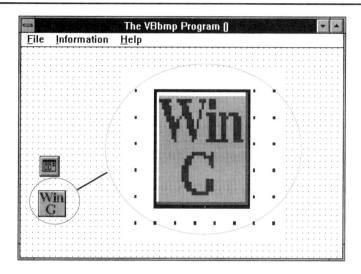

- Implement the menu of the frmVBBMP form with the Properties settings shown in Table 8.2. The menus of the frmVBBMP form are shown in Figures 8.4, 8.5, and 8.6.

TABLE 8.2: The Menu of the frmVBBMP Form

Caption	Name
&File	mnuFile
...&Open BMP File...	mnuOpen
...E&xit	mnuExit
Information	mnuInformation
...&Width of Loaded BMP Picture	mnuBMPWidth
...&Height of Loaded BMP Picture	mnuBMPHeight
...&Other Information	mnuOtherInformation
&Help	mnuHelp
...&Help...	mnuHelpMe
...&About...	mnuAbout

8

FIGURE 8.4:

The File menu

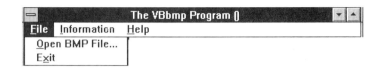

FIGURE 8.5:

The Information menu

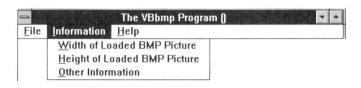

FIGURE 8.6:

The Help menu

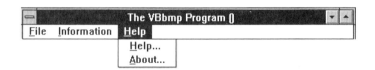

The General Declarations Section of the frmVBBMP Form

You'll now enter the code of the General Declarations section of the frmVBBMP form.

- Enter the following code in the frmVBBMP form:

```
Option Explicit

Dim gBMPHandle As Integer

Const SRCAND = &H8800C6      ' dest = source AND dest
Const SRCCOPY = &HCC0020     ' dest = source
Const SRCERASE = &H440328    ' dest = source AND (NOT dest)
```

```
Const SRCINVERT = &H660046 ' dest = source XOR dest
Const SRCPAINT = &HEE0086  ' dest = source OR dest
```

This code first declares the gBMPHandle variable. As you'll soon see, this variable will hold the handle of the BMP file that the VBBMP program loads. Because you declared this variable inside the General Declarations section of the frmVBBMP form, it is accessible from any procedure inside the frmVBBMP form.

The rest of the statements that you entered are declarations of constants. You'll learn about the use of these constants later in this chapter.

The Form_Load( ) Procedure of the frmVBBMP Form

You'll now write the code of the Form_Load( ) procedure of the frmVBBMP form. This procedure is executed whenever the user starts the VBBMP program.

- Enter the following code inside the Form_Load( ) procedure of the frmVBBMP form:

```
Private Sub Form_Load( )

    Me.ScaleMode = 3 'Pixels

    ' Tell the TegoSoft WinG control
    ' in which window to draw
    Tegwing1.hWndDisplay = Me.hWnd

    ' Open a WinG session
    Tegwing1.OpenWinG

End Sub
```

This code first sets the ScaleMode property of the frmVBBMP form to 3:

```
Me.ScaleMode = 3 'Pixels
```

This statement causes the program to report distances in units of pixels.

8

The next statement sets the hWndDisplay property of the WinG control to the hWnd property of the frmVBBMP form:

```
' Tell the TegoSoft WinG control
' in which window to draw
Tegwing1.hWndDisplay = Me.hWnd
```

So from now on, whenever you slam the contents of the WinG virtual window, they will go into the frmVBBMP form.

The next statement in the Form_Load( ) procedure opens a WinG session:

```
' Open a WinG session
Tegwing1.OpenWinG
```

Because you set the hWndDisplay property of the WinG control to the hWnd property of the frmVBBMP form, the size of the WinG window that you opened is the same as the size of the frmVBBMP form.

The Code of the Form_Unload( ) Procedure of the frmVBBMP Form

- Enter the following code in the Form_Unload( ) procedure of the frmVBBMP form:

```
Private Sub Form_Unload(Cancel As Integer)

    ' Close the WinG session
    Tegwing1.CloseWinG

    ' Close the BMP
    Tegwing1.CloseBMP gBMPHandle

End Sub
```

When the user terminates the VBBMP program, the Form_Unload( ) procedure is automatically executed. The first statement that you entered closes the WinG session:

```
' Close the WinG session
Tegwing1.CloseWinG
```

While running the VBBMP program, the user may have loaded a BMP file. Thus, the second statement in the Form_Unload( ) procedure closes the BMP file by using the CloseBMP method of the WinG control:

```
' Close the BMP
Tegwing1.CloseBMP gBMPHandle
```

Note that the CloseBMP method requires a parameter— it needs to know which BMP file to close. You supplied the gBMPHandle variable as the parameter of the CloseBMP method. As you'll soon see, when you open the BMP file, the handle of the loaded BMP file is stored inside this variable.

The Code of the Exit Item of the File Menu

- Enter the following code in the mnuExit_Click( ) procedure of the frmVBBMP form:

```
Private Sub mnuExit_Click( )

    Unload Me

End Sub
```

This statement unloads the frmVBBMP form (which causes the VBBMP program to terminate).

Loading and Displaying the BMP File

You'll now write the procedures that load and display the BMP file.

The mnuOpen_Click( ) procedure is executed whenever the user selects Open BMP File from the File menu.

- Write the following code in the mnuOpen_Click( ) procedure of the frmVBBMP form:

```
Private Sub mnuOpen_Click( )
```

8

```
' Selecting a file (with the common dialog box)

' Set an error trap prior to displaying
' the Open dialog box.
On Error GoTo OpenError

' Set the items of the File Type list box
CommonDialog1.Filter = _
    "All Files (*.*) ¦ *.* ¦Bitmap Files (*.bmp)¦*.bmp"

' Set the default File Type
CommonDialog1.FilterIndex = 2

' Display the common dialog box
CommonDialog1.Action = 1

' No need to trap errors any more,
' so remove the error trap
On Error GoTo 0

''' MsgBox CommonDialog1.FileName

' Close previous loaded BMP file (if any)
Tegwing1.CloseBMP gBMPHandle

' Open the selected BMP file
gBMPHandle = Tegwing1.OpenBMP(CommonDialog1.FileName)

If gBMPHandle = 0 Then
   MsgBox "Can't open the " _
         + CommonDialog1.FileName _
         + " file.", vbInformation, "Error"
   Exit Sub
End If

Me.Caption = "TheVBbmp Program - (" + _
              CommonDialog1.FileName + ")"

DisplayBMP (gBMPHandle)

' Exit this procedure
Exit Sub
```

```
OpenError:
' The user pressed the Cancel key of
' the common dialog box, or an error occurred.

' Exit this procedure
Exit Sub

End Sub
```

The code you entered lets the user select a BMP file, and then displays the BMP file.

First an error trap is set:

```
' Set an error trap prior to displaying
' the Open dialog box.
On Error GoTo OpenError
```

If an error occurs, the program will immediately jump to the OpenError label:

```
OpenError:
' The user pressed the Cancel key of
' the common dialog box, or an error occurred.

' Exit this procedure
Exit Sub
```

In other words, if an error occurs, the procedure will terminate.

The Filter property of the common dialog box is then set:

```
' Set the items of the File Type list box
CommonDialog1.Filter = _
    "All Files (*.*) | *.* |Bitmap Files (*.bmp)|*.bmp"
```

Then the default File Type is set:

```
' Set the default File Type
CommonDialog1.FilterIndex = 2
```

Later, when the Open dialog box is displayed, these statements cause the Open common dialog to appear as shown in Figure 8.7.

The common dialog box is now ready to be displayed, so display it as an Open dialog box by setting the Action property to 1:

```
' Display the common dialog box
CommonDialog1.Action = 1
```

8

FIGURE 8.7:

The Open common dialog box. The default displayed files are BMP files.

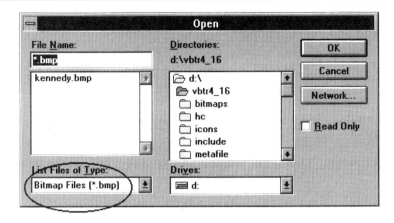

When you designed the form, you set the Cancel property of the common dialog box to True. This means that if the user clicks the Cancel button of the Open dialog box, an error will occur (and as a result of the error-trapping statement, the procedure will be terminated). Also, if an error occurs while the Open common dialog box is displayed, the error-trapping statement causes the procedure to be terminated. If no error occurred and the user did not click the Cancel button, the next statement in the procedure is executed.

Because there is no need to trap errors anymore, you remove the error trapping mechanism:

```
' No need to trap errors any more,
' so remove the error trap
On Error GoTo 0
```

Then you execute the CloseBMP method to close the previously loaded BMP file (if any):

```
' Close previous loaded BMP file (if any)
Tegwing1.CloseBMP gBMPHandle
```

You load the BMP file that was selected by the user as follows:

```
' Open the selected BMP file
gBMPHandle = Tegwing1.OpenBMP(CommonDialog1.FileName)
```

Note that the return value of the OpenBMP method is assigned to the gBMPHandle variable. So from now on, you refer to the BMP file as gBMPHandle. Also note that

Loading a BMP File

To load a BMP file, use the TegoSoft WinG control's OpenBMP method as in the following (fictitious) example:

```
gBMPHandle = Tegwing1.OpenBMP("C:\Try\MyBMP.BMP")
```

In the preceding statement, the file MyBMP.BMP that resides inside the C:\Try directory is loaded. The return value from the OpenBMP method is assigned to a variable. You refer to the loaded BMP file by the value that was returned from the OpenBMP method. For example, to close the loaded BMP file (that is, to remove it from memory), you would use the following statement:

```
Tegwing1.CloseBMP gBMPHandle
```

If the value returned by the OpenBMP method is less than or equal to 0, it means that the BMP file was not loaded successfully.

8

the OpenBMP method takes one parameter, the path and name of the BMP file that will be loaded with the OpenBMP method.

An If statement is then executed to examine whether the BMP file was loaded successfully:

```
If gBMPHandle <= 0 Then
    MsgBox "Can't open the " _
            + CommonDialog1.FileName _
            + " file.", vbInformation, "Error"
    Exit Sub
End If
```

If the BMP file was loaded successfully, the Caption property of the frmVBBMP form is set so that the caption will indicate which BMP file is currently loaded:

```
Me.Caption = "TheVBbmp Program - (" + _
            CommonDialog1.FileName + ")"
```

All right! It is now time to display the loaded BMP file:

```
DisplayBMP (gBMPHandle)
```

You'll write the code of the DisplayBMP( ) function later in this chapter.

Finally, you terminate the procedure:

```
' Exit this procedure
Exit Sub
```

Writing the Code of the Form_Paint( ) Procedure of the frmVBBMP Form

The Form_Paint( ) procedure of the frmVBBMP form is executed whenever Windows decides that there is a need to redraw the frmVBBMP form. For example, suppose that currently the frmVBBMP form is displayed as shown in Figure 8.8.

FIGURE 8.8:

The frmVBBMP form during runtime

Now suppose that the user drags the window shown in Figure 8.8 to the left, so that the frmVBBMP form looks during runtime as shown in Figure 8.9.

FIGURE 8.9:

Dragging the form to the left

If the user drags the window back to the right, it will appear as shown in Figure 8.10.

FIGURE 8.10:

Dragging the window of Figure 8.9 back to the right

As you can see in Figure 8.10, the area that was hidden is now blank. Windows knows that you probably want to redraw the window, so it automatically executes the Form_Paint( ) procedure. Thus, you have to write code inside the Form_Paint( ) procedure that redraws the frmVBBMP form.

- Enter the following code in the Form_Paint( ) procedure of the frmVBBMP form:

```
Private Sub Form_Paint( )

    If gBMPHandle > 0 Then
        DisplayBMP (gBMPHandle)
    End If

End Sub
```

This procedure uses an If statement to examine the value of gBMPHandle. Recall that gBMPHandle holds the handle of the loaded BMP file. If the value of gBMPHandle is greater than 0, it means that there is a loaded BMP file. Thus, the code under the If statement uses the DisplayBMP( ) function to display the loaded BMP file.

The Code of the Form_Resize ( ) Procedure of the frmVBBMP Form

Whenever the user resizes the frmVBBMP form, the Form_Resize( ) procedure of the frmVBBMP form is executed. You'll now write the code of the Form_Resize( ) procedure.

- Enter the following code in the Form_Resize( ) procedure of the frmVBBMP form:

```
Private Sub Form_Resize( )

    If gBMPHandle <= 0 Then
        Exit Sub
    End If

    ' Close the WinG session
    Tegwing1.CloseWinG
```

```
Tegwing1.hWndDisplay = Me.hWnd
' Open a WinG session
Tegwing1.OpenWinG

DisplayBMP (gBMPHandle)
```

End Sub

The code you entered first uses an If statement to examine the value of gBMPHandle:

```
If gBMPHandle <= 0 Then
   Exit Sub
End If
```

So if gBMPHandle is less than or equal to 0, it means that no BMP file is loaded, and hence there is no point in executing the rest of the statements of the Form_Resize ( ) procedure.

If a BMP file has been loaded, the rest of the statements inside the Form_Resize( ) procedure are executed.

The current WinG session is closed:

```
' Close the WinG session
Tegwing1.CloseWinG
```

You close the WinG session because you want to start a new WinG session:

```
Tegwing1.hWndDisplay = Me.hWnd

' Open a WinG session
Tegwing1.OpenWinG
```

Why did you open a new WinG session? Because the frmVBBMP window has a new size, and you want the WinG window to have the same size as the frmVBBMP form.

Finally, the DisplayBMP( ) function is executed to display the BMP picture:

```
DisplayBMP (gBMPHandle)
```

8

The Code of the DisplayBM( ) Function

You'll now write the code of the DisplayBMP( ) function. Recall that you executed the DisplayBMP( ) function in three places: from within the Form_Load( ) procedure, from within the Form_Paint( ) procedure, and from within the Form_Resize( ) procedure.

Here is how you add the DisplayBMP( ) function to the frmVBBMP form:

- Display the window that displays the code of the frmVBBMP form, and select Procedure from the Insert menu of Visual Basic.

Visual Basic responds by displaying the Insert Procedure dialog box (see Figure 8.11).

FIGURE 8.11:

The Insert Procedure dialog box

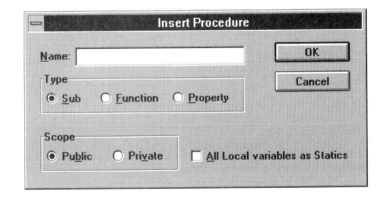

- Type DisplayBMP as the name of the new function, and select the Function radio button.

The Insert Procedure dialog box should now look as shown in Figure 8.12.

- Click the OK button of the Insert Procedure dialog box.

FIGURE 8.12:

Adding the DisplayBMP( ) function

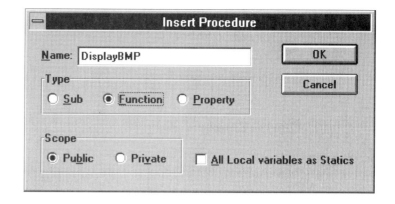

Visual Basic responds by inserting the DisplayBMP( ) function inside the general section of the frmVBBMP form.

- Write the following code inside the DisplayBMP( ) function. Note that you have to add the parameter of the DisplayBMP( ) function (on the first line of the function) as shown below. In other words, when Visual Basic wrote the first and last lines of the DisplayBMP( ) function, it did not write the parameter of this function.

```
Public Sub DisplayBMP(BMPHandle As Integer)

Dim XTarget, YTarget As Integer
Dim WidthTarget, HeightTarget As Integer
Dim XSource, YSource As Integer
Dim WidthSource, HeightSource As Integer
Dim StretchType As Long
Dim BMPSourceHandle As Integer

    XTarget = 0
    YTarget = 0
    WidthTarget = Tegwing1.WinGWidth
    HeightTarget = Tegwing1.WinGHeight
    XSource = 0
    YSource = 0
    WidthSource = Tegwing1.GetBMPWidth(BMPHandle)
    HeightSource = Tegwing1.GetBMPHeight(BMPHandle)
    StretchType = SRCCOPY
    BMPSourceHandle = BMPHandle
```

8

```
' Copy the BMP file into WinG
Tegwing1.CopyBMP2WinG XTarget, YTarget, _
            WidthTarget, HeightTarget, _
            BMPSourceHandle, _
            XSource, YSource, _
            WidthSource, HeightSource, _
            StretchType

' SlamIt
Tegwing1.SlamIt

End Sub
```

NOTE The parameter you are passing to the DisplayBMP( ) function is the value of the gBMPHandle variable. That is, you are passing this function the handle of the BMP file that was loaded. Of course, gBMPHandle is a global variable that was declared inside the General Declarations section of the frmVBBMP form. As such, it is accessible from within the DisplayBMP( ) function. You could have written this function without any parameters, because it has access to the gBMPHandle variable. We wrote the DisplayBMP( ) function with a parameter simply to emphasize that the DisplayBMP( ) function displays the BMP file that was loaded.

The code you entered first declares various local variables:

```
Dim XTarget, YTarget As Integer
Dim WidthTarget, HeightTarget As Integer
Dim XSource, YSource As Integer
Dim WidthSource, HeightSource As Integer
Dim StretchType As Long
Dim BMPSourceHandle As Integer
```

The DisplayBMP( ) function displays the loaded BMP file. In the above variable names, the loaded BMP file is referred to as the source. The source is copied into WinG. Thus, WinG is referred to as the target (or destination). Refer to Figure 8.13 for a pictorial representation of the operations of the DisplayBMP( ) function.

FIGURE 8.13:

The operations of the DisplayBMP( ) function

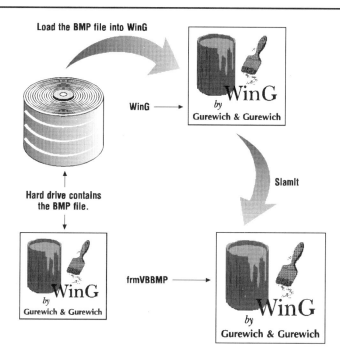

The XTarget and YTarget variables are the (*x*,*y*) coordinates of the upper-left corner of the WinG window. The BMP that you loaded from the hard drive is rectangular. Because you want to copy this file from the hard drive into the WinG window so that its upper-left corner is at the (0,0) point of the window, you set the XTarget and YTarget variables to 0:

```
XTarget = 0
YTarget = 0
```

Then the variables that hold the width and the height of the target are set to the width and height of WinG:

```
WidthTarget = Tegwing1.WinGWidth
HeightTarget = Tegwing1.WinGHeight
```

Because you want to copy the entire loaded BMP file, the (*x*,*y*) coordinates of the source are (0,0). Thus, you set the XSource and YSource variables to 0:

```
XSource = 0
YSource = 0
```

8

Again, you want to copy the entire loaded BMP file, so you set the WidthSource and HeightSource variables to the width and height of the loaded BMP file by using the GetBMPWidth( ) and GetBMPHeight( ) methods as follows:

```
WidthSource = Tegwing1.GetBMPWidth(BMPHandle)
HeightSource = Tegwing1.GetBMPHeight(BMPHandle)
```

There are two more variables that you have to set before copying the loaded BMP file to the WinG window:

```
StretchType = SRCCOPY
BMPSourceHandle = BMPHandle
```

The StretchType variable is set to SRCCOPY. Recall that in the General Declarations section you declared various constants, including SRCCOPY. When you want to copy the source to the destination as-is (without manipulating the picture in any way), you use SRCCOPY as the type of stretching.

BMPSourceHandle holds the handle of the loaded BMP, hence you set this variable to BMPHandle. (BMPHandle was passed as a parameter to the DisplayBMP( ) function.)

So what have you accomplished so far? You prepared variables that indicate the co-ordinates of the upper-left corner of the source, the width and height of the source, the upper-left corner of the target, and the width and height of the target. You are now ready to copy the contents of the source (the loaded BMP file) into the target (the WinG virtual window). Because the loaded BMP file does not necessarily have the same size as the target, you'll have to stretch the picture so that it will cover the entire area of the WinG window. You accomplish that by using the CopyBMP2 WinG( ) method as follows:

```
' Copy the BMP file into WinG
   Tegwing1.CopyBMP2WinG XTarget, YTarget, _
             WidthTarget, HeightTarget, _
             BMPSourceHandle, _
             XSource, YSource, _
             WidthSource, HeightSource, _
             StretchType
```

That's it! You've copied the loaded BMP into the WinG window.

Now you can slam the contents of WinG into the frmVBBMP form:

```
' SlamIt
Tegwing1.SlamIt
```

The Code of the About Menu Item

You'll now write the code that will be executed when the user selects the About menu item.

- Enter the following code in the mnuAbout_Click( ) procedure of the frmVBBMP form:

```
Private Sub mnuAbout_Click( )

    frmAbout.Show 1

End Sub
```

This statement displays the frmAbout form as a modal window, which requires the user to respond before the program can continue (because you supplied 1 as the parameter of the Show method):

```
frmAbout.Show 1
```

Later in this chapter you'll design the frmAbout form.

The Code of the Help Menu

8

When the user selects Help from the Help menu, a Help window appears. You'll now write the code that displays this window.

- Enter the following code in the mnuHelpMe_Click( ) procedure of the frmVBBMP form:

```
Private Sub mnuHelpMe_Click( )

    frmHelp.Show 1

End Sub
```

This statement displays the frmHelp form as a modal window (because you supplied 1 as the parameter of the Show method):

```
frmHelp.Show 1
```

Later in this chapter you'll design the frmHelp form.

Designing the frmAbout Form

You'll now design the frmAbout form.

- Implement the frmAbout form with the settings shown in Table 8.3. When you complete implementing the form, it should look as shown in Figure 8.14.

TABLE 8.3: The Properties of the frmAbout Form

Object: Form
Object Name: frmAbout

Property	Value
BorderStyle	1 'Fixed Single
Caption	"About"
Height	5910
Left	1095
MaxButton	'False
MinButton	0 'False
Picture	Use C:\WinGPrg\CH07\About 01.BMP or a similar BMP file.
Top	660
Width	5985

Object: CommandButton
Object Name: cmdOK

Property	Value
Caption	"&OK"
Height	495
Left	4320
Top	3480
Width	735

8

FIGURE 8.14:
The frmAbout form in design mode

The Code of the OK Button of the frmAbout Form

You'll now write the code of the cmdOK_Click( ) procedure of the frmAbout form.

- Enter the following code in the cmdOK_Click( ) procedure of the frmAbout form:

```
Private Sub cmdOK_Click( )
    Unload Me

End Sub
```

This code simply unloads (closes) the frmAbout form.

Designing the frmHelp Form

You'll now design the frmHelp form.

• Implement the frmHelp form (the Help window of the VBBMP program) with the Properties settings shown in Table 8.4. When you complete implementing the form, it should look as shown in Figure 8.15.

TABLE 8.4: The Properties of the frmHelp Form

Object: Form
Object Name: frmHelp

Property	Value
BorderStyle	3 'Fixed Double
Caption	"Help"
Height	5850
Left	990
MaxButton	0 'False
MinButton	0 'False
Picture	Use C:\WinGPrg\CH16\Help02.BMP or a similar BMP file.
Top	630
Width	6255

Object: CommandButton
Object Name: cmdOK

Property	Value
Caption	"&OK"
Height	495
Left	5280
Top	4800
Width	495

FIGURE 8.15:

The frmHelp form in design mode

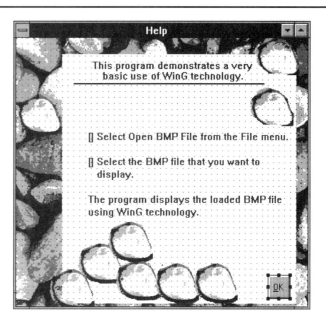

The Code of the cmdOK_Click( ) Procedure of the frmHelp Form

8

You'll now write the code of the cmdOK_Click( ) procedure of the frmHelp form.

- Enter the following code in the cmdOK_Click( ) procedure of the frmHelp form:

```
Private Sub cmdOK_Click( )

    Unload Me

End Sub
```

This code is executed whenever the user clicks the OK button of the Help form. It simply closes the Help window.

Implementing the Information Menu

Recall that the DisplayBMP( ) function you wrote earlier in the chapter needs to know the height and width of the loaded BMP file, and hence you extracted the height and width of the loaded BMP file by using the GetBMPWidth( ) and GetBMPHeight( ) methods. This program also has another use for the height and width values: it displays them via the Information menu. The Information menu is provided for examining the size and format of the BMP picture.

When the user selects the Height of Loaded BMP Picture menu item from the Information menu, the VBBMP program displays the height of the loaded BMP file. So again you'll utilize the GetBMPHeight( ) method.

- Enter the following code in the mnuBMPHeight_Click( ) procedure of the frmVBBMP form:

```
Private Sub mnuBMPHeight_Click( )

Dim HeightSource As Integer
Dim Msg As String

If gBMPHandle = 0 Then
     Msg = "No BMP file was loaded yet."
Else

  HeightSource = Tegwing1.GetBMPHeight(gBMPHandle)

  Msg =  _
     "The height of the loaded BMP is:" + _
       Str(HeightSource)

End If

MsgBox Msg, vbInformation, "Information"

End Sub
```

This code first declares local variables:

```
Dim HeightSource As Integer
Dim Msg As String
```

Then an If statement is executed to find out whether there is a loaded BMP file:

```
If gBMPHandle = O Then
    Msg = "No BMP file was loaded yet."
Else
  HeightSource = Tegwing1.GetBMPHeight(gBMPHandle)

  Msg = _
      "The height of the loaded BMP is:" + _
      Str(HeightSource)

End If
```

If no BMP file has been loaded, the Msg variable is updated with the string "No BMP file was loaded yet."

If a BMP file was loaded already, the code under the Else is executed. This code extracts the height of the loaded BMP file:

```
HeightSource = Tegwing1.GetBMPHeight(gBMPHandle)
```

and then the Msg variable is updated:

```
Msg = _
    "The height of the loaded BMP is:" + _
    Str(HeightSource)
```

Finally, the Msg variable is displayed with a message box:

```
MsgBox Msg, vbInformation, "Information"
```

In a similar manner you extract and display the width of the loaded BMP file whenever the user selects Width of Loaded BMP File from the Information menu.

- Enter the following code in the mnuBMPWidth_Click( ) procedure of the frmVBBMP form:

```
Private Sub mnuBMPWidth_Click( )

Dim WidthSource As Integer
Dim Msg As String

If gBMPHandle = O Then
    Msg = "No BMP file was loaded yet."
Else
    WidthSource = Tegwing1.GetBMPWidth(gBMPHandle)
    Msg = _
```

8

```
        "The width of the loaded BMP is:" + _
        Str(WidthSource)
    End If

    MsgBox Msg, vbInformation, "Information"

    End Sub
```

This code is essentially the same as the code that you entered in the frmBMPHeight_Click( ) procedure. Of course, now you are extracting the width of the loaded BMP file, so you use the GetBMPWidth( ) method.

The Number of Colors in the Loaded BMP File

As stated in the previous chapter, the BMP files that you can load with the VBBMP program are BMP pictures that were originally saved as 256-color BMP files. (Paintbrush offers this option in its Save As dialog box.)

You'll now write code that is executed whenever the user selects Other Information from the Information menu.

- Enter the following code in the mnuOtherInformation_Click( ) procedure of the frmVBBMP form:

```
Private Sub mnuOtherInformation_Click( )

Dim NumberOfColors As Integer

Dim Msg As String

If gBMPHandle <= 0 Then
    Msg = "No BMP file was loaded!"
Else
    NumberOfColors = Tegwing1.GetBMPNumOfColors(gBMPHandle)

    Msg = "Number of colors in the loaded BMP file: "
    Msg = Msg + Str(NumberOfColors)
End If

MsgBox Msg, vbInformation, "Colors"
```

```
End Sub
```

This code first determines whether a BMP file is loaded, and if so, executes the GetBMPNumOfColors( ) method to determine the number of colors in the loaded BMP file:

```
NumberOfColors = Tegwing1.GetBMPNumOfColors(gBMPHandle)
```

The version of the WinG control that is included on this book's CD-ROM can only handle 256-color BMP files, so the GetBMPNumOfColors method will always report 256 colors.

As an experiment, you can perform the following steps:

- Start Paintbrush.

- Draw something with Paintbrush, and save it as a 16-color BMP file.

- Start the VBBMP program.

- Select Load BMP File from the File menu of the VBBMP program, and select the 16-color BMP file that you just saved.

As you can see, you cannot load a 16-color BMP file.

8

Executing the VBBMP Program

You've finished writing the code of the VBBMP program.

- Save your work, execute the VBBMP program, and verify its proper operations.

Summary

In this chapter you wrote the code of the VBBMP program by using Visual Basic/WinG. As you saw, the VBBMP program loads a BMP file into memory, then copies the loaded BMP file into the WinG virtual window, and finally slams the contents of WinG into the screen.

PART III

Multimedia

CHAPTER

NINE

Determining the Multimedia Capabilities of Your PC

So far in this book, you've started to learn how to use and apply WinG technology. In this chapter you'll temporarily leave the subject of WinG, and learn about multimedia.

Chances are, you bought this book because you've seen just how exciting good multimedia and games software can be, and you want to apply your Visual Basic skills—and WinG technology—in creating dazzling multimedia and games programs of your own. This chapter lays the groundwork for multimedia programming by outlining the major types of multimedia devices and multimedia files involved. More important, in this chapter you'll examine the multimedia capabilities of your PC. That is, you'll learn how to perform tests that examine the multimedia devices of your PC.

What Is Multimedia?

If you ask most computer users that question, they will say it means sound, animation, and probably lots of interaction. Strictly speaking, multimedia capability is defined as the ability of a computer to work with input and output media beyond the usual disk, keyboard, and monitor. The media can be devices such as a sound card that is capable of playing WAV files, a sound card that is capable of playing MIDI files, a CD-ROM drive that is capable of playing CD audio, a monitor and a monitor card that is capable of displaying movies, and other media.

NOTE **Most CD-ROM drives can be used both for reading CD data and for playing CD audio.**

Playing and Recording WAV Files

A WAV file (it might be named, for example, Mysong.WAV) contains a recording of sound. A waveform is a visual representation of a sound's amplitude (volume) and duration (length), such as you might see on an oscilloscope display. The digital information in a WAV file represents the same properties of a sound. (As you'll see, MIDI files produce sound in a very different way.) Typically, you record WAV files using a sound card and its controlling software. In this respect, the sound card is no different than an ordinary tape recorder. That is, a mechanical tape recorder has buttons such as Play, Rewind, Fast Forward, Record, and so on. When you're using a sound card with a PC, the software displays a window with "buttons" such as Play, Rewind, Fast Forward, Record, and so on. Instead of physically pressing the buttons, you click them.

When you record sound with a tape recorder, the sound is recorded with a microphone, which converts the movement of air into an analog electrical signal, and these electrical impulses are saved into a magnetic cassette. When you record sound with a sound card, you use the sound card's microphone, and the recording (further converted into digital information by the sound card's electronics) is saved as a WAV file into the hard drive.

You can purchase either internal or external sound cards. An internal sound card must be installed into one of the slots of the PC. An external sound card is connected to one of the ports of the PC. Figure 9.1 is a schematic showing an external sound card, and Figure 9.2 shows an internal sound card.

FIGURE 9.1:
External sound card connected to a PC

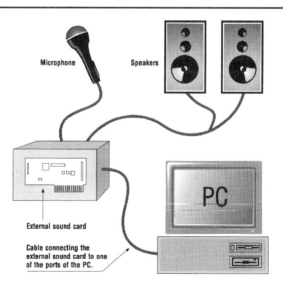

Notice that for both types of sound card the hardware includes speakers as well as a microphone. You record sound by playing it within range of the sound card's microphone. When you play the recording, the sound card sends the information (converted back to analog voltages) directly to the connected speakers.

FIGURE 9.2:
Internal sound card connected
to a PC

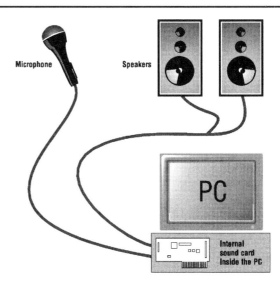

In subsequent chapters you'll learn how to write programs that let your user play and record sound by using the sound card.

About WAV files

You've seen that recordings made with a sound card are saved as WAV files. Some sound cards also let you save the recording in other formats, such as VOC files, SND files, and so on, but the most popular and acceptable format is the WAV file.

WAV files can be recorded in either mono or stereo format. Also, the quality of the recording depends on a couple of factors. One is the sampling rate at which the recording was performed—that is, how frequently a "snapshot" of the sound is taken. You can record WAV files at sampling rates of 11 kHz (kiloHertz, or thousands of cycles per second), 22 kHz and 44 kHz. The higher the sampling rate, the better the quality of the recording. However, higher sampling rates also mean a larger resulting WAV file. A recording made using an 8 kHz sampling rate has a sound quality similar to that of a phone transmission. With a sampling rate of 11 kHz, you get a recorded sound quality similar to that of an inexpensive tape recorder. A 22 kHz recording sounds like a recording made with an expensive tape recorder. A 44 kHz recording sounds like a CD audio.

Another factor that determines the quality of the recording is whether the WAV file is recorded in 8-bit or 16-bit format. In an 8-bit recording, each sample is represented by 8 bits of data. In a 16-bit recording, each sample is represented by 16 bits. Like sampling the sound at a higher rate, representing each sample with a better resolution results in a more detailed rendering of the sound. A WAV file that was recorded as a 16-bit WAV file has better quality than an 8-bit WAV file, but the 16-bit WAV file is double the size of a WAV file that contains the same recording with 8-bit resolution.

Playing and Recording MIDI Files

Typically, a sound card that is capable of playing WAV files can also play MIDI files. MIDI stands for Musical Instrument Digital Interface, an industry-wide standard for connecting computers to various kinds of synthesizers, including sound boards. This standard defines a large number of preset "voices" for musical instruments. A MIDI file (named, for example, MySong.MID) contains synthesized music in the form of instructions to activate these voices. That is, a WAV file can contain any sound that can be recorded by a microphone (such as human voice, music, special sound effects). On the other hand, a MIDI file can only play music or preset special sound effects. A sound card that supports MIDI playback has circuitry that simulates music instruments such as piano, drums, guitar, and so on. So naturally, the sound card can only play the instruments that the electronic circuitry was designed to play. A sound card's MIDI circuitry supports a smaller part of the standard than, say, a Yamaha DX-7 synthesizer (but after all, compare their prices).

9

MIDI files are much smaller than WAV files, because instead of representing the entire sound, MIDI files contain only instructions to the sound card that tell it which instrument to play, the duration of the playback, the musical notes, the tempo (playback speed), and so on.

A very short MIDI file can contain instructions that tell the sound card to play music by playing several instruments simultaneously. Thus, a MIDI file can create very impressive results. For example, a MIDI file can play music that sounds as if a whole orchestra is playing.

To record MIDI files by yourself you need special MIDI hardware and software that lets you play music on a musical keyboard and record it into a MIDI file. You can then use the MIDI software to edit this file—for example, by adding instruments, changing the notes of the music, and so on. As you can see, the main talent required for authoring MIDI files is not the talent to use the MIDI hardware/software, but the artistic talent to write the music. MIDI recording hardware/software is not part of a standard "multimedia computer" configuration. It's typically purchased in stores that specialize in musical instruments. Many people are wondering what wonderful music would have been written had giants like Mozart and other musicians had access to MIDI and PC technology.

In subsequent chapters of this book you'll learn how to play MIDI files from within your programs.

Playing and Recording Movie AVI Files

AVI stands for Audio-Visual Interleaving. An AVI file (named, for example, My-Movie.AVI) contains a movie—both the frames of the movie and the sound track of the movie.

To play a movie file, you need a PC that has a 386 processor or better, and you need a monitor (and monitor card) that is a VGA or better.

You'll be able to listen to the sound track of the movie provided that your PC is also equipped with a sound card. That is, the sound track of the movie is a WAV file.

To record a movie AVI file by yourself, you need to install a video capture card in one of the slots of your PC. A camcorder is then attached to the video capture card. When you use the camcorder, the movie is captured as an AVI file into your hard drive (see schematic in Figure 9.3).

You can also connect a VCR machine to the video capture card and convert a videotape to an AVI file.

In subsequent chapters of this book you'll learn how to play movie AVI files from within your programs.

Playing CD Audio

An audio CD is typically purchased in a record store. Most CD-ROM drives are also capable of playing CD audio. The CD-ROM drive in this case simply serves as a

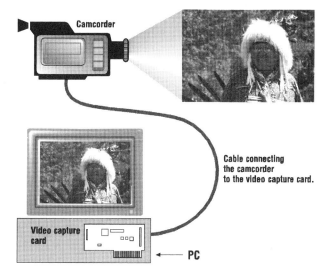

FIGURE 9.3:

Generating AVI movie files with a camcorder and a video capture card

CD player. However, instead of physically pressing the mechanical buttons of the CD player, the user clicks the buttons of the CD audio player program.

In subsequent chapters of this book you'll learn how to play CD audio from within your programs.

Other Media

The multimedia devices that were discussed in the previous sections are considered the major multimedia devices. Nevertheless, some vendors classify other products as multimedia devices. For example, a scanner is also considered a multimedia device.

A VCR player is also considered a multimedia device. In this case, the program that lets the user play the VCR has buttons just like the mechanical buttons of a regular VCR device.

Nowadays, you can purchase a TV card. A TV card is a circuit board that you insert into one of the slots of the PC; its accompanying software lets the user click buttons like those on a TV remote control. Thus, the user can view television on the monitor of the PC.

Examining the Multimedia Capabilities of Your PC

After purchasing and installing multimedia hardware, you also need to install the corresponding software drivers for each devices. For example, after installing the sound card, the user has to install the corresponding WAV driver and the corresponding MIDI driver. You can quickly determine whether you've correctly set up a multimedia device and its driver software in a Windows system. Here's how to make that test:

- Start the Media Player program, which usually resides inside the Accessories group of programs (see Figure 9.4).

FIGURE 9.4:
The icon of the Media Player program.

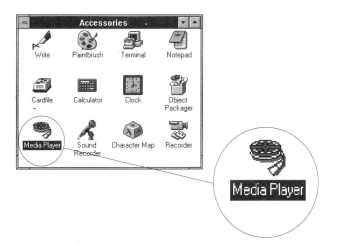

Window responds by executing the Media Player program (see Figure 9.5).

- Select the Device menu.

Media Player displays the Device menu, as shown in Figure 9.6.

FIGURE 9.5:

The Media Player program

FIGURE 9.6:

The Device menu of Media player. The items listed in the Device menu are the multimedia devices that the PC is capable of playing.

In Figure 9.6, the Device menu contains the following devices:

```
CD Audio
MIDI Sequencer
Sound
Video for Windows
```

This means that the PC on which we made this test is set up to play CD Audio, MIDI files, Sound (WAV files), and movie AVI files. For each of these devices, both the hardware and the software has been installed properly.

If you don't see a device listed in the Device menu of Media Player, it means that Windows is not configured to play that device. Why? Well, maybe the hardware is missing, maybe one of the drivers is missing, or maybe something else is missing. But the point is that a multimedia device that does not appear as a menu item inside the Device menu of Media Player will not be able to operate properly.

Note that typically, the multimedia hardware comes with a software application that enables you to experiment with the multimedia device. For example, a sound card typically comes with software that lets you record and play WAV files. In some cases, this software will operate properly from Windows, but you will not see Sound listed in the Device menu of Media Player. This still means that something

9

is wrong with the sound card installation (hardware, software, or both). Remember, you want all Windows applications to be able to utilize the sound card. And the only way to be sure of that is to see the Sound item in the Device menu of Media Player.

Summary

In this chapter you looked briefly at the major types of multimedia devices and files, and you learned how to use the Device menu of Media Player to verify your computer's multimedia capabilities.

Later in this book you'll learn how to write programs that utilize multimedia devices, and how to combine multimedia and WinG technologies for designing powerful games, virtual reality, and multimedia applications.

CHAPTER

TEN

Executing the WinGMult Program

10

In this chapter you'll execute the WinGMult.EXE program, an application that uses WinG and Multimedia/WAV technologies. You'll write the code for this application in Chapter 11.

NOTE   The WinGMult.EXE program plays WAV files through a sound card. Thus, it is assumed that your PC has a sound card installed. As described in the previous chapter, you can use the Media Player application to determine whether your sound card has been installed correctly.

Executing the WinGMult.EXE Program

The WinGMult.EXE program resides in the \WinGPrg\EXE directory of the book's CD-ROM.

* Execute the WinGMult.EXE program. You'll see the window shown in Figure 10.1.

FIGURE 10.1:

The window of the WinGMult.EXE program

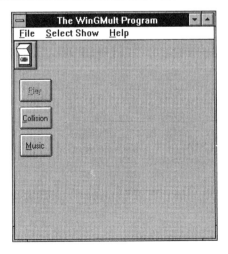

The WinGMult program presents three menus: File, Select Show, and Help. These menus are shown in Figures 10.2, 10.3, and 10.4.

FIGURE 10.2:

The File menu of the WinGMult program

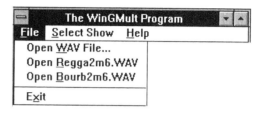

FIGURE 10.3:

The Select Show menu of the WinGMult program

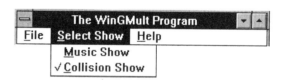

FIGURE 10.4:

The Help menu of the WinGMult program

- Minimize the window of the WinGMult program. The icon of the WinGMult program appears, as shown in Figure 10.5.

10

The WinGMult program has an Exit switch in the upper-left corner of its window. To terminate the WinGMult program, you have to click the Exit switch:

- Double-click the WinGMult program icon to restore the application window to its full size.

- Click the Exit switch.

FIGURE 10.5:

The icon of the WinGMult program

WinGMult responds by displaying the dialog box shown in Figure 10.6.

- Click the No button (because you don't want to terminate the WinGMult program now).

FIGURE 10.6:

The WinGMult program's Exit dialog box

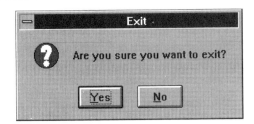

Loading WAV Files with the WinGMult Program

You'll now use the WinGMult program to load a WAV file.

- Select Open WAV File from the File menu of the WinGMult program.

WinGMult responds by displaying the Open dialog box shown in Figure 10.7.

The Open dialog box that lets the
user selects a WAV file

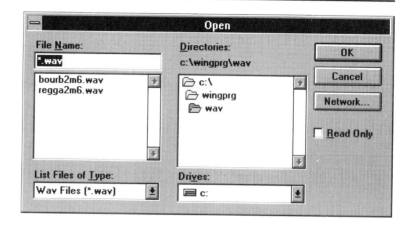

- You can now select a WAV file, but for now, just click the Cancel button.

As shown back in Figure 10.2, the File menu contains the Open Regga2m6.WAV
item and the Open Bourb2m6.WAV item.

NOTE The Open Regga2m6.WAV item and the Open Bourb2m6.WAV item
are included in the File menu for the sole purpose of making the
development process easier. That is, the WinGMult program utilizes
WAV files. As you develop the program, you develop some code and
then execute the program to verify its proper operation. Then you add
more code and verify that the code that you developed works
properly, and so on. The File menu contains the items that open the
Regga2m6.WAV and the Bourb2m6.WAV files, so that while
developing this program, you won't no need to go through the long
process of selecting Open WAV File from the File menu and then
selecting a WAV file.

- Select the Open Regga2m6.WAV item from the File menu.

WinGMult responds by opening the Regga2m6.WAV file, and the caption of the window now displays the name of the opened WAV file (see Figure 10.8).

FIGURE 10.8:

The caption of the window displays the name of the WAV file that was selected

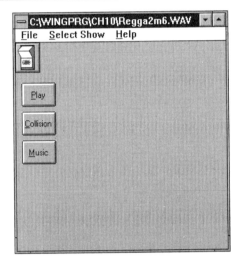

Also, after you select the WAV file, the Play button becomes enabled.

• Click the Play button.

The WinGMult program responds by starting a show. As you can see in Figure 10.9, the show consists of displaying two planets approaching each other. While the planets approach each other, the sound card plays the WAV file that was selected.

Figure 10.10 shows the two planets just before impact, and Figure 10.11 shows the planets (or what is left of them) after the collision.

FIGURE 10.9:

The Collision show displays two planets approaching each other.

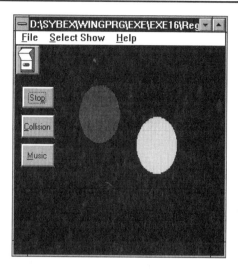

FIGURE 10.10:

The planets just before the collision

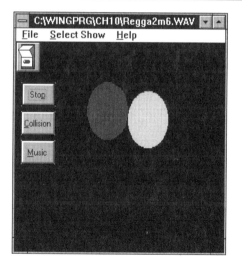

10

Once the fragments of the planets reach the ground, a broom appears and sweeps them up (see Figure 10.12).

FIGURE 10.11:

The planets after the collision

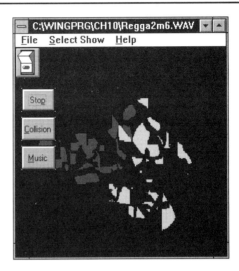

FIGURE 10.12:

Cleaning the window of the
WinGMult program

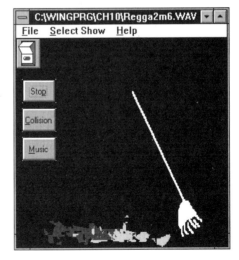

Once the window of the WinGMult program is clean, the broom is broken to several pieces (see Figure 10.13), and the pieces of the broom start to form the word END (see Figure 10.14).

FIGURE 10.13:

The broom is broken into several pieces.

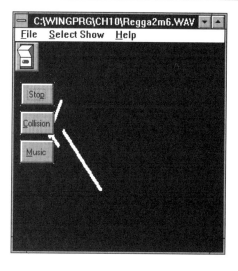

FIGURE 10.14:

The broom's pieces form the word END.

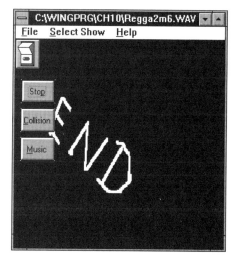

The Collision show continues in an endless loop. You can stop it by clicking the Stop button (when you clicked the Play button, the caption of this button changed to Stop). However, instead of stopping the show now, try out the Music show instead:

- Click the Music button.

WinGMult responds by switching to the Music show, which displays a man playing his bass fiddle (see Figure 10.15).

FIGURE 10.15:

Playing the bass (the Music show).

Displaying an Animated Icon

While the show is going on, you can minimize the WinGMult window :

- Minimize the window of the WinGMult program while the show is in progress.

WinGMult responds by minimizing the window. Note that the show is still being displayed inside the program icon.

- Restore the size of the WinGMult window.
- Click the Collision button to switch to the Collision show.

WinGMult responds by switching to the Collision show.

- While the Collision show is in progress, minimize the window of WinGMult.

The icon of the WinGMult program is minimized, and the Collision show is now displayed inside the program icon.

The Help and About Windows of the WinGMult Program

- Select the Help item from the Help menu.

WinGMult responds by displaying the Help window, as shown in Figure 10.16.

FIGURE 10.16:

The Help window

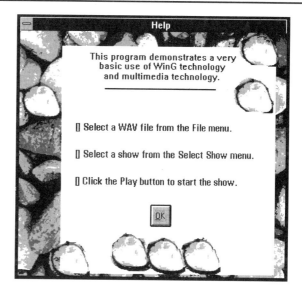

- Click the OK button of the Help window to close the Help window.

WinGMult responds by closing the Help window.

- Select the About item from the Help menu.

WinGMult responds by displaying the About window.

- Click the OK button of the About window to close the About window.

WinGMult responds by closing the About window.

10

Resizing the Window of the WinGMult Program

One of the interesting features of the WinGMult program is that it lets the user resize the window of the application while the show is in progress.

- While the Collision show is in progress, resize the WinGMult window.

Figures 10.17 and 10.18 show the WinGMult window in two different sizes while the Collision show is in progress.

FIGURE 10.17:

Enlarging the window while the Collision show is in progress

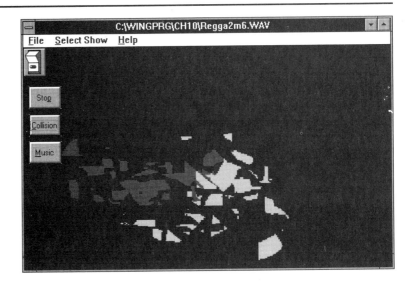

Executing Several Instances of the WinGMult Program

The user can execute several instances of the WinGMult program.

- While the WinGMult program is running, execute another instance of the WinGMult program.

FIGURE 10.18:

Shrinking the window while the
Collision show is in progress

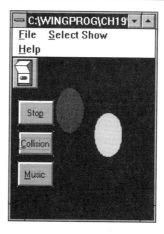

FIGURE 10.19:

Two instances of the WinGMult
program. In both instances the
Collision show is in progress

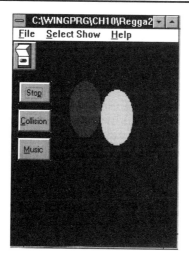

10

Figure 10.19 shows two instances of the WinGMult program. In both instances the
Collision show is in progress.

- Experiment with the WinGMult program, and then click the Exit switch to
  terminate the program.

Summary

In this chapter you executed the WinGMult program. As you saw, the WinGMult program uses WinG and multimedia technologies. In the next chapter you'll write the code of the WinGMult program.

ELEVEN

Writing the WinG/Multimedia Program

In this chapter you'll write the code of the WinGMult.EXE program, which you executed in the previous chapter. This application uses WinG and Multimedia/WAV technologies. There are no new WinG topics in this chapter. Instead, you'll apply the WinG concepts that you've learned in previous chapters to write the code of the WinGMult program.

Creating the Project for the WinGMult Program

You first need to create the project of the WinGMult program:

- Select New Project from the File menu of Visual Basic.

- Save the new form as WinGMult.FRM and the new project file as WinG-Mult.MAK, both in the C:\WinGPrg\Ch10 directory.

Implementing the frmWinGMult Form

You'll now implement the frmWinGMult form, which is the application window of the WinGMult program.

- Implement the frmWinGMult form using the Properties settings listed in Table 11.1. Once you've completed implementing the form, it should look as shown in Figure 11.1.

TABLE 11.1: The Properties of the frmWinGMult Form

Object: Form
Object Name: frmWinGMult

Property	Value
BackColor	Light gray
Caption	"The WinGMult Program"
Height	5025
Icon	C:\WinGMult\Icons\WinGMult.ICO
Left	1470
Top	615
Width	4620

Object: CommandButton
Object Name: cmdMusic

Property	Value
Caption	"&Music"
Height	495
Left	120
Top	2040
Width	735

Object: CommandButton
Object Name: cmdCollision

Property	Value
Caption	"&Collision"
Height	495
Left	120
Top	1440
Width	735

TABLE 11.1 : The Properties of the frmWinGMult Form

Object: CommandButton
Object Name: cmdPlayStop

Property	Value
Caption	"&Play"
Enabled	0 'False
Height	495
Left	120
Top	840
Width	735

Object: Common Dialog
Object Name: CommonDialog1

Property	Value
Left	1560
Top	2040
CancelErr	True

Object: TegoSoft Switch Control
Object Name: swExit

Property	Value
Height	630
Left	0
Top	0
Width	525
Value	-1 'True

Object: WinG
Object Name: Tegwing1

Property	Value
Left	2160
Top	2040

11

TABLE 11.1: The Properties of the frmWinGMult Form

Object: TegoSoft Multimedia control
Object Name: Tegomm1

Property	Value
Height	465
Left	480
Top	3360
Width	3510
Bevelwidth	4

FIGURE 11.1:
The frmWinGMult form in design mode

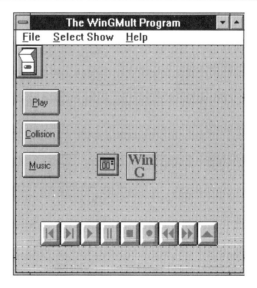

The TegoSoft WinG control, TegoSoft Switch control, and the TegoSoft Multimedia control appear inside the frmWinGMult form. For each of these, follow the basic procedure outlined in Chapter 4 first to add the control's icon to Visual Basic's Tools window and then to place the control in the form:

- Select Custom Controls from the Tools menu in Visual Basic and then click the appropriate name to add the control's icon to the Tools window.

- Select the icon and then click anywhere in the form to place the control there.

Figure 11.2 shows the TegoSoft WinG control's icon in the Tools window, and Figure 11.3 shows the control placed in the form. Figure 11.4 shows the TegoSoft Switch control's icon in the Tools window, and Figure 11.5 shows the control placed in the form. Figure 11.6 shows the TegoSoft Multimedia control's icon in the Tools window, and Figure 11.7 shows the control placed in the form.

FIGURE 11.2:

The icon of the TegoSoft WinG control inside the tools window

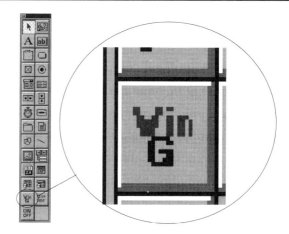

11

FIGURE 11.3:
The TegoSoft WinG control inside
the form

FIGURE 11.4:
The icon of the TegoSoft Switch
control inside the tools window

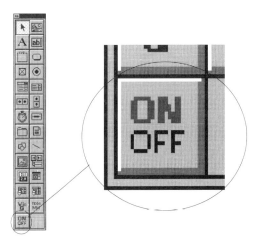

FIGURE 11.5:

The TegoSoft Switch control inside the form

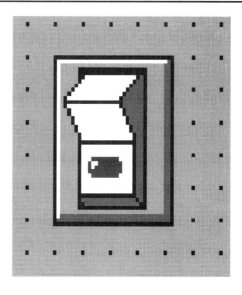

FIGURE 11.6:

The icon of the TegoSoft Multimedia control inside the tools window

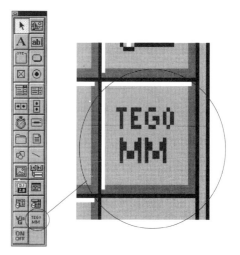

FIGURE 11.7:

The TegoSoft Multimedia control inside the form

- Implement the menu of the frmWinGMult form with the settings shown in Table 11.2. The menus of the frmWinGMult form are shown in Figures 11.8, 11.9 and 11.10.

TABLE 11.2: The Menus of the frmWinGMult Form

Menu Caption	Name	Other Properties
&File	mnuFile	
... Open &WAV File...	mnuOpenWAV	
...Open &Regga2m6.WAV	mnuReg	
...Open &Bourb2m6.WAV	mnuOpenBour	
...−	mnuSep	
...E&xit	mnuExit	
Select Show	mnuSelectShow	
...&Select Show	mnuMusicShow	
...&Collision Show	mnuCollisionShow	Checked = − 1 'True
&Help	mnuHelp	
...&Help...	mnuHelpMe	
...&About...	mnuAbout	

FIGURE 11.8:

The File menu of the frmWinGMult form

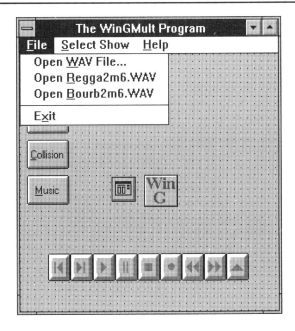

FIGURE 11.9:

The Select Show menu of the frmWinGMult form

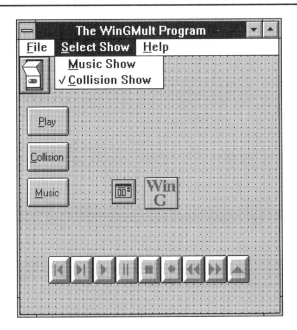

FIGURE 11.10:
The Help menu of the frmWinGMult
form

The General Declarations Section of the frmWinGMult Form

You'll now write the code inside the General Declarations section of the frmWinG-Mult form.

- Enter the following code within the General Declarations section of the frmWinGMult form:

```
Option Explicit

Const SRCAND = &H8800C6   ' dest = source AND dest
Const SRCCOPY = &HCC0020  ' dest = source
Const SRCERASE = &H440328 ' dest = source AND (NOT dest)
Const SRCINVERT = &H660046 ' dest = source XOR dest
Const SRCPAINT = &HEE0086  ' dest = source OR dest
```

```
Dim gBMPHandle As Integer

Dim gWavWasLoaded As Integer

Dim gMusicShow
Dim gCollisionShow
```

This code declares various constants:

```
Const SRCAND = &H8800C6  ' dest = source AND dest
Const SRCCOPY = &HCC0020 ' dest = source
Const SRCERASE = &H440328  ' dest = source AND (NOT dest)
Const SRCINVERT = &H660046 ' dest = source XOR dest
Const SRCPAINT = &HEE0086  ' dest = source OR dest
```

As you'll see later in this chapter, these constants can be used as the last parameter of the CopyBMP2WinG method of the WinG control.

The code then declares global variables:

```
Dim gBMPHandle As Integer
Dim gWavWasLoaded As Integer
Dim gMusicShow
Dim gCollisionShow
```

Because these variables are declared in the General Declarations section, they are accessible from any procedure and function of the frmWinGMult form.

The Code of the Form_Load( ) Procedure of the frmWinGMult Form

The Form_Load( ) procedure is executed upon starting the WinGMult program.

- Enter the following code inside the Form_Load( ) procedure of the frmWinG-Mult form:

```
Private Sub Form_Load( )

    gWavWasLoaded = 0

    gCollisionShow = 1
    gMusicShow = 0
```

11

```
Tegomm1.UpdateInterval = 200
Tegomm1.Visible = False

Me.ScaleMode = 3 'Pixels
```

End Sub

This code first sets the gWavWasLoaded global variable to 0:

```
gWavWasLoaded = 0
```

This global variable serves as a flag that indicates whether the user has loaded a WAV file. Because no WAV file has been loaded when the program starts, gWavWasLoaded is set to 0. Actually, Visual Basic automatically initializes the variables to 0 upon starting the program, but setting the variable to 0 inside the Form_Load( ) procedure makes the program easier to read and understand.

The gCollisionShow and gMusicShow variables are set as follows:

```
gCollisionShow = 1
gMusicShow = 0
```

The gCollisionShow and gMusicShow variables serve as flags that indicate which show is selected. That is, if the Collision show is selected, gCollisionShow is equal to 1 and gMusicShow is equal to 0. And if the Music show is selected, gCollision-Show equals 0 and gMusicShow equals 1. Upon starting the program, the default selection is the Collision show. This is the reason for setting gCollisionShow to 1 and gMusicShow to 0.

The next statement sets the UpdateInterval property of the Multimedia control to 200:

```
Tegomm1.UpdateInterval = 200
```

As you'll soon see, the UpdateInterval property determines how often the Multi-media control's Tegomm1_StatusUpdate( ) procedure is executed. Setting the Up-dateInterval property to 200 means that every 200 milliseconds, the Tegomm1_StatusUpdate( ) procedure is executed automatically. You'll write the code of the Te-gomm1_StatusUpdate( ) procedure later in this chapter.

In this program, there is no need to make the Multimedia control visible, so you set its Visible property to False:

```
Tegomm1.Visible = False
```

You set the ScaleMode property of the frmWinGMult form to 3:

```
Me.ScaleMode = 3 'Pixels
```

This means that the units used in the program are expressed in pixels.

The Code of the Exit Item
of the File Menu

You'll now attach code to the Exit item of the File menu.

- Enter the following code inside the mnuExit_Click( ) procedure of the frmWinGMult form:

```
Private Sub mnuExit_Click( )

        Unload Me

End Sub
```

When the user selects Exit from the File menu, the mnuExit_Click( ) procedure is automatically executed. The code you entered unloads the frmWinGMult form.

Attaching Code to the
Click Event of the Exit Switch

You'll now attach code to the Click event of the Exit switch.

- Type the following code inside the swExit_Click( ) procedure of the frmWinG-Mult form:

```
Private Sub swExit_Click( )

' User clicked the Exit switch

Dim Answer

Answer = MsgBox("Are you sure you want to exit?", _
                vbQuestion + vbYesNo, "Exit")
```

```
If Answer = vbYes Then
   Unload Me
Else
   swExit.Value = True
End If

End Sub
```

The swExit_Click( ) procedure is automatically executed whenever the user clicks the Exit switch. The code you entered displays a message box with Yes and No buttons in it, and depending on which button the user clicks to close the dialog box, the Answer variable is updated accordingly:

```
Answer = MsgBox("Are you sure you want to exit?", _
               vbQuestion + vbYesNo, "Exit")
```

So if the user clicks the Yes button of the message box, the Answer variable is updated with the value vbYes. And if the user clicks the No button, the Answer variable is updated with the value vbNo.

The Answer variable is then examined with an If...Else statement:

```
If Answer = vbYes Then
   Unload Me
Else
   swExit.Value = True
End If
```

If the user has selected Yes from the Exit dialog box, the form is unloaded. If the user has selected No, the code under the Else statement is executed, setting the Value property of the Exit Switch control to True. That is, once the user clicks the Exit switch control, the Value property of the switch control toggles from True to False and vice-versa. Because the user indicated that the program should not be terminated, the Value property of the switch is set back to True. When the Value property of the switch is True, the red LED lamp of the switch is On.

The Code of the Form_Unload( ) Procedure

The Form_Unload( ) procedure is executed when the form is about to unload itself. The user can terminate the program by doing any one of the following:

- Selecting Exit from the File menu.

- Clicking the icon that appears on the upper-left corner of the frmWinGMult form and then selecting Close from the system menu that pops up.

- Clicking the Exit switch and then clicking the Yes button from the Exit dialog box that pops up.

You'll now add the code that implements the Form_Unload( ) procedure:

- Type the following code inside the Form_Unload( ) procedure:

```
Private Sub Form_Unload(Cancel As Integer)

    ' Close the WinG session
    Tegwing1.CloseWinG

    ' Close the BMP
    Tegwing1.CloseBMP gBMPHandle

End Sub
```

This code closes the WinG session. As you'll soon see, during the execution of the program, a WinG session is opened. Thus, upon termination of the program, the WinG session is closed:

```
Tegwing1.CloseWinG
```

Also, as you'll see later, during the execution of the program, a BMP file is loaded. So when terminating the program, the BMP file is closed:

```
Tegwing1.CloseBMP gBMPHandle
```

Attaching Code to the Open WAV File Item of the File Menu

11

You'll now attach code to the Open WAV File item of the File menu. When the user selects the Open WAV File item from the File menu, the WinGMult program lets the user selects a WAV file.

- Enter the following code inside the mnuOpenWAV_Click( ) procedure:

```
Private Sub mnuOpenWAV_Click( )

Dim Msg As String

' Selecting a file (with the common dialog box)

' Set an error trap prior to displaying
' the Open dialog box.
On Error GoTo OpenError

' Set the items of the File Type list box
CommonDialog1.Filter = _
    "All Files (*.*) | *.* |Wav Files (*.wav)|*.wav"

' Set the default File Type
CommonDialog1.FilterIndex = 2

' Display the dialog box as an Open dialog box
CommonDialog1.Action = 1

' No need to trap errors any more,
' so remove the error trap
On Error GoTo 0

''' MsgBox CommonDialog1.FileName
```

```
Tegomm1.DeviceType = "WaveAudio"
Tegomm1.FileName = CommonDialog1.FileName
Tegomm1.Command = "Open"

If Tegomm1.Error <> 0 Then
   Msg = "Can't open the "
   Msg = Msg + CommonDialog1.FileName + " file. "
   MsgBox Msg, vbInformation, "Error"
   Exit Sub
Else
   Me.Caption = CommonDialog1.FileName

    ' Tell the TegoSoft WinG control
    ' in which window to draw
    Tegwing1.hWndDisplay = Me.hWnd

   ' Open a WinG session
   Tegwing1.OpenWinG

   cmdPlayStop.Enabled = True
   cmdPlayStop.Caption = "&Play"

End If

' Exit this procedure
Exit Sub

OpenError:
' The user pressed the Cancel key of
' the common dialog box, or an error occurred.

' Exit this procedure
Exit Sub

End Sub
```

The code you entered sets an error trap:

```
On Error GoTo OpenError
```

11

So from now on, if an error occurs, the program will immediately execute the statements that are placed after the OpenError label. Let's examine these statements:

```
OpenError:
' The user pressed the Cancel key of
' the common dialog box, or an error occurred.

' Exit this procedure
Exit Sub
```

Recall that in designing the form you set the CancelError property of the common dialog control to True. This means that if the user clicks the Cancel button of the Open dialog box, an error will occur, and the program will immediately jump to the OpenError label. The code under the OpenError label terminates the procedure.

After setting the error trap, the code that you typed sets the Filter property of the common dialog box:

```
' Set the items of the File Type list box
CommonDialog1.Filter = _
    "All Files (*.*) ¦ *.* ¦Wav Files (*.wav)¦*.wav"
```

Then the default file type is set:

```
' Set the default File Type
CommonDialog1.FilterIndex = 2
```

The common dialog box is now ready, so the Action property of the common dialog box is set to 1 (which causes the dialog box to pop up as an Open dialog box):

```
CommonDialog1.Action = 1
```

Now the error trap is no longer needed:

```
' Remove the error trap
On Error GoTo 0
```

OK, the user has selected a WAV file. Now it is time to open a multimedia session for the selected WAV file.

The DeviceType of the Multimedia control is set to WaveAudio:

```
Tegomm1.DeviceType = "WaveAudio"
```

Summary: Using the Multimedia Control to Play and Record WAV Files

To use the multimedia control for playing and recording WAV files, you first need to set the DeviceType property of the multimedia control to WaveAudio as in the following:

```
Tegomm1.DeviceType = "WaveAudio"
```

The next step is to set the FileName property of the multimedia control to the name and path of the WAV file as in the following:

```
Tegomm1.FileName = "C:\Try\MySong.WAV"
```

Once the DeviceType and FileName properties of the multimedia control are set, you can issue the Open command as follows:

```
Tegomm1.Command = "Open"
```

Of course, you also have to tell the Multimedia control which WAV file to play. You accomplish this by setting the FileName property of the Multimedia control to the name and path of the WAV file:

```
Tegomm1.FileName = CommonDialog1.FileName
```

In the preceding statement, you set the FileName property of the Multimedia control to the name and path of the WAV file that was selected by the user with the common dialog box.

Finally, the Open command is issued as follows:

```
Tegomm1.Command = "Open"
```

The Error property of the Multimedia control is then examined to see whether the WAV session was opened successfully:

```
If Tegomm1.Error <> 0 Then
   Msg = "Can't open the "
   Msg = Msg + CommonDialog1.FileName + " file. "
   MsgBox Msg, vbInformation, "Error"
   Exit Sub
Else
```

11

```
Me.Caption = CommonDialog1.FileName

' Tell the TegoSoft WinG control
' in which window to draw
Tegwing1.hWndDisplay = Me.hWnd

' Open a WinG session
Tegwing1.OpenWinG

cmdPlayStop.Enabled = True
cmdPlayStop.Caption = "&Play"

End If
```

The Error property reports the result of the last command that was issued to the Multimedia control. The last command that was issued was the Open command. Thus, the Error property reports whether the Open command was executed successfully.

The Error Property of the Multimedia Control

The Error property of the Multimedia control reports whether the last command that was issued to the multimedia control was executed successfully.

The following code issues the Open command and then an If statement is executed to examine whether the Open command was executed successfully.

```
Tegomm1.Command = "Open"

If Tegomm1.Error <> 0 Then
    ..........................
    ... Error occurred ...
    ..........................
Else
    ..........................
    ... No error occurred ...
    ..........................
End If
```

The code under the If statement displays a message telling the user that the WAV file cannot be opened:

```
If Tegomm1.Error <> 0 Then
   Msg = "Can't open the "
   Msg = Msg + CommonDialog1.FileName + " file. "
   MsgBox Msg, vbInformation, "Error"
   Exit Sub
Else
   ....
   ....
   ....
End If
```

The code under the Else is executed provided that the WAV session was opened successfully. As you'll see later, the program simultaneously plays a WAV file and displays a sequence of pictures. The pictures are displayed using WinG technology. Thus, the code under the Else opens a WinG session:

```
' Tell the TegoSoft WinG control
' in which window to draw
Tegwing1.hWndDisplay = Me.hWnd

' Open a WinG session
Tegwing1.OpenWinG
```

The cmdPlayStop button serves as both a Play button and a Stop button. Because the WAV file was open successfully, the user should be able to click the cmdPlayStop button. Thus, you need to enable the cmdPlayStop button:

```
cmdPlayStop.Enabled = True
```

Also, the cmdPlayStop button now serves as a Play button, so you need to set its Caption property accordingly:

```
cmdPlayStop.Caption = "&Play"
```

Finally, the procedure is terminated:

```
Exit Sub
```

Opening Other WAV Files from the File Menu

11

You'll now attach code to the Open Regga2m6.WAV item of the File menu.

- Enter the following code within the mnuReg_Click( ) procedure:

```
Private Sub mnuReg_Click( )

Dim FileName As String
Dim Msg As String

FileName = App.Path
If Right(FileName, 1) <> "\" Then
    FileName = FileName + "\"
End If
FileName = FileName + "Regga2m6.WAV"

Tegomm1.DeviceType = "WaveAudio"
Tegomm1.FileName = FileName
Tegomm1.Command = "Open"

If Tegomm1.Error <> 0 Then
    Msg = "Can't open the "
    Msg = Msg + FileName + " file. "
    MsgBox Msg, vbInformation, "Error"
    Exit Sub
Else
    Me.Caption = FileName

    ' Tell the TegoSoft WinG control
    ' in which window to draw
    Tegwing1.hWndDisplay = Me.hWnd

    ' Open a WinG session
    Tegwing1.OpenWinG

    cmdPlayStop.Enabled = True
    cmdPlayStop.Caption = "&Play"

End If

End Sub
```

This code is very similar to the code you entered within the mnuOpenWAV_Click( ) procedure. However, while the mnuOpenWAV_Click( ) procedure lets the user open any WAV file, the mnuReg_Click( ) procedure opens a specific file—namely, the Regga2m6.WAV file—as follows:

```
FileName = App.Path
If Right(FileName, 1) <> "\" Then
   FileName = FileName + "\"
End If
FileName = FileName + "Regga2m6.WAV"
```

In the preceding code, FileName is assigned the value of App.Path (which is the path and filename of the application):

```
FileName = App.Path
```

Then, an If statement is executed to examine whether the last character of the string inside FileName is the "\" character. If it's not, the statement under the If adds the "\" character:

```
FileName = App.Path
If Right(FileName, 1) <> "\" Then
   FileName = FileName + "\"
End If
```

Finally, the name of the WAV file is added to the FileName string:

```
FileName = FileName + "Regga2m6.WAV"
```

For example, if the program resides inside the root directory of C:, then App.Path is equal to C:. The statement under the If adds a "\" to FileName, so now FileName equals "C:"+"\"="C:\". Finally, the name of the WAV file is added, so that File-Name equals "C:\"+"Regga2m6.WAV"="C:\Regga2m6.WAV".

As you can see, the code you entered requires the WAV file to reside in the same directory as the program.

- Type the following code inside the mnuOpenBour_Click( ) procedure:

```
Private Sub mnuOpenBour_Click( )

Dim FileName As String
Dim Msg As String

FileName = App.Path
If Right(FileName, 1) <> "\" Then
   FileName = FileName + "\"
```

```
   End If
   FileName = FileName + "Bourb2m6.WAV"

   Tegomm1.DeviceType = "WaveAudio"
   Tegomm1.FileName = FileName
   Tegomm1.Command = "Open"

   If Tegomm1.Error <> 0 Then
      Msg = "Can't open the "
      Msg = Msg + FileName + " file. "
      MsgBox Msg, vbInformation, "Error"
      Exit Sub
   Else
      Me.Caption = FileName

         ' Tell the TegoSoft WinG control
         ' in which window to draw
         Tegwing1.hWndDisplay = Me.hWnd

         ' Open a WinG session
         Tegwing1.OpenWinG

      cmdPlayStop.Enabled = True
      cmdPlayStop.Caption = "&Play"

   End If

End Sub
```

This code is very similar to the mnuReg_Click( ) procedure. The only difference is that now you are opening the Bourb2m6.WAV file:

```
FileName = App.Path
If Right(FileName, 1) <> "\" Then
   FileName - FileName + "\"
End If
FileName = FileName + "Bourb2m6.WAV"
```

Again, the program can reside in any drive and any directory, but the WAV file has to reside in the same directory where the program resides.

Resizing the Application Window

The Form_Resize( ) procedure is automatically executed whenever the user changes the size of the application window.

- Enter the following code within the Form_Resize( ) procedure:

```
Private Sub Form_Resize( )

    If gBMPHandle <= 0 Then
        Exit Sub
    End If

    ' Close the WinG session
    Tegwing1.CloseWinG

    Tegwing1.hWndDisplay = Me.hWnd
    ' Open a WinG session
    Tegwing1.OpenWinG

End Sub
```

This code checks the value of gBMPHandle:

```
If gBMPHandle <= 0 Then
    Exit Sub
End If
```

The gBMPHandle variable holds the handle of the loaded BMP file. If no BMP file has been loaded, the If condition is satisfied, and the procedure terminates.

If a BMP file has been loaded already, the current WinG session is closed:

```
' Close the WinG session
Tegwing1.CloseWinG
```

And then a new WinG session is opened:

```
Tegwing1.hWndDisplay = Me.hWnd

' Open a WinG session
Tegwing1.OpenWinG
```

11

So putting it all together, when the user changes the size of the application's window, a new WinG session is opened. This way, the size of WinG is always the same size as the size of the application's window.

Playing and Stopping the Playback

You'll now attach code to the cmdPlayStop button. Recall that this button serves as both the Play button and the Stop button.

- Enter the following code within the cmdPlayStop_Click( ) procedure:

```
Private Sub cmdPlayStop_Click( )

    If cmdPlayStop.Caption = "&Play" Then
        Tegomm1.Command = "Play"
        cmdPlayStop.Caption = "Sto&p"
        gWavWasLoaded = 1
    Else
        Tegomm1.Command = "Stop"
        cmdPlayStop.Caption = "&Play"
        gWavWasLoaded = 0
    End If

End Sub
```

The code you entered uses an If...Else statement to determine whether the user clicked the button while it serves as a Play or as a Stop button:

```
If cmdPlayStop.Caption = "&Play" Then
    ..............................
    ... User clicked the Play button
    ..............................
Else
    ..............................
    ... User clicked the Stop button
    ..............................
End If
```

If the user clicked the Play button, the statements under the If statement are executed. The Play command is issued to the Multimedia control:

```
Tegomm1.Command = "Play"
```

So now the program plays the WAV file. Because now the playback is in progress, the Caption of the cmdPlayStop button is set to Sto&p:

```
cmdPlayStop.Caption = "Sto&p"
```

Finally, the gWavLoaded variable is set to 1, as an indication that a WAV file playback is in progress:

```
gWavWasLoaded = 1
```

The code under the Else statement is executed if the user clicked the Stop button. This code issues the Stop command to the Multimedia control:

```
Tegomm1.Command = "Stop"
```

The Caption property of the cmdPlayStop button is then changed to &Play:

```
cmdPlayStop.Caption = "&Play"
```

And finally, the gWavWasLoaded flag is set to 0 (because the WAV playback is not in progress):

```
gWavWasLoaded = 0
```

Attaching Code to the Collision Show Item of the Select Show Menu

The user can run either the Collision show or the Music show by selecting the appropriate item from the Select Show menu. You'll now attach code to the Collision Show item of the Select Show menu.

- Enter the following code inside the mnuCollisionShow_Click( ) procedure:

```
Private Sub mnuCollisionShow_Click( )

    gCollisionShow = 1
    gMusicShow = 0
```

```
        mnuMusicShow.Checked = False
        mnuCollisionShow.Checked = True

    End Sub
```

This code sets the gCollisionShow variable to 1:

```
    gCollisionShow = 1
```

The gCollisionShow variable serves as a flag that indicates which show is selected.

Also, the gMusicShow variable serves as a flag that indicates that the Music show is or is not selected. The mnuCollisionShow_Click( ) procedure is executed whenever the user selects the Collision Show item from the Select Show menu, so the code you entered sets the gMusicShow flag to 0:

```
    gMusicShow = 0
```

Finally, the check mark that appears to the left of the Music Show menu item is removed:

```
    mnuMusicShow.Checked = False
```

and a check mark is placed next to the Collision menu item:

```
    mnuCollisionShow.Checked = True
```

Attaching Code to the Collision Command Button

Whenever the user clicks the Collision button, the program should behave in the same manner as when the user selects Collision Show from the Select Show menu.

- Enter the following code within the cmdCollision_Click( ) procedure:

```
Private Sub cmdCollision_Click( )

    mnuCollisionShow_Click

End Sub
```

Attaching Code to the Music Show Item of the Select Show Menu

You'll now attach code to the Music Show item of the Select Show menu.

- Enter the following code inside the mnuMusicShow_Click( ) procedure:

```
Private Sub mnuMusicShow_Click( )

    gCollisionShow = 0
    gMusicShow = 1
    mnuMusicShow.Checked = True
    mnuCollisionShow.Checked = False

End Sub
```

This code is very similar to the code you entered inside the mnuCollision_Click( ) procedure. However, now you've set the flags and menu items to indicate that the Music show is selected.

Attaching Code to the Music Button

You'll now attach code to the Music button. Whenever the user clicks the Music button, the program should behave in the same manner as when the user selects Music Show from the Select Show menu.

- Enter the following code inside the cmdMusic_Click( ) procedure:

```
Private Sub cmdMusic_Click( )

    mnuMusicShow_Click

End Sub
```

Attaching Code to the StatusUpdate Event of the Multimedia Control

During design time you set the UpdateInterval property of the Multimedia control to 200. This means that the StatusUpdate event occurs every 200 milliseconds. So the Tegomm1_StatusUpdate( ) procedure is automatically executed every 200 milliseconds.

- Enter the following code inside the Tegomm1_StatusUpdate( ) procedure:

```
Private Sub Tegomm1_StatusUpdate( )

    If gWavWasLoaded = 1 Then
        If gMusicShow = 1 Then
            MusicShow
        End If

        If gCollisionShow = 1 Then
            CollisionShow
        End If

    End If

End Sub
```

An If statement is used to examine whether the playback of a WAV file is in progress. If so, the statements under the If statement are executed. Two inner If statements are executed to determine which show should be displayed. If the Music show is selected, the MusicShow procedure is executed:

```
If gMusicShow = 1 Then
    MusicShow
End If
```

And if the Collision show is selected, the CollisionShow procedure is executed:

```
If gCollisionShow = 1 Then
    CollisionShow
End If
```

Later in this chapter you'll implement the MusicShow and CollisionShow procedures.

Attaching Code to the Done Event of the Multimedia Control

You'll now attach code to the Done event of the Multimedia control.

- Enter the following code inside the Tegomm1_Done( ) procedure:

```
Private Sub Tegomm1_Done( )

    If Tegomm1.Length = Tegomm1.Position Then

        Tegomm1.Command = "Prev"
        Tegomm1.Command = "Play"

    End If

End Sub
```

The Done event occurs whenever the Multimedia control completes executing a command. For example, after issuing the Play command, the Multimedia control plays the WAV file. When the entire WAV file has been played, the Done event occurs, and the Tegomm1_Done( ) procedure is executed.

An If statement is executed to verify that the Done event has occurred:

```
If Tegomm1.Length = Tegomm1.Position Then

    .................................
    ... The entire WAV file was played
    .................................

End If
```

The code under the If statement issues the Prev command and the Play command:

```
Tegomm1.Command = "Prev"
Tegomm1.Command = "Play"
```

So putting it all together, when the WAV file is played in its entirety, the code inside the Tegomm1_Done( ) procedure rewinds the WAV file and then playback starts all over again.

The CollisionShow( ) Procedure

11

Once the user clicks the Play button, the loaded WAV file is played, and the show is displayed. As you saw, the code that displays the show is executed from within the Tegomm1_StatusUpdate( ) procedure. The code you entered in the Tegomm1_StatusUpdate( ) procedure executes either the CollisionShow() procedure or the MusicShow( ) procedure. You'll now write the code of the CollisionShow( ) procedure:

- Make sure the Code window of the frmWinGMult form is selected, select Procedure from the Insert menu to display the Insert Procedure dialog box, type **CollisionShow** as the Name of the new procedure (see Figure 11.11), and finally, click the OK button of the Insert Procedure dialog box.

Visual Basic responds by inserting the CollisionShow( ) procedure inside the general section of the frmWinGMult form.

- Enter the following code within the CollisionShow procedure:

```
Public Sub CollisionShow( )

Static FrameNumber As Integer
Dim Msg As String
Dim FileName As String
```

FIGURE 11.11:
Inserting the CollisionShow procedure

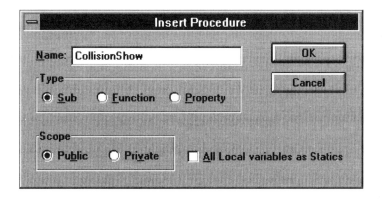

```
' Close previous loaded BMP file (if any)
Tegwing1.CloseBMP gBMPHandle

If (Right(App.Path, 1)) <> "\" Then
   FileName = App.Path + "\"
Else
   FileName = App.Path
End If

FileName = FileName + _
           "Bil" + _
           Format(FrameNumber) + ".BMP"

gBMPHandle = Tegwing1.OpenBMP(FileName)

If gBMPHandle <= 0 Then
   Msg = "Can't open the "
   Msg = Msg + FileName + " file. "
   Msg = Msg + _
     "(Make sure the BMP file is a 256-color BMP file)."

   MsgBox Msg, vbInformation, "Error"

   End
End If

DisplayBMP (gBMPHandle)

FrameNumber = FrameNumber + 1
If FrameNumber = 42 Then
   FrameNumber = 0
End If

End Sub
```

This code declares a static variable:

```
Static FrameNumber As Integer
```

As you'll soon see, FrameNumber holds the frame number of the show. Because FrameNumber is a static variable, its value is retained even after the CollisionShow procedure is terminated. For example, if FrameNumber is currently equal to 3, and the CollisionShow procedure is terminated and then executed again, FrameNumber will still be equal to 3.

11

The next statement that you typed closes the loaded BMP file:

```
' Close previous loaded BMP file (if any)
Tegwing1.CloseBMP gBMPHandle
```

In the following code, a new BMP file is loaded, so the preceding statement unloads the BMP file that was previously loaded. (No harm is done if you try to close a BMP file that has not been loaded yet.)

Then the name of the BMP file that will be loaded is constructed:

```
If (Right(App.Path, 1)) <> "\" Then
    FileName = App.Path + "\"
Else
    FileName = App.Path
End If
FileName = FileName + "Bil" + Format(FrameNumber) + ".BMP"
```

For example, if FrameNumber is equal to 0 (its value when the CollisionShow procedure is executed for the very first time) and the WinGMult program is executed from the C:\WinGPrg\CH10 directory, FileName is constructed to hold the C:\WinGPrg\CH10\Bil0.BMP file. If FrameNumber is equal to 1, FileName is constructed with the path and name of the Bil1.BMP file. If FrameNumber is equal to 2, FileName is constructed with the path and name of the Bil2.BMP file, and so on.

Next, the BMP file is opened using the OpenBMP method:

```
gBMPHandle = Tegwing1.OpenBMP(FileName)
```

The result of the OpenBMP method is examined, and if the BMP file was not loaded successfully, the procedure is terminated:

```
If gBMPHandle <= 0 Then
    Msg = "Can't open the "
    Msg = Msg + FileName + " file. "
    Msg = Msg + _
        "(Make sure the BMP file is a 256-color BMP file)."

    MsgBox Msg, vbInformation, "Error"
    End
End If
```

Now that the BMP file was loaded, you display the contents of the loaded BMP file:

```
DisplayBMP (gBMPHandle)
```

Later in this chapter you'll write the code of the DisplayBMP procedure.

Then FrameNumber is increased by 1:

```
FrameNumber = FrameNumber + 1
```

So when executing the CollisionShow procedure for the first time (which means that FrameNumber is equal to 0), the Bil0.BMP file is loaded.

After 200 milliseconds, the Tegomm1_StatusUpdate( ) procedure is executed again, and the CollisionShow procedure is executed. But because FrameNumber is now equal to 1, the Bil1.BMP file is loaded.

An If statement is executed to make sure that FrameNumber does not exceed 42:

```
If FrameNumber = 42 Then
    FrameNumber = 0
End If
```

So putting it altogether, every 200 milliseconds a new BMP file is loaded. The sequence of BMP files that are loaded is as follows:

Bil0.BMP

Bil1.BMP

Bil2.BMP

...

...

...

Bil41.BMP

Bil0.BMP

Bil1.BMP

and so on...

The MusicShow Procedure

You'll now write the code of the MusicShow procedure. Recall that if the Music Show item of the Select Show menu is selected and the Play button was clicked, then the Tegomm1_StatusUpdate( ) procedure executes the MusicShow procedure every 200 milliseconds.

- Make sure that the Code window of the frmWinGMult form is selected, select Procedure from the Insert menu to display the Insert Procedure dialog box, type **MusicShow** as the Name of the new procedure (see Figure 11.12), and finally, click the OK button of the Insert Procedure dialog box.

FIGURE 11.12:
Inserting the MusicShow procedure

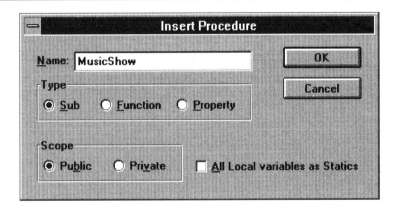

Visual Basic responds by inserting the MusicShow procedure inside the general section of the frmWinGMult form.

- Enter the following code inside the MusicShow procedure:

```
Public Sub MusicShow( )

Static FrameNumber As Integer
Dim Msg As String
Dim FileName As String

' Close previous loaded BMP file (if any)
Tegwing1.CloseBMP gBMPHandle

If (Right(App.Path, 1)) <> "\" Then
   FileName = App.Path + "\"
Else
   FileName = App.Path
End If
```

```
FileName = FileName + _
         "Dance" + Format(FrameNumber) + _
         ".BMP"

gBMPHandle = Tegwing1.OpenBMP(FileName)

If gBMPHandle <= 0 Then
   Msg = "Can't open the "
   Msg = Msg + FileName + " file. "
   Msg = Msg + _
      "(Make sure the BMP file is a 256-color BMP file)."

   MsgBox Msg, vbInformation, "Error"

   End
End If

DisplayBMP (gBMPHandle)

FrameNumber = FrameNumber + 1
If FrameNumber = 6 Then
   FrameNumber = 0
End If

End Sub
```

This code is very similar to the code you entered in the CollisionShow procedure. In fact, the only difference between the two procedures is that CollisionShow loads and displays the Bil?.BMP files, where ? stands for a number between 0 and 41, and MusicShow loads and displays the Dance? files, where ? stands for a number between 0 and 5.

The BMP files are loaded in the following sequence:

Dance0.BMP

Dance1.BMP

Dance2.BMP

Dance3.BMP

Dance4.BMP

11

Dance5.BMP

Dance0.BMP

Dance1.BMP

and so on...

Loading BMP Files

As you saw in the CollisionShow and MusicShow procedures, the code that you typed loads the BMP files from the drive from within the CollisionShow and MusicShow procedures. This means that during the animation, the program is involved in loading BMP files from the drive.

Alternatively, you may choose to load the BMP files only once during the life of the program. For example, you can load the Dance0.BMP file and assign the handle of the loaded BMP file to a variable called gBMPHandle[0]. Similarly, you load the files Dance1.BMP, Dance2.BMP, Dance3.BMP, Dance4.BMP and Dance5.BMP and assign the handles of the loaded files to gBMPHandle[1], gBMPHandle[2], gBMPHandle[3], gBMPHandle[4] and gBMPHandle[5]. The MusicShow procedure will then be able to display the BMP files without having to load the BMP files prior to displaying them.

NOTE The CollisionShow and MusicShow procedures assume that the BMP files reside in the same directory from which the program was executed. Also, the BMP files are assumed to be 256-color BMP files.

The DisplayBMP Procedure

The CollisionShow and MusicShow procedures both execute the DisplayBMP procedure. You'll now write the code of this procedure.

- Make sure that the Code window of the frmWinGMult form is selected, select Procedure from the Insert menu to display the Insert Procedure dialog box, type **DisplayBMP** as the Name of the new procedure (see Figure 11.13), and finally, click the OK button of the Insert Procedure dialog box.

Visual Basic responds by inserting the DisplayBMP procedure inside the general section of the frmWinGMult form.

FIGURE 11.13:
Inserting the DisplayBMP procedure

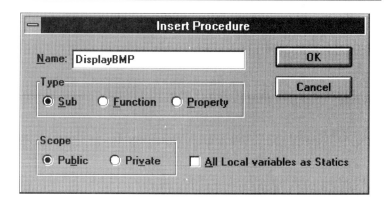

- Type the following code inside the DisplayBMP procedure:

```
Public Sub DisplayBMP(BMPHandle)

Dim XTarget, YTarget As Integer
Dim WidthTarget, HeightTarget As Integer
Dim XSource, YSource As Integer
Dim WidthSource, HeightSource As Integer
Dim StretchType As Long
Dim BMPSourceHandle As Integer
```

11

```
        XTarget = 0
        YTarget = 0
        WidthTarget = Tegwing1.WinGWidth
        HeightTarget = Tegwing1.WinGHeight
        XSource = 0
        YSource = 0
        WidthSource = Tegwing1.GetBMPWidth(BMPHandle)
        HeightSource = Tegwing1.GetBMPHeight(BMPHandle)
        StretchType = SRCCOPY
        BMPSourceHandle = BMPHandle

        ' Copy the BMP file into WinG
        Tegwing1.CopyBMP2WinG XTarget, YTarget, _
                WidthTarget, HeightTarget, _
                BMPSourceHandle, _
                XSource, YSource, _
                WidthSource, HeightSource, _
                StretchType

        ' SlamIt
        Tegwing1.SlamIt

    End Sub
```

Don't forget to include the parameter (BMPHandle) in the first line of the DisplayBMP procedure:

```
Public Sub DisplayBMP(BMPHandle)
...
...
...
End Sub
```

The code you entered first sets the values of the various parameters needed for the CopyBMP2WinG method:

```
        XTarget = 0
        YTarget = 0
        WidthTarget = Tegwing1.WinGWidth
        HeightTarget = Tegwing1.WinGHeight
        XSource = 0
        YSource = 0
        WidthSource = Tegwing1.GetBMPWidth(BMPHandle)
        HeightSource = Tegwing1.GetBMPHeight(BMPHandle)
        StretchType = SRCCOPY
        BMPSourceHandle = BMPHandle
```

Then the CopyBMP2WinG method is executed, copying the contents of the loaded BMP file to WinG:

```
' Copy the BMP file into WinG
    Tegwing1.CopyBMP2WinG XTarget, YTarget, _
                WidthTarget, HeightTarget, _
                BMPSourceHandle, _
                XSource, YSource, _
                WidthSource, HeightSource, _
                StretchType
```

Finally, the contents of WinG are slammed into the screen:

```
' SlamIt
    Tegwing1.SlamIt
```

Attaching Code to the About Menu Item

You'll now attach code to the About menu item.

- Enter the following code inside the mnuAbout_Click( ) procedure of the frmWinGMult form:

```
Private Sub mnuAbout_Click( )

    'Display the About window
    frmAbout.Show 1

End Sub
```

This code displays the frmAbout form as a modal window. (Later in this chapter you'll implement the frmAbout form.)

Attaching Code to the
Help Menu Item

You'll now attach code to the Help menu item.

- Enter the following code inside the mnuHelpMe_Click( ) procedure of the frmWinGMult form:

```
Private Sub mnuHelpMe_Click( )

    ' Display the Help window
    frmHelp.Show 1

End Sub
```

This code displays the frmHelp form as a modal window. (Later in this chapter you'll implement the frmHelp form.)

Implementing the
About Window

You'll now implement the frmAbout form.

- Implement the frmAbout form using the Properties settings listed in Table 11.3. When you've completed implementing the form, it should look as shown in Figure 11.14.

TABLE 11.3: The Properties of the frmAbout Form

Object: Form
Name: frmAbout

Property	Value
BorderStyle	1 'Fixed Single
Caption	"About"
Height	5910
Left	1095

TABLE 11.3: The Properties of the frmAbout Form (continued)

Property	Value
MaxButton	0 'False
MinButton	0 'False
Picture	C:\WinGPrg\CH10\About01.BMP
Top	660
Width	5985

Object: CommandButton
Name: cmdOK

Property	Value
Caption	"&OK"
Height	495
Left	4320
Top	3480
Width	735

Attaching Code to the OK Button of the frmAbout Form

- Enter the following code inside the cmdOK_Click( ) procedure of the frmAbout form:

```
Private Sub cmdOK_Click( )

    Unload Me

End Sub
```

This code is executed whenever the user clicks the OK button of the About window; it unloads the About form.

FIGURE 11.14:

The frmAbout form in design mode

Implementing the Help Window

You'll now implement the frmHelp form.

- Implement the frmHelp form using the Properties settings listed in Table 11.4. When you've completed implementing the form, it should look as shown in Figure 11.15.

TABLE 11.4: The Properties of the frmHelp Form

Object: Form
Name: frmHelp

Property	Value
BackColor	&H00C0C0C0&
BorderStyle	3 'Fixed Double
Caption	"Help"
Height	5850
Left	990
MaxButton	0 'False
MinButton	0 'False
Picture	C:\WinGPrg\CH10\Help.BMP
Top	630
Width	6255

Object: CommandButton
Name: cmdOK

Property	Value
Caption	"&OK"
Height	495
Left	3000
Top	3840
Width	495

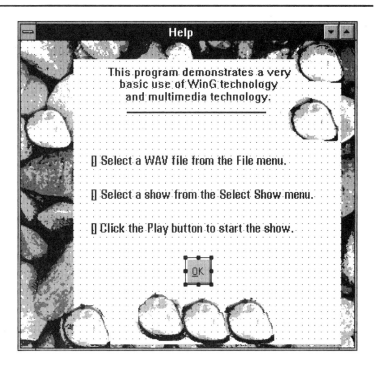

FIGURE 11.15:

The frmHelp form in design mode

Attaching Code to the OK Button of the frmHelp Form

- Enter the following code inside the cmdOK_Click( ) procedure of the frmHelp form:

```
Private Sub cmdOK_Click( )

    Unload Me

End Sub
```

This code is executed whenever the user clicks the OK button of the Help window; it unloads the Help form.

Summary

In this chapter you learned how to utilize the TegoSoft Multimedia control (from this book's CD-ROM) for playing WAV files. As demonstrated with the WinGMult program, you used WinG technology and multimedia technology to implement an animation program that plays back a WAV file while displaying a sequence of BMP files.

CHAPTER

TWELVE

Extracting Information about WAV Files

In this chapter you'll execute the WAVInfo.EXE program, which demonstrates how you can use the TegoSoft Multimedia control for extracting information about the recording settings of WAV files—specifically, the sampling rate at which the file was recorded, whether it's an 8-bit or a 16-bit recording, and whether it was recorded in mono or stereo mode. This chapter also looks briefly at what each of these characteristics means. In the next chapter, you'll implement the WAVInfo.EXE program yourself.

Executing the WAVInfo.EXE Program

You'll now execute the WAVInfo.EXE program, which resides in the \WingPrg\EXE directory of this book's CD-ROM.

- Execute the WAVInfo.EXE program.

Windows responds by displaying the window shown in Figure 12.1.

As shown in Figure 12.1, the File Name label has the caption "No WAV was loaded." So let's load a WAV file:

- Select Open WAV File from the File menu.

WAVInfo responds by displaying the Open dialog box as shown in Figure 12.2.

FIGURE 12.1:

The window of the WAVInfo.EXE program

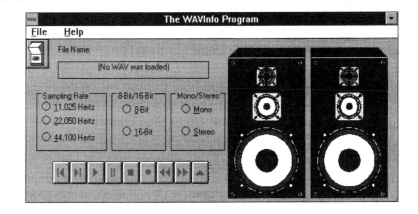

FIGURE 12.2:

The Open WAV File dialog box

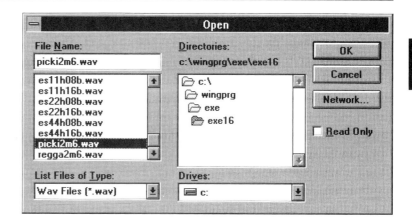

- Select the Picki2m6.WAV file from the \WinGPrg\EXE directory and then click the OK button of the Open dialog box.

WAVInfo responds by loading the Picki2m6.WAV file. As shown in Figure 12.3, the various option buttons of the application window are selected. These buttons reflect the recording settings of the loaded WAV file, in this case, the settings of the Picki2m6.WAV file. As you can see, the Picki2m6.WAV file was recorded with a sampling rate of 22,025 Hz, it's an 8-bit WAV file, and it's a Mono WAV file. (The topics of sampling rate, 8-bit versus 16-bit WAV files, and Mono/Stereo recording will be discussed later in this chapter.)

FIGURE 12.3:

The Pick12M6.WAV file loaded into the WAVInfo program window

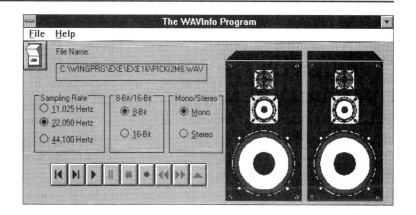

FIGURE 12.4:

The menu that pops up after selecting Template WAV Files from the File menu

EM11H08B.WAV (Mono, 11 KHz, 8-bit)
ES11H08B.WAV (Stereo, 11 KHz, 8-bit)
EM11H16B.WAV (Mono, 11 KHz, 16-bit)
ES11H16B.WAV (Stereo, 11 KHz, 16-bit)
EM22H08B.WAV (Mono, 22 KHz, 8-bit)
ES22H08B.WAV (Stereo, 22 KHz, 8-bit)
EM22H16B.WAV (Mono, 22 KHz, 16-bit)
ES22H16B.WAV (Stereo, 22 KHz, 16-bit)
EM44H08B.WAV (Mono, 44 KHz, 8-bit)
ES44H08B.WAV (Stereo, 44 KHz, 8-bit)
EM44H16B.WAV (Mono, 44 KHz, 16-bit)
ES44H16B.WAV (Stereo, 44 KHz, 16-bit)

• Click the Play button (the third button from the left).

WAVInfo responds by playing the WAV file. Notice that during the playback, the speaker cones are vibrating, which gives a realistic touch.

• Experiment with the other buttons of the Multimedia control.

• Select Template WAV File from the File menu.

WAVInfo responds by displaying another menu (see Figure 12.4).

As shown in Figure 12.4, the menu lists 12 different WAV files. These WAV files do not contain any recording in them, hence the name "template WAV files." Their only purpose is to help you learn about multimedia programming, and in subsequent chapters you'll learn more about these WAV files. For now, you can load these WAV files and notice that they have the recording characteristics shown in Table 12.1.

TABLE 12.1: Recording Characteristics of the Template WAV Files

File Name	Sampling Rate	Mono/Stereo	8-bit/16-bit
EM11H08B.WAV	11,025 Hertz	Mono	8-bit
ES11H08B.WAV	11,025 Hertz	Stereo	8-bit
EM11H16B.WAV	11,025 Hertz	Mono	16-bit
ES11H16B.WAV	11,025 Hertz	Stereo	16-bit
EM22H08B.WAV	22,050 Hertz	Mono	8-bit
ES22H08B.WAV	22,050 Hertz	Stereo	8-bit
EM22H16B.WAV	22,050 Hertz	Mono	16-bit
ES22H16B.WAV	22,050 Hertz	Stereo	16-bit
EM44H08B.WAV	44,100 Hertz	Mono	8-bit
ES44H08B.WAV	44,100 Hertz	Stereo	8-bit
EM44H16B.WAV	44,100 Hertz	Mono	16-bit
ES44H16B.WAV	44,100 Hertz	Stereo	16-bit

12

The Naming Convention for the Template WAV Files

The various template WAV filenames were constructed as follows:

- The first character is E, to indicate that the WAV file does not contain any recording in it. (E stand for empty.)

- The second character is M or S. M stand for Mono, and S stands for Stereo.

- The next three characters can be 11H, 22H or 44H. 11H indicates that a sampling rate of 11,025 Hertz was used for the recording, 22H indicates that a sampling rate of 22,050 Hertz was used for the recording, and 44H indicates that a sampling rate of 44,100 Hertz was used for the recording.

- The next three characters can be 08B or 16B. 08B indicates that the WAV file was recorded as an 8-bit WAV file, and 16B indicates that the WAV file was recorded as a 16-bit WAV file.

The Help window is shown in Figure 12.5 and the About window is shown in Figure 12.6.

- Experiment with the WAVInfo program's options and then click the Exit switch to terminate the program.

FIGURE 12.5:
The Help window of the WAVInfo program

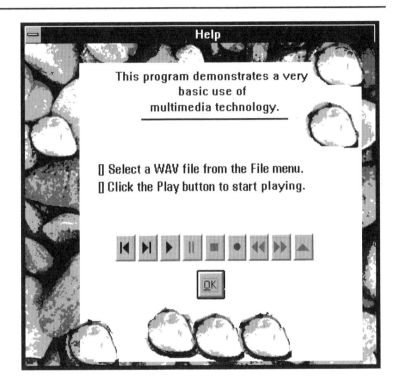

Sampling Rates

As noted in Chapter 9, WAV files can be recorded at different sampling rates. Essentially, what happens during the recording of a WAV file is this: The sound card's microphone picks up a sound and converts it into an electrical signal—an analog voltage that varies continuously over time. Then the sound card's circuitry "reads"

FIGURE 12.6:
The About window of the WAVInfo program

this signal at fixed intervals and converts it into a series of digital values. These values are then stored into a WAV file. The digital value at each interval is known as a *sample*, and the frequency of the intervals is known as the *sampling rate*. Of course, these intervals are very small; they are measured in thousandths of a second.

For example, a sampling rate of 11,025 Hz means that every 1/11,025=0.0000907 seconds (or 0.0907 milliseconds, or 90.7 microseconds), the sound card samples the sound.

The principle of sampling the sound is illustrated in the schematic of Figure 12.7. The steps are as follows:

1. Sound is introduced to the microphone. The microphone picks up the sound, and generates an electronic signal. The magnitude of the electronic signal is measured in units of volts.

2. The sound card has electronic circuitry called an amplifier, which amplifies the incoming voltage signal from the microphone. So in step 2, the sound is converted to a voltage and amplified. The resulting signal is shown as the upper graph in Figure 12.7.

3. The sound card samples the signal. The black dots in the lower graph of Figure 12.7 indicate the digital values of the samples.

4. The sound card saves the samples into the WAV file.

FIGURE 12.7:

Sampling sound and saving the samples into a WAV file

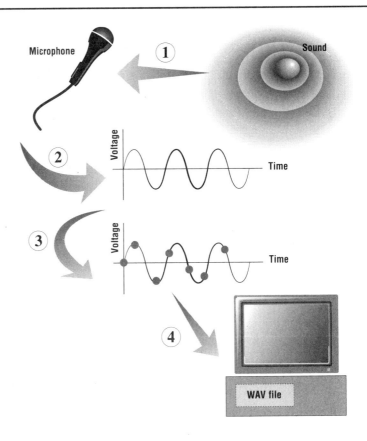

12

Note that in the WAV file, some of the information that existed in the original analog signal that represents the sound is lost forever. That is, the WAV file "knows" the values of the samples (which represent the values of the sound at certain times). But the values of the sound in between the samples are not recorded.

Now you can appreciate the importance of the sampling rate. If (to take an extreme case) the sound card sampled the incoming sound every hour, the WAV file would obviously be useless, and the resulting sound when the WAV file is played back would not resemble the original sound. However, if you sample the sound very frequently, the WAV file contains enough information about the original sound; and when played back, the WAV file will sound like the original. The higher the sampling rate, the better the sound quality of the resulting WAV file.

8-bit and 16-bit Recording

Typically, a sound card records sound in the so-called 8-bit recording mode. In this mode, each sample is saved as a byte (8 bits). Basically, in an 8-bit recording, the incoming signal is scaled so that each sample can have an integer value between 0 and 255. So 0 represents the most negative value that the signal can have (that is, the lowest point on the voltage scale shown in Figure 12.7's graphs), and 255 represents the maximum value (that is, the highest point on the voltage scale). A value of 128 (the mid-point) represents the no-signal value (silence). So what happens when the signal is between integer values? For example, what happens when the signal has a value of 32.1? The value is rounded to 32. Again, this means that the WAV file is not an exact replica of the original sound, which will affect the playback quality.

Some sound cards can record in the so-called 16-bit recording mode. In this mode, each sample is saved as two bytes (16 bits). When recording in 16-bit mode, the maximum value of an incoming sample is divided into approximately 64,000 parts. Thus, when recording with 16-bit technique, the resolution of the recording is much better than with the 8-bit recording technique.

Mono and Stereo Recording

Another difference between sound cards is that some can record a WAV file as a stereo rather than a mono recording. The principle of mono recording is what we've just described: Each sample is saved into the WAV file. In an 8-bit recording, each byte in the WAV file represents a single sample. In a 16-bit recording, each sample is represented by a two-byte value in the WAV file.

When recording in stereo mode, you can view the microphone as two microphones. The sound that is picked up by the microphone from the left side of the room is sampled, and these samples are saved into the WAV file as the "left channel." At the same time, the sound that is picked up from the right side of the microphone is sampled, and these samples are saved into the WAV file as the "right channel."

So when recorded in mono mode, the WAV file looks as follows:

Sample #1

Sample #2

Sample #3

Sample #4

.....

.....

.....

... and so on.

And when recorded in stereo mode, the WAV file looks as follows:

Sample #1 from the left side

Sample #1 from the right side

Sample #2 from the left side

Sample #2 from the right side

Sample #3 from the left side

Sample #3 from the right side

Sample #4 from the left side

Sample #4 from the right side

.....

.....

.....

... and so on.

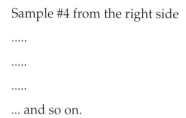

Tradeoffs—Which Is Better?

Note the tradeoff that exists when recording WAV files. When you record with a higher sampling rate, the quality of the recording is better than with a lower sampling rate, but the size of the WAV file is larger (because during the recording, many more samples are taken each second).

Also, when recording in stereo mode, the size of the WAV file is twice that of the mono WAV file.

And finally, the size of a 16-bit recording WAV file is twice the size of an 8-bit recording, because in 8-bit recording, each sample occupies one byte, while in 16-bit recording, each sample occupies two bytes.

So which recording settings should you use? It depends on your application. If you are trying to impress somebody with your singing, then record it with your sound card's best possible recording quality (typically, 44,100 Hertz, Stereo, 16-bit). If hard drive space is a consideration, then record the WAV file as an 11,025 Hertz, mono, 8-bit recording.

For comparison purposes, note that telephone equipment transmits voice at a quality similar to a WAV file recorded at 8,000 Hz, in mono and 8-bit mode. A CD Audio recording has a quality similar to that of a WAV file recorded at 44,100 Hz, in stereo and 16-bit mode. An ordinary portable tape recorder typically has a quality similar to that of a WAV file recorded at 22,050 Hz, in mono and 8-bit mode.

Summary

In this chapter you execute the WAVInfo program. This program loads a WAV file, analyzes it, and displays the recording settings. As stated, WAV files can be recorded at various sampling rates, in mono or stereo mode, and as an 8-bit or a 16-bit recording.

CHAPTER

THIRTEEN

13

Writing the WAVInfo Application

In this chapter you'll write the WAVInfo.EXE program that you executed in the previous chapter. This program demonstrates how you can use the TegoSoft Multimedia control from this book's CD-ROM to extract information about the recording settings of WAV files.

Creating the Project of the WAVInfo Application

You first need to create the project of the WAVInfo application.

- Start Visual Basic and select New Project from the File menu.

- Save the new form as WAVInfo.FRM and the new project file as WAVInfo.MAK, both in the C:\WinGPrg\CH12 directory.

TABLE 13.1: The Properties of the frmWAVInfo Form

Object: Form

Name: frmWAVInfo

Property	Value
BackColor	Light gray
BorderStyle	1 'Fixed Single
Caption	"The WAVInfo Program"
Height	4215
Icon	C:\WinG\Icons\WAVInfo.ICO
Left	645
MaxButton	0 'False
Top	255
Width	8430

TABLE 13.1: The Properties of the frmWAVInfo Form (continued)

Object: Frame

Name: fraSamplingRate

Comment: First place the frame inside the form, and then place the opt11KHz, opt22KHz, and opt44KHz option buttons inside the fraSamplingRate frame.

Property	Value
BackColor	Light gray
Caption	"Sampling Rate"
Height	1335
Left	240
Top	1080
Width	1575

Object: OptionButton

Name: opt11KHz

Comment: Place this option button inside the fraSamplingRate frame.

Property	Value
BackColor	Light gray
Caption	"&11,025 Hertz"
Height	255
Left	120
Top	240
Width	1215

Object: OptionButton

Name: opt22KHz

Comment: Place this option button inside the fraSamplingRate frame.

Property	Value
BackColor	Light gray
Caption	"&22,050 Hertz"
Height	375
Left	120
Top	480
Width	1335

TABLE 13.1: The Properties of the frmWAVInfo Form (continued)

Object: OptionButton

Name: opt44KHz

Comment: Place this option button inside the fraSamplingRate frame.

Property	Value
BackColor	Light gray
Caption	"&44,100 Hertz"
Height	375
Left	120
Top	840
Width	1335

Object: Frame

Name: fraMonoStereo

Comment: First place the frame inside the form, and then place the optMono and optStereo option buttons inside the fraMonoStereo frame.

Property	Value
BackColor	Light gray
Caption	"Mono/Stereo"
Height	1335
Left	3240
Top	1080
Width	1215

Object: OptionButton

Name: optMono

Comment: Place the optMono option button inside the fraMonoStereo frame.

Property	Value
BackColor	Light gray
Caption	"&Mono"
Height	375
Left	240
Top	240
Width	855

TABLE 13.1: The Properties of the frmWAVInfo Form (continued)

Object: OptionButton

Name: optStereo

Comment: Place the optStereo option button inside the fraMonoStereo frame.

Property	Value
BackColor	Light gray
Caption	"&Stereo"
Height	375
Left	240
Top	720
Width	855

Object: Frame

Name: fra8Bit16Bit

Comment: First place the frame inside the form, and then place the opt8Bit and opt16Bit option buttons inside the fra8Bit16Bit frame.

Property	Value
BackColor	Light gray
Caption	"8-Bit/16-Bit"
Height	1335
Left	1920
Top	1080
Width	1215

Object: OptionButton

Name: opt16Bit

Comment: Place this option button inside the fra8Bit16Bit frame.

Property	Value
BackColor	Light gray
Caption	"&16-Bit"
Height	375
Left	240
Top	720
Width	735

TABLE 13.1: The Properties of the frmWAVInfo Form (continued)

Object: OptionButton

Name: opt8Bit

Comment: Place this option button inside the fra8Bit16Bit frame.

Property	Value
BackColor	Light gray
Caption	"&8-Bit"
Height	375
Left	240
Top	240
Width	735

Object: Image

Name: imgSpk01

Property	Value
Stretch	−1 'True
Height	375
Left	3000
Picture	C:\WinGPrg\CH12\SPK01.BMP
Top	120
Visible	0 'False
Width	495

Object: Image

Name: imgSpk02

Property	Value
Stretch	−1 'True
Height	375
Left	2400
Picture	C:\WinGPrg\CH12\SPK02.BMP
Top	120
Visible	0 'False
Width	495

TABLE 13.1: The Properties of the frmWAVInfo Form (continued)

Object: Image
Name: imgSpeakers

Property	Value
Height	3435
Left	4440
Picture	C:\WinGPrg\CH12\SPK01.BMP
Top	120
Width	3795

Object: CommonDialog
Name: CommonDialog1

Property	Value
CancelError	True
Left	3600
Top	0

Object: Label
Name: Label1

Property	Value
BackColor	Light gray
Caption	"File Name:"
Height	255
Left	720
Top	120
Width	855

13

TABLE 13.1: The Properties of the frmWAVInfo Form (continued)

Object: Label
Name: lblFileName

Property	Value
Alignment	2 'Center
BackColor	Light gray
BorderStyle	1 'Fixed Single
Caption	(No WAV was loaded)
Height	375
Left	720
Top	480
Width	3375

Object: TegoSoft Multimedia Control
Name: Tegomm1

Property	Value
Height	495
Left	600
Top	2640
Width	3510

Object: TegoSoft Switch Control
Name: swExit

Property	Value
Height	630
Left	0
Top	0
Width	525
value	−1 'True

- Implement the frmWAVInfo form with the Properties settings shown in Table 13.1. When you're finished, the form should look as shown in Figure 13.1.

FIGURE 13.1:

The frmWAVInfo form in design mode

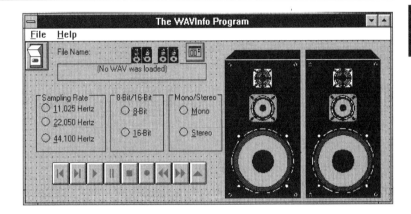

The TegoSoft Multimedia OCX control and the TegoSoft OCX Switch control appear inside the frmWinGMult form. For each of these, follow the basic procedure outlined in Chapter 4 to add the control's icon to Visual Basic's Tools window and place the control in the form:

- Select Custom Controls from the Tools menu in Visual Basic and then click the appropriate name to add the control's icon to the Tools window.

- Double-click the icon in the Toolbox window to place the control inside the form.

The icon of the Multimedia control inside the Tools window appears in Figure 13.2. Once you place the Multimedia control inside the form, it appears as shown in Figure 13.3.

The icon of the Switch control inside the Tools window appears in Figure 13.4. Once you place the Switch control inside the form, it appears as shown in Figure 13.5.

FIGURE 13.2:

The Multimedia control inside the
Tools window

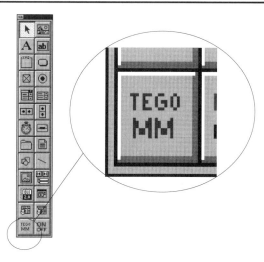

FIGURE 13.3:

The Multimedia control inside the
form

FIGURE 13.4:

The Switch control inside the Tools
window

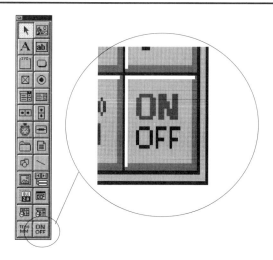

FIGURE 13.5:

The Switch control inside the form

- Implement the menu of the frmWAVInfo form. The menus are shown in Figures 13.6, 13.7 and 13.8. Figures 13.9 and 13.10 show the menu arrangements.

FIGURE 13.6:

The File menu

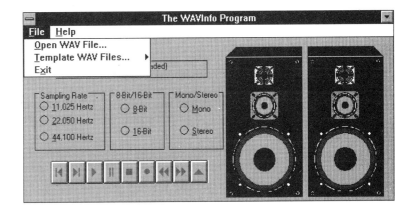

FIGURE 13.7:

The Help menu

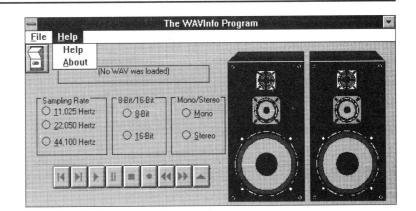

FIGURE 13.8:

The Template WAV Files submenu of
the File menu

EM11H08B.WAV (Mono, 11 KHz, 8-bit)
ES11H08B.WAV (Stereo, 11 KHz, 8-bit)
EM11H16B.WAV (Mono, 11 KHz, 16-bit)
ES11H16B.WAV (Stereo, 11 KHz, 16-bit)
EM22H08B.WAV (Mono, 22 KHz, 8-bit)
ES22H08B.WAV (Stereo, 22 KHz, 8-bit)
EM22H16B.WAV (Mono, 22 KHz, 16-bit)
ES22H16B.WAV (Stereo, 22 KHz, 16-bit)
EM44H08B.WAV (Mono, 44 KHz, 8-bit)
ES44H08B.WAV (Stereo, 44 KHz, 8-bit)
EM44H16B.WAV (Mono, 44 KHz, 16-bit)
ES44H16B.WAV (Stereo, 44 KHz, 16-bit)

FIGURE 13.9:

The menus as they appear in the
Menu Editor

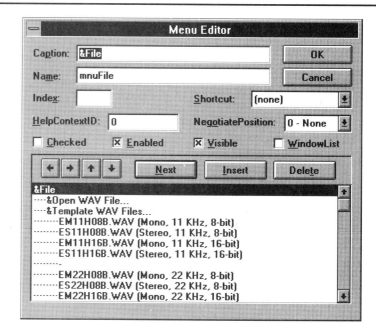

The name of each menu is constructed according to its Caption property. For example, mnuFile corresponds to the File menu, mnuOpenWAVFile corresponds to the Open WAV File menu, and mnuExit corresponds to the Exit menu. Similarly,

FIGURE 13.10:

The menus as they appear in the Menu Editor (continued)

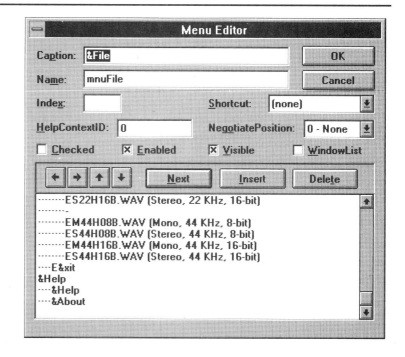

mnuEM11H08B corresponds to the EM11H08B.WAV (Mono, 11KHz, 8-bit) menu item and so on.

The General Declarations Section of the frmWAVInfo Form

- Enter the following code inside the General Declarations section of the frmWAVInfo form:

```
Option Explicit
```

This statement forces you to declare variables. That is, if you use a variable without first declaring it, Visual Basic will prompt you with an error.

The Form_Load( ) Procedure of the frmWAVInfo Form

When you start the WAVInfo program, the frmWAVInfo form is loaded, and the Form_Load( ) procedure is executed.

- Enter the following code inside the Form_Load( ) procedure of the frmWAVInfo form:

```
Private Sub Form_Load( )

    Tegomm1.UpdateInterval = 50

End Sub
```

This statement sets the UpdateInterval property of the Multimedia control to 50, so that every 50 milliseconds the Tegomm1_StatusUpdate( ) procedure is automatically executed. You'll write the code of the Tegomm1_StatusUpdate( ) procedure later in this chapter.

Attaching Code to the Open WAV File Menu Item

You'll now attach code to the Open WAV File menu item. Whenever the user selects this menu item, the mnuOpenWAVFile_Click( ) procedure is executed.

- Enter the following code inside the mnuOpenWAVFile_Click( ) procedure of the frmWAVInfo form:

```
Private Sub mnuOpenWAVFile_Click()

Dim Msg As String

' Selecting a file (with the common dialog box)

' Set an error trap prior to displaying
' the Open dialog box.
On Error GoTo OpenError
```

```
' Set the items of the File Type list box
CommonDialog1.Filter = _
    "All Files (*.*) ¦ *.* ¦Wav Files (*.wav)¦*.wav"

' Set the default File Type
CommonDialog1.FilterIndex = 2

' Display the dialog box as an Open dialog box
CommonDialog1.Action = 1

' No need to trap errors any more,
' so remove the error trap
On Error GoTo 0

''' MsgBox CommonDialog1.FileName

Tegomm1.DeviceType = "WaveAudio"
Tegomm1.FileName = CommonDialog1.FileName
Tegomm1.Command = "Open"

If Tegomm1.Error <> 0 Then
   Msg = "Can't open the "
   Msg = Msg + CommonDialog1.FileName + " file. "
   MsgBox Msg, vbInformation, "Error"
   Exit Sub
Else
   UpdateParameters
End If

' Exit this procedure
Exit Sub

OpenError:
' The user pressed the Cancel key of
' the common dialog box, or an error occurred.

' Exit this procedure
Exit Sub

End Sub
```

The code that you typed sets an error trap:

```
On Error GoTo OpenError
```

This statement causes the program to execute the statements that follow the OpenError label immediately whenever an error occurs (or the user clicks the Cancel button) during the time the Open dialog box is displayed.

The code under the OpenError label terminates the procedure:

```
OpenError:
' The user pressed the Cancel key of
' the common dialog box, or an error occurred.

' Exit this procedure
Exit Sub
```

The code after the error-trapping statement sets the common dialog box as follows:

```
' Set the items of the File Type list box
CommonDialog1.Filter = _
    "All Files (*.*) ¦ *.* ¦Wav Files (*.wav)¦*.wav"

' Set the default File Type
CommonDialog1.FilterIndex = 2
```

These statements set the dialog box so that it will be easier to select WAV files.

Now that the common dialog box is ready, you set the Action property to 1:

```
' Display the dialog box as an Open dialog box
CommonDialog1.Action = 1
```

This statement causes the common dialog box to appear as an Open dialog box.

Once the user selects a file, the program continues with the execution of the statements in this procedure, and there is no need to trap errors any more. So the code that you entered removes the error trapping:

```
' No need to trap errors any more,
' so remove the error trap
On Error GoTo 0
```

The filename that was selected with the common dialog box is stored as the FileName property of the common dialog box. The following statements open a WAV session with the selected WAV file:

```
Tegomm1.DeviceType = "WaveAudio"
Tegomm1.FileName = CommonDialog1.FileName
Tegomm1.Command = "Open"
```

The If…Else statements are executed to determine whether the WAV session was opened successfully:

```
If Tegomm1.Error <> 0 Then
    Msg = "Can't open the "
    Msg = Msg + CommonDialog1.FileName + " file. "
    MsgBox Msg, vbInformation, "Error"
    Exit Sub
Else
    UpdateParameters
End If
```

Note that if the WAV session was opened successfully, the code under the Else is executed. This code executes the UpdateParameters procedure, which sets the option buttons according to the WAV file that was opened. You'll write the code of the UpdateParameters procedure later in this chapter.

Finally, the Exit Sub statement is executed to terminate the procedure:

```
' Exit this procedure
Exit Sub
```

Attaching Code to the Exit Menu Item

You'll now attach code to the Exit menu item.

- Enter the following code inside the mnuExit_Click( ) procedure of the frmWAVInfo form:

```
Private Sub mnuExit_Click()

    Unload Me

End Sub
```

This code unloads the frmWAVInfo form (which causes the program to terminate).

Attaching Code to the Exit Switch

You'll now attach code to the Exit switch of the frmWAVInfo form.

- Enter the following code inside the swExit_Click( ) procedure of the frmWAVInfo form:

```
Private Sub swExit_Click()

' User clicked the Exit switch

Dim Answer

Answer = MsgBox("Are you sure you want to exit?", _
               vbQuestion + vbYesNo, "Exit")

If Answer = vbYes Then
   Unload Me
Else
   swExit.Value = True
End If

End Sub
```

The code first displays a message box:

```
Answer = MsgBox("Are you sure you want to exit?", _
               vbQuestion + vbYesNo, "Exit")
```

The message box asks the user to click the Yes or No button. The response is saved in the Answer variable.

If...Else statements are then executed to examine the user's response:

```
If Answer = vbYes Then
   Unload Me
Else
   swExit.Value = True
End If
```

If the user clicked the Yes button, the code under the If statement is executed, terminating the application.

If the user clicked the No button, the Value property of the Exit switch is set back to True.

Loading the Mono, 11,025 Hz, 8-Bit WAV file

13

You'll now write the code that loads the EM11H08B.WAV file.

- Enter the following code inside the mnuEM11H08B_Click( ) procedure of the frmWAVInfo form:

```
Private Sub mnuEM11H08B_Click()

Dim FileName

    ' Open the EM11H08B.WAV file
    ' Mono, 11,025 Hz, 8-bit
    Tegomm1.DeviceType = "WaveAudio"

    FileName = App.Path
    If Right(FileName, 1) <> "\" Then
        FileName = FileName + "\"
    End If
    FileName = FileName + "EM11H08B.WAV"
    Tegomm1.FileName = FileName

    Tegomm1.Command = "Open"
    If Tegomm1.Error <> O Then
        MsgBox "Can't open " + FileName, vbCritical, "ERROR"
        Exit Sub
    End If

    UpdateParameters

End Sub
```

This code first sets the DeviceType property of the Multimedia control to play WAV files:

```
Tegomm1.DeviceType = "WaveAudio"
```

245

Then it sets FileName property of the Multimedia control to the path and filename of the EM11H08B.WAV file:

```
FileName = App.Path
    If Right(FileName, 1) <> "\" Then
        FileName = FileName + "\"
    End If
    FileName = FileName + "EM11H08B.WAV"
    Tegomm1.FileName = FileName
```

Note that the EM11H08B.WAV file is assumed to reside in the directory from which the application is executed.

The Open command is issued:

```
Tegomm1.Command = "Open"
```

And then an If statement is executed to find out whether the WAV session was opened successfully:

```
If Tegomm1.Error <> 0 Then
    MsgBox "Can't open " + FileName, vbCritical, "ERROR"
    Exit Sub

End If
```

Finally, the UpdateParameters procedure is executed:

```
UpdateParameters
```

The UpdateParameters procedure updates the option buttons according to the loaded WAV file. You'll write the code of this procedure later in this chapter.

The procedures that load the other types of WAV files work in the same way; only the filenames of the loaded WAV files are different.

Loading the Stereo, 11,025 Hz, 8-Bit WAV File

You'll now write the code that loads the ES11H08B.WAV file.

- Enter the following code inside the mnuES11H08B_Click( ) procedure of the frmWAVInfo form:

```
Private Sub mnuES11H08B_Click()

Dim FileName

    ' Open the ES11H08B.WAV file
    ' Stereo, 11,025 Hz, 8-bit
    Tegomm1.DeviceType = "WaveAudio"

    FileName = App.Path
    If Right(FileName, 1) <> "\" Then
        FileName = FileName + "\"
    End If
    FileName = FileName + "ES11H08B.WAV"
    Tegomm1.FileName = FileName

    Tegomm1.Command = "Open"
    If Tegomm1.Error <> 0 Then
        MsgBox "Can't open " + FileName, vbCritical, "ERROR"
        Exit Sub
    End If

    UpdateParameters

End Sub
```

This procedure works in the same way as the mnuEM11H08B_Click( ) procedure described above.

Loading the Mono, 11,025 Hz, 16-Bit WAV file

You'll now write the code that loads the EM11H16B.WAV file.

- Enter the following code inside the mnuEM11H168B_Click( ) procedure of the frmWAVInfo form:

```
Private Sub mnuEM11H16B_Click()

Dim FileName
```

```
' Open the EM11H16B.WAV file
' Mono, 11,025 Hz, 16-bit
Tegomm1.DeviceType = "WaveAudio"

FileName = App.Path
If Right(FileName, 1) <> "\" Then
    FileName = FileName + "\"
End If
FileName = FileName + "EM11H16B.WAV"
Tegomm1.FileName = FileName

Tegomm1.Command = "Open"
If Tegomm1.Error <> 0 Then
    MsgBox "Can't open " + FileName, vbCritical, "ERROR"
    Exit Sub
End If

UpdateParameters
```

```
End Sub
```

This procedure works in the same way as the mnuEM11H08B_Click( ) procedure described above.

Loading the Stereo, 11,025 Hz, 16-Bit WAV file

You'll now write the code that loads the ES11H16B.WAV file.

- Enter the following code inside the mnuES11H168B_Click( ) procedure of the frmWAVInfo form:

```
Private Sub mnuES11H16B_Click()

Dim FileName

    ' Open the ES11H16B.WAV file
    ' Stereo, 11,025 Hz, 16-bit
    Tegomm1.DeviceType = "WaveAudio"

    FileName = App.Path
```

```
If Right(FileName, 1) <> "\" Then
    FileName = FileName + "\"
End If
FileName = FileName + "ES11H16B.WAV"
Tegomm1.FileName = FileName

Tegomm1.Command = "Open"
If Tegomm1.Error <> 0 Then
    MsgBox "Can't open " + FileName, vbCritical, "ERROR"
    Exit Sub
End If

UpdateParameters

End Sub
```

This procedure works in the same way as the mnuEM11H08B_Click( ) procedure described above.

Loading the Mono, 22,050 Hz, 8-Bit WAV File

You'll now write the code that loads the EM22H08B.WAV file.

• Enter the following code inside the mnuEM22H088B_Click( ) procedure of the frmWAVInfo form:

```
Private Sub mnuEM22H08B_Click()

Dim FileName

    ' Open the EM22H08B.WAV file
    ' Mono, 22,050 Hz, 8-bit
    Tegomm1.DeviceType = "WaveAudio"

    FileName = App.Path
    If Right(FileName, 1) <> "\" Then
        FileName = FileName + "\"
    End If
    FileName = FileName + "EM22H08B.WAV"
    Tegomm1.FileName = FileName
```

```
Tegomm1.Command = "Open"
If Tegomm1.Error <> 0 Then
   MsgBox "Can't open " + FileName, vbCritical, "ERROR"
   Exit Sub
End If

UpdateParameters

End Sub
```

This procedure works in the same way as the mnuEM11H08B_Click( ) procedure described above.

Loading the Stereo, 22,050 Hz, 8-Bit WAV File

You'll now write the code that loads the ES22H08B.WAV file.

- Enter the following code inside the mnuES22H088B_Click( ) procedure of the frmWAVInfo form:

```
Private Sub mnuES22H08B_Click()

Dim FileName

   ' Open the ES22H08B.WAV file
   ' Stereo, 22,050 Hz, 8-bit
   Tegomm1.DeviceType = "WaveAudio"

   FileName = App.Path
   If Right(FileName, 1) <> "\" Then
      FileName = FileName + "\"
   End If
   FileName = FileName + "ES22H08B.WAV"
   Tegomm1.FileName = FileName

   Tegomm1.Command = "Open"
   If Tegomm1.Error <> 0 Then
      MsgBox "Can't open " + FileName, vbCritical, "ERROR"
      Exit Sub
   End If
```

```
        UpdateParameters

End Sub
```

This procedure works in the same way as the mnuEM11H08B_Click( ) procedure described above.

Loading the Mono, 22,050 Hz, 16-Bit WAV File

You'll now write the code that loads the EM22H16B.WAV file.

• Enter the following code inside the mnuEM22H168B_Click( ) procedure of the frmWAVInfo form:

```
Private Sub mnuEM22H16B_Click()

Dim FileName

    ' Open the EM22H16B.WAV file
    ' Mono, 22,050 Hz, 16-bit
    Tegomm1.DeviceType = "WaveAudio"

    FileName = App.Path
    If Right(FileName, 1) <> "\" Then
       FileName = FileName + "\"
    End If
    FileName = FileName + "EM22H16B.WAV"
    Tegomm1.FileName = FileName

    Tegomm1.Command = "Open"
    If Tegomm1.Error <> 0 Then
       MsgBox "Can't open " + FileName, vbCritical, "ERROR"
       Exit Sub
    End If

    UpdateParameters

End Sub
```

This procedure works in the same way as the mnuEM11H08B_Click( ) procedure described above.

Loading the Stereo, 22,050 Hz, 16-Bit WAV File

You'll now write the code that loads the ES22H16B.WAV file.

- Enter the following code inside the mnuES22H168B_Click( ) procedure of the frmWAVInfo form:

```
Private Sub mnuES22H16B_Click()

Dim FileName

    ' Open the ES22H16B.WAV file
    ' Stereo, 22,050 Hz, 16-bit
    Tegomm1.DeviceType = "WaveAudio"

    FileName = App.Path
    If Right(FileName, 1) <> "\" Then
        FileName = FileName + "\"
    End If
    FileName = FileName + "ES22H16B.WAV"
    Tegomm1.FileName = FileName

    Tegomm1.Command = "Open"
    If Tegomm1.Error <> O Then
        MsgBox "Can't open " + FileName, vbCritical, "ERROR"
        Exit Sub
    End If

    UpdateParameters

End Sub
```

This procedure works in the same way as the mnuEM11H08B_Click( ) procedure described above.

Loading the Mono, 44,100 Hz, 8-Bit WAV File

You'll now write the code that loads the EM44H08B.WAV file.

- Enter the following code inside the mnuEM244H08B_Click( ) procedure of the frmWAVInfo form:

```
Private Sub mnuEM44H08B_Click()

Dim FileName

    ' Open the EM44H08B.WAV file
    ' Mono, 44,100 Hz, 8-bit
    Tegomm1.DeviceType = "WaveAudio"

    FileName = App.Path
    If Right(FileName, 1) <> "\" Then
        FileName = FileName + "\"
    End If
    FileName = FileName + "EM44H08B.WAV"
    Tegomm1.FileName = FileName

    Tegomm1.Command = "Open"
    If Tegomm1.Error <> 0 Then
        MsgBox "Can't open " + FileName, vbCritical, "ERROR"
        Exit Sub
    End If

    UpdateParameters

End Sub
```

This procedure works in the same way as the mnuEM11H08B_Click( ) procedure described above.

Loading the Stereo, 44,100 Hz, 8-Bit WAV File

You'll now write the code that loads the ES44H08B.WAV file.

- Enter the following code inside the mnuES244H08B_Click( ) procedure of the frmWAVInfo form:

```
Private Sub mnuES44H08B_Click()

Dim FileName
```

```
' Open the ES44H08B.WAV file
' Stereo, 44,100 Hz, 8-bit
Tegomm1.DeviceType = "WaveAudio"

FileName = App.Path
If Right(FileName, 1) <> "\" Then
    FileName = FileName + "\"
End If
FileName = FileName + "ES44H08B.WAV"
Tegomm1.FileName = FileName

Tegomm1.Command = "Open"
If Tegomm1.Error <> 0 Then
    MsgBox "Can't open " + FileName, vbCritical, "ERROR"
    Exit Sub
End If

UpdateParameters
```

```
End Sub
```

This procedure works in the same way as the mnuEM11H08B_Click( ) procedure described above.

Loading the Mono, 44,100 Hz, 16-Bit WAV File

You'll now write the code that loads the EM44H16B.WAV file.

- Enter the following code inside the mnuEM44H16B_Click( ) procedure of the frmWAVInfo form:

```
Private Sub mnuEM44H16B_Click()

Dim FileName

    ' Open the EM44H16B.WAV file
    ' Mono, 44,100 Hz, 16-bit
    Tegomm1.DeviceType = "WaveAudio"

    FileName = App.Path
```

```
    If Right(FileName, 1) <> "\" Then
        FileName = FileName + "\"
    End If
    FileName = FileName + "EM44H16B.WAV"
    Tegomm1.FileName = FileName

    Tegomm1.Command = "Open"
    If Tegomm1.Error <> 0 Then
        MsgBox "Can't open " + FileName, vbCritical, "ERROR"
        Exit Sub
    End If

    UpdateParameters

End Sub
```

13

This procedure works in the same way as the mnuEM11H08B_Click( ) procedure described above.

Loading the Stereo, 44,100 Hz, 16-Bit WAV File

You'll now write the code that loads the ED44H16B.WAV file.

- Enter the following code inside the mnuDM44H16B_Click( ) procedure of the frmWAVInfo form:

```
Private Sub mnuES44H16B_Click()

Dim FileName

    ' Open the ES44H16B.WAV file
    ' Stereo, 44,100 Hz, 16-bit
    Tegomm1.DeviceType = "WaveAudio"

    FileName = App.Path
    If Right(FileName, 1) <> "\" Then
        FileName = FileName + "\"
    End If
    FileName = FileName + "ES44H16B.WAV"
    Tegomm1.FileName = FileName
```

```
Tegomm1.Command = "Open"
If Tegomm1.Error <> 0 Then
    MsgBox "Can't open " + FileName, vbCritical, "ERROR"
    Exit Sub
End If

UpdateParameters
```

End Sub

This procedure works in the same way as the mnuEM11H08B_Click( ) procedure described above.

Attaching Code to the Done Event of the Multimedia Control

You'll now attach code to the Done event of the Multimedia control. This event occurs whenever the control has completed executing a command.

- Enter the following code inside the Tegomm1_Done( ) procedure of the frmWAVInfo form:

Private Sub Tegomm1_Done( )

```
If Tegomm1.Position = Tegomm1.Length Then

    Tegomm1.Command = "Prev"

End If
```

End Sub

The code that you typed uses an If statement to determine whether the Done event occurred because the Multimedia control has played the entire WAV file:

```
If Tegomm1.Position = Tegomm1.Length Then

    Tegomm1.Command = "Prev"

End If
```

If the WAV file was played in its entirety, the Prev command is issued. This command rewinds the WAV file.

Attaching Code to the StatusUpdate Event of the Multimedia Control

13

You'll now attach code to the StatusUpdate event of the Multimedia control.

- Enter the following code inside the Tegomm1_StatusUpdate( ) procedure of the frmWAVInfor form:

```
Private Sub Tegomm1_StatusUpdate( )

Static ToggleIt

    If Tegomm1.Mode = 526 Then
        If ToggleIt = 0 Then
            ToggleIt = 1
            imgSpeakers.Picture = imgSpk01.Picture
        Else
            ToggleIt = 0
            imgSpeakers.Picture = imgSpk02.Picture
        End If
    End If

End Sub
```

This code declares a static variable:

```
Static ToggleIt
```

Thus, the ToggleIt static variable retains its value even after the Tegomm1_StatusUpdate( ) procedure is terminated.

An If statement is then executed to examine the value of the Mode property of the Multimedia control:

```
If Tegomm1.Mode = 526 Then
```

```
.............................
... Playback is in progress ....
.............................
```

```
End If
```

When the Mode property is equal to 526, it means that playback is in progress.

Summary: The Multimedia Control's StatusUpdate Event and Mode Property

The StatusUpdate event is executed every 50 milliseconds because you set the UpdateInterval property of the Multimedia control to 50.

The Mode property of the Multimedia control is used for determining the status of the WAV session. When the Mode property is equal to 526, it means that playback is in progress.

A series of inner If...Else statements are executed:

```
If Tegomm1.Mode = 526 Then

    If ToggleIt = 0 Then
        ToggleIt = 1
        imgSpeakers.Picture = imgSpk01.Picture
    Else
        ToggleIt = 0
        imgSpeakers.Picture = imgSpk02.Picture
    End If

End If
```

The inner If...Else statements toggle the value of the ToggleIt variable. If ToggleIt is equal to 0, its value is changed to 1. And if ToggleIt is equal to 1, its value is changed to 0. Because ToggleIt is a static variable, its value is maintained even after the Tegomm1_StatusUpdate( ) procedure is terminated. So when Tegomm1_StatusUpdate( ) is executed again, ToggleIt has the same value that it had during the last execution of the procedure.

In designing the program, you made the imgSpk01 and imgSpk02 image controls invisible. During playback, the Picture property of the imgSpeakers is assigned with the Picture property of the imgSpk01 and imgSpk02 image controls. That is, during the playback, the imgSpeakers control holds the following sequence of BMP pictures:

SPK01.BMP

SPK02.BMP

SPK01.BMP

SPK02.BMP

SPK01.BMP

SPK02.BMP

… and so on.

Take a look at the SPK01.BMP and SPK02.BMP pictures (Figures 13.11 and 13.12). At first glance, these two pictures appear to be identical. However, the Spk02.BMP picture was generated from the Spk01.BMP picture by first moving the speaker cones slightly and then saving the picture as Spk02.BMP. So during runtime, it looks as if the speaker cones are vibrating.

NOTE The speaker cones in the image control vibrate during the playback because the Picture property of the imgSpeakers image control is changed. Why didn't we use WinG technology for that purpose? Because the number of monitor operations this animation requires is so small that the user will not notice any flickering or performance problems.

FIGURE 13.11:

The Spk01.BMP picture.

FIGURE 13.12:

The Spk02.BMP picture.

The UpdateParameters Procedure

You'll now create the UpdateParameters procedure.

- Select Procedure from the Insert menu and name the new procedure UpdateParameters.

13

Visual Basic responds by inserting the UpdateParameters procedure inside the general section of the frmWAVInfo form.

Recall that you executed the UpdateParameters procedure from within the procedures that load the WAV files. For example, you executed the UpdateParameters procedure from within the mnuOpenWAVFile_Click( ) procedure.

- Enter the following code inside the UpdateParameters procedure:

```
Public Sub UpdateParameters()

        opt11KHz.Value = False
        opt22KHz.Value = False
        opt44KHz.Value = False
        If Tegomm1.SamplingRate = 11025 Then
            opt11KHz.Value = True
        End If
        If Tegomm1.SamplingRate = 22050 Then
            opt22KHz.Value = True
        End If
        If Tegomm1.SamplingRate = 44100 Then
            opt44KHz.Value = True
        End If

        optMono.Value = False
        optStereo.Value = False
        If Tegomm1.Channels = 1 Then
            optMono.Value = True
        End If
        If Tegomm1.Channels = 2 Then
            optStereo.Value = True
        End If

        opt8Bit.Value = False
        opt16Bit.Value = False
```

```
If Tegomm1.BitsPerSample = 8 Then
    opt8Bit.Value = True
End If
If Tegomm1.BitsPerSample = 16 Then
    opt16Bit.Value = True
End If

lblFileName.Caption = Tegomm1.FileName
```

```
End Sub
```

This code sets the Value properties of the 11,025 Hertz, 22,050 Hertz, and 44,100 Hertz option buttons to False:

```
opt11KHz.Value = False
opt22KHz.Value = False
opt44KHz.Value = False
```

Then an If statement is executed to determine whether the 11,025 Hertz option button should be shown selected:

```
If Tegomm1.SamplingRate = 11025 Then
opt11KHz.Value = True
End If
```

The SamplingRate property of the Multimedia control is read-only. That is, you can read its value, but you cannot set its value. The SamplingRate property indicates the sampling rate used to record the WAV file. The Multimedia control makes this determination by examining the header file of the WAV file that was opened during the execution of the Open command.

Summary: The SamplingRate Property of the Multimedia Control

The SamplingRate property of the Multimedia control indicates which sampling rate was used to record the WAV file. SamplingRate is a read-only property. You can read the value of this property but you cannot set its value.

In a similar manner an If statement is used to determine whether the WAV file was recorded with a sampling rate of 22,050 Hz:

```
If Tegomm1.SamplingRate = 22050 Then

    opt22KHz.Value = True

End If
```

13

And another If statement is executed to determine whether the WAV file was recorded with a sampling rate of 44,100 Hz:

```
If Tegomm1.SamplingRate = 44100 Then

    opt44KHz.Value = True

End If
```

The next statements set the Value property of the Mono and Stereo option buttons to False:

```
optMono.Value = False
optStereo.Value = False
```

and then two If statements determine the value of the Channels property:

```
If Tegomm1.Channels = 1 Then
    optMono.Value = True
End If
If Tegomm1.Channels = 2 Then
    optStereo.Value = True
End If
```

The Channels property indicates the number of channels used for recording the WAV file. When this property is equal to 1, it means that the WAV file was recorded in mono, and when the property is equal to 2, it means that the WAV file was recorded in stereo.

Summary: The Channels Property of the Multimedia Control

The Channels property of the Multimedia control is a read-only property that determines whether the WAV file was recorded in mono or stereo. When the Channels property is equal to 1, it means that the WAV file was recorded in mono. When the Channels property is equal to 2, it means that the WAV file was recorded in stereo.

In a similar manner, the Value properties of the 8-Bit and 16-Bit option buttons are set to False:

```
opt8Bit.Value = False
opt16Bit.Value = False
```

And then two If statements are executed to determine whether the WAV file was recorded as an 8-Bit or as a 16-Bit recording:

```
If Tegomm1.BitsPerSample = 8 Then
    opt8Bit.Value = True
End If

If Tegomm1.BitsPerSample = 16 Then
    opt16Bit.Value = True
End If
```

Summary: The BitsPerSample Property of the Multimedia Control

The BitsPerSample property of the Multimedia control is a read-only property that indicates whether the WAV file was recorded as an 8-bit or as a 16-bit recording. When BitsPerSample is equal to 8, it means that the WAV file is an 8-bit recording. When BitsPerSample is equal to 16, it means that the WAV file is a 16-bit recording.

The last statement sets the Caption property of the lblFileName label to the name of the WAV file:

```
lblFileName.Caption = Tegomm1.FileName
```

Attaching Code to the Help Menu

When the user clicks the Help item from the Help menu, the mnuHelpMe_Click( ) procedure is executed.

- Enter the following code inside the mnuHelpMe_Click( ) procedure of the frmWAVInfo form:

```
Private Sub mnuHelpMe_Click()

    frmHelp.Show 1

End Sub
```

This code displays the frmHelp form as a modal window. You'll implement the frmHelp form later in this chapter.

Attaching Code to the About Menu Item

You'll now attach code to the About menu item of the Help menu.

- Enter the following code inside the mnuAbout_Click( ) procedure of the frmWAVInfo form:

```
Private Sub mnuAbout_Click()

    frmAbout.Show 1

End Sub
```

This code displays the frmAbout form as a modal window. You'll implement the frmAbout form later in this chapter.

Implementing the frmHelp Form

You'll now implement the frmHelp form.

- Implement the frmHelp form with the Properties settings shown in Table 13.2. When you complete implementing the form, it should look as shown in Figure 13.13. When implementing the frmHelp form, you'll use the Help.BMP file from this book's CD-ROM(in the C:\WinGPrg\ch12 directory).

TABLE 13.2: The Properties of the frmHelp Form

Object: Form
Name: frmHelp

Property	Value
BackColor	Light gray
BorderStyle	3 'Fixed Double
Caption	"Help"
Height	5850
Left	990
MaxButton	0 'False
MinButton	0 'False
Picture	C:\WinGProg\CH12\Help.BMP
Top	630
Width	6255

Object: CommandButton
Name: cmdOK

Property	Value
Caption	"&OK"
Height	495
Left	3000
Top	3840
Width	495

FIGURE 13.13:

The frmHelp form in design mode

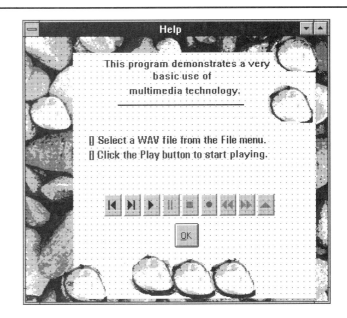

13

Attaching Code to the OK Button of the frmHelp Form

You'll now attach code to the OK button of the frmHelp form.

- Enter the following code inside the cmdOK_Click( ) procedure of the frmHelp form:

```
Private Sub cmdOK_Click()

    Unload Me

End Sub
```

The code that you typed unloads the frmHelp form.

Implementing the frmAbout Form

You'll now implement the frmAbout form.

- Implement the frmAbout form with the Properties settings shown in Table 13.3. When you complete implementing the form, it should look as shown in Figure 13.14. Table 13.3 instructs you to use the About01.BMP file, located in the C:\WinGPrg\Ch12 directory.

TABLE 13.3: The Properties of the frmAbout Form

Object: Form
Name: frmAbout

Property	Value
BorderStyle	1 'Fixed Single
Caption	"About"
Height	5910
Left	1095
MaxButton	0 'False
MinButton	0 'False
Picture	C:\WinGPrg\CH12\About01.BMP
Top	660
Width	5985

Object: CommandButton
Name: cmdOK

Property	Value
Caption	"&OK"
Height	495
Left	4320
Top	3480
Width	735

FIGURE 13.14:

The frmHelp form in design mode

Attaching Code to the OK Button of the About Window

You'll now attach code to the OK button of the frmAbout form.

- Enter the following code inside the cmdOK_Click( ) procedure of the frmAbout form:

```
Private Sub cmdOK_Click()

    Unload Me

End Sub
```

The code that you typed unloads the frmAbout form.

Summary

In this chapter you implemented the WAVInfo application. As you saw, the WAV-Info application utilizes various read-only properties of the TegoSoft Multimedia control to determine how the WAV file was recorded. The SamplingRate property indicates the sampling rate, the Channels property indicates whether the WAV file was recorded as a mono or a stereo WAV file, and the BitsPerSample property indicates whether the WAV file was recorded as an 8-bit or a 16-bit recording.

CHAPTER

FOURTEEN

Recording Wav Files

14

In this chapter you'll execute the Record.EXE program, which lets you record WAV files. As you'll see, this program demonstrates how to let the user record WAV files by selecting the recording settings (sampling rate, mono/stereo, 8-bit/16-bit). In the next chapter you'll implement this program.

Executing the Record.EXE Program

Start the Record.EXE program from the \WinGPrg\EXE directory of this book's CD-ROM. You'll see the window shown in Figure 14.1.

FIGURE 14.1:
The Record.EXE program Window

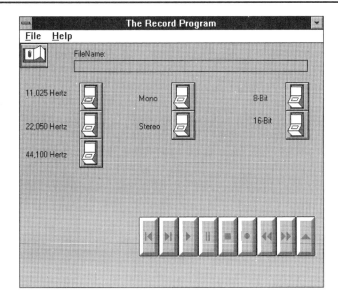

The Record.EXE program has a File menu (Figure 14.2) and a Help menu (Figure 14.3).

Notice in Figure 14.1 that the FileName label is empty, because no WAV file has been loaded yet. For the same reason, none of the switches are turned On.

FIGURE 14.2:

The File menu

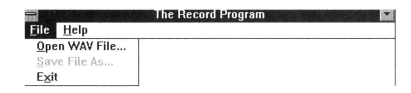

FIGURE 14.3:

The Help menu

The icon of the Record.EXE program is shown in Figure 14.4.

FIGURE 14.4:

The icon of the Record.EXE program

- Select Open WAV File from the File menu, and you'll see the Open dialog box shown in Figure 14.5.

- Select the C:\WinGPrg\WAV\Picki2M6.WAV file and then click the OK button.

FIGURE 14.5:

The Open dialog box

FIGURE 14.5:

The Open dialog box

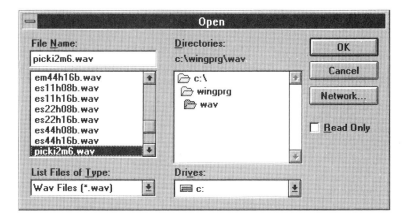

Record.EXE opens a WAV session for the Picki2M6.WAV file, and its window now looks as shown in Figure 14.6. Notice that the switches' LEDs are lit to indicate the recording settings of the WAV file. The sampling rate of this WAV file is 22,050 Hz, and it is a mono 8-bit WAV file.

FIGURE 14.6:

The application's window after opening a WAV session

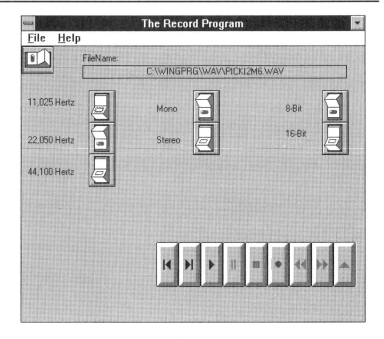

- Try to click any of the recording setting switches. For example, try to set the sampling rate to 11,025 Hz.

Record.EXE refuses to accept the new sampling rate. The only active sampling rate switch (the switch with the red LED turned On) is the 22,050 Hertz switch.

- Click the Play button of the Multimedia control (the third button from the left).

Record.EXE responds by playing the WAV file and displays an animation show (see Figure 14.7).

14

FIGURE 14.7:

During playback, an animation show is displayed.

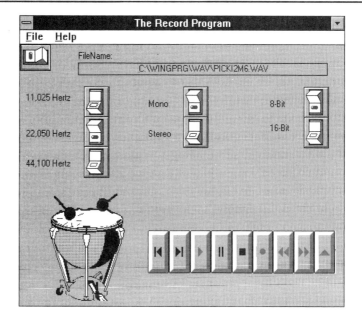

The fourth button from the left of the Multimedia control is the Pause button, and the fifth button from the left is the Stop button. To see the difference between these two buttons, do the following:

- Rewind the WAV file (click the first button from the left).

- Click the Play button.

- While the playback is in progress, click the Pause button.

Record.EXE responds by pausing the playback. As you can see, the animation is paused, and you see the last displayed frame of the animation.

- Click the Pause button again.

Record.EXE resumes the playback. You can see that the fourth button from the left on the Multimedia control toggles between Pause and Resume.

- While playback is in progress, click the Stop button.

Record.EXE stops the playback, and no frame of the animation is displayed.

Recording with the Record.EXE Program

The sixth button from the left on the Multimedia control is the Record button. Here is how you record:

- Click the Rewind button (first button from the left).
- Click the Record button, and then speak into the microphone of your sound card.

Record.EXE responds by recording your voice into the WAV file. During the recording, an animation show is displayed (Figure 14.8).

- Click the Pause button to pause the recording.

Record.EXE responds by pausing the recording. The last frame of the recording animation is displayed.

- Click the same button to resume the recording.
- Click the Stop button to stop the recording.

Record.EXE responds by stopping the recording. No frame of the recording animation is displayed.

- Click the Rewind button (the first button from the left).
- Click the Play button (third button from the left) to play the WAV file.

The recording was inserted into the WAV file starting at the current file position. If you rewound the WAV file before clicking Record, the recording was inserted at the beginning of the file.

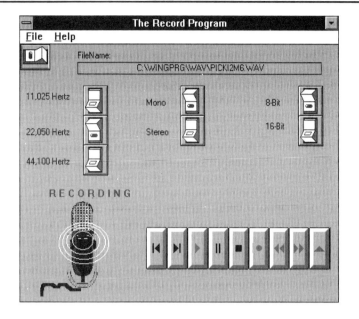

FIGURE 14.8:
During recording, an animation
show is displayed.

Examining the Header Section
of a WAV File

What recording settings will be used for the recording you just made? The same settings that the loaded WAV has. If you load a 11,025 Hz, mono, 8-bit WAV file, then any recording you insert into the file will be made with those settings.

The recording settings are embedded within the WAV file. That is, the WAV file's header includes various bytes that indicate the recording settings.

You can use the DOS DEBUG program to look at the values of these bytes in the template WAV files on the CD-ROM; this information is essential to the program's method of letting the user select recording settings.

- In Windows, double-click the MS-DOS Prompt program icon. At the DOS prompt, enter **DEBUG C:\WinGPrg\WAV\EM11H08B.WAV**.

(This step assumes that you have a path to your DOS directory, and that the DEBUG.EXE program resides there.) DOS executes the DEBUG program and displays the DEBUG prompt (the "-" character)

- At the DEBUG prompt, enter **D**.

DEBUG responds by displaying the first 128 bytes of the C:\WinGPrg\WAV\ EM11H08B.WAV file (see Figure 14.9).

FIGURE 14.9:

The first 128 bytes of the C:\WinGPrg\WAV\EM11H08B.WAV file (displayed with DEBUG).

```
Microsoft(R) MS-DOS(R) Version 6.22
       (C)Copyright Microsoft Corp 1981-1994.

C:\WINDOWS>DEBUG C:\wingPrg\WAV\em11h08b.wav
-D
3483:0100 52 49 46 46 AC 15 00 00-57 41 56 45 66 6D 74 20   RIFF....WAVEfmt
3483:0110 10 00 00 00 01 00 01 00-11 2B 00 00 11 2B 00 00   .........+...+..
3483:0120 01 00 08 00 64 61 74 61-88 15 00 00 80 80 80 80   ....data........
3483:0130 80 80 80 80 80 80 80 80-80 80 80 80 80 80 80 80   ................
3483:0140 80 80 80 80 80 80 80 80-80 80 80 80 80 80 80 80   ................
3483:0150 80 80 80 80 80 80 80 80-80 80 80 80 80 80 80 80   ................
3483:0160 80 80 80 80 80 80 80 80-80 80 80 80 80 80 80 80   ................
3483:0170 80 80 80 80 80 80 80 80-80 80 80 80 80 80 80 80   ................
```

00-57 41 56 4

00-11 2B 00 0

61-88 15 00 0

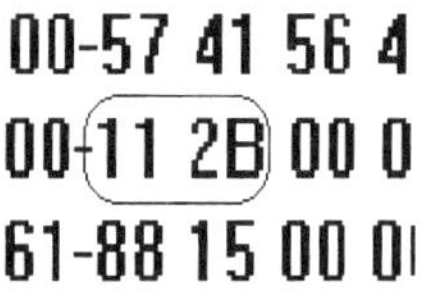

The 25th byte is 11, and the 26th byte is 2B. These are hexadecimal numbers. To see what they mean, you first have to reverse their order. So 11 2B becomes:

2B 11

To convert 2B11 to the decimal numbering system, use the following calculations:

2B11 = 2*16*16*16 + 11*16*16 + 1*16 + 1

or

8192 + 2816 + 16 + 1 = 11025

So as you might have guessed, the 25th and 26th bytes of the C:\WinGPrg\WAV\ EM11H08B.WAV file indicate that the sampling rate of this WAV file is 11,025 Hz. Similarly, the other bytes at the beginning of the WAV file indicate its other recording parameters.

- At the DEBUG prompt, enter Q to quit the DEBUG program.

- At the DOS prompt, enter EXIT to terminate the DOS shell session.

Letting Your User Select the Recording Settings

To let your user select recording settings, your program can display groups of option buttons:

Sampling Rate:

- 11,025 Hertz

- 22,050 Hertz

- 44,100 Hertz

Mono/Stereo:

- Mono

- Stereo

8-bit/16-bit:

- 8-bit

- 16-bit

Once the user has selected the appropriate option buttons, your program will create and save a dummy WAV file with a header section like the one you've just looked at, containing byte values corresponding to the selected recording settings. You can find the values that your program has to use in these headings by using DEBUG program to examine the various template WAV files on the CD-ROM.

279

Summary: The Template WAV Files

The various E???H??B.WAV files in the C:\WinGPrg\WAV directory are template WAV files representing various recording settings. Each character in the filename is significant. For example, let's look at the EM11H08B.WAV file.

- E indicates that the WAV file is empty.

- M indicates that the WAV file was recorded as a mono file. Another possibility for the second character is S for stereo.

- The third, fourth and fifth characters of the template WAV file indicate the sampling rate. For example, 11H indicate that the WAV files was recorded at 11,025 Hz, 22H indicate that the WAV file was recorded at 22,050 Hz, and 44H indicate that the WAV file was recorded at a sampling rate of 44,100 Hz.

- The last three characters of the filename indicate whether the file was recorded as 8-bit (08B), or as a 16-bit (16B).

Note that the E??H??B.WAV files are not completely empty. If you insert a new recording into a completely empty WAV file (one that contains only the header section and no samples), you may have trouble saving the new recorded WAV file into the hard drive. That is, each E??H??B.WAV file must have at least one recorded sample in it. Of course, it can be a sample of silence.

As you'll see when we construct the Record.EXE program in the next chapter, once a dummy WAV file has been saved, your program can open a WAV session with that file and let the user record into it. The recording will be made with the same recording settings as the opened WAV file.

The last step in the process of recording WAV files is to ask the user to name the file.

Recording with the Template WAVFiles

The Record.EXE program lets you record WAV files with a variety of recording settings by using the template WAV files.

- Select Open WAV File from the File menu and you'll see the Open dialog box.

- Select an E??H??B.WAV file from the C:\WinGPrg\WAV directory.

When Record.EXE loads the selected WAV file, notice that it also sets the various switches according to the file's header section.

- Click the Record button, and speak into the microphone. Then click the Stop button to stop the recording.

The WAV file now contains your recording. However, it is saved only in memory; it has not yet been saved into the hard drive.

- Select Save File As from the File menu.

- When Record.EXE displays the Save File As dialog box (Figure 14.10), save the file as TRY.WAV file.

- Experiment with the Record.EXE program and then click the Exit switch (at the upper-left corner of the window) to terminate the program.

FIGURE 14.10:
The Save File As dialog box for saving your recording

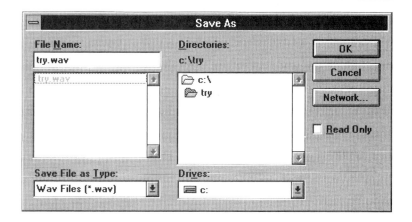

Summary

In this chapter you executed the Record.EXE program, which you'll implement in the next chapter. As you saw, this program loads an existing WAV file and records into it, using the file's recording settings.

When designing programs that let your user select the recording settings, you can select the appropriate template WAV file (according to the user's recording selection), and then let the user record into the loaded WAV file. The recording will be performed with the same recording settings of the loaded WAV file.

Alternatively, during runtime you can generate and save a dummy WAV file that has a header file that corresponds to the user's recording settings. Then load the WAV file and let the user record into the WAV file. This way, your program does not have to use prerecorded template WAV files.

CHAPTER

FIFTEEN

Writing the Record Application

15

In this chapter you'll write the Record program that you executed in the previous chapter. As you saw, this program lets you record WAV files at various settings.

Creating the Record Project

As usual, the first step is to create the project of the Record application.

- Start the Visual Basic program.

- Select New Project from the File menu. Save the new form as Record.FRM and the new project file as Record.MAK, both in the C:\WinGPrg\CH14 directory.

- Implement the frmRecord form with the settings listed in Table 15.1. When you're finished, the form should look as shown in Figure 15.1.

TABLE 15.1: The Properties of the frmRecord Form

Object: Form
Name: frmRecord

Property	Value
BackColor	Light gray
BorderStyle	1 'Fixed Single
Caption	"The Record Program"
Height	5925
Icon	C:\WinGPrg\Icons\Record.ICO
Left	1095
MaxButton	'False
Top	525
Width	6840

TABLE 15.1: The Properties of the frmRecord Form (continued)

Object: CommonDialog
Name: CommonDialog1

Property	Value
CancelError	−1 'True
Left	5760
Top	2640

Object: Image
Name: imgGraph

Property	Value
Height	2250
Left	360
Top	2880
Width	2160

Object: Switch
Name: swExit

Property	Value
Height	525
Left	0
Top	0
Width	630
Value	−1 'True
horizontal	−1 'True

15

TABLE 15.1: The Properties of the frmRecord Form (continued)

Object: Label
Name: lblFileName

Property	Value
Alignment	2 'Center
BackColor	Light gray
BorderStyle	1 'Fixed Single
Caption	"No WAV File"
Height	255
Left	1200
Top	360
Width	5175

Object: Label
Name: Label8

Property	Value
BackColor	Light gray
Caption	"FileName:"
Height	255
Left	1200
Top	120
Width	735

Object: Multimedia Control
Name: Tegomm1

Property	Value
Height	855
Left	2640
Top	3720
Width	3915
Bevelwidth	5

TABLE 15.1: The Properties of the frmRecord Form (continued)

Object: Label
Name: Label7

Property	Value
BackColor	Light gray
Caption	"16-Bit"
Height	255
Left	5160
Top	1560
Width	615

Object: Label
Name: Label6

Property	Value
BackColor	Light gray
Caption	"8-Bit"
Height	255
Left	5160
Top	1080
Width	615

Object: Label
Name: Label5

Property	Value
BackColor	Light gray
Caption	"Stereo"
Height	255
Left	2640
Top	1680
Width	615

15

TABLE 15.1: The Properties of the frmRecord Form (continued)

Object: Label
Name: Label4

Property	Value
BackColor	Light gray
Caption	"Mono"
Height	255
Left	2640
Top	1080
Width	615

Object: Label
Name: Label3

Property	Value
BackColor	Light gray
Caption	"44,100 Hertz"
Height	255
Left	120
Top	2280
Width	1095

Object: Label
Name: Label2

Property	Value
BackColor	Light gray
Caption	"22,050 Hertz"
Height	255
Left	120
Top	1680
Width	1095

TABLE 15.1: The Properties of the frmRecord Form (continued)

Object: Label
Name: Label1

Property	Value
BackColor	Light gray
Caption	"11,025 Hertz"
Height	255
Left	120
Top	960
Width	1095

Object: Switch
Name: sw16Bit

Property	Value
Height	630
Left	5880
Top	1440
Width	525

Object: Switch
Name: sw8Bit

Property	Value
Height	630
Left	5880
Top	840
Width	525

Object: Switch
Name: swStereo

Property	Value
Height	630
Left	3360
Top	1440
Width	525

15

TABLE 15.1: The Properties of the frmRecord Form (continued)

Object: Switch
Name: swMono

Property	Value
Height	630
Left	3360
Top	840
Width	525

Object: Switch
Name: sw44KHz

Property	Value
Height	630
Left	1320
Top	2040
Width	525

Object: Switch
Name: sw22KHz

Property	Value
Height	630
Left	1320
Top	1440
Width	525

Object: Switch
Name: sw11KHz

Property	Value
Height	630
Left	1320
Top	840
Width	525

FIGURE 15.1:

The frmRecord form in design mode

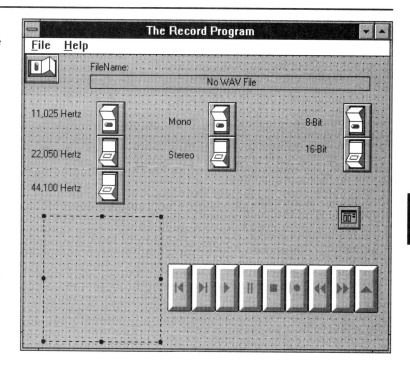

NOTE

In designing the frmRecord form you set the Bevelwidth property of the Multimedia control to 5. This property determines how much "3D effect" the Multimedia control will have. It is included for cosmetic purposes only, to make the control look fancier.

- Implement the menu of the frmRecord with the settings listed in Table 15.2. The menus of the frmRecord form are shown in Figures 15.2 and 15.3.

TABLE 15.2: The frmRecord Form's Menus

Caption	Name
&File	mnuFile
...&Open WAV File...	mnuOpenWAVFile
...&Save File As...	mnuSaveFileAs
...E&xit	mnuExit
&Help	mnuHelp
...&Help	mnuHelpMe
...&About	mnuAbout

FIGURE 15.2:
The File menu of the frmRecord form

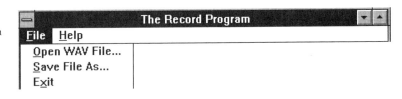

FIGURE 15.3:
The Help menu of the frmRecord form

The General Declarations Section of the frmRecord Form

- Enter the following code in the General Declarations section of the frmRecord form:

```
Option Explicit
```

This statement forces you to declare the variables in the program. If you use a variable without first declaring it, Visual Basic will prompt you with an error.

The Form_Load() Procedure of the frmRecord Form

frmRecord is the form that is first loaded upon executing the Record program. Thus, upon executing the Record program, the Form_Load() procedure is run.

- Enter the following code in the Form_Load() procedure of the frmRecord form:

```
Private Sub Form_Load()

    Tegomm1.UpdateInterval = 150
    mnuSaveFileAs.Enabled = False

End Sub
```

15

This code sets the UpdateInterval property of the Multimedia control to 150 milliseconds:

```
Tegomm1.UpdateInterval = 150
```

So from now on, the Tegomm1_StatusUpdate() procedure will be executed automatically every 150 milliseconds. You'll write the code of the Tegomm1_StatusUpdate() procedure later in this chapter.

You also disabled the Save File As menu item:

```
mnuSaveFileAs.Enabled = False
```

As you'll see later in this chapter, once a WAV file is loaded, you'll enable the Save File As menu item, so that the user can save the loaded WAV file by another name.

Attaching Code to the Exit Menu Item

You'll now attach code to the Exit menu item.

- Enter the following code in the mnuExit_Click() procedure of the frmRecord form:

```
Private Sub mnuExit_Click()

    Unload Me

End Sub
```

This code unloads the frmRecord form, which causes the Record program to terminate.

Attaching Code to the Exit Switch

You'll now attach code to the Exit switch.

- Enter the following code in the swExit_Click( ) procedure of the frmRecord form:

```
Private Sub swExit_Click()

' User clicked the Exit switch

Dim Answer

Answer = MsgBox("Are you sure you want to exit?", _
                vbQuestion + vbYesNo, "Exit")

If Answer = vbYes Then
   Unload Me
Else
   swExit.Value = True
End If

End Sub
```

This code first displays a message box that asks the user to click a Yes or No button:

```
Answer = MsgBox("Are you sure you want to exit?", _
                vbQuestion + vbYesNo, "Exit")
```

An If...Else statement is then executed to examine the user's response to the message box:

```
If Answer = vbYes Then
   Unload Me
Else
   swExit.Value = True
End If
```

If the user clicked the Yes button, the frmRecord form is unloaded (which causes the program to terminate). If the user clicked No, the program sets the Value property of the Exit switch back to True (in the True state, the red LED lamp of the switch is On).

Attaching Code to the Open WAV File Item of the File Menu

You'll now attach code to the Open WAV File item of the File menu.

- Enter the following code in the mnuOpenWAVFile_Click( ) procedure of the frmRecord form:

```
Private Sub mnuOpenWAVFile_Click()

Dim Msg As String

' Selecting a file (with the common dialog box)
' Set an error trap prior to displaying
' the Open dialog box.
On Error GoTo OpenError

' Set the items of the File Type list box
CommonDialog1.Filter = _
    "All Files (*.*) ¦ *.* ¦Wav Files (*.wav)¦*.wav"

' Set the default File Type
CommonDialog1.FilterIndex = 2

' Display the dialog box as an Open dialog box
CommonDialog1.Action = 1

' No need to trap errors any more,
' so remove the error trap
On Error GoTo 0

''' MsgBox CommonDialog1.FileName
```

15

```
Tegomm1.DeviceType = "WaveAudio"
Tegomm1.FileName = CommonDialog1.FileName
Tegomm1.Command = "Open"

If Tegomm1.Error <> 0 Then
   Msg = "Can't open the "
   Msg = Msg + CommonDialog1.FileName + " file. "
   MsgBox Msg, vbInformation, "Error"
   Exit Sub
Else
   mnuSaveFileAs.Enabled = True
   UpdateParameters
End If

' Exit this procedure
Exit Sub

OpenError:
' The user pressed the Cancel key of
' the common dialog box, or an error occurred.

' Exit this procedure
Exit Sub

End Sub
```

This code first sets an error trap:

```
' Set an error trap prior to displaying
' the Open dialog box.
On Error GoTo OpenError
```

So if an error occurs while the Open dialog box is displayed (or if the user clicks the Cancel button), the program immediately jumps to the OpenError label.

The code that follows the OpenError label terminates the procedure:

```
OpenError:
' The user pressed the Cancel key of
' the common dialog box, or an error occurred.

' Exit this procedure
Exit Sub
```

Before displaying the Open dialog box, we prepare the dialog box:

```
' Set the items of the File Type list box
CommonDialog1.Filter = _
    "All Files (*.*) ¦ *.* ¦Wav Files (*.wav)¦*.wav"

' Set the default File Type
CommonDialog1.FilterIndex = 2
```

And finally, the dialog box is displayed as an Open dialog box:

```
' Display the dialog box as an Open dialog box
CommonDialog1.Action = 1
```

If an error occurred when the user selected a file from the Open dialog box, the procedure is terminated. If no error occurred, the next statement is executed:

15

```
' No need to trap errors any more,
' so remove the error trap
On Error GoTo 0
```

This statement terminates the error-trapping mechanism.

The file that was selected by the user is stored in the FileName property of the dialog box.

A WAV session is then opened with the selected WAV file:

```
Tegomm1.DeviceType = "WaveAudio"
Tegomm1.FileName = CommonDialog1.FileName
Tegomm1.Command = "Open"
```

And then an If statement is executed to examine whether the WAV session was opened successfully:

```
If Tegomm1.Error <> 0 Then
    Msg = "Can't open the "
    Msg = Msg + CommonDialog1.FileName + " file. "
    MsgBox Msg, vbInformation, "Error"
    Exit Sub
Else
    mnuSaveFileAs.Enabled = True
    UpdateParameters
End If
```

The statements under Else are executed provided that the WAV session was opened successfully. Because a WAV file was loaded, the user should be able to save the file under another name. The following code enables the Save File As menu:

```
mnuSaveFileAs.Enabled = True
```

Also, under the Else statement, the UpdateParameters procedure is executed:

```
UpdateParameters
```

The UpdateParameters procedure updates the status of the switches. For example, if the opened WAV file was recorded at 11,025 Hz, the Value property of the sw11KHz switch is set to True, and the Value properties of the sw22KHz and sw44KHz switches are set to False. You'll write the code of the UpdateParameters procedure later in this chapter.

Attaching Code to the Save File As Item of the File Menu

You'll now attach code to the Save File As item of the File menu.

- Enter the following code in the mnuSaveFileAs_Click( ) procedure of the frmRecord form:

```
Private Sub mnuSaveFileAs_Click()

Dim Msg As String

Dim OriginalFileName

OriginalFileName = Tegomm1.FileName

' Set an error trap prior to displaying
' the Open dialog box.
On Error GoTo SaveAsError

' Set the items of the File Type list box
CommonDialog1.Filter = _
    "All Files (*.*) ¦ *.* ¦Wav Files (*.wav)¦*.wav"

' Set the default File Type
CommonDialog1.FilterIndex = 2
```

```
' Display the dialog box as a Save As dialog box
CommonDialog1.Action = 2

' No need to trap errors any more,
' so remove the error trap
On Error GoTo 0

''' MsgBox CommonDialog1.FileName

Tegomm1.FileName = CommonDialog1.FileName
Tegomm1.Command = "Save"

If Tegomm1.Error <> 0 Then
   Msg = "Can't save the "
   Msg = Msg + CommonDialog1.FileName + " file. "
   MsgBox Msg, vbInformation, "Error"

   Tegomm1.FileName = OriginalFileName

   Exit Sub
End If

' Exit this procedure
Exit Sub

SaveAsError:
' The user pressed the Cancel key of
' the common dialog box, or an error occurred.

' Exit this procedure
Exit Sub

End Sub
```

This code updates the OriginalFileName variable with the name of the currently open WAV file:

```
OriginalFileName = Tegomm1.FileName
```

Then an error trap is set:

```
' Set an error trap prior to displaying
' the Open dialog box.
On Error GoTo SaveAsError
```

So if an error occurs while the Save As dialog box is displayed (or if the user clicks the Cancel button), the program will immediately jump to the SaveAsError label.

The Save As dialog box is then prepared:

```
' Set the items of the File Type list box
CommonDialog1.Filter = _
    "All Files (*.*) ¦ *.* ¦Wav Files (*.wav)¦*.wav"

' Set the default File Type
CommonDialog1.FilterIndex = 2
```

Finally, the dialog box is displayed as a Save As dialog box:

```
' Display the dialog box as a Save As dialog box
CommonDialog1.Action = 2
```

Once the user closes the Save As dialog box there is no need to trap errors anymore, so the program executes the next statement:

```
' No need to trap errors any more,
' so remove the error trap
On Error GoTo 0
```

The file that was selected by the user is stored in the FileName property of the common dialog box.

The WAV file is then saved as follows:

```
Tegomm1.FileName = CommonDialog1.FileName
Tegomm1.Command = "Save"
```

Summary: Renaming Template WAV Files

Once you have opened a WAV session, you can save the WAV file under another name as follows:

```
Tegomm1.FileName = CommonDialog1.FileName
Tegomm1.Command = "Save"
```

This is the principle used by the Record program to let the user select a template WAV file, record into that file, and then save it.

An If statement is executed to examine whether an error occurred during execution of the Record command:

```
If Tegomm1.Error <> 0 Then
   Msg = "Can't save the "
   Msg = Msg + CommonDialog1.FileName + " file. "
   MsgBox Msg, vbInformation, "Error"

   Tegomm1.FileName = OriginalFileName

   Exit Sub
End If
```

These statements display a message box telling the user that the file cannot be saved, and then the FileName property of the Multimedia control is updated with the original WAV filename.

15

Attaching Code to the Done Event of the Multimedia Control

You'll now attach code to the Done event of the Multimedia control, which occurs when the Multimedia control completes executing a command.

- Enter the following code inside the Tegomm1_Done( ) procedure of the frmRecord form:

```
Private Sub Tegomm1_Done()

   imgGraph.Picture = LoadPicture("")

   If Tegomm1.Position = Tegomm1.Length Then
      Tegomm1.Command = "Prev"
   End If

End Sub
```

While playing back the WAV file, the program also displays an animation clip of drums. When the playback is completed, the Done event occurs and the drum animation is terminated. Another animation show is displayed during recording.

When the recording is completed (that is, when the user clicks the Stop button), the Done event occurs and the recording animation is stopped. The first statement in the Tegomm1_Done( ) procedure clears the picture of the imgGraph image control:

```
imgGraph.Picture = LoadPicture("")
```

So when the playback or recording is completed, the window of the Record program will not display any picture.

An If statement is then executed to find out whether the Done event occurred because the entire WAV file was played:

```
If Tegomm1.Position = Tegomm1.Length Then
    Tegomm1.Command = "Prev"
End If
```

If the Position property of the Multimedia control is equal to the Length property of the Multimedia control, it means that the entire WAV file was played, and the If condition is satisfied. The code under the If statement rewinds the WAV file:

```
Tegomm1.Command = "Prev"
```

Attaching Code to the StatusUpdate Event of the Multimedia Control

You'll now attach code to the StatusUpdate event of the Multimedia control. Inside the Form_Unload( ) procedure you set the UpdateInterval property of the Multimedia control to 150. This means that every 150 milliseconds the Tegomm1_StatusUpdate() procedure is executed.

- Enter the following code in the Tegomm1_StatusUpdate( ) procedure of the frmRecord form:

```
Private Sub Tegomm1_StatusUpdate()

Static FrameNumber
```

```
Dim BMPFileName

UpdateParameters

' Playing
If Tegomm1.Mode = 526 Then

   FrameNumber = FrameNumber + 1
   If FrameNumber = 8 Then
      FrameNumber = 0
   End If

   BMPFileName = App.Path
   If Right(BMPFileName, 1) <> "\" Then
      BMPFileName = BMPFileName + "\"
   End If
   BMPFileName = BMPFileName + _
                 "GR" + _
                 Format(FrameNumber) + _
                 ".BMP"

   imgGraph.Picture = LoadPicture(BMPFileName)

End If

' Recording
If Tegomm1.Mode = 527 Then

   FrameNumber = FrameNumber + 1
   If FrameNumber = 8 Then
      FrameNumber = 0
   End If

   BMPFileName = App.Path
   If Right(BMPFileName, 1) <> "\" Then
      BMPFileName = BMPFileName + "\"
   End If
   BMPFileName = BMPFileName + _
                 "Mic" + _
                 Format(FrameNumber) + _
                 ".BMP"
```

15

```
    imgGraph.Picture = LoadPicture(BMPFileName)

  End If

  End Sub
```

This code first declares a static variable:

```
Static FrameNumber
```

During the execution of the Tegomm_StatusUpdate( ) procedure, the value of Fra-meNumber is changed. However, because FrameNumber is a static variable, its value is maintained. This means that the next time the Tegomm1_StatusUpdate( ) procedure is executed, FrameNumber will have the same value it had at the end of the previous execution of the procedure.

Then the UpdateParameters procedure is executed:

```
UpdateParameters
```

You'll write the code of this procedure later in this chapter. It updates the switches according to the recording settings of the loaded WAV file. So every 150 millisec-onds the switches are updated. If the user changes the setting of the switches, the switches are returned to their original values by the UpdateParameters procedure inside the Tegomm1_StatusUpdate( ) procedure.

Two If statements are then executed to see if either a playback or a recording is in progress:

```
If Tegomm1.Mode = 526 Then
  ...............................
  ... Playback is in progress ...
  ...............................
End If

If Tegomm1.Mode = 527 Then
  ................................
  ... Recording is in progress ...
  ................................
End If
```

TIP

The Mode property of the Multimedia control indicates the control's status. When this property is equal to 526, it means that playback is in progress. When it is equal to 527, it means that recording is in progress.

The code that is executed when playback is in progress causes the playback animation to appear. First the FrameNumber static variable is increased by 1:

```
FrameNumber = FrameNumber + 1
```

Because there are a total of eight frames in the playback animation (GR0.BMP, GR1.BMP, GR2.BMP, ..., GR7.BMP), an If statement is executed to make sure that FrameNumber does not exceed 7:

```
If FrameNumber = 8 Then
    FrameNumber = 0
End If
```

Then the filename of the BMP file is constructed:

```
BMPFileName = App.Path
If Right(BMPFileName, 1) <> "\" Then
    BMPFileName = BMPFileName + "\"
End If
BMPFileName = BMPFileName + _
              "GR" + _
              Format(FrameNumber) + _
              ".BMP"
```

For example, if the Record program is executed from the C:\WinGPrg\CH14 directory and FrameNumber is currently equal to 3, then BMPFileName is assigned to C:\WinGPrg\CH14\GR3.BMP.

Then, the BMP file is loaded:

```
imgGraph.Picture = LoadPicture(BMPFileName)
```

So during the playback, the following sequence of BMP pictures is displayed: GR0.BMP, GR1.BMP, ..., GR7.BMP, GR0.BMP, ..., GR7.BMP, and so on.

> **NOTE**
>
> The animation show is displayed using conventional Visual Basic code, without WinG technology. As you can see in the Record program, the animation is "smooth," and there is no real need to use WinG technology for the animation. So when will you use WinG to perform animation? When the complexity of the animation requires it. For example, in 3D virtual reality animation, each frame has to be calculated based on the previous frame and based on the user's actions. In such a case (as you'll see later in this book), conventional Visual Basic code cannot perform the tasks fast enough, and you'll have to use WinG technology.

The code of the second If statement inside the Tegomm1_StatusUpdate( ) procedure is executed when recording is in progress. This code is very similar to the code under the first If statement. FrameNumber is incremented and an If statement is used to make sure that FrameNumber does not exceed 7:

```
FrameNumber = FrameNumber + 1
If FrameNumber = 8 Then
    FrameNumber = 0
End If
```

Then the name of the BMP file is constructed:

```
BMPFileName = App.Path
    If Right(BMPFileName, 1) <> "\" Then
        BMPFileName = BMPFileName + "\"
    End If
    BMPFileName = BMPFileName + _
                "Mic" + _
                Format(FrameNumber) + _
                ".BMP"
```

Finally, the BMP file is loaded and is assigned to the Picture property of the imgGraph image control:

```
imgGraph.Picture = LoadPicture(BMPFileName)
```

So the following BMP files are displayed during the recording: Mic0.BMP, Mic1.BMP, ..., Mic7.BMP, Mic0.BMP, Mic1.BMP, ..., Mic7.BMP, and so on.

The UpdateParameters()
Procedure

You'll now add the UpdateParameters( ) procedure.

- Select Procedure from the Insert menu, name the new procedure UpdatePara-meters, and then click the OK button of the Insert dialog box.

Visual Basic responds by inserting the UpdateParameters procedure inside the General section of the frmRecord form.

- Enter the following code inside the UpdateParameters procedure of the frmRecord form:

```
Public Sub UpdateParameters()

        sw11KHz.Value = False
        sw22KHz.Value = False
        sw44KHz.Value = False
        If Tegomm1.SamplingRate = 11025 Then
            sw11KHz.Value = True
        End If
        If Tegomm1.SamplingRate = 22050 Then
            sw22KHz.Value = True
        End If
        If Tegomm1.SamplingRate = 44100 Then
            sw44KHz.Value = True
        End If

        swMono.Value = False
        swStereo.Value = False
        If Tegomm1.Channels = 1 Then
            swMono.Value = True
        End If
        If Tegomm1.Channels = 2 Then
            swStereo.Value = True
        End If

        sw8Bit.Value = False
        sw16Bit.Value = False
        If Tegomm1.BitsPerSample = 8 Then
            sw8Bit.Value = True
        End If
```

15

```
If Tegomm1.BitsPerSample = 16 Then
   sw16Bit.Value = True
End If

lblFileName.Caption = Tegomm1.FileName

End Sub
```

This code sets the Value properties of the switches according to the loaded WAV files. For example, to set the Sampling Rate switches, the Value properties of the switches are set to False:

```
sw11KHz.Value = False
sw22KHz.Value = False
sw44KHz.Value = False
```

and then a series of If statements is executed to determine which switch should have its Value property set to True:

```
If Tegomm1.SamplingRate = 11025 Then
   sw11KHz.Value = True
End If

If Tegomm1.SamplingRate = 22050 Then
   sw22KHz.Value = True
End If

If Tegomm1.SamplingRate = 44100 Then
   sw44KHz.Value = True
End If
```

In a similar way, the rest of the code set the mono/stereo switches and the 8/16 bit switches.

Attaching Code to the Help Menu Item

You'll now attach code to the Help item of the Help menu.

- Enter the following code in the mnuHelpMe_Click( ) procedure of the frmRecord form:

```
Private Sub mnuHelpMe_Click()
```

```
        frmHelp.Show 1

    End Sub
```

This code displays the frmHelp form as a modal window. You'll implement the frmHelp form later in this chapter.

Attaching Code to the About Menu Item

You'll now attach code to the About item of the Help menu.

- Enter the following code in the mnuAbout_Click( ) procedure of the frmRecord form:

```
Private Sub mnuAbout_Click()

    frmAbout.Show 1

End Sub
```

This code displays the frmAbout form as a modal window. You'll implement the frmAbout form later in this chapter.

Implementing the frmHelp Form

You'll now implement the frmHelp form.

- Implement the frmHelp form with the settings listed in Table 15.3. When you're finished, the form should look as shown in Figure 15.4.

TABLE 15.3: The Properties of the frmHelp Form

Object: Form
Name: frmHelp

Property	Value
BackColor	Light gray
BorderStyle	3 'Fixed Double
Caption	"Help"
Height	5850
Left	990
MaxButton	0 'False
MinButton	0 'False
Picture	C:\WinGPrg\CH14\Help.BMP
Top	630
Width	6255

Object: CommandButton
Name: cmdOK

Property	Value
Caption	"&OK"
Height	495
Left	3000
Top	3840
Width	495

FIGURE 15.4:
The frmHelp form in design mode

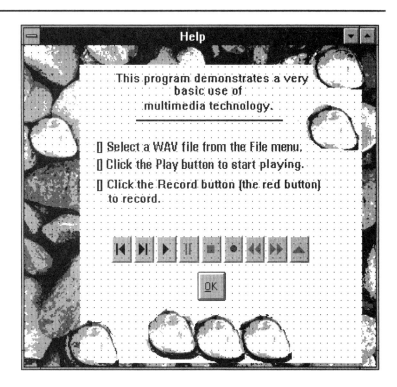

Attaching Code to the OK Button of the Help Window

You'll now attach code to the OK button of the frmHelp form.

- Enter the following code in the cmdOK_Click( ) procedure of the frmHelp form:

```
Private Sub cmdOK_Click()

    Unload Me

End Sub
```

This code unloads the frmHelp form.

Implementing the frmAbout Form

You'll now implement the frmAbout form.

- Implement the frmAbout form with the settings listed in Table 15.4. When you're finished, the form should look as shown in Figure 15.5.

TABLE 15.4: The Properties of the frmAbout Form

Object: Form
Name: frmAbout

Property	Value
BorderStyle	1 'Fixed Single
Caption	"About"
Height	5910
Left	1095
MaxButton	0 'False
MinButton	'False
Picture	C:\WinGPrg\CH14\About.BMP
Top	660
Width	5985

Object: CommandButton
Name: cmdOK

Property	Value
Caption	"&OK"
Height	495
Left	4320
Top	3480
Width	735

FIGURE 15.5:

The frmAbout form in design mode

15

Attaching Code to the OK Button of the About Window

You'll now attach code to the OK button of the frmAbout form.

- Enter the following code in the cmdAbout_Click( ) procedure of the frmAbout form:

```
Private Sub cmdOK_Click()

    Unload Me

End Sub
```

This code unloads the frmAbout form.

Did the User Modify the WAV File?

Typically, programs that let the user save files need to determine whether there is a file to be saved before exiting. For example, suppose the user loads a WAV file, records into it, and then tries to exit the program. Before exiting, the program should ask the user if the modified WAV file should be saved.

You can implement this feature as follows:

- Declare a variable inside the General Declarations section. For example, you can include the following statement:

```
Dim gSaveBeforeExit
```

- Inside the Form_Load( ) procedure of the frmRecord form you can initialize the gSaveBeforeExit variable to False:

```
gSaveBeforeExit = False
```

- In the Form_Unload() procedure of the frmRecord form, use an If statement that examines whether the file has to be saved:

```
If gSaveBeforeExit = True then
    ...........................................
    ... Prompt the user with a message box
    ... that tells the user that the WAV file was
    ... modified, and ask the user if the WAV file
    ... should be saved.
    ...........................................
End If
```

- If the user wants to save the modified WAV file, use the same code that you used inside the mnuSaveFileAs_Click( ) procedure to save the file.

- Once a WAV file has been saved, you have to set the gSaveFileAs flag to False. So inside the mnuSaveFileAs_Click( ) procedure write the following code:

```
gSaveBeforeExit = False
```

That is, if the user has saved the WAV file, set to False the flag that will be examined when the program is terminated.

During the recording, the WAV file is modified. The gSaveBeforeExit variable is the flag that indicates the WAV file has been modified. This means that you have to set this variable to True. So use the following statement inside the second If statement of the Tegomm1_StatusUpdate( ) procedure.

```
gSaveBeforeExit = True
```

Summary

In this chapter you implemented the Record program, which lets the user record a WAV file and select recording settings for it. However, the program does this by a method that you should be able to improve upon in your own programs.

In the Record program's current form, the user begins a recording and chooses settings for it by first selecting Open from the program's File menu. Most users, however, would expect a New option to create a new file. This program uses Open because its underlying method of implementing the selections is to first load a template WAV file that has the required recording settings. The user then records into the loaded WAV file and saves the recording under a new name.

A more user-friendly design would include a New item in the File menu. Once the user selected New, your program would display option buttons for the recording settings and then, based on the user's selections, generate a template WAV file with the appropriate settings. It would then open a WAV session for the WAV file that was generated.

15

CHAPTER

SIXTEEN

Playing MIDI Files

16

In this chapter you'll execute the Pool.EXE program, which plays MIDI files. It demonstrates how to use the Multimedia control for playing MIDI files, and how to change the tempo of a MIDI file. In the next chapter you'll implement the Pool program yourself.

Executing the Pool.EXE Program

Begin by starting the Pool.EXE program, which resides in the \EXE directory of the book's CD. You'll see the window shown in Figure 16.1.

FIGURE 16.1:

The window of the Pool.EXE program

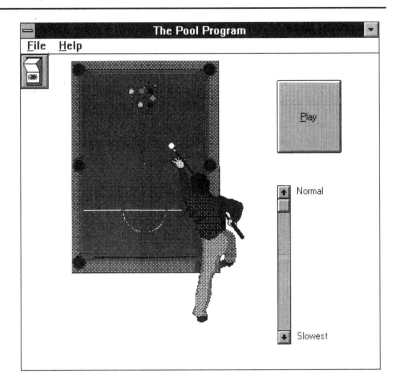

- Click the Play button.

Pool.EXE responds by starting an animation show. During the animation, a MIDI file is played in the background. Also notice that the caption of the Play button has changed to Stop (see Figure 16.2).

FIGURE 16.2:
During playback, the Play button becomes the Stop button.

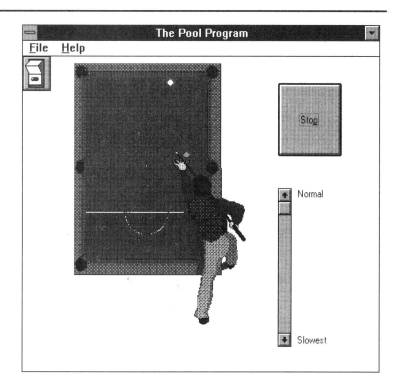

- Click the Stop button.

Pool.EXE responds by stopping the playback. You can now click the Play button again to resume the playback.

The animation show consists of 47 frames. Figure 16.3 shows one frame of the show.

FIGURE 16.3:

The Pool1.BMP picture

The Tempo of a MIDI File

Each MIDI file has its own "natural" tempo, which represents the playback speed of the MIDI file. Unlike WAV files, which contain recording of sound, MIDI files contain instructions for synthesizing music. As such, you can achieve various music effects by changing the tempo of the MIDI files.

- Click the Play button to play the MIDI file.

- While the playback is in progress, change the scroll bar position.

As you can see, the animation show and the playback speed of the MIDI file are changed according to the scroll bar position.

- Experiment with the Pool.EXE program and then click its Exit switch to terminate the program.

Summary: Modifying the Tempo of WAV and Midi Files

A WAV file contains an actual recording (just like an ordinary tape cassette). As such, if you play a WAV file slower or faster than its "natural" playback speed, it will sound like a cassette played on a broken tape deck. Voices and instruments will be pitched either too high or too low.

On the other hand, a MIDI file is a synthesized music file, and as such, can be played with a modified tempo (faster or slower). In fact, when designing games and multimedia programs, very often you'll find that changing the tempo of a MIDI file produces an impressive sound effect. In the Pool.EXE program, a scroll bar is provided for changing the tempo of the MIDI file. The scroll bar also changes the speed of the animation. So, as you slow down the animation, the animation is displayed in "slow motion" and the MIDI file is played slower.

16

Summary

In this chapter you executed the Pool.EXE program, which you'll write in the next chapter. This program demonstrates how to use the Multimedia control for playing MIDI files, and how to change the tempo of a MIDI file.

CHAPTER

SEVENTEEN

Designing the Pool Program

In this chapter you'll design the Pool.EXE program that you executed in the previous chapter. As you saw, the Pool program plays a MIDI file, and it lets the user modify the playback speed.

Creating the Project of the Pool Program

Start by creating the project of the Pool program.

- Start Visual Basic and select New Project from the File menu.

- Save the new form as Pool.FRM and the new project file as Pool.MAK, both in the C:\WinGPrg\CH16 directory.

- Implement the frmPool form with the Properties settings listed in Table 17.1. When you're finished, the form should look as shown in Figure 17.1.

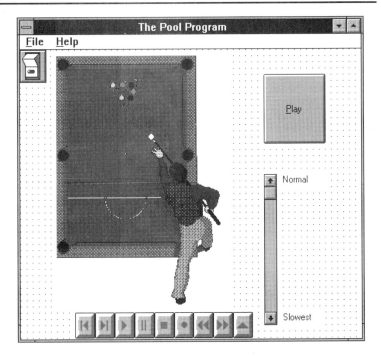

TABLE 17.1 : The Properties of the frmPool Form

Object: Form
Name: frmPool

Property	Value
BorderStyle	1 'Fixed Single
Caption	"The Pool Program"
Height	6435
Icon	C:\WinGPrg\Icons\Pool.ICO
Left	1185
MaxButton	0 'False
Top	150
Width	6840

Object: Vertical scroll bar
Name: vsbSpeed

Property	Value
Height	2895
LargeChange	100
Left	4800
Max	500
Min	50
SmallChange	10
Top	2400
Value	50
Width	255

Object: CommandButton
Name: cmdPlayStop

Property	Value
Caption	"&Play"
Height	1335
Left	4800

17

TABLE 17.1: The Properties of the frmPool Form (continued)

Top	480
Width	1215

Object: Label
Name: Label1

Property	Value
Caption	"Normal"
Height	255
Left	5160
Top	2400
Width	855

Object: Label
Name: Label2

Property	Value
Caption	"Slowest"
Height	255
Left	5160
Top	5040
Width	735

Object: Image
Name: imgPool

Property	Value
Height	4875
Left	960
Picture	C:\WinGPrg\BMP\Pool\Pool0.BMP
Top	120
Width	3450

TABLE 17.1 : The Properties of the frmPool Form (continued)

Object: Multimedia control

Name: Tegomm1

Property	Value
Height	495
Left	1080
Top	5160
Width	3510
Bevelwidth	4

Object: Switch

Name: swExit

Property	Value
Height	630
Left	0
Top	0
Width	525
value	−1 'True

- Implement the menu of the frmPool form according to Table 17.2. The menus of the frmPool form are shown in Figures 17.2 and 17.3.

TABLE 17.2 : The Menus of the frmPool Form

Caption	Name
&File	mnuFile
...E&xit	mnuExit
&Help	mnuHelp
...&About...	mnuAbout

FIGURE 17.2:

The File menu of the frmPool form

FIGURE 17.3:

The Help menu of the frmPool form

The General Declarations Section of the frmPool Form

You'll now write code for the General Declarations section.

- Enter the following code in the General Declarations section of the frmPool form:

```
' Force variable declarations
Option Explicit

' Name of the MIDI file to be played.
Const MIDI_FILENAME = "PICKIN6.Mid"

' Variable, to save the original Tempo
' of the MIDI file.
Dim gNormalTempo
```

This code forces variable declarations:

```
' Force variable declarations
Option Explicit
```

As you'll soon see, the Pool program plays a MIDI file. In the General Declarations section you declared the MIDI file that will be played as follows:

```
' Name of the MIDI file to be played.
Const MIDI_FILENAME = "PICKIN6.Mid"
```

Also, as you'll soon see, the Pool program changes the tempo of the MIDI file. The original tempo of the MIDI file will be stored as the gNormalTempo variable. So in the General Declarations section you declared this variable:

```
' Variable to save the original Tempo
' of the MIDI file.
Dim gNormalTempo
```

The Form_Load( ) Procedure of the frmPool Form

You'll now write the code of the Form_Load() procedure of the frmPool form.

• Enter the following code in the frmPool form:

```
Private Sub Form_Load()

Dim FileName As String

' Make the Multimedia control invisible
Tegomm1.Visible = False

' Set the UpdateInterval property of the
' Multimedia control to the Value property
' of the scroll bar.
Tegomm1.UpdateInterval = vsbSpeed.Value

' Set the Multimedia control so that it
' will play MIDI files.
Tegomm1.DeviceType = "Sequencer"

' Tell the Multimedia control the
' name of the file to be played.
FileName = App.Path
If Right(FileName, 1) <> "\" Then
    FileName = FileName + "\"
End If
FileName = FileName + MIDI_FILENAME
Tegomm1.FileName = FileName

' Issue the Open command
Tegomm1.Command = "Open"
```

```
' Save the original tempo of the MIDI file
gNormalTempo = Tegomm1.Tempo

If Tegomm1.Error <> 0 Then

End If

End Sub
```

This code first makes the Multimedia control invisible:

```
' Make the Multimedia control invisible
Tegomm1.Visible = False
```

The UpdateInterval property of the Multimedia control is then set to the Value property of the Speed vertical scroll bar:

```
' Set the UpdateInterval property of the
' Multimedia control to the Value property
' of the scroll bar.
Tegomm1.UpdateInterval = vsbSpeed.Value
```

The Tegomm1_StatusUpdate()procedure (which you'll write later in this chapter) is executed automatically every X milliseconds, where X is the value of the Update-Interval property. In the statement above you set the UpdateInterval property to the Value property of the scroll bar. So if, for example, the scroll bar is set to 100, the Tegomm1_StatusUpdate() procedure is executed every 100 milliseconds.

The Multimedia control is then set to play MIDI files:

```
' Set the Multimedia control so that it
' will play MIDI files.
Tegomm1.DeviceType = "Sequencer"
```

Summary: Setting the Multimedia Control to Play MIDI Files

To set the TegoSoft Multimedia control so that it will play MIDI files, set its DeviceType property as follows:

```
Tegomm1.DeviceType = "Sequencer"
```

The next statements in the Form_Load() procedure set the name of the MIDI file:

```
' Tell the Multimedia control the
' name of the file to be played.
FileName = App.Path
If Right(FileName, 1) <> "\" Then
    FileName = FileName + "\"
End If
FileName = FileName + MIDI_FILENAME
Tegomm1.FileName = FileName
```

App.Path is the name of the directory from which the Pool application is executed. So as you can see from the preceding statement, it is assumed that the MIDI file resides in the same directory as the application.

Then the Open command is issued to open a MIDI session:

```
' Issue the Open command
Tegomm1.Command = "Open"
```

An If statement is then issued to examine whether the MIDI session was opened successfully:

```
If Tegomm1.Error <> 0 Then
    MsgBox "Can't open the file: " + _
            FileName, vbCritical, "Error"
    End
End If
```

17

The Tempo property of the Multimedia control represents the playback speed of the MIDI file. The next statement saves the original value of the Tempo property:

```
' Save the original tempo of the MIDI file
gNormalTempo = Tegomm1.Tempo
```

Attaching Code to the Exit Item of the File Menu

You'll now attach code to the Exit menu of the File menu.

- Enter the following code in the mnuExit_Click( ) procedure of the frmPool form:

```
Private Sub mnuExit_Click()
```

```
' User clicked the Exit menu item
' Terminate the application
    Unload Me

End Sub
```

This code unloads the frmPool form and causes the program to terminate.

Attaching Code to the Exit Switch of the frmPool Form

You'll now attach code to the Exit switch of the frmPool form.

- Enter the following code in the swExit_Click( ) procedure of the frmPool form:

```
Private Sub swExit_Click()

' User clicked the Exit switch

Dim Answer

' Display a message box that asks
' the user if he/she wants to exit.
Answer = MsgBox("Are you sure you want to exit?", _
                vbQuestion + vbYesNo, "Exit")

' Analyze user's respond to the message box
If Answer = vbYes Then
    ' Terminate the application
    Unload Me
Else
    ' Set the red LED of the switch ON
    ' (During normal operation of the
    ' program the red LED is ON)
    swExit.Value = True
End If

End Sub
```

This code displays a message box:

```
' Display a message box that asks
' the user if he/she wants to exit.
Answer = MsgBox("Are you sure you want to exit?", _
                vbQuestion + vbYesNo, "Exit")
```

The user can click the Yes button of the message box (to terminate the application), or click the No button (to cancel the exit request). The user's response is then analyzed:

```
' Analyze user's respond to the message box
If Answer = vbYes Then
   ' Terminate the application
   Unload Me
Else
   ' Set the red LED of the switch ON
   ' (During normal operation of the
   ' program the red LED is ON)
   swExit.Value = True
End If
```

17

Attaching Code to the Change Event of the Speed Scroll Bar

You'll now attach code to the Change event of the Speed scroll bar.

- Enter the following code inside the vsbSpeed_Change( ) procedure of the frmSpeed form:

```
Private Sub vsbSpeed_Change()

Tegomm1.UpdateInterval = vsbSpeed.Value

Tegomm1.Tempo= _
    (vsbSpeed.Min/vsbSpeed.Value)*gNormalTempo

End Sub
```

The vsbSpeed_Change() procedure is executed whenever the user changes the scroll bar position. The first statement sets the UpdateInterval property of the Multimedia control to the new Value property of the scroll bar:

```
Tegomm1.UpdateInterval = vsbSpeed.Value
```

Next, the Tempo property of the Multimedia control is changed according to the new Value property of the scroll bar:

```
Tegomm1.Tempo= _
    (vsbSpeed.Min/vsbSpeed.Value)*gNormalTempo
```

This statement decreases the Tempo when the Value property of the scroll bar is increased, and vice-versa. When the Value property of the scroll bar is at its minimum, the Tempo property is set to gNormalTempo.

Attaching Code to the Play/Stop Command of the frmPool Form

The cmdPlayStop button serves as both the Play and Stop buttons. You'll now attach code to the cmdPlayStop button.

- Enter the following code inside the cmdPlayStop_Click( ) procedure of the frmPool form:

```
Private Sub cmdPlayStop_Click()

If cmdPlayStop.Caption = "&Play" Then
   cmdPlayStop.Caption = "Sto&p"
   Tegomm1.Command = "Prev"
   Tegomm1.Command = "Play"
Else
   cmdPlayStop.Caption = "&Play"
   Tegomm1.Command = "Stop"
End If

End Sub
```

This code uses an If...Else statement to determine the current Caption of the button. If the Caption is equal to &Play, it means that the user clicked the Play button. Thus, the If condition is satisfied, which changes the Caption to Sto&p. Also, because the user clicked the Play button, the MIDI file is rewound and then played:

```
If cmdPlayStop.Caption = "&Play" Then
    cmdPlayStop.Caption = "Sto&p"
    Tegomm1.Command = "Prev"
    Tegomm1.Command = "Play"
Else
    .....
    .....
    .....
End If
```

Summary: Playing, Rewinding, and Stopping MIDI Files with the TegoSoft Multimedia Control

To play a MIDI file, issue the Play command as follows:

```
Tegomm1.Command = "Play"
```

To rewind the MIDI file, issue the Prev command as follows:

```
Tegomm1.Command = "Prev"
```

To stop the playback, issue the Stop command as follows:

```
cmdPlayStop.Caption = "&Play"
Tegomm1.Command = "Stop"
```

The code under the Else statement is executed if the user clicks the Stop button. This code sets the Caption of the button to &Play, and then the Stop command is issued to stop the playback:

```
cmdPlayStop.Caption = "&Play"
Tegomm1.Command = "Stop"
```

Note that the code that causes the Multimedia control to play MIDI files is very similar to the code that causes the Multimedia control to play WAV files.

17

Summary: Playing, Rewinding, and Stopping MIDI Files with the TegoSoft Multimedia Control (continued)

When playing a WAV file (e.g., C:\Try\MyWAV.WAV), you have to execute the following statements:

```
Tegomm1.FileName = "C:\Try\MyWAV.WAV"
Tegomm1.DeviceType = "WaveAudio"

Tegomme.Command="Open"
Tegomme.Command="Play"
```

To play a MIDI file (e.g., C:\Try\MyMIDI.MID), execute the following statements:

```
Tegomm1.FileName = "C:\Try\MyMIDI.MID"
Tegomm1.DeviceType = "Sequencer"
Tegomme.Command="Open"
Tegomme.Command="Play"
```

As you can see, the only difference between playing WAV files and MIDI files is that the DeviceType property of the Multimedia control has to be set differently. (And of course, the FileName property of the Multimedia control is set to the name of a WAV file when playing WAV files and to the name of a MIDI file when playing MIDI files.)

Attaching Code to the Done Event of the Multimedia Control

You'll now attach code to the Done event of the Multimedia control.

- Enter the following code inside the Tegomm1_Done( ) procedure of the frmPool form:

```
Private Sub Tegomm1_Done()

' Was the entire file played?
If Tegomm1.Position = Tegomm1.Length Then
    ' Rewind the file
```

```
        Tegomm1.Command = "Prev"
        ' Play the file
        Tegomm1.Command = "Play"
    End If

    End Sub
```

This code uses an If statement to examine whether the Done event occurred because the entire file was played, and if so, the file is rewound:

```
Tegomm1.Command = "Prev"
```

Then the file is played all over again:

```
Tegomm1.Command = "Play"
```

Attaching Code to the StatusUpdate Event of the Multimedia Control

17

You'll now attach code to the StatusUpdate event of the Multimedia control. Recall that the UpdateInterval property of the Multimedia control is updated with the Value property of the scroll bar. So for example, if this property is equal to 100, the Tegomm1_StatusUpdate( ) procedure is executed automatically every 100 milliseconds.

- Enter the following code inside the Tegomm1_StatusUpdate( ) procedure of the frmPool form:

```
Private Sub Tegomm1_StatusUpdate()

Static FrameNumber
Dim NextFrame As String

' Playback is in progress?
If Tegomm1.Mode = 526 Then

    ' Next frame to be displayed
    FrameNumber = FrameNumber + 1
    If FrameNumber = 48 Then
        FrameNumber = 0
    End If
    NextFrame = Left(App.Path, 2)
```

```
    NextFrame = _
            NextFrame + _
            "\WinGPrg\BMP\Pool\Pool" + _
            Format(FrameNumber) + _
            ".BMP"

    ' Display the frame
    imgPool.Picture = LoadPicture(NextFrame)

End If

End Sub
```

This code first declares a static variable:

```
Static FrameNumber
```

This means that FrameNumber retains its value even after the Tegomm1_StatusUpdate() procedure is executed. So when the procedure is executed for the first time, FrameNumber is set to 0. The next time Tegomm1_StatusUpdate() is executed, FrameNumber is equal to the value that it had during the last execution of the procedure.

An If statement is then executed to examine whether playback is in progress:

```
If Tegomm1.Mode = 526 Then
    .............................
    ... Playback is in progress ...
    .............................
End If
```

If playback is in progress, the code under the If causes the animation show to be displayed. FrameNumber is increased by 1:

```
FrameNumber = FrameNumber + 1
```

The animation is composed of 47 frames. Thus, an If statement is executed to make sure that FrameNumber does not exceed 47:

```
If FrameNumber = 48 Then
    FrameNumber = 0
End If
```

The name of the BMP file to be displayed is then constructed:

```
NextFrame = Left(App.Path, 2)
NextFrame = _
```

```
NextFrame + _
"\WinGPrg\BMP\Pool\Pool" + _
Format(FrameNumber) + _
".BMP"
```

For example, if FrameNumber currently is equal to 15, then NextFrame is equal to C:\WinGPrg\BMP\Pool\Pool15.BMP (assuming that the Pool program is executed from the C: drive).

Finally, the Picture property of the imgPool image is assigned with the BMP file whose filename is FrameNumber:

```
' Display the frame
imgPool.Picture = LoadPicture(NextFrame)
```

So putting it altogether, if playback is in progress, the following sequence of BMP pictures is displayed:

Pool0.BMP

Pool1.BMP

...

Pool47.BMP

Pool0.BMP

Pool1.BMP

...

Pool47.BMP

...and so on

As you saw by running the program in the previous chapter, the player hits the white ball, which proceeds to hit the rest of the balls. The player is so lucky (or talented), that with a single stroke, all the balls are hit and pushed to the pockets of the pool table.

Attaching Code to the About Item of the Help Menu

You'll now attach code to the About menu item of the frmPool form.

- Enter the following code inside the mnuAbout_Click( ) procedure of the frmPool form:

```
Private Sub mnuAbout_Click()

    frmAbout.Show 1

End Sub
```

This code displays the frmAbout form as a modal window whenever the user selects the About menu item. (You'll implement the frmAbout form in the next section).

Implementing the About Window

You'll now implement the frmAbout form.

- Implement the frmAbout form with the Properties settings listed in Table 17.3. When you're finished, the form should look as shown in Figure 17.4.

TABLE 17.3: The Properties of the frmAbout Form

Object: Form
Name: frmAbout

Property	Value
BorderStyle	1 'Fixed Single
Caption	"About"
Height	5910
Left	1095
MaxButton	'False
MinButton	0 'False
Picture	C:\WinGPrg\CH16\About.BMP

TABLE 17.3: The Properties of the frmAbout Form (continued)

Object: Form	
Name: frmAbout	
Top	660
Width	5985

Object: CommandButton	
Name: cmdOK	
Property	**Value**
Caption	"&OK"
Height	495
Left	4320
Top	3480
Width	735

17

FIGURE 17.4:

The frmAbout form in design mode

Attaching Code to the OK Button of the frmAbout Form

You'll now attach code to the OK button of the frmAbout form.

- Enter the following code in the cmdOK_Click( ) procedure of the frmAbout form:

```
Private Sub cmdOK_Click()

    Unload Me

End Sub
```

This code unloads the frmAbout form. Thus, when the user clicks the OK button of the About form, the About window closes itself.

Summary

In this chapter you implemented the Pool program. As you saw, the Pool program plays a MIDI file by using the Multimedia control. You learned that the code used for playing a WAV file is very similar to that for playing a MIDI file. You also learned that the Tempo property of the Multimedia control (when a MIDI session is opened) serves as the property that holds the playback speed of the MIDI file, and that this property can be modified to play the MIDI file at various playback speeds.

As an exercise, you can enhance the Pool program so that it will display another animation show. The Pool program that is provided on the book's CD also includes a check box next to the scroll bar. When you check this box, you'll see fish swimming to the music.

CHAPTER

EIGHTEEN

Playing Movie Files

18

In this chapter you'll execute the MyMovie.EXE program, which plays movie files on your PC. You'll design the MyMovie program yourself in the next chapter.

Executing the MyMovie.EXE Program

Begin by executing the MyMovie.EXE program, which resides in the \WinGPrg \EXE directory of the book's CD-ROM. You'll see the window shown in Figure 18.1.

The MyMovie program has three menus: File, Display Options, and Help. These menus are shown in Figures 18.2, 18.3, and 18.4.

FIGURE 18.1:

The window of the MyMovie.EXE program

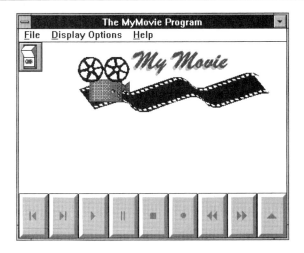

In the \WinGPrg\AVI directory you'll find various movie files. Here is how you play a movie file:

- Select Open Movie (AVI) File from the File menu. You'll see an Open dialog box that lets you select an AVI file.

- Select the \WinGPrg\AVI\Bush.AVI file, and the MyMovie program opens a session for the Bush.AVI movie file.

FIGURE 18.2:

The File menu of the MyMovie.EXE program

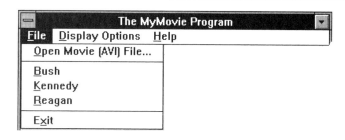

FIGURE 18.3:

The Display Options menu of the MyMovie.EXE program

FIGURE 18.4:

The Help menu of the MyMovie.EXE program

18

- Click the Play button of the Multimedia control (the third button from the left), and you'll see the Bush.AVI movie (Figure 18.5).

As shown in Figure 18.2, the File menu also contains the Bush, Kennedy, and Reagan menu items. Selecting the Bush item from the File menu has the same effect as selecting Open Movie (AVI) File from the File menu and then selecting the Bush.AVI file.

- Select the Kennedy item from the File menu, and MyMovie loads the Kennedy.AVI file.

- Click the Play button of the Multimedia control, and MyMovie plays the Kennedy.AVI movie (see Figure 18.6).

- Select the Reagan item from the File menu, and MyMovie loads the Reagan.AVI file.

FIGURE 18.5:

Playing the Bush.AVI movie in a separate window

FIGURE 18.6:

Playing the Kennedy.AVI movie in a separate window

- Click the Play button of the Multimedia control, and MyMovie plays the Reagan.AVI movie (see Figure 18.7).

As shown in Figure 18.4, the MyMovie program has an About menu item.

- Click the About menu item from the Help menu, and MyMovie displays the About window (see Figure 18.8).

- Click the OK button of the About window to close the About window.

FIGURE 18.7:

Playing the Reagan.AVI movie in a separate window

FIGURE 18.8:

The About window of the MyMovie program

18

Selecting the Window in Which the Movie Will Be Displayed

So far, you've displayed the movies in a separate window. For example, when you played the Bush movie, the movie was played in its own separate window. The My-Movie program also includes the Display Options menu, which lets the user choose a window in which to display the movie.

- Select the Use a Different Window item from the Display Options menu.

MyMovie responds by removing the check mark from this menu item. In other words, this menu item is checked (selected) by default (see Figure 18.3). As you saw, when this menu item checked, the movie is played in a different window.

- Now that the Use a Different Window menu item is not selected, select the Bush item from the File menu.

- Click the Play button of the Multimedia control.

MyMovie responds by playing the Bush movie. As shown in Figure 18.9, the movie is displayed inside the window of the MyMovie program.

FIGURE 18.9:

Playing the Bush movie inside the window of the MyMovie program

- Select the Kennedy item from the File menu and then click the Play button of the Multimedia control.

MyMovie responds by playing the Kennedy movie. As shown in Figure 18.10, the Kennedy movie is displayed inside the window of the MyMovie program.

FIGURE 18.10:

Playing the Kennedy movie inside the window of the MyMovie program

18

- Select the Reagan item from the File menu and then click the Play button of the Multimedia control.

MyMovie responds by playing the Reagan movie. As shown in Figure 18.11, the Reagan movie is displayed inside the window of the MyMovie program.

The icon of the MyMovie window is shown in Figure 18.12. You'll now examine the icon of the separate window that displays the movies. Thus, you need to instruct the MyMovie program to display the movies in a different window:

- Select the Use a Different Window menu item.

- Select Bush from the File menu.

- Click the Play button of the Multimedia control.

FIGURE 18.11:

Playing the Reagan movie inside the window of the MyMovie program

FIGURE 18.12:

The icon of the MyMovie program

- While the Bush movie is playing, minimize the window in which the movie is displayed.

As shown in Figure 18.13, the movie is now played inside the icon.

FIGURE 18.13:

The icon of the separate window that displays the movies. If playback is in progress and the window is minimized, the movie is displayed inside the icon.

Using the Forward, Backward, Rewind, and the End Buttons of the Multimedia Control

Once you load a movie file, you can use the Forward and Backward buttons of the Multimedia control. The Forward button is the second button from the right, and the Backward button is the third button from the right. Here is how you use the Forward and Backward buttons:

- Select Bush from the File menu (but do NOT click the Play button).
- Click the Forward button several items.

As you click the Forward button, the MyMovie program displays the next frame of the movie for each click.

- Click the Backward button several items.

As you click the Backward button, the MyMovie program displays the previous frame of the movie for each click.

The Rewind button is the first button from the left of the Multimedia control. This button lets you display the first frame of the movie. The End button (the second button from the left) of the Multimedia control lets you display the last frame of the movie.

18

- Click the Rewind button.

MyMovie responds by displaying the first frame of the movie.

- Click the End button.

MyMovie responds by displaying the last frame of the movie.

- Experiment with the MyMovie program and then click its Exit switch to terminate the program.

Summary

In this chapter you executed the MyMovie program, which uses the Multimedia control to display movies. As you saw, you can display the movies in the application window, or in a separate window.

You also learned that the MyMovie program lets the user display the first or last frame of the movie, or display the frames one after another by clicking the Forward and Backward buttons.

In the next chapter you'll implement the MyMovie program.

CHAPTER

NINETEEN

Writing the MyMovie Program

19

In this chapter you'll write the MyMovie program that you executed in the previous chapter. As you saw in the previous chapter, the MyMovie program lets the user select a movie file and then plays the movie.

Creating the Project for the MyMovie Program

Start by creating the project of the MyMovie program.

- Start Visual Basic and select New Project from the File menu.

- Save the new form as MyMovie.FRM in the C:\WinGPrg\CH18 directory and the new project file as MyMovie.MAK in the same directory.

- Implement the frmMyMovie form with the Properties settings listed in Table 19.1. When you're finished, the form should look as shown in Figure 19.1.

TABLE 19.1: The Properties of the frmMyMovie Form

Object: Form	
Name: frmMyMovie	
Property	**Value**
Caption	"The MyMovie Program"
Height	4890
Icon	C:\WinGPrg\Icons\MyMovie.ICO
Left	1005
MaxButton	0 'False
Picture	C:\WinGPrg\CH18\MyMovie.BMP
Top	1200
Width	6030

TABLE 19.1: The Properties of the frmMyMovie Form (continued)

Object: CommonDialog
Name: CommonDialog1

Property	Value
CancelError	−1 'True
Left	600
Top	2160

Object: Multimedia Control
Name: Tegomm1

Property	Value
Height	975
Left	0
Top	3240
Width	5940
bevelwidth	5

Object: Switch
Name: swExit

Property	Value
Height	630
Left	0
Top	0
Width	525
value	−1 'True

19

FIGURE 19.1:
The frmMyMovie form in design mode

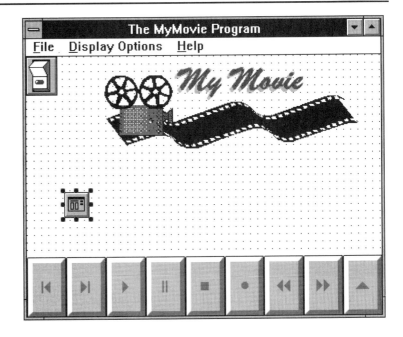

• Implement the menus of the frmMyMovie form according to Table 19.2.

TABLE 19.2: The Menus of the frmMyMovie Form

Caption	Name
&File	mnuFile
...&Open Movie (AVI) File...	mnuOpenMovieFile
..."-"	mnuSpe1
...&Bush	mnuBush
...&Kennedy	mnuKennedy
...&Reagan	mnuReagan
..."-"	mnuSep2
...E&xit	mnuExit
&Display Options	mnuDisplayOptions

TABLE 19.2: The Menus of the frmMyMovie Form (continued)

Caption	Name
...Use a Different Window	mnuDifferentWindow
	Checked = –1 'True
&Help	mnuHelp
...&About..	mnuAbout

The General Declarations Section of the frmMyMovie Form

You'll now enter code in the General Declarations section of the frmMyMovie form.

- Enter the following code in the General Declarations section of the frmMy-Movie form:

```
Option Explicit

Dim gWhichDisplay
```

This code uses the Option Explicit statement to force variable declarations. You also declared the gWhichDisplay global variable. The value of this variable determines which window will be used for displaying the movies.

19

The Form_Load() Procedure of the frmMyMovie Form

You'll now write the code of the Form_Load( ) procedure of the frmMyMovie form.

- Enter the following code in the Form_Load( ) procedure of the frmMyMovie form:

```
Private Sub Form_Load()
```

gWhichDisplay = 1

```
End Sub
```

This code sets the value of the gWhichDisplay variable to 1. As you'll see later in this chapter, setting this variable to 1 instructs the program to show the movies in a separate window, rather than the application window.

Attaching Code to the Exit Menu Item

You'll now attach code to the Exit item of the File menu.

- Enter the following code in the mnuExit_Click( ) procedure of the frmMyMovie form:

```
Private Sub mnuExit_Click()

    Unload Me

End Sub
```

This code unloads the frmMyMovie form (which causes the program to terminate).

Attaching Code to the Exit Switch

You'll now attach code to the Exit switch of the frmMyMovie form.

- Enter the following code inside the swExit_Click( ) procedure of the frmMyMovie form:

```
Private Sub swExit_Click()
```

```
' User clicked the Exit switch

Dim Answer

' Display a message box that asks
' the user if he/she wants to exit.
Answer = MsgBox("Are you sure you want to exit?", _
                vbQuestion + vbYesNo, "Exit")

' Analyze user's respond to the message box
If Answer = vbYes Then
   ' Terminate the application
   Unload Me
Else
   ' Set the red LED of the switch ON
   ' (During normal operation of the
   ' program the red LED is ON)
   swExit.Value = True
End If

End Sub
```

This code is executed whenever the user clicks the Exit switch. The code displays a message box that asks the user whether to continue with the process of terminating the program. If the user clicks the Yes button, the Unload Me statement is executed, which causes the program to terminate.

19

Attaching Code to the Open Movie (AVI) File Item of the File Menu

You'll now attach code to the Open Movie (AVI) File item of the File menu.

- Enter the following code in the mnuOpenMovieFile Click( ) procedure of the frmMyMovie form:

```
Private Sub mnuOpenMovieFile_Click()

Dim Msg As String

' Selecting a file (with the common dialog box)
```

```
' Set an error trap prior to displaying
' the Open dialog box.
On Error GoTo OpenError

' Set the items of the File Type list box
CommonDialog1.Filter = _
    "All Files (*.*) ¦ *.* ¦AVI Files (*.avi)¦*.avi"

' Set the default File Type
CommonDialog1.FilterIndex = 2

' Display the dialog box as an Open dialog box
CommonDialog1.Action = 1

' No need to trap errors any more,
' so remove the error trap
On Error GoTo 0

''' MsgBox CommonDialog1.FileName

Tegomm1.DeviceType = "AVIVideo"
Tegomm1.FileName = CommonDialog1.FileName

If gWhichDisplay = 0 Then
    Tegomm1.hWndDisplay = Me.hWnd
End If

If gWhichDisplay = 1 Then
    Tegomm1.hWndDisplay = 0
End If

Tegomm1.Command = "Open"

If Tegomm1.Error <> 0 Then
    Msg = "Can't open the "
    Msg = Msg + CommonDialog1.FileName + " file. "
    MsgBox Msg, vbInformation, "Error"
    Exit Sub
Else
    Me.Caption = _
        "MyMovie - (" + CommonDialog1.FileName + ")"
End If

' Exit this procedure
```

```
Exit Sub

OpenError:
' The user pressed the Cancel key of
' the common dialog box, or an error occurred.

' Exit this procedure
Exit Sub

End Sub
```

This code first sets an error trap:

```
On Error GoTo OpenError
```

So if an error occurs (or the user clicks the Cancel button) while the Open dialog box is displayed, the program will immediately jump to the OpenError label in this procedure.

Next, the Open dialog box is prepared to open AVI files:

```
' Set the items of the File Type list box
CommonDialog1.Filter = _
    "All Files (*.*) ¦ *.* ¦Avi Files (*.avi)¦*.avi"

' Set the default File Type
CommonDialog1.FilterIndex = 2
```

And then the common dialog box is displayed as an Open dialog box:

```
' Display the dialog box as an Open dialog box
CommonDialog1.Action = 1
```

Because at this point in the procedure the AVI file has been selected, there is no need to trap errors any more:

```
' No need to trap errors any more,
' so remove the error trap
On Error GoTo 0
```

The selected AVI file is now stored as the FileName property of the common dialog box.

The Multimedia control is then prepared for playing AVI files:

```
Tegomm1.DeviceType = "AVIVideo"
Tegomm1.FileName = CommonDialog1.FileName
```

You then execute two If statements:

19

```
If gWhichDisplay = 0 Then
    Tegomm1.hWndDisplay = Me.hWnd
End If
```

Summary: Using the TegoSoft Multimedia Control to Play AVI Files

To set the Multimedia control to play AVI movie files, use the following statement:

```
Tegomm1.DeviceType = "AVIVideo"
```

```
If gWhichDisplay = 1 Then
    Tegomm1.hWndDisplay = 0
End If
```

The hWndDisplay property of the Multimedia control determines which window will be used for displaying the movie files. Me.hWnd is the window handle of the frmMyMovie form. So if gWhichDisplay is equal to 0, the movie will be shown inside the frmMyMovie form.

When gWhichDisplay is equal to 1, the second If statement is satisfied. The code under the second If statement sets the hWndDisplay property of the Multimedia control to 0:

```
Tegomm1.hWndDisplay = 0
```

Finally, the Open command is issued to the Multimedia control:

```
Tegomm1.Command = "Open"
```

Summary: The hWndDisplay Property of the TegoSoft Multimedia Control

The hWndDisplay property of the Multimedia control determines which window will be used for displaying the movies. If you set the hWndDisplay property to 0, the movies will be shown in a separate window.

For example, if you set the hWndDisplay property of the Multimedia control to the hWnd property of a form called frmMyForm, as in the following:

```
Tegomm1.hWndDisplay = frmMyForm.hWnd
```

the movies will be displayed inside the frmMyForm window.

An If statement is then executed to examine whether the AVI file was opened successfully:

```
If Tegomm1.Error <> 0 Then
    Msg = "Can't open the "
    Msg = Msg + CommonDialog1.FileName + " file. "
    MsgBox Msg, vbInformation, "Error"
    Exit Sub
Else
    Me.Caption = _
        "MyMovie - (" + CommonDialog1.FileName + ")"
End If
```

As you can see from the preceding statements, the Caption of the frmMyMovie form is set to the name of the AVI file, provided that the AVI session was opened successfully.

Attaching Code to the Bush Item of the File Menu

You'll now attach code to the Bush item of the File menu.

19

- Enter the following code in the mnuBush_Click( ) procedure of the frmMyMovie form:

```
Private Sub mnuBush_Click()

Dim FileName As String
Dim Msg As String

FileName = Left(App.Path, 2)
FileName = FileName + "\WinGPrg\AVI\Bush.AVI"

Tegomm1.DeviceType = "AVIVideo"
Tegomm1.FileName = FileName

If gWhichDisplay = 0 Then
    Tegomm1.hWndDisplay = Me.hWnd
End If

If gWhichDisplay = 1 Then
    Tegomm1.hWndDisplay = 0
End If

Tegomm1.Command = "Open"

If Tegomm1.Error <> 0 Then
    Msg = "Can't open the "
    Msg = Msg + FileName + " file. "
    MsgBox Msg, vbInformation, "Error"
    Exit Sub
Else
    Me.Caption = "MyMovie - (" + FileName + ")"
End If

End Sub
```

This code is very similar to the code you entered in the mnuOpenMovieFile_Click( ) procedure. However, it does not need the common dialog box to select the file. Instead, the Bush.AVI file is opened as follows:

```
FileName = Left(App.Path, 2)
FileName = FileName + "\WinGPrg\AVI\Bush.AVI"

Tegomm1.DeviceType = "AVIVideo"
Tegomm1.FileName = FileName
```

```
If gWhichDisplay = 0 Then
   Tegomm1.hWndDisplay = Me.hWnd
End If

If gWhichDisplay = 1 Then
   Tegomm1.hWndDisplay = 0
End If

Tegomm1.Command = "Open"
```

Note that in the preceding statements, the BUSH.AVI file is assumed to reside in the X:\WinGPrg\AVI directory (where X represents the letter of the drive from which the program is executed).

An If statement is then executed to determine whether the BUSH.AVI file was opened successfully:

```
If Tegomm1.Error <> 0 Then
   Msg = "Can't open the "
   Msg = Msg + FileName + " file. "
   MsgBox Msg, vbInformation, "Error"
   Exit Sub
Else
   Me.Caption = "MyMovie - (" + FileName + ")"
End If
```

Attaching Code to the Kennedy Item of the File Menu

19

You'll now attach code to the Kennedy item of the File menu.

- Enter the following code inside the mnuKennedy_Click( ) procedure of the frmMyMovie form:

```
Private Sub mnuKennedy_Click()

Dim FileName As String
Dim Msg As String
```

```
FileName = Left(App.Path, 2)
FileName = FileName + "\WinGPrg\AVI\Kennedy.AVI"

Tegomm1.DeviceType = "AVIVideo"
Tegomm1.FileName = FileName

If gWhichDisplay = 0 Then
   Tegomm1.hWndDisplay = Me.hWnd
End If

If gWhichDisplay = 1 Then
   Tegomm1.hWndDisplay = 0
End If

Tegomm1.Command = "Open"

If Tegomm1.Error <> 0 Then
   Msg = "Can't open the "
   Msg = Msg + FileName + " file. "
   MsgBox Msg, vbInformation, "Error"
   Exit Sub
Else
   Me.Caption = "MyMovie - (" + FileName + ")"
End If

End Sub
```

This code is very similar to the code that you attached to the Bush menu item. In fact, the only difference is that now you are loading the Kennedy.AVI file:

```
FileName = Left(App.Path, 2)
FileName = FileName + "\WinGPrg\AVI\Kennedy.AVI"
```

Attaching Code to the Reagan Item of the File Menu

You'll now attach code to the Reagan item of the File menu.

- Enter the following code inside the mnuReagan_Click( ) procedure of the frmMyMovie form:

```
Private Sub mnuReagan_Click()

Dim FileName As String
Dim Msg As String

FileName = Left(App.Path, 2)
FileName = FileName + "\WinGPrg\AVI\Reagan.AVI"

Tegomm1.DeviceType = "AVIVideo"
Tegomm1.FileName = FileName

If gWhichDisplay = 0 Then
    Tegomm1.hWndDisplay = Me.hWnd
End If

If gWhichDisplay = 1 Then
    Tegomm1.hWndDisplay = 0
End If

Tegomm1.Command = "Open"

If Tegomm1.Error <> 0 Then
    Msg = "Can't open the "
    Msg = Msg + FileName + " file. "
    MsgBox Msg, vbInformation, "Error"
    Exit Sub
Else
    Me.Caption = "MyMovie - (" + FileName + ")"
End If

End Sub
```

This code is very similar to the code that you attached to the Bush and Kennedy menu items. In fact, the only difference is that now you are loading the Reagan.AVI file:

```
FileName = Left(App.Path, 2)
FileName = FileName + "\WinGPrg\AVI\Reagan.AVI"
```

Attaching Code to the Use a Different Window Menu Item

You'll now attach code to the Use a Different Window menu item.

- Enter the following code in the mnuDifferentWindow_Click( ) procedure of the frmMyMovie form:

```
Private Sub mnuDifferentWindow_Click()

If mnuDifferentWindow.Checked = True Then
   mnuDifferentWindow.Checked = False
   gWhichDisplay = 0
Else
   mnuDifferentWindow.Checked = True
   gWhichDisplay = 1
End If

End Sub
```

Recall that in the code you've entered so far, when you opened an AVI file you use two If statements to determine the value of gWhichWindow, and based on that value you set the hWndDisplay property of the Multimedia control.

The code in the mnuDifferentWindow_Click( ) procedure toggles the check mark of the Use a Different Window menu item. If currently the menu item has a check mark, the check mark is removed. And if the menu item is unchecked, then the check mark is added:

```
If mnuDifferentWindow.Checked = True Then
   mnuDifferentWindow.Checked = False
   gWhichDisplay = 0
Else
   mnuDifferentWindow.Checked = True
   gWhichDisplay = 1
End If
```

Also notice that the gWhichDisplay variable is set according to the current status of the Use a Different Window menu item.

Attaching Code to the About Item of the Help Menu

You'll now attach code to the About item of the Help menu.

- Enter the following code inside the mnuAbout_Click( ) procedure of the frmMyMovie form:

```
Private Sub mnuAbout_Click()

    frmAbout.Show 1

End Sub
```

This code displays the frmAbout window as a modal window. Next you'll implement the frmAbout form.

Implementing the frmAbout Form

You'll now implement the frmAbout form.

- Implement the frmAbout form with the Properties settings listed in Table 19.3. When you're finished, the form should look as shown in Figure 19.2.

Attaching Code to the OK Button of the frmAbout Form

You'll now attach code to the OK button of the frmAbout form.

19

TABLE 19.3: The Properties of the frmAbout Form

Object: Form
Name: frmAbout

Property	Value
BorderStyle	1 'Fixed Single
Caption	"About"
Height	5910
Left	1095
MaxButton	0 'False
MinButton	0 'False
Picture	C:\WinGPrg\CH18\About.BMP
Top	660
Width	5985

Object: CommandButton
Name: cmdOK

Property	Value
Caption	"&OK"
Height	495
Left	4320
Top	3480
Width	735

- Enter the following code in the cmdOK_Click( ) procedure of the frmAbout form:

```
Private Sub cmdOK_Click()

    Unload Me

End Sub
```

This code unloads the About window.

FIGURE 19.2:

The frmAbout form in design mode

Summary

In this chapter you implemented the MyMovie program. As you saw, using the Multimedia control for playing AVI movie files is very similar to the way you use the Multimedia control for playing WAV files and MIDI files.

You also saw that you can write code to determine which window will be used for displaying the movies, by setting the hWndDisplay property of the Multimedia control.

19

CHAPTER

TWENTY

Playing CD Audio

20

In this chapter you'll execute the MyCD.EXE program, which plays conventional audio CDs through the CD-ROM drive. You'll design the MyCD program in the next chapter.

Executing the MyCD.EXE Program

Most of this book's programs can be run directly from the CD-ROM. Before executing the MyCD.EXE program, however, you need to make sure it resides on your hard drive. Why? Because you'll use the CD-ROM drive for playing an audio CD. Also be sure to insert an audio CD into your CD-ROM drive before you begin.

CD Audio as a Multimedia Capability

The ability to play audio CDs adds an additional medium to a computer's multimedia capability.

When it's playing an audio CD, the CD-ROM drive is on its own! That is, once you issue the Play command, the drive plays the CD without any instructions from the computer. So if you execute a program while playing an audio CD, you will not notice any degradation of the program's performance, because no computer resources are used in playing the CD.

One popular application is simply to listen to relaxing music while doing work on the PC. Another possibility, if you have an audio CD that contains (for example) educational material, is to create a program that will display a sequence of graphics while the CD is playing. But remember that a PC system typically has only one CD-ROM drive. So the program that accompanies the CD audio must reside on your hard drive, not the CD-ROM drive.

Typically, if your audio is not too long, it's best to record your audio as a WAV file and include it on a data CD that contains the program. (This of course makes sense, because producing a CD audio could be an expensive venture).

- Execute the MyCD.EXE program from your hard drive. You'll see the window shown in Figure 20.1.

FIGURE 20.1:
The window of the MyCD.EXE program

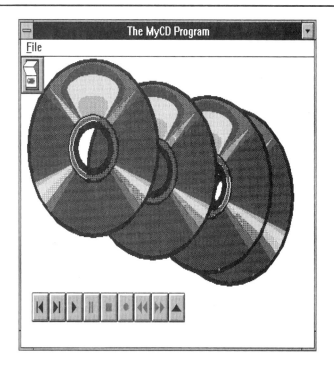

The MyCD program has one menu, the File menu, shown in Figure 20.2.

FIGURE 20.2:
The File menu of the MyCD.EXE program.

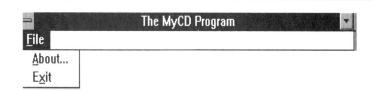

- Select the About item from the File menu. You'll see the About window (see Figure 20.3).

FIGURE 20.3:

The About window of the MyCD
program

- Click the OK button of the About window to close the window.

You'll now use the buttons of the Multimedia control to play the audio CD.

- Click the Play button of the Multimedia control (the third button from the left). MyCD responds by playing the CD.

- Experiment with the MyCD program, and then click its Exit switch to terminate the program.

Playing Audio CDs with the TegoSoft Multimedia Control

The rightmost button of the TegoSoft Multimedia control serves as the Eject button. The user can eject the CD from the CD-ROM drive by clicking this button, if the drive has a mechanical eject feature. The Eject button is automatically dimmed if the CD-ROM drive does not have this feature.

The second button from the left of the Multimedia control lets the user advance to the next track of the CD, and the first button from the left lets the user move backward one track.

Summary

In this chapter you executed the MyCD program, a program that plays CD audio. In the next chapter you'll implement the MyCD program yourself.

20

CHAPTER

TWENTY-ONE

Implementing the MyCD Application

In this chapter you'll implement the MyCD program that you executed in the previous chapter. As you'll soon see, the code that you'll use for playing CD audio with the Multimedia control is very similar to the code that is used when using the Multimedia control for playing WAV files, MIDI files, and movie AVI files.

Creating the Project for the MyCD Program

As usual, begin by creating the project of the MyCD program.

- Start Visual Basic and select New Project from the File menu.

- Save the new form as MyCD.FRM and the new project file as MyCD.MAK, both in the C:\WinGPrg\CH20 directory.

- Implement the frmMyCD form with the Properties settings listed in Table 21.1. When you're finished, the form should look as shown in Figure 21.1.

TABLE 21.1: The Properties of the frmMyCD Form

Object: Form	
Name: frmMyCD	
Property	**Value**
Caption	"The MyCD Program"
Height	5565
Icon	C:\WinGPrg\Icons\MyCD.ICO
Left	1035
MaxButton	0 'False
Picture	C:\WinGPrg\CH20\MyCD.BMP
Top	1170
Width	6840

21

TABLE 21.1: The Properties of the frmMyCD Form (continued)

Object: Multimedia control
Name: Tegomm1

Property	Value
Height	495
Left	240
Top	3960
Width	3510

Object: Switch
Name: swExit

Property	Value
Height	630
Left	0
Top	0
Width	525
Value	−1 'True

FIGURE 21.1:

The frmMyCD form in design mode.

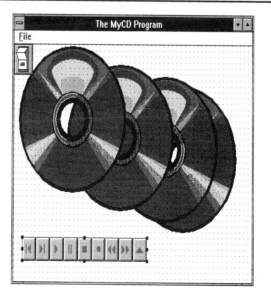

- Implement the menu of the frmMyCD form with the settings listed in Table 21.2.

TABLE 21.2: The Menu of the frmMyCD Form

Caption	Name
&File	mnuFile
...&About...	mnuAbout
...E&xit	mnuExit

Attaching Code to the Form_Load( ) Procedure of the frmMyCD Form

Next we'll attach code to the Load event of the frmMyCD form.

- Enter the following code in the Form_Load( ) procedure of the MyCD form:

```
Private Sub Form_Load( )

Tegomm1.DeviceType = "CDAudio"
Tegomm1.Command = "Open"


End Sub
```

This code first sets the DeviceType property of the Multimedia control to CDAudio:

```
Tegomm1.DeviceType = "CDAudio"
```

This means that the Multimedia control is set to play CD audio.

Then we issue the Open command to the Multimedia control:

```
Tegomm1.Command = "Open"
```

Attaching Code to the Exit Item of the File Menu

Now we need to attach code to the Exit item of the File menu.

- Enter the following code in the mnuExit_Click( ) procedure of the frmMyCD form:

```
Private Sub mnuExit_Click( )

    Unload Me

End Sub
```

This code unloads the frmMyCD form (which causes the MyCD program to terminate).

Attaching Code to the Exit Switch of the frmMyCD Form

Now we attach code to the Switch control of the frmMyCD form.

- Enter the following code in the swExit_Click( ) procedure of the frmMyCD form:

```
Private Sub swExit_Click( )

' User clicked the Exit switch

Dim Answer

' Display a message box that asks
' the user if he/she wants to exit.
Answer = MsgBox("Are you sure you want to exit?", _
                vbQuestion + vbYesNo, "Exit")

' Analyze user's respond to the message box
If Answer = vbYes Then
   ' Terminate the application
   Unload Me
Else
   ' Set the red LED of the switch ON
   ' (During normal operation of the
```

```
            ' program the red LED is ON)
            swExit.Value = True
        End If

    End Sub
```

The code you just added is executed whenever the user clicks the Exit switch. This code displays a message box that asks the user to confirm the exit request.

Attaching Code to the About Menu Item

You'll now attach code to the About item of the File menu.

- Enter the following code in the mnuAbout_Click( ) procedure of the frmMyCD form:

```
Private Sub mnuAbout_Click( )

    frmAbout.Show 1

End Sub
```

This code displays the frmAbout form as a modal window. You'll implement the frmAbout form in the following section.

Implementing the frmAbout Form

Now we'll implement the frmAbout form.

- Implement the frmAbout form with the Properties settings listed in Table 21.3. When you're finished, the form should look as shown in Figure 21.2.

TABLE 21.3: The Properties of the frmAbout Form

Object: Form
Name: frmAbout

Property	Value
BorderStyle	1 'Fixed Single
Caption	"About"
Height	5910
Left	1095
MaxButton	0 'False
MinButton	0 'False
Picture	C:\WinGPrg\CH20\frmAbout.BMP
Top	660
Width	5985

Object: CommandButton
Name: cmdOK

Property	Value
Caption	"&OK"
Height	495
Left	4320
Top	3480
Width	735

Attaching Code to the OK Button of the frmAbout Form

We'll now attach code to the OK button of the frmAbout form.

FIGURE 21.2:

The frmAbout form in design mode

- Enter the following code in the cmdOK_Click( ) procedure of the frmAbout form:

```
Private Sub cmdOK_Click( )

    Unload Me

End Sub
```

This code unloads the frmAbout form.

Using Your Own Buttons with the Multimedia Control

The MyCD program uses the buttons of the Multimedia control and thus sets the control's Visible property to True (its default value). Alternatively, you can set the Visible property of the Multimedia control to False, and place your own buttons instead of using the buttons of the Multimedia control. For example, you can place a button, set its Name property to &Play, and attach the following code to the cmdPlay_Click() procedure:

```
Private cmdPlay_Click()

        Tegomm1.Command = "Play"

End Sub
```

When designing a program that sets the Visible property of the multimedia control to False, you can execute the following statement from the Form_Load() procedure:

```
Tegomm1.Visible = False
```

One advantage of making your own buttons is that they can contain text such as Play, Stop, and so on. This will make your program easier to use for people who aren't familiar with the standard CD player button symbols.

Summary

In this chapter you implemented the MyCD program. As you saw, the code for using the Multimedia control to play CD audio is very similar to the code for playing other media (WAV, MIDI, and movie AVI files).

PART IV

Sprites and Animation

CHAPTER

TWENTY-TWO

22

Sprites—What They Are and How to Create Them

In this chapter you'll learn what sprites are, what they are used for, and how to create them.

What Is a Sprite?

In a nutshell, a *sprite* is a graphic object, used in animation, whose background (the rectangular area surrounding the image) has been made transparent so that it automatically "accepts" whatever background image it's placed against.

To understand this concept, let's consider an example. Assume that you are creating an animation show in which a tank prepares for combat with aliens from outer space. During the animation show, the tank is shown moving around the screen.

Figure 22.1 shows a picture of a beach. The ocean is displayed in the upper part of the picture.

FIGURE 22.1:
The beach
(\WinGPrg\CH23\BkGnd0.BMP)

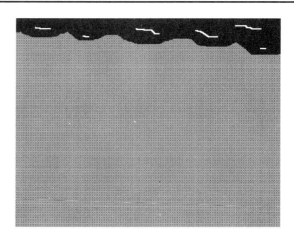

Now suppose you want to display a tank on the beach. In other words, you want to take a picture such as the one shown in Figure 22.2 and place it on the beach as shown in Figure 22.3.

Now suppose that during the animation, the tank advances toward the user, as shown in Figure 22.4. Naturally, as the tank advances, its size increases.

FIGURE 22.2:

A picture of a tank

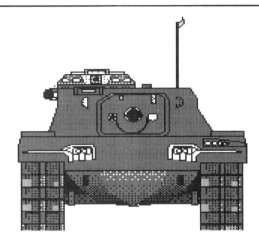

FIGURE 22.3:

Placing the tank on the beach

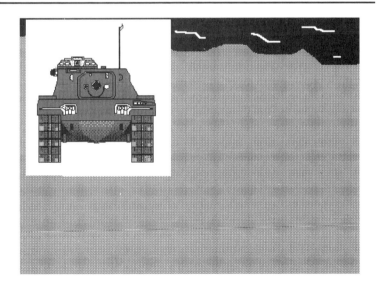

As you can see from Figures 22.3 and Figure 22.4, there is something fundamentally wrong with these images. The background of the tank pictures is white, and this makes the animation looks very bad. The white background is the portion of the drawing program's drawing area that is not occupied by the tank image.

FIGURE 22.4:

The tank advancing toward the user

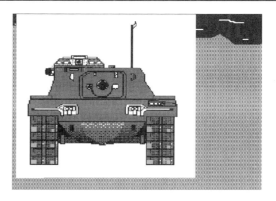

The correct way to display the tank of Figure 22.3 is as shown in Figure 22.5.

FIGURE 22.5:

The tank sprite automatically "accepts" the background.

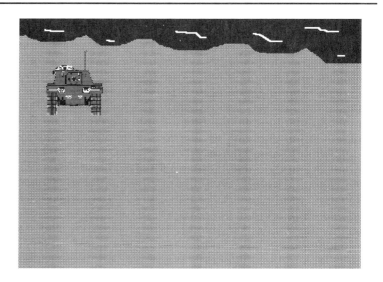

As you can see, the white background of the tank has been changed. The new background is whatever it should be according to the location of the tank. In Figure 22.6, trees were added to the background. As shown in Figure 22.6, the background of the tank consists of a portion of the ocean and the sand of the beach, as well as portions of the trees.

FIGURE 22.6:
The background of the tank consists of ocean, sand, and trees.

Furthermore, as your program moves the tank around the beach, and as the tank size increases, the tank's background is changed according to the background picture on which the tank is displayed.

In this example, the tank is a sprite. To summarize, a sprite is a graphic object used in animation. As you move the sprite, its background automatically accepts the background on which it is displayed.

The tank shown in Figure 22.2 (TankF0.BMP) is included on this book's CD-ROM in the \WinGPrg\CH23 directory. The following steps instruct you to use the Paintbrush program. However, you can use any similar program, such as the Win 95 Paint Program, for performing the steps. Of course, with other programs you'll need to adjust the procedure slightly.

- Use Paintbrush to load and view the tank.

- Select Zoom In from the View menu of Paintbrush. The mouse cursor changes to a rectangle.

- Place the mouse cursor inside an area of the picture which you want to view in a zoomed mode, and then click the mouse. You'll see the area where you clicked enlarged, as shown in Figure 22.7.

- You can click the scroll bars of the window shown in Figure 22.7 to view other portions of the picture in a zoomed mode.

FIGURE 22.7:

Zooming in on an area of the tank

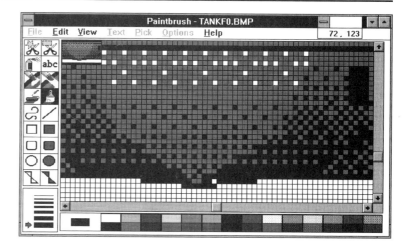

- Select Zoom Out from the View menu of Paintbrush to return to a normal view of the picture.

As shown in Figure 22.7, the tank is painted with a composite color! Moreover, as you'll see in subsequent chapters, the tank picture is stretched. Yes, this will cause the picture's colors to appear distorted.

NOTE Why did we use composite colors? In this case, we *wanted* the distortion they produce. Tanks are heavy machines that generate a lot of heat, and as you view a moving tank, the air around the hot tank creates a similar appearance to the distorted composite colors of the tank seen during the animation. Unless you have a similar application where you want the distortion to occur on purpose, you should use solid colors with sprites.

Creating the Sprites

You'll now learn how to create sprites. In particular, you'll learn how the TankF0 sprite and another file called MTankF0.BMP (which is called the *mask* file) were created. As you'll soon see, creating a sprite amounts to knowing how to use Paintbrush or a similar drawing program. All the BMP sprite files that are required for the programs you'll design in subsequent chapters are included on the book's CD-ROM. This chapter shows you how these files were created, so that you'll be able to create such sprite files in your own future projects.

Your first step in creating a sprite is to draw a BMP picture with Paintbrush (or a similar drawing program).

- Select New from the File menu in Paintbrush. You'll see a new empty drawing area.

- Select Image Attributes from the Options menu. Paintbrush displays the Image Attributes dialog box, where you can set the size of your BMP picture.

- Click the Default button of the Image Attributes dialog box. Paintbrush sets the area of the BMP to its default settings.

- Use your artistic talent to draw the image that you'll use as your sprite.

For example, Figure 22.8 shows the picture of the TankF0 sprite.

FIGURE 22.8:

The picture of the TankF0 sprite in Paintbrush

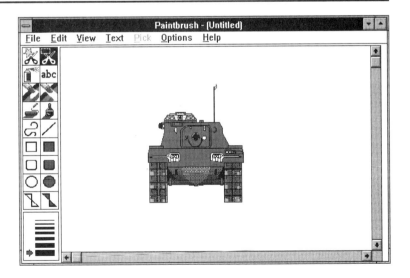

- Save your picture to the hard drive as a 256-color BMPfile. (In the following steps you are going to manipulate this image, so it is a good idea to save your work now in case something goes wrong.)

Note that the size of the BMP picture shown in Figure 22.8 is Paintbrush's default size. Obviously, this is a very large area, and the TankF0 sprite does not have to be that large. Generally, it is easiest to create the image at the default size and then resize it as needed. We'll do that in the next section.

NOTE   When creating sprites, make the sprite area as small as possible. Don't forget that during the execution of your program the sprite is enlarged and moved around. The image is a bitmap; and a bigger image means a bigger file size. The smaller the sprite, the faster your program will be able to manipulate it.

In some of the following steps you'll perform Paintbrush operations using the keyboard, not the mouse. This is simply because the keyboard gives you greater precision.

Also, during the operations, you'll need to make written notes of various locations and distances. Whenever you need to do this, take the following steps:

- Select Cursor Position from the View menu of Paintbrush.

- The small Cursor Position window appears in the upper-right corner of the Paintbrush window, displaying the current position of the mouse cursor. Write these mouse coordinates on a piece of paper.

Resizing the BMP Image

Once you've drawn an image to be used as a sprite, the next step is to make it as small as possible. You'll now do this with the TankF0.BMP picture. Begin by making sure this file is open in Paintbrush.

- Click the Pick tool (on the upper right of the Paintbrush Tools window, it's selected in Figure 22.8). The mouse cursor changes to a cross.

- Place this cursor at the point that will be the lower-right corner of the sprite. (See Figure 22.9.)

- Hold down the left mouse button, and move the mouse upward and to the left. As you move the mouse, a dashed rectangle is drawn according to your

FIGURE 22.9:

Placing the mouse cursor at the point that will be the lower-right corner of the sprite

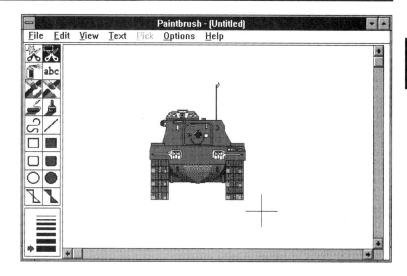

movements. Move the mouse so that the rectangle encloses the entire tank, and then release the mouse button.

- Place the mouse cursor inside the dashed rectangle, hold down the mouse left button, and move the mouse. As you do this, the entire area is dragged. Move the tank to the upper-left corner of the Paintbrush window. The window should now look like Figure 22.10.

You can now set a new size for the BMP area of the sprite:

- With the Pick tool selected, place the mouse cursor at the point that will be the lower-right corner of the sprite area.

- Make sure that a check mark appears to the left of the Cursor Position item of the View menu (so that you'll be able to see the cursor coordinates). Then press and hold down the Insert key on your keyboard, and write the mouse coordinates on a piece of paper. (Do not release the Insert key yet.)

The numbers you just wrote down are the coordinates of the point where the mouse cursor is located at the time you pressed the Insert key.

- Keep the Insert key pressed down. On paper, add 1 to the numbers that you wrote down. For example, if the coordinates are (200, 150), the mouse cursor

Moving the tank to the upper-left corner of the window

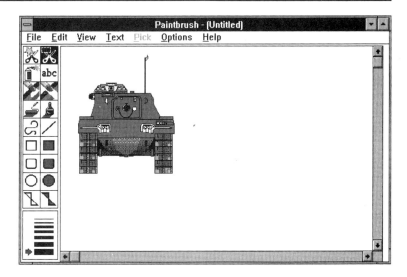

is located at a point 201 pixels from the left edge of the window and 151 pixels from the top. This is because the coordinates are zero-based; the upper-left corner is at coordinate (0,0).

- While the Insert key is pressed down, press the up-arrow on your keyboard.

- With the Insert key still held down, press the left-arrow on your keyboard.

- As you press the up or left arrow keys on your keyboard simultaneously with the Insert key, a dashed rectangle is drawn. Keep pressing these keys until the upper-left corner of the rectangle is at the (0,0) point (the upper-left corner of the Paintbrush window).

- Release the Insert key and select Copy from the Edit menu.

Paintbrush responds by copying the area that was enclosed by the dashed rectangle into the Clipboard.

- Select Image Attributes from the Options menu of Paintbrush. You'll see the Image Attributes dialog box.

- Click the Pels option button to tell Paintbrush to use Pixels as units.

- Inside the Width and Height boxes of the Image Attributes dialog box, type the numbers that you wrote on a piece of paper, and then click the OK button.

- When Paintbrush asks whether to create a new Picture, click the Yes button; and when Paintbrush asks whether to save the previous picture, click No.

22

Paintbrush creates a new drawing area with the size you specified in the Image Attributes dialog box. Figure 22.11 shows this new, resized area.

FIGURE 22.11:

The empty new small area that will be used for the sprite

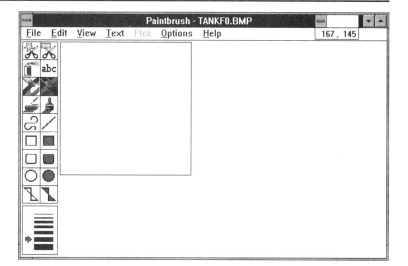

- Select Paste from the Edit menu, and Paintbrush copies the contents of the Clipboard into the new area (see Figure 22.12).

- Save the resized image as a 256-color BMP file. (This is required for using the file with the Sprite control from the accompanying CD-ROM. It's also generally the best format that you can assume your program's users will be able to display.)

When saving the BMP file, do not use more than seven characters for its filename. For example, you can save the file as 1234567.BMP. In the next section you'll learn why you cannot use eight characters for the name of a sprite's BMP file.

FIGURE 22.12:

The picture that will be used as the sprite, with its new size

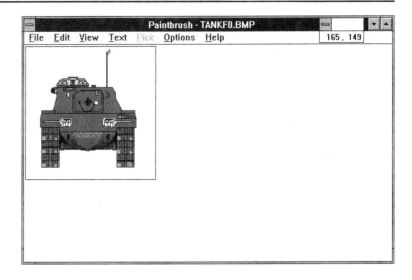

Creating the Mask for the Sprite

In the preceding steps you created half of the sprite. Why only half? When using sprites, you need two BMP files—one for the image, and another for its *mask*. You'll now create this second BMP file. As you'll see, the second BMP file is generated from the first BMP file.

- Using the Save As option, save the BMP file as another 256-color BMP file, but prefix its filename with the character M. For example, if you saved the BMP file as 1234567.BMP, save the new copy of the file as M1234567.BMP.

In the case of the tank sprite, the first BMP file was saved as TankF0.BMP, and the second file as MTankF0.BMP. So far, the TankF0.BMP file is identical to the MTankF0.BMP file. You'll now make several changes to the MTankF0.BMP file.

- Click the red color in the color palette, and then click the Fill Area tool (the left tool on the fourth row of the Tools window).

- Click anywhere outside the tank.

Paintbrush responds by filling the background area with red. (See Figure 22.13.)

FIGURE 22.13:

Filling the background area of the sprite with red

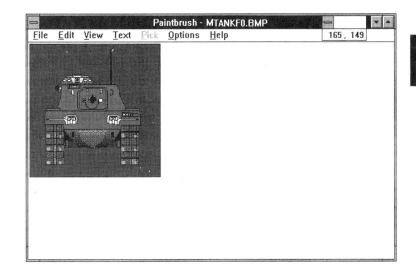

As you can see, the red paint does not leak into the tank, because the entire tank is enclosed by a color other than red. In other words, there are no openings from which the red paint can leak into the tank. If you are using a drawing that has an opening, the red paint will leak into the figure.

To overcome the leaking problem, select Undo from the Edit menu (to remove the red paint that was filled), close the opening in the picture, and then fill the background again.

- Make sure that the background color of Paintbrush is set to white. That is, right-click the mouse on the white box in the Paintbrush color palette.

- Click the black color of the Paintbrush palette to set the foreground color to black.

- Click the Erase Color tool (the left tool on the third row) in the Paintbrush Tools window.

- Now drag the mouse inside the MTankF0.BMP picture. Because you set the background color to white and the foreground color to black, as you drag the mouse, the black color is erased and replaced with white.

The preceding steps illustrate how you replace the black color of the picture with white. Figure 22.14 shows the tank after replacing the black with white.

FIGURE 22.14:

The tank after replacing the black color with white

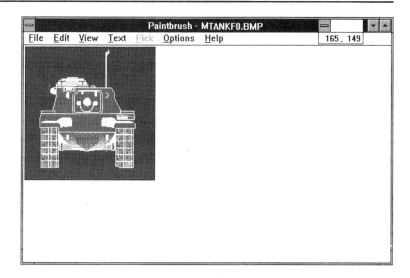

The picture of the tank also contains the colors light gray, gray, and yellow. Figure 22.15 shows the tank after removing all of these colors. Only the red background color remains.

There is one more thing to do—replace the red background with black:

FIGURE 22.15:

The tank after removing all the colors (except the red background)

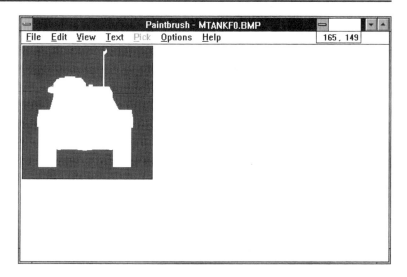

- Click the black color in the Paintbrush palette to set black as the foreground color.

- Click the Fill Color tool of Paintbrush, and then click inside the background area of the tank picture.

The tank mask BMP picture is now ready, so you can save the picture as MTankF0.BMP, a 256-color bitmap. Figure 22.16 shows the complete MTankF0.BMP mask file.

FIGURE 22.16:

The complete MTankF0.BMP mask file

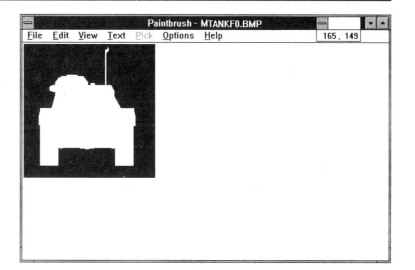

Now you can see why we had to first fill the background with red or some other color—so that you'll be able to erase black inside the tank. A mask BMP picture must have a black background. When you erase the black color of the tank, you don't want to erase any of the background; so initially the background must be some nonblack color. Once you've finished erasing all the colors, you must fill the background with black.

Now here is the essence of a mask BMP file: Every black pixel that appears in Figure 22.16 will be replaced during the animation with the corresponding pixel from the background image (in this example, the beach picture) that the black pixel covers. For example, if the tank picture covers a background that contains red pixels, then any black pixel that covers a red pixel is automatically replaced by a red pixel.

Characteristics of a Mask BMP File

A mask BMP file must have the following characteristics:

- The filename must start with the letter M, and the remaining characters must be the same as those of the sprite's filename. For example, if the original sprite name is 1234567.BMP, then the mask BMP filename must be: M1234567.BMP.

- The BMP file must be saved as a 256-color BMP file.

- The background color of the BMP picture must be filled with black.

- Any color that appeared in the original picture must be replaced with white.

And of course this applies to other colors in the background.

In effect, the black pixels are transparent—the pixels that are located under the black pixels of the mask BMP file replace the black pixels.

Now that you know how sprites are constructed, you can now move on in the next chapter to try out a program that uses sprites.

The process of making a mask BMP file is actually very easy and very quick. With a little practice, you'll be able to generate mask BMP files in a few minutes or less.

Summary

In this chapter you learned what sprites are and how they are used. You learned that the BMP file of the sprite must be 256-color BMP file, and that it must have a file name with seven or less characters. You also learned that a mask BMP file is needed. This mask file also must be saved as a 256-color BMP file, and it has the same filename as the original BMP file, but prefixed with the character M.

In this chapter you learned how to use Paintbrush for generating the mask BMP file from the original BMP file. However, you can use any similar drawing program for creating your sprites and mask BMP files.

CHAPTER
TWENTY-THREE

23

Using Sprites for Animation

In this chapter you'll execute the MySprite program, which uses sprites for animation. In the next chapter you'll start implementing this program.

Executing the MySprite Program

The MySprite.EXE program resides in the \WinGPrg\EXE directory of the accompanying CD-ROM.

- Execute the MySprite.EXE program. You'll see the window shown in Figure 23.1.

FIGURE 23.1:

The window of the MySprite.EXE program

The MySprite program has a File menu, shown in Figure 23.2. You terminate the MySprite program by selecting Exit from the File menu.

The MySprite program also includes the Display Control item in the Control Panel menu (see Figure 23.3).

FIGURE 23.2:

The File menu of the MySprite program

FIGURE 23.3:

The Display Control menu item of the MySprite program

- Select the Display Control menu item; you'll see the Control Panel window shown in Figure 23.4.

FIGURE 23.4:

The Control Panel window

The Control Panel window has a File menu with two menu items, Exit and About (see Figure 23.5).

- Select the About menu item. MySprite displays the About window (see Figure 23.6).

FIGURE 23.5:

The File menu of the Control Panel window

FIGURE 23.6:

The About window of the MySprite program

• Click the About window's OK button to close the window.

Moving the Tank

As shown in Figure 23.4, the Control Panel window has five option buttons:

Forward

Backward

From Left to Right

From Right to Left

No Tank Motion

- Click the Forward button.

MySprite responds by starting an animation show in which the tank advances forward toward the user. For example, Figures 23.7 and 23.8 show the tank in two positions during the Forward animation.

FIGURE 23.7:

The tank as the Forward animation begins

FIGURE 23.8:

The tank as the Forward animation continues

NOTE As discussed in the previous chapter, the background of the tank picture "accepts" the background picture. For example, in Figure 23.8 the tank hides a portion of the tree. But the rest of the tree (the part that is not hidden by the tank) is displayed.

- Click the Backward option button.

MySprite responds by starting an animation show where the tank is shown to move backward (away from the user). For example, Figures 23.9 and 23.10 show the tank in two positions during the Backward animation.

- Click the From Left to Right option button.

MySprite starts an animation show in which the tank moves from left to right. For example, Figures 23.11 and 23.12 show the tank in two positions during the left-to-right animation.

- Click the From Right to Left option button.

FIGURE 23.9:
The tank as the Backward animation begins

FIGURE 23.10:
The tank as the Backward animation continues

MySprite starts an animation show in which the tank moves from right to left.

FIGURE 23.11:
The tank as the From Left to Right animation begins

FIGURE 23.12:
The tank as the From Left to Right animation continues

Setting the Speed of the Tank Motion

The scroll bar in the Control Panel window lets the user control the speed at which the tank is moving.

- Set the scroll bar to various positions and note how the speed of the tank changes accordingly.

23

Background Sound Effects

If you have a sound card installed in your PC, then during the animation, you'll hear sound effects played through the sound card (the sound of a moving tank).

- Experiment with the MySprite program's options and then click the Exit Program button to terminate the program.

Summary

The MySprite program demonstrates how sprites are used for performing animation. You'll start implementing the MySprite program in the next chapter. As you'll see, using the Sprite control lets you perform animation with great ease.

CHAPTER

TWENTY-FOUR

24

Using Sprites from within Your Programs (Part I)

In this chapter you'll start implementing the MySprite program, which illustrates how you can use sprites in performing animation.

Creating the MySprite Project

As usual, the first step is to create the MySprite project.

- Start Visual Basic and select New Project from the File menu.

- Save the new form as MySprite.FRM and the new project file as MySprite.MAK, both in the C:\WinGPrg\CH23 directory.

- Implement the frmMySprite form with the Properties settings listed in Table 24.1. When you're finished, the form should look as shown in Figure 24.1.

TABLE 24.1: The Properties of the frmMySprite Form

Object: Form
Name: frmMySprite

Property	Value
ScaleMode	3 'Pixel
BorderStyle	1 'Fixed Single
Caption	"The MySprite Program"
Height	5775
Icon	C:\WinGPrg\Ch23\MySprite.ICO
Left	2775
MaxButton	'False
Top	720
Width	6675

Object: Timer
Name: Timer1

Property	Value
Interval	50
Left	1920
Top	240

TABLE 24.1: The Properties of the frmMySprite Form (continued)

Object: Multimedia control
Name: Tegomm1

Property	Value
Height	495
Left	2760
Top	360
Width	3510

Object: Sprite control
Name: sprBack

Property	Value
Autosize	−1 'True
Left	0
Top	0
Spritefilename	"c:\wingprg\Ch23\BkGnd0.BMP"
Transparent	0 'False
Spriteheight	340
Spritewidth	440
Transparent	0 'False

Object: Sprite
Name: sprTank

Property	Value
Autosize	False
Left	600
Top	600
Spritefilename	"c:\wingprg\Ch23\TankF0.BMP"
Spriteleft	40
Spritetop	40
Spriteheight	81
Spritewidth	81
Transparent	True

24

FIGURE 24.1:

The frmMySprite in design mode

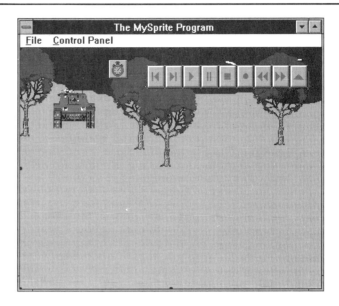

A few features of the frmMySprite form are worth particular attention:

- The ScaleMode property of frmMySprite is set to 3 (Pixel). This is required because the WinG objects that you'll use in the MySprite program use pixels as the unit for distances and coordinates. Thus, by setting Pixel as the ScaleMode property of the frmMySprite form, you don't have to convert twips or other units to pixels when communicating with the WinG objects.

- You are placing the Multimedia control inside the form, which enables you to add background music to the program. (You'll write the code to do this in a later chapter.) Figure 24.2 shows the icon of the Multimedia OCX control inside the Tools window. If you don't see this icon in your Tools window, add it by selecting Custom Controls from the Options menu and then use the Browse button to select the TegoSoft Multimedia OCX control from the \Windows\System directory.

- You're placing two sprite controls in the frmMySprite form. The icon of the Sprite control inside the Tools window of Visual Basic is shown in Figure 24.3. Name one sprite sprBack and the other sprite sprTank. As implied by these names, one sprite serves as the background, and the other serves as the sprite of the tank. It is essential to understand that the order in which you place the sprites determines which one serves as a background. Because

FIGURE 24.2:

The icon of the Multimedia OCX control in the Tools window of Visual Basic

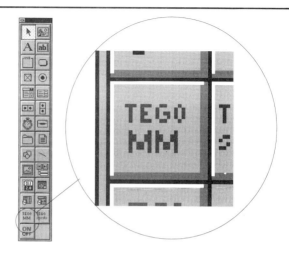

FIGURE 24.3:

The icon of the Sprite OCX control in the Tools window of Visual Basic

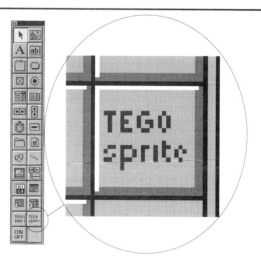

sprBack will be the background, you must place it in the form before you place the sprTank sprite. As shown in Table 24.1, the AutoSize property of the sprBack sprite is set to True. This means that the sprBack sprite will contain the background BMP picture without stretching the BMP. The size of the form was set so that it encloses the entire BMP picture.

- You are setting the Spritefilename property of the sprBack sprite to c:\winGprg\Ch23\BkGnd0.BMP. (The Maskfilename property of sprBack is then automatically set to c:\winGprg\Ch23\MBkGnd0.BMP.) The BkGnd0.BMP picture is shown in Figure 24.4. Because you set the Transparent property of the sprBack sprite to False, the setting of this sprite's Maskfilename property does not matter.

FIGURE 24.4:

The BkGnd0.BMP picture, which serves as the background picture of the MySprite program

NOTE When you place sprites in a form, one of the sprites serves as the background. Set the Transparent property of the background sprite to False.

- The Autosize property of the sprTank sprite is set to False. This means that the BMP picture used for this sprite is stretched to fit the size of the sprite control.

- The Transparent property of the sprTank sprite is set to True (the default setting). This means that the black pixels of this sprite's mask BMP file will be replaced by the pixels of the background sprite that they cover.

- You are setting the Spritefilename property of the sprTank sprite to c:\wingprg\Ch23\TankF0.BMP, and the Maskfilename is then automatically set to c:\wingprg\Ch23\MTankF0.BMP. Figure 24.5 shows the TankF0.BMP picture, and Figure 24.6 shows the MTankF0.BMP picture.

24

FIGURE 24.5:

The TankF0.BMP picture, which serves as the picture of the sprTank sprite and is animated during the execution of the MySprite program

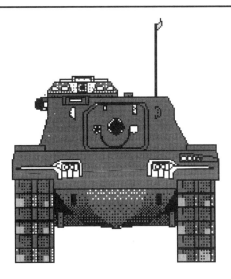

FIGURE 24.6:

The MTankF0.BMP image, used as the mask file for the sprTank sprite

Implementing the Menu of the frmMySprite Form

You'll now implement the menu of the frmMySprite form.

- Implement the menu of the frmMySprite form with the settings shown in Table 24.2. When you're finished, the menu should look as shown in Figures 24.7 and 24.8.

TABLE 24.2: The Menus of the frmMySprite Form

Caption	Name
&File	mnuFile
E&xit	mnuExit
&Control Panel	mnuControlPanel
...&Display Control	mnuDisplayControl

FIGURE 24.7:

The File menu of the frmMySprite form

FIGURE 24.8:

The Display Control menu of the frmMySprite form

The General Declarations Section of the frmMySprite Form

You'll now add code to the General Declarations section of the frmMySprite form.

- Enter the following code within the General Declarations section of the frmMySprite form:

```
Option Explicit
```

As usual, the Option Explicit statement forces variable declarations.

Attaching Code to the Form_Load( ) Procedure of the frmMySprite Form

The frmMySprite form is loaded upon starting the MySprite program. Now you'll add the code that performs this loading:

- Enter the following code in the Form_Load( ) procedure of the frmMySprite form:

```
Private Sub Form_Load( )
```

```
Dim Path

  Tegomm1.Visible = False
  gDirection = "NoMotion"

  ' Extract the directory name from
  ' which this application is executed
  Path = App.Path
  If Right(Path, 1) <> "\" Then
     Path = Path + "\"
  End If

  ' Initialize the sprite controls.
  sprBack.InitializeSprite Me.hWnd
  sprTank.InitializeSprite Me.hWnd

  ' Open the sprites used in show.
  gBkGnd0 = sprBack.OpenSprite(Path + "BkGnd0.bmp")
  gTankF0 = sprBack.OpenSprite(Path + "TankF0.bmp")
  gTankF1 = sprBack.OpenSprite(Path + "TankF1.bmp")
  gTankR0 = sprBack.OpenSprite(Path + "TankR0.bmp")
  gTankR1 = sprBack.OpenSprite(Path + "TankR1.bmp")
  gTankL0 = sprBack.OpenSprite(Path + "TankL0.bmp")
  gTankL1 = sprBack.OpenSprite(Path + "TankL1.bmp")
  gTankB0 = sprBack.OpenSprite(Path + "TankB0.bmp")
  gTankB1 = sprBack.OpenSprite(Path + "TankB1.bmp")

End Sub
```

This code first makes the Multimedia control invisible:

```
Tegomm1.Visible = False
```

You then set the gDirection variable to NoMotion:

```
gDirection = "NoMotion"
```

The gDirection variable serves as a flag, indicating the direction in which the tank should move. This variable is declared in a separate BAS module, which you'll create in the next section.

The Path variable is then set as follows:

```
' Extract the directory name from
' which this application is executed
Path = App.Path
```

```
If Right(Path, 1) <> "\" Then
    Path = Path + "\"
End If
```

In other words, Path is set to the directory name from which the program is executed. For example, if the MySprite.EXE program resides inside the C:\ directory, then App.Path is equal to C:\. And if the application is executed from the C:\WinG\CH23 directory, then App.Path is equal to C:\WinG\CH23, and Path is set to C:\WinG\CH23\ (the \ character is added).

You then used each Sprite control's InitializeSprite method:

```
' Initialize the sprite controls.
sprBack.InitializeSprite Me.hWnd
sprTank.InitializeSprite Me.hWnd
```

24

The Sprite control uses WinG technology. This means that the BMP pictures are drawn in a virtual WinG window, whose contents are then slammed into the window of your application. Which window? The window whose hWnd property you supplied to the InitializeSprite method. In the preceding two statements you supplied Me.hWnd as the parameter of the InitializeSprite method. This means that the contents of WinG will be slammed into the window of the frmMySprite form.

Sprites and WinG

Sprites use WinG technology, which means that the contents of a WinG window are slammed into your application's window. Thus, use the InitializeSprite method to specify the destination window.

As an example, suppose your program uses five sprite controls, named sprBackground, sprMySprite, sprHerSprite, sprHisSprite, and sprOurSprite.

In the Form_Load( ) procedure you have to execute the following statements:

```
sprBackground.InitilizeSprite Me.hWnd
sprMySprite.InitializeSprite Me.hWnd
sprHerSprite.InitializeSprite Me.hWnd
sprHisSprite.InitializeSprite Me.hWnd
sprOurSprite.InitializeSprite Me.hWnd
```

Sprites and WinG (continued)

These statements set the window that will accept the WinG contents to the Me form (that is, the form from which the procedure is executed). Naturally, you can supply other window handles as the parameter of the InitializeSprite method.

The last block of statements that you added to the Form_Load( ) procedure opens the sprites:

```
' Open the sprites used in the show.
gBkGnd0 = sprBack.OpenSprite(Path + "BkGnd0.bmp")
gTankF0 = sprBack.OpenSprite(Path + "TankF0.bmp")
gTankF1 = sprBack.OpenSprite(Path + "TankF1.bmp")
gTankR0 = sprBack.OpenSprite(Path + "TankR0.bmp")
gTankR1 = sprBack.OpenSprite(Path + "TankR1.bmp")
gTankL0 = sprBack.OpenSprite(Path + "TankL0.bmp")
gTankL1 = sprBack.OpenSprite(Path + "TankL1.bmp")
gTankB0 = sprBack.OpenSprite(Path + "TankB0.bmp")
gTankB1 = sprBack.OpenSprite(Path + "TankB1.bmp")
```

In these statements, you use the OpenSprite method, which opens a sprite. The value returned by the OpenSprite method is the handle of the opened sprite. For example, the following statement opens the sprite whose BMP file is the BkGnd0.BMP file:

```
gBkGnd0 = sprBack.OpenSprite(Path + "BkGnd0.bmp")
```

gBkGnd0 is now the handle of the sprite. The gBkGnd variable is declared in a separate BAS module, which you'll create in the following section.

So the preceding statements open all the sprites that will be used by the program. But wait a minute! Didn't we already set the Spritefilename property of the sprBack control to the BkGnd0.BMP file? Yes, we did (see Table 24.1). But we did this only so that you'll be able to see the picture of the background during design time. In other words, the Spritefilename property is included for the sole purpose of making the picture visible during design time. During runtime, you must open the sprites by using the OpenSprite method.

In a similar manner, in the Form_Load( ) procedure you open the following sprites:

```
gTankF0 = sprBack.OpenSprite(Path + "TankF0.bmp")
gTankF1 = sprBack.OpenSprite(Path + "TankF1.bmp")
gTankR0 = sprBack.OpenSprite(Path + "TankR0.bmp")
gTankR1 = sprBack.OpenSprite(Path + "TankR1.bmp")
gTankL0 = sprBack.OpenSprite(Path + "TankL0.bmp")
gTankL1 = sprBack.OpenSprite(Path + "TankL1.bmp")
gTankB0 = sprBack.OpenSprite(Path + "TankB0.bmp")
gTankB1 = sprBack.OpenSprite(Path + "TankB1.bmp")
```

24

Again, gTankF0, gTankF1, …, gTankB1 (variables that you'll declare in the next section) are the returned values from the OpenSprite method. So from now on, your code will refer to the TankF0.BMP picture as gTank0, the TankF1.BMP picture as gTankF1, and so on.

TankF0.BMP and TankF1.BMP are the BMP pictures that show the tank advancing toward the user. Figure 24.9 shows the TankF0.BMP picture on the left and the TankF1.BMP picture on the right. At first glance, these images look identical. Looking closely, however, you can see a couple of small differences. The flag of the antenna in TankF1.BMP is at a slightly different location than in the TankF0.BMP picture. Also, we've modified the tank's track or chain (its "wheels") a bit. The TankF1.BMP picture was generated by modifying the TankF0.BMP picture.

FIGURE 24.9:

The TankF0.BMP (frame 1 of 2 when moving forward) and TankF1.BMP (frame 2 of 2) pictures

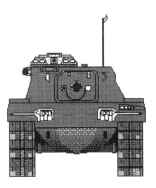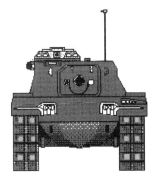

As you'll see during the implementation of the MySprite program, when the tank is moving forward, its size is increased, and the following sequence of BMP pictures is shown:

TankF0.BMP

TankF1.BMP

TankF0.BMP

TankF1.BMP

…and so on.

To summarize, the sprTank sprite does not serve as a background sprite. As such, you set the Transparent property of this control to True (see Table 24.1). This means that you have to provide a mask file for the sprite.

In the Form_Load( ) procedure you opened a sprite as follows:

```
gTankF0 = sprBack.OpenSprite(Path + "TankF0.bmp")
```

So because the sprite is used as a foreground sprite, it must have a mask BMP file. Thus, the preceding statement opens both TankF0.BMP and MTankF0.BMP. (The MTankF0.BMP file must reside in the same directory as the TankF0.BMP file).

Similarly, you opened the sprite whose BMP file is TankF1.BMP and whose mask BMP file is MTankF1.BMP. Figure 24.10 shows the MTankF0.BMP and MTankF1.BMP pictures.

The rest of the OpenSprite statements that you entered in the Form_Load( ) procedure of the frmMySprite form open other sprites:

```
gTankR0 = sprBack.OpenSprite(Path + "TankR0.bmp")
gTankR1 = sprBack.OpenSprite(Path + "TankR1.bmp")
gTankL0 = sprBack.OpenSprite(Path + "TankL0.bmp")
gTankL1 = sprBack.OpenSprite(Path + "TankL1.bmp")
gTankB0 = sprBack.OpenSprite(Path + "TankB0.bmp")
gTankB1 = sprBack.OpenSprite(Path + "TankB1.bmp")
```

TankR0.BMP and TankR1.BMP are the pictures of the tank when the tank is going from left to right. Figures 24.11 shows these two frames. Again, these two images look identical at first glance. However, after close examination you may notice that the flag on the antenna and also the tank's chain are slightly different in these two pictures. In addition, on the right, exhaust fumes are coming out of the tank (which further gives the illusion that the tank is moving).

FIGURE 24.10:

The mask files (MTankF0.BMP and MTankF1.BMP) of the TankF0.BMP and TankF1.BMP pictures

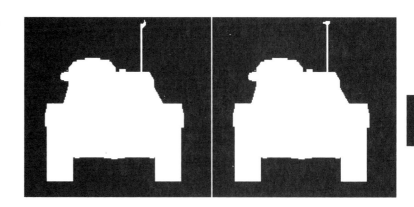

24

FIGURE 24.11:

The TankR0.BMP (frame 1 of 2 when moving to the right) and TankR1.BMP (frame 2 of 2) pictures

> **TIP**
>
> The interesting thing about animation is that small details, like making the flag of the tank waving, are what create a realistic impression.

Figure 24.12 shows the mask BMP files of the TankR0.BMP and TankR1.BMP pictures.

FIGURE 24.12:

The mask files (MTankR0.BMP and MTankR1.BMP) of the TankR0.BMP and TankR1.BMP pictures

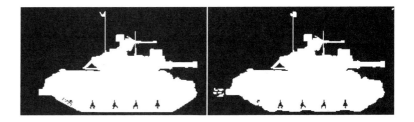

The TankL0.BMP and TankL1.BMP pictures, shown in Figure 24.13, are the pictures of the tank when it is moving from right to left. Again, although these two images look identical, they have slight differences like those in the other pairs.

Figure 24.14 shows the mask BMP files of the TankL0.BMP and TankL1.BMP pictures.

TankB0.BMP and TankB1.BMP (Figure 24.15) are the pictures of the tank when the tank is going backward (away from the user). Again, notice that the differences between them are very slight. Figures 24.16 shows the mask BMP files of the TankB0.BMP and TankB1.BMP pictures.

FIGURE 24.13:

The TankL0.BMP (frame 1 of 2 when moving to the left) and TankL1.BMP (frame 2 of 2) pictures

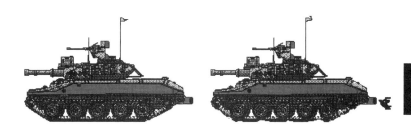

24

FIGURE 24.14:

The mask files (MTankL0.BMP and MTankL1.BMP) of the TankL0.BMP and TankL1.BMP pictures

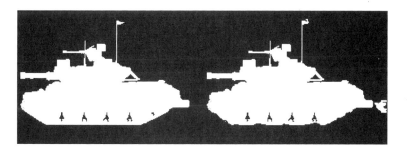

FIGURE 24.15:

The TankB0.BMP (frame 1 of 2 when moving backward) and TankB1.BMP (frame 2 of 2) pictures

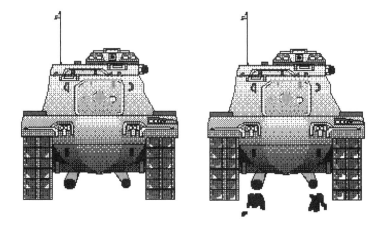

FIGURE 24.16:

The mask files (MTankB0.BMP and MTankB1.BMP) of the TankB0.BMP and TankB1.BMP pictures

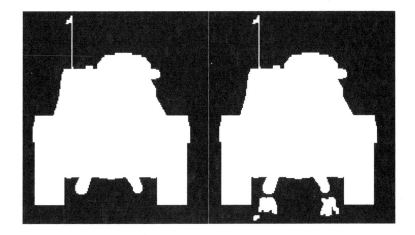

Adding the MySprite.BAS module to the MySprite.MAK Project

As mentioned earlier, the MySprite project needs an additional module, MySprite.BAS, for declaring global variables. You'll now add this module to the MySprite.MAK project:

- Select Module from the Insert menu of Visual Basic.

Visual Basic responds by inserting a new BAS module into the MySprite.MAK project.

- Select Save As from the File menu of Visual Basic and save the new module as MySprite.BAS in the C:\WinGPrg\CH23 directory.

- Enter the following code in the General Declarations section of the MySprite.BAS module:

```
Option Explicit

Public gDirection

' Background
Public gBkGnd0 As Long

' Tank moving forward toward the user
Public gTankF0 As Long
Public gTankF1 As Long

' Tank moving from left to right
Public gTankR0 As Long
Public gTankR1 As Long

' Tank moving backward away from the user
Public gTankB0 As Long
Public gTankB1 As Long

' Tank moving from right to left
Public gTankL0 As Long
Public gTankL1 As Long
```

24

This code declares variables that, as you've seen in the previous section, are used to hold the handles of the sprites. We declare them as Public in a separate BAS module to make them accessible from any procedure of any form of the frmMySprite.MAK project. In the next chapter you'll see that the MySprite project includes another form (the frmControlPanel form). So these variables are accessible from any procedure of the frmControlPanel form as well as from any procedure of frmMySprite.

Attaching Code to the Form_Unload( ) Procedure

You'll now attach code to the Form_Unload( ) procedure of the frmMySprite form.

- Enter the following code in the Form_Unload( ) procedure of the frmMySprite form:

```
Private Sub Form_Unload(Cancel As Integer)

    ' Free all the sprites of the show.
    sprBack.CloseSprite (gBkGnd0)
    sprBack.CloseSprite (gTankF0)
    sprBack.CloseSprite (gTankF1)
    sprBack.CloseSprite (gTankR0)
    sprBack.CloseSprite (gTankR1)
    sprBack.CloseSprite (gTankL0)
    sprBack.CloseSprite (gTankL1)
    sprBack.CloseSprite (gTankB0)
    sprBack.CloseSprite (gTankB1)

    Unload frmControlPanel

End Sub
```

As you saw earlier in this chapter, the code in the Form_Load( ) procedure uses the OpenSprite method to open various sprites. When you open a sprite, the computer dedicates a certain amount of memory to the opened sprite. What happens to this memory space when you terminate the application? It remains occupied, and Windows cannot use it for any other purpose. Moreover, if you run the program again, a new block of memory will be allocated to the sprites.

As you can see, it is necessary to free the memory occupied by the sprites when the program is terminated. A good place to put the code that frees this memory is in the Form_Unload( ) procedure, which is executed whenever frmMySprite is unloaded. The code you entered frees the memory by using the CloseSprite method of the Sprite control. For example, the following statement frees the memory area occupied by the gBkGnd0 sprite:

```
sprBack.CloseSprite (gBkGnd0)
```

and similar statements free other memory occupied by the sprites.

The last statement unloads the frmControlPanel form:

```
Unload frmControlPanel
```

In the next chapter you'll implement the frmControlPanel form. When the frmMySprite form is terminated, the frmControlPanel form is unloaded.

24

TIP

The Form_Unload( ) procedure is a good focal point to write code that performs "clean-up." This procedure is executed when the user clicks the window's Control box and then selects Close from the system menu that pops up. The procedure is also executed if the form is closed by executing the Unload statement.

Summary: Opening and Closing Sprites

Typically, you open sprites inside the Form_Load( ) procedure. For example, the following code opens three sprites:

```
gBkGnd0 = sprBack.OpenSprite(Path + "BkGnd0.bmp")
gTankF0 = sprBack.OpenSprite(Path + "TankF0.bmp")
gTankF1 = sprBack.OpenSprite(Path + "TankF1.bmp")
```

This means that before terminating the program (usually inside the Form_Unload( ) procedure) you have to execute the following statements:

```
sprBack.CloseSprite (gBkGnd0)
sprBack.CloseSprite (gTankF0)
sprBack.CloseSprite (gTankF1)
```

Attaching Code to the Exit Menu of the frmMySprite Form

You'll now attach code to the Exit menu item of the frmMySprite form.

- Enter the following code in the mnuExit_Click( ) procedure of the FrmMySprite form:

```
Private Sub mnuExit_Click( )

    Unload frmControlPanel
    Unload Me

End Sub
```

This code unloads the two forms that are included in the MySprite project. (As stated, in the next chapter you'll implement the frmControlPanel form.)

Summary

In this chapter you started to implement the MySprite program. In the next chapter you'll continue to implement this program.

As you saw in this chapter, you placed two sprite controls inside the form. One sprite serves as the background picture of the animation (sprBackground), and the other serves as the animated sprite (sprTank).

During design time, you can set the Spritefilename property of the Sprite controls, so that you'll be able to see (as you're designing) how the sprite will look at runtime. During runtime, however, you need to use the InitializeSprite method (to tell the Sprite control where to slam the contents of WinG) and the OpenSprite method to open sprites. The returned value from the OpenSprite method is assigned to a variable, and as you'll see in the next chapter, this variable is used to refer to the BMP picture of the sprite.

CHAPTER

TWENTY-FIVE

Using Sprites from within Your Programs (Part II)

In this chapter you'll continue implementing the MySprite program that you started in the previous chapter. As you'll see, the code that performs the animation is actually very short and easy!

Implementing the frmControlPanel Form

The animation show of the MySprite program is performed within the frmMySprite form. The MySprite program has another form, named frmControl-Panel, that is used as a control panel to let the user manipulate the show. You'll now implement the frmControlPanel form.

- Select Form from the Insert menu of Visual Basic.

Visual Basic responds by adding a new form to the project.

- Save the new form as Control.FRM in the C:\WinGPrg\CH23 directory.

- Implement the frmControlPanel form with the Properties settings listed in Table 25.1. When you're finished, the form should look as shown in Figure 25.1.

- Implement the menu of the frmControlPanel form with the settings listed in Table 25.2.

TABLE 25.1: The Properties of the frmControlPanel Form

Object: Form	
Name: frmControlPanel	
Property	**Value**
BackColor	Light gray
Caption	"Control Panel"
Height	6015
Icon	C:\WinGPrg\CH23\MySprite.ICO
Left	165
MaxButton	0 'False
Top	405
Width	2340

TABLE 25.1: The Properties of the frmControlPanel Form (continued)

Object: Timer
Name: Timer1

Property	Value
Interval	250
Left	240
Top	4680

Object: Horizontal Scroll Bar
Name: hsbSpeed
Comment: The Min property is greater than the Max property.

Property	Value
Height	255
Left	120
Max	1
Min	10
Top	2760
Value	10
Width	2055

Object: CommandButton
Name: cmdExitProgram

Property	Value
Caption	"E&xit Program"
Height	495
Left	840
Top	4680
Width	1215

25

TABLE 25.1: The Properties of the frmControlPanel Form (continued)

Object: Frame
Name: fraTankDirection

Property	Value
BackColor	Light gray
Caption	"Tank Direction"
Height	2175
Left	120
Top	120
Width	2055

Object: Option Button
Name: optForward

Property	Value
BackColor	Light gray
Caption	"&Forward"
Height	255
Left	120
Top	240
Width	1815

Object: Option Button
Name: optBackward

Property	Value
BackColor	Light gray
Caption	"&Backward"
Height	375
Left	120
Top	480
Width	1815

TABLE 25.1: The Properties of the frmControlPanel Form (continued)

Object: Option Button
Name: optLeft

Property	Value
BackColor	Light gray
Caption	"From Right to &Left"
Height	255
Left	120
Top	1200
Width	1815

Object: Option Button
Name: optRight

Property	Value
BackColor	Light gray
Caption	"From Left to &Right"
Height	255
Left	120
Top	840
Width	1695

Object: Option Button
Name: optNoMotion

Property	Value
BackColor	Light gray
Caption	"&No Tank Motion"
Height	375
Left	120
Top	1680
Value	-1 'True
Width	1695

25

TABLE 25.1: The Properties of the frmControlPanel Form (continued)

Object: Line control
Name: Line1
Comment: The purpose of the Line control is cosmetic.

Property	Value
X1	1800
X2	120
y1	1560
y2	1560

Object: Label
Name: lblSpeed

Property	Value
BackColor	Light gray
Caption	"Speed: "
Height	255
Left	120
Top	2400
Width	1215

FIGURE 25.1:

The frmControlPanel form in design mode

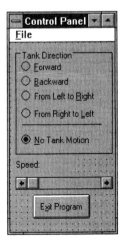

TABLE 25.2: The Menu of the frmControlPanel Form

Caption	Name
&File	mnuFile
...&About...	mnuAbout
...E&xit	mnuExit

Before writing the code of the frmControlPanel form, we first need to add code to the frmMySprite form. The code that you'll add here will cause the frmMySprite form to repaint itself whenever repainting is necessary. As you'll soon see, the frmControlPanel window is displayed as a nonmodal window. This means that once you display the frmControlPanel window, you can return to the frmMySprite window without first closing the frmControlPanel window. When returning to the frmMySprite window, you want Windows to repaint the frmMySprite window with its original contents.

Attaching Code to the Paint Event of the frmMySprite Form

The Paint event occurs whenever Windows determines that there is a need to re-paint the window. For example, upon starting the application, the frmMySprite form is displayed. This means that the Paint event is generated, and the Form_Paint( ) procedure of frmMySprite is executed. You'll now write code in the Form_Paint( ) procedure of frmMySprite( ).

- Enter the following code in the Form_Paint( ) procedure of the frmMySprite form:

```
Private Sub Form_Paint( )

    ' Draw the sprBack sprite inside WinG
    sprBack.SpriteHandle = gBkGnd0
    sprBack.DrawSprite
```

```
' Slam WinG into the screen
sprBack.SlamIt
```

```
End Sub
```

Recall that in designing the form, the only reason you assigned the BkGnd0.BMP picture to the sprBack sprite and the TankF0.BMP picture to the sprTank sprite is to be able to see these pictures during design time. In the previous chapter you wrote code in the Form_Load( ) procedure that prepares the handles of the sprites. The code you've just entered in the Form_Paint( ) procedure actually displays the contents of the sprBack Sprite control.

Here is how you display the background picture:

```
' Draw the sprBack sprite inside WinG
sprBack.SpriteHandle = gBkGnd0
sprBack.DrawSprite
```

Inside the Form_Load( ) procedure you extracted gBkGnd0, the handle of the sprite. The statements above set the SpriteHandle to gBkGnd0 and then execute the DrawSprite method.

Recall that WinG technology is used with sprites. When you use sprites, a virtual WinG window is created. The DrawSprite method draws the contents of the sprite into the WinG window. Currently, the sprite contains the BkGnd0.BMP picture because SpriteHandle is set to gBkGnd0.

Sprites and WinG Technology

Sprites use WinG technology. This means that before displaying the drawing in the window of the application, your code draws it in the WinG window. You start by assigning to the Sprite control the handle of the sprite whose BMP picture you want to draw in WinG.

For example, assuming that gBkGnd0 is the handle of the sprite that contains the BkGnd0.BMP picture, the following statement uses the SpriteHandle property to assign to the Sprite control the handle of the BkGnd0.BMP picture:

```
sprBack.SpriteHandle = gBkGnd0
```

Sprites and WinG Technology (continued)

Once the Sprite control has been assigned a handle, the DrawSprite method is executed to draw the BMP file inside the WinG window:

```
sprBack.DrawSprite
```

Well, now WinG is ready, so you can slam its contents into the application's window:

```
' Slam WinG into the screen
sprBack.SlamIt
```

The result is shown in Figure 25.2.

25

FIGURE 25.2:

The result of slamming the contents of WinG (the BkGnd0.BMP picture) into the screen

Attaching Code to the Display Control Menu Item of the frmMySprite Form

When the user selects the Display Control menu item, the frmControlPanel form is displayed. This form lets the user manipulate the tank movements. You'll now attach code to the Display Control menu item.

- Enter the following code in the mnuDisplayControl_Click( ) procedure of the frmMySprite form:

```
Private Sub mnuDisplayControl_Click( )

    frmControlPanel.Show

End Sub
```

This code displays the frmControlPanel form. Because you did not supply 1 as the parameter of the Show method, the frmControlPanel window is displayed as a nonmodal window.

Attaching Code to the Timer Event

The frmMySprite form has a timer called Timer1. You'll now attach code to the Timer event of the Timer1 control. This code is responsible for displaying the animation shows. At first glance, the code looks complex and long. However, as you'll soon see, it is actually very easy to write and understand. The code is long only because it is responsible for the four animation shows: Forward, Backward, Left to Right, and Right To Left.

- Type the following code in the Timer1_Timer( ) procedure of the frmMySprite form:

```
Private Sub Timer1_Timer( )

    Static TankFrame

    ' Don't perform animation when the
```

```
' program's window is minimized.
If Me.WindowState = 1 Then
    Exit Sub
End If

' Don't perform animation when the
' No Tank Motion option button is selected.
If gDirection = "NoMotion" Then
      Exit Sub
End If

' Draw the section of the background where the
' Tank sprite is located.
sprBack.SpriteHandle = gBkGnd0
sprBack.PartialDraw sprTank.SpriteLeft, _
                    sprTank.SpriteTop, _
                    sprTank.SpriteWidth, _
                    sprTank.SpriteHeight

' Perform the forward animation
If gDirection = "Forward" Then
    ' Show tank going forward (toward the user).
    sprTank.StretchBottom _
          11 - frmControlPanel.hsbSpeed.Value

    sprTank.StretchRight _
          11 - frmControlPanel.hsbSpeed.Value

    TankFrame = TankFrame + 1

    If TankFrame >= 2 Then TankFrame = 0
    Select Case TankFrame
          Case 0
          sprTank.SpriteHandle = gTankF0
          Case 1
          sprTank.SpriteHandle = gTankF1
    End Select
    sprTank.DrawSprite

    If sprTank.SpriteHeight >= 250 Then
        ' Draw the background
        sprBack.SpriteHandle = gBkGnd0
        sprBack.DrawSprite

        ' Set initial size of sprite
```

25

```
            sprTank.SpriteWidth = 81
            sprTank.SpriteHeight = 81

            ' Place tank at initial point
            sprTank.SpriteLeft = 40
            sprTank.SpriteTop = 40
        End If

        ' Slam WinG into the screen.
        sprBack.SlamIt

        Exit Sub

    End If

    ' Perform the Left to Right animation
    If gDirection = "LeftToRight" Then
        ' Show tank going from left to right.
        sprTank.SpriteLeft = _
            sprTank.SpriteLeft + _
            (11 - frmControlPanel.hsbSpeed.Value)

        TankFrame = TankFrame + 1
        If TankFrame >= 2 Then TankFrame = 0
        Select Case TankFrame
            Case 0
            sprTank.SpriteHandle = gTankR0
            Case 1
            sprTank.SpriteHandle = gTankR1
        End Select
        sprTank.DrawSprite

        If sprTank.SpriteLeft >= 450 Then
            ' Draw the background
            sprBack.SpriteHandle = gBkGnd0
            sprBack.DrawSprite

            ' Set initial size of sprite
            frmMySprite.sprTank.SpriteWidth = 209
            frmMySprite.sprTank.SpriteHeight = 121

            ' Place tank at initial point
            frmMySprite.sprTank.SpriteLeft = 20
            frmMySprite.sprTank.SpriteTop = 200
        End If
```

```
    ' Slam WinG into the screen.
    sprBack.SlamIt

    Exit Sub

End If

' Perform the Right to Left animation
If gDirection = "RightToLeft" Then
    ' Show tank going from right to left.
    sprTank.SpriteLeft = _
        sprTank.SpriteLeft - _
        (11 - frmControlPanel.hsbSpeed.Value)

    TankFrame = TankFrame + 1
    If TankFrame >= 2 Then TankFrame = 0
    Select Case TankFrame
        Case 0
            sprTank.SpriteHandle = gTankL0
        Case 1
            sprTank.SpriteHandle = gTankL1
    End Select
    sprTank.DrawSprite

    If sprTank.SpriteLeft <= 0 Then
        ' Draw the background
        sprBack.SpriteHandle = gBkGnd0
        sprBack.DrawSprite

        ' Set initial size of sprite
        frmMySprite.sprTank.SpriteWidth = 193
        frmMySprite.sprTank.SpriteHeight = 137

        ' Place tank at initial point
        frmMySprite.sprTank.SpriteLeft = 300
        frmMySprite.sprTank.SpriteTop = 80
    End If

    ' Slam WinG into the screen.
    sprBack.SlamIt

    Exit Sub

End If
```

```
' Perform the backward animation
If gDirection = "Backward" Then

    ' Show tank going backward (away from the user).
    sprTank.StretchBottom _
        -(11 - frmControlPanel.hsbSpeed.Value)

    sprTank.StretchRight _
        -(11 - frmControlPanel.hsbSpeed.Value)

    TankFrame = TankFrame + 1

    If TankFrame >= 2 Then TankFrame = 0
    Select Case TankFrame
        Case 0
        sprTank.SpriteHandle = gTankB0
        Case 1
        sprTank.SpriteHandle = gTankB1
    End Select
    sprTank.DrawSprite

    If sprTank.SpriteHeight <= 150 Then
        ' Draw the background
        sprBack.SpriteHandle = gBkGnd0
        sprBack.DrawSprite

        ' Set initial size of sprite
        frmMySprite.sprTank.SpriteWidth = 255
        frmMySprite.sprTank.SpriteHeight = 241

        ' Place tank at initial point
        frmMySprite.sprTank.SpriteLeft = 200
        frmMySprite.sprTank.SpriteTop = 80
    End If

    ' Slam WinG into the screen.
    sprBack.SlamIt

    Exit Sub
End If

End Sub
```

This code is responsible for the animation. First a static variable is declared:

```
Static TankFrame
```

An If statement is then executed to examine whether the frmMySprite form is minimized:

```
' Don't perform animation when the
' program's window is minimized.
If Me.WindowState = 1 Then
   Exit Sub
End If
```

This code causes the Timer1_Timer( ) procedure to terminate if the window is minimized. So when the window is minimized, no animation is shown.

The user manipulates the tank movements by selecting the appropriate option button inside the frmControlPanel form. As you'll see later in this chapter, when the user selects the No Tank Motion button, the gDirection variable is updated with the string NoMotion.

An If statement is executed to examine whether the gDirection variable is set to No-Motion:

```
' Don't perform animation when the
' No Tank Motion option button is selected.
If gDirection = "NoMotion" Then
   Exit Sub
End If
```

If the user selected the No Tank Motion option button, the Timer1_Timer( ) procedure is terminated, and no animation is performed.

The next block of statements draws the background picture in the WinG window. But wait a minute—we've already done that! Why do we need to draw the background picture inside WinG again? There is no need to draw the entire background picture inside WinG. But suppose the tank was displayed at a certain location on the background. During the next execution of the Timer1_Timer( ) procedure, the tank is moved to a new location. What happens to the area that was covered by the tank's previous location? You need to write code that replaces this area with the appropriate section from the original background picture. The area that has to be redrawn inside WinG is shown in Figure 25.3.

FIGURE 25.3:

Before you place the tank in its new location in the WinG window, make sure to draw the original section of the background that was covered by the tank.

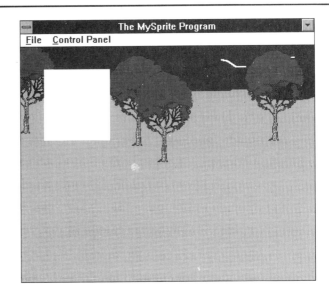

NOTE

When using sprite technology for performing animation, you move the sprite from one location to another location. So you have to "erase" the area that was covered by the old location of the sprite. That is, you have to replace the area that was covered by the old location of the sprite with the original section of the background.

So here is how you draw the original area of the background:

```
' Draw the section of the background where the
' Tank sprite is located.
sprBack.SpriteHandle = gBkGnd0

sprBack.PartialDraw sprTank.SpriteLeft, _
                    sprTank.SpriteTop, _
                    sprTank.SpriteWidth, _
                    sprTank.SpriteHeight
```

In this code you set the SpriteHandle property of the sprBack sprite to the handle that corresponds to the BkGnd0.BMP picture. You then execute the PartialDraw method to draw, in the WinG window, the portion of the BMP picture currently stored in the SpriteHandle property (that is, the BkGnd0.BMP picture) that is specified by the parameters of the PartialDraw method. As you can see, these parameters specify the coordinates and size of the tank picture (the sprTank sprite).

Summary: Drawing Part of the Background into WinG

The coordinates and size of the tank sprite are as follows:

```
sprTank.SpriteLeft
sprTank.SpriteTop
sprTank.SpriteWidth
sprTank.SpriteHeight
```

To draw a portion of the background picture in WinG at the location where the tank sprite is located, use the following statements:

```
sprBack.SpriteHandle = gBkGnd0

sprBack.PartialDraw sprTank.SpriteLeft, _
                    sprTank.SpriteTop, _
                    sprTank.SpriteWidth, _
                    sprTank.SpriteHeight
```

The only reason you draw a partial section of the background is to enable slow PCs to perform the animation fast. In other words, instead of drawing the entire background picture for each tank movement, you execute the PartialDraw method to draw only the section that was covered by the old location of the tank.

With faster PCs (those with 80486 or Pentium chips), the reduction in animation speed will not be noticeable even if you draw the entire background picture for each tank movement. If you decide that you want to draw the entire background picture for each tank movement, then use the following code instead of the PartialDraw method:

```
' Draw the entire background
sprBack.SpriteHandle = gBkGnd0
sprBack.DrawSprite
```

25

The next block of statements executes an If statement to see whether the gDirection variable is equal to Forward:

```
If gDirection = "Forward" Then

    ..................................
    ... Perform the forward animation ...
    ..................................

End If
```

As you'll see later in this chapter, when the user selects the Forward option button, the gDirection variable is updated with the Forward string. So when the Timer1_Timer( ) procedure is executed, the code under the If statement is executed, and this code is responsible for the forward animation (showing the tank advancing toward the user). Here is the code of the forward animation:

```
' Perform the forward animation
If gDirection = "Forward" Then
    ' Show tank going forward (toward the user).
    sprTank.StretchBottom _
            11 - frmControlPanel.hsbSpeed.Value

    sprTank.StretchRight _
            11 - frmControlPanel.hsbSpeed.Value

    TankFrame = TankFrame + 1
    If TankFrame >= 2 Then TankFrame = 0
    Select Case TankFrame
            Case 0
            sprTank.SpriteHandle = gTankF0
            Case 1
            sprTank.SpriteHandle = gTankF1
    End Select
    sprTank.DrawSprite

    If sprTank.SpriteHeight >= 250 Then
        ' Draw the background
        sprBack.SpriteHandle = gBkGnd0
        sprBack.DrawSprite

        ' Set initial size of sprite
        sprTank.SpriteWidth = 81
        sprTank.SpriteHeight = 81
```

```
        ' Place tank at initial point
        sprTank.SpriteLeft = 40
        sprTank.SpriteTop = 40
    End If

        ' Slam WinG into the screen.
        sprBack.SlamIt

        Exit Sub

    End If
```

The StretchBottom method is executed:

```
sprTank.StretchBottom _
         11 - frmControlPanel.hsbSpeed.Value
```

The speed scroll bar inside the frmControlPanel determines how fast the tank is moving. The Max property of the speed scroll bar is 1 and the Min property is set to 10. So when the scroll bar position is at the extreme left, the Value property of the scroll bar is 10, and when the scroll bar is at its extreme right position, the Value property is 1. In the preceding statement, you supplied

```
11 - frmControlPanel.hsbSpeed.Value
```

as the parameter of the StretchBottom method. So when the scroll bar is at its extreme left position, the parameter that you supplied is:

$$11 - 10 = 1$$

and when the scroll bar is at its extreme right position, the parameter that you supplied is:

$$11 - 1 = 10$$

The parameter of the StretchBottom method indicates the number of pixels by which the picture of the sprTank picture should be stretched. In other words, when the speed scroll bar is at its extreme left position, the bottom of the sptTank picture is stretched one pixel downward. And when the speed control is at its extreme right position, the sprTank picture is stretched 10 pixels downward.

Once the bottom of the sprTank picture has been stretched downward according to the speed scroll bar position, the right side of the sprite is stretched. Again, the amount of stretching depends on the scroll bar position:

```
sprTank.StretchRight _
        11 - frmControlPanel.hsbSpeed.Value
```

So putting it all together, the size of the sprTank Sprite control is increased. This control contains the picture of the tank, and therefore the tank picture size is increased. The following code determines which tank BMP picture will be displayed inside the sprTank control:

```
TankFrame = TankFrame + 1
   If TankFrame >= 2 Then TankFrame = 0
   Select Case TankFrame
        Case 0
        sprTank.SpriteHandle = gTankF0
        Case 1
        sprTank.SpriteHandle = gTankF1
   End Select
```

Recall that you declared TankFrame as a static variable. So when the Timer1_Timer( ) procedure is run for the first time, TankFrame is equal to 0. The TankFrame variable is increased by 1 and an If statement is executed to make sure that the only possible values that TankFrame can have are 0 and 1.

A Select Case statement is executed to assign the appropriate handle to the SpriteHandle property of the sprTank sprite—either gTankF0 (which corresponds to TankF0.BMP) or gTankF1 (which corresponds to TankF1.BMP).

Finally, the contents of the sprTank control are drawn inside the WinG virtual window:

```
sprTank.DrawSprite
```

The last thing needed for the Forward animation is an If statement that makes sure the tank picture does not grow beyond the borders of the window:

```
If sprTank.SpriteHeight >= 250 Then
      ' Draw the background
      sprBack.SpriteHandle = gBkGnd0
      sprBack.DrawSprite

      ' Set initial size of sprite
      sprTank.SpriteWidth = 81
```

```
      sprTank.SpriteHeight = 81

      ' Place tank at initial point
      sprTank.SpriteLeft = 40
      sprTank.SpriteTop = 40
   End If
```

These statements examine the value of the SpriteHeight property, and if this property exceeds 250 pixels, the entire background picture is drawn inside WinG:

```
' Draw the background
sprBack.SpriteHandle = gBkGnd0
sprBack.DrawSprite
```

and the sprite's size and coordinates are initialized to the initial location and size:

25

```
' Set initial size of sprite
sprTank.SpriteWidth = 81
sprTank.SpriteHeight = 81

' Place tank at initial point
sprTank.SpriteLeft = 40
sprTank.SpriteTop = 40
```

So far, the area covered by the old location of the sprite has been redrawn in the WinG window, the size of the sprTank has been increased, and the contents of the sprTank sprite have been drawn in WinG. It is now time to slam the contents of WinG into the application window:

```
' Slam WinG into the screen.
sprBack.SlamIt
```

The Exit Sub statement is then executed to terminate the procedure:

```
Exit Sub
```

On the next execution of the Timer1_Timer( ) procedure, the size of the sprTank control is increased again, so now the tank appears larger. This process continues, and it gives the user the illusion that the tank is advancing forward.

The Left-To-Right Animation

The next block of statements in the Timer1_Timer( ) procedure is very similar to the code that performs the Forward animation. However, now the tank is shown to move from left to right. Let's go over the code quickly.

An If statement is used to determine the value of gDirection:

```
If gDirection = "LeftToRight" Then
    .......................................
    ... Perform the Left to Right animation ...
    .......................................
End If
```

The code under the If statement changes the value of the Left property of the Sprite control according to the speed scroll's bar position:

```
sprTank.SpriteLeft = _
    sprTank.SpriteLeft + _
    (11 - frmControlPanel.hsbSpeed.Value)
```

Then we determine whether the TankR0.BMP picture or the TankR1.BMP picture should be displayed:

```
TankFrame = TankFrame + 1
    If TankFrame >= 2 Then TankFrame = 0
    Select Case TankFrame
        Case 0
            sprTank.SpriteHandle = gTankR0
        Case 1
            sprTank.SpriteHandle = gTankR1
    End Select
```

The sprite is drawn inside WinG:

```
sprTank.DrawSprite
```

An If statement is executed to make sure that the sprite was not moved too far to the left:

```
If sprTank.SpriteLeft >= 450 Then
    ' Draw the background
    sprBack.SpriteHandle = gBkGnd0
    sprBack.DrawSprite

    ' Set initial size of sprite
    frmMySprite.sprTank.SpriteWidth = 209
    frmMySprite.sprTank.SpriteHeight = 121

    ' Place tank at initial point
    frmMySprite.sprTank.SpriteLeft = 20
    frmMySprite.sprTank.SpriteTop = 200
End If
```

In these statements, if the sprite was moved too far to the left, its coordinates and size are initialized.

Finally, the WinG contents are slammed:

```
' Slam WinG into the screen.
sprBack.SlamIt
```

The Right-To-Left Animation

The next block of code in the Timer1_Timer( ) procedure is responsible for performing the right-to-left animation. This code is very similar to the left-to-right animation code. Of course, now the animation shows the tank moving from right to left, so the SpriteLeft property is decreased in each execution of the Timer1_Timer( ) procedure:

```
sprTank.SpriteLeft = _
        sprTank.SpriteLeft - _
        (11 - frmControlPanel.hsbSpeed.Value)
```

And now the TankL0.BMP and TankL1.BMP pictures are drawn:

```
TankFrame = TankFrame + 1
If TankFrame >= 2 Then TankFrame = 0
    Select Case TankFrame
            Case 0
            sprTank.SpriteHandle = gTankL0
            Case 1
            sprTank.SpriteHandle = gTankL1
    End Select
sprTank.DrawSprite
```

The Backward Animation

The last block of statements in the Timer1_Timer( ) procedure performs the Backward animation. This code is similar to the previous animation code you've added.

You accomplish the Backward animation by stretching the sprite from its bottom by a negative number:

```
sprTank.StretchBottom _
        -(11 - frmControlPanel.hsbSpeed.Value)
```

and stretching the sprite from its right side by a negative number:

```
sprTank.StretchRight _
        -(11 - frmControlPanel.hsbSpeed.Value)
```

Then the TankB0.BMP and TankB1.BMP pictures are drawn in the WinG window:

```
TankFrame = TankFrame + 1

    If TankFrame >= 2 Then TankFrame = 0
    Select Case TankFrame
        Case 0
        sprTank.SpriteHandle = gTankB0
        Case 1
        sprTank.SpriteHandle = gTankB1
    End Select
    sprTank.DrawSprite
```

You've now finished writing the code of the frmMySprite form. In the next section you'll write the code of the frmControlPanel form.

The General Declarations Section of the frmControlPanel Form

As usual, we begin with the General Declarations section:

- Enter the following code in the General Declarations section of the frmControlPanel form:

```
Option Explicit
```

This statement forces variable declarations.

The Load Event of the frmControlPanel Form

Next we attach code to the Load event of the frmControlPanel form.

• Enter the following code in the Form_Load( ) procedure of the frmControl-Panel form:

```
Private Sub Form_Load( )

    If gDirection = "Forward" Then
        frmControlPanel.optForward.Value = True
    End If

    If gDirection = "Backward" Then
        frmControlPanel.optBackward.Value = True
    End If

    If gDirection = "LeftToRight" Then
        frmControlPanel.optRight.Value = True
    End If

    If gDirection = "RightToLeft" Then
        frmControlPanel.optLeft.Value = True
    End If

    If gDirection = "NoMotion" Then
        frmControlPanel.optNoMotion.Value = True
    End If

    lblSpeed.Caption = _
        "Speed: " + Str(110 - hsbSpeed.Value * 10) + " mph"

End Sub
```

This code executes If statements that determine which option button should be selected. For example, if gDirection is equal to Forward, then the optForward option button is selected:

```
If gDirection = "Forward" Then

    frmControlPanel.optForward.Value = True
End If
```

Also, the speed label is updated so that it displays the current position of the speed scroll bar:

```
lblSpeed.Caption = _
    "Speed: " + Str(110 - hsbSpeed.Value * 10) + " mph"
```

25

Note that when you designed the scroll bar, you set the Min property of the scroll bar to 10, and the Max property to 1. So if the scroll bar is at its extreme left side, for example, the Value property of the scroll bar is equal to 10. This means that the Caption of the speed label shows the following speed:

$$110 - 10 \times 10 = 110 - 100 = 10$$

And if the scroll bar is at its extreme right position, the Value property of the scroll bar is equal to 1. This means that the Caption of the speed label shows the following speed:

$$110 - 1 \times 10 = 110 - 10 = 100$$

The Exit Program Button of the frmControlPanel Form

You'll now attach code to the Exit button of the frmControlPanel form.

- Enter the following code in the cmdExitProgram_Click( ) procedure of the frmControlPanel form:

```
Private Sub cmdExitProgram_Click( )

    Unload frmMySprite

End Sub
```

This code unloads the frmMySprite form.

The Exit Menu of the frmControlPanel Form

You'll now attach code to the Exit menu of the frmControlPanel form.

- Enter the following code in the mnuExit_Click( ) procedure of the frmControlPanel form:

```
Private Sub mnuExit_Click( )

    cmdExitProgram_Click

End Sub
```

This code executes the cmdExitProgram_Click( ) procedure of the frmControlPanel form. So clicking the Exit Program button has the same effect as selecting Exit from the File menu.

The Forward Option Button of the frmControlPanel Form

You'll now attach code to the Forward option button of the frmControlPanel form.

- Enter the following code in the optForward_Click( ) procedure of the frmControlPanel form:

```
Private Sub optForward_Click( )

        gDirection = "Forward"

        ' Draw the background
        frmMySprite.sprBack.SpriteHandle = gBkGnd0
        frmMySprite.sprBack.DrawSprite

        ' Set initial size of sprite
        frmMySprite.sprTank.SpriteWidth = 81
        frmMySprite.sprTank.SpriteHeight = 81

        ' Place tank at initial point
        frmMySprite.sprTank.SpriteLeft = 40
        frmMySprite.sprTank.SpriteTop = 40

End Sub
```

This code is executed whenever the user clicks the Forward option button. First the gDirection variable is set to Forward:

```
gDirection = "Forward"
```

The background picture is redrawn inside the WinG window:

```
' Draw the background
frmMySprite.sprBack.SpriteHandle = gBkGnd0
frmMySprite.sprBack.DrawSprite
```

The size of the sprTank sprite is then set to its initial size:

```
' Set initial size of sprite
frmMySprite.sprTank.SpriteWidth = 81
frmMySprite.sprTank.SpriteHeight = 81
```

And the sprite is placed at the starting point:

```
' Place tank at initial point
frmMySprite.sprTank.SpriteLeft = 40
frmMySprite.sprTank.SpriteTop = 40
```

As you saw earlier in this chapter, the code in the Timer1_Timer( ) procedure of the frmMySprite form executes an If statement that checks the value of gDirection, and if gDirection is equal to Forward, the Forward animation is displayed. Here you set the sprTank to its initial size and location because you want the Forward animation to start at a certain initial location.

How can you determine the initial size and location of the sprTank sprite? During the visual design of the frmMySprite form, you can highlight the sprTank sprite, and examine the Properties window. As you can see in Figure 25.4, the Properties window of the sprTank sprite (when SpriteFileName is equal to the TankF0.BMP picture) shows that the Left and Top properties of the control are set to 40, and the SpriteHeight and SpriteWidth properties are set to 81. The code that you typed inside the optForward_Click( ) procedure sets the size and location of the sprTank to these settings.

FIGURE 25.4:

The Properties window of the Sprite control

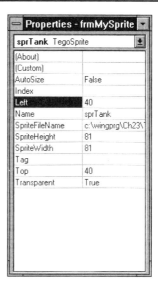

Properties - frmMySprite	
sprTank TegoSprite	
(About)	
(Custom)	
AutoSize	False
Index	
Left	40
Name	sprTank
SpriteFileName	c:\wingprg\Ch23\
SpriteHeight	81
SpriteWidth	81
Tag	
Top	40
Transparent	True

NOTE During design time, the top and left coordinates of the upper-left corner of the Sprite control are denoted as Left and Top (see Figure 24.5 in the previous chapter). During runtime, the Left and Top properties of the Sprite control are denoted as SpriteLeft and SpriteTop.

The Backward Option Button of the frmControlPanel Form

You'll now attach code to the Backward option button of the frmControlPanel form.

- Enter the following code in the optBackward_Click( ) procedure of the frmControlPanel form:

```
Private Sub optBackward_Click( )
```

```
            gDirection = "Backward"

            ' Draw the background
            frmMySprite.sprBack.SpriteHandle = gBkGnd0
            frmMySprite.sprBack.DrawSprite

            ' Set initial size of sprite
            frmMySprite.sprTank.SpriteWidth = 255
            frmMySprite.sprTank.SpriteHeight = 241

            ' Place tank at initial point
            frmMySprite.sprTank.SpriteLeft = 200
            frmMySprite.sprTank.SpriteTop = 80

    End Sub
```

This code is very similar to the code that you entered in the optForward_Click( ) procedure. First the gDirection variable is set to Backward:

```
    gDirection = "Backward"
```

The background picture is drawn inside WinG:

```
    ' Draw the background
    frmMySprite.sprBack.SpriteHandle = gBkGnd0
    frmMySprite.sprBack.DrawSprite
```

And finally, we set the initial size and initial location of the sprTank sprite:

```
    ' Set initial size of sprite
            frmMySprite.sprTank.SpriteWidth = 255
            frmMySprite.sprTank.SpriteHeight = 241

            ' Place tank at initial point
            frmMySprite.sprTank.SpriteLeft = 200
            frmMySprite.sprTank.SpriteTop = 80
```

Again, you can determine the initial size and location of the sprite for the Backward animation as follows:

- Set the SpriteFileName property of the Sprite control to the C:\WinGPrg\CH23\TankB0.BMP file.

- Highlight the sprTank sprite.

- Drag and size the sprTank sprite to the initial location and initial size where you want the Backward animation to start.

- Display the Properties window of the sprTank sprite and write down its Left, Top, SpriteHeight, and SpriteWidth properties.

- In the Timer1_Timer( ) procedure of the frmMySprite form (under the If statement that performs the Backward animation) and in the cmdBackward_Click( ) procedure of the frmControlPanel form, set the initial size and location for the Backward animation.

The Left To Right Option Button of the frmControlPanel Form

25

You'll now attach code to the Left To Right option button of the frmControlPanel form.

- Enter the following code in the optLeft_Click( ) procedure of the frmControlPanel form:

```
Private Sub optLeft_Click( )

        gDirection = "RightToLeft"

        ' Draw the background
        frmMySprite.sprBack.SpriteHandle = gBkGnd0
        frmMySprite.sprBack.DrawSprite

        ' Set initial size of sprite
        frmMySprite.sprTank.SpriteWidth = 193
        frmMySprite.sprTank.SpriteHeight = 137

        ' Place tank at initial point
        frmMySprite.sprTank.SpriteLeft = 300
        frmMySprite.sprTank.SpriteTop = 80

    ' Slam WinG into the screen.
    frmMySprite.sprBack.SlamIt


End Sub
```

This code is similar to the code you entered in the optForward_Click( ) and optBackward_Click( ) procedures of the frmControlPanel form. Of course, here you set the initial size and location of the Sprite control for the Right to Left animation.

The Right To Left Option Button of the frmControlPanel Form

You'll now attach code to the Right To Left option button of the frmControlPanel form.

Enter the following code in the optRight_Click( ) procedure of the frmControlPanel form:

```
Private Sub optRight_Click( )

        gDirection = "LeftToRight"

        ' Draw the background
        frmMySprite.sprBack.SpriteHandle = gBkGnd0
        frmMySprite.sprBack.DrawSprite

        ' Set initial size of sprite
        frmMySprite.sprTank.SpriteWidth = 209
        frmMySprite.sprTank.SpriteHeight = 121

        ' Place tank at initial point
        frmMySprite.sprTank.SpriteLeft = 20
        frmMySprite.sprTank.SpriteTop = 200

    ' Slam WinG into the screen.
    frmMySprite.sprBack.SlamIt


    End Sub
```

This code is similar to the code you entered in the optForward_Click( ), optBackward_Click( ), and optLeft_Click( ) procedures of the frmControlPanel form. Here you set the initial size and location of the Sprite control for the Left to Right animation.

The No Tank Motion Option Button of the frmControlPanel Form

You'll now attach code to the No Tank Motion option button of the frmControl-Panel form.

- Enter the following code in the optNoMotion_Click( ) procedure of the frmControlPanel form:

```
Private Sub optNoMotion_Click( )

    gDirection = "NoMotion"

End Sub
```

25

This code sets the value of the gDirection variable to NoMotion. Recall that inside the Timer1_Timer( ) procedure of the frmMySprite form you execute an If statement that checks the value of gDirection. If gDirection is equal to NoMotion, no animation is performed.

The About Menu of the frmControlPanel Form

You'll now attach code to the About menu of the frmControlPanel form.

- Enter the following code in the mnuAbout_Click( ) procedure of the frmControlPanel form:

```
Private Sub mnuAbout_Click( )

    frmAbout.Show 1

End Sub
```

This code displays the About window as a modal window (the parameter of the Show method is equal to 1). You'll implement the frmAbout form in the next section.

Implementing the frmAbout Form

You'll now implement the frmAbout form.

- Select Form from the Insert menu of Visual Basic, and save the new form as About.FRM in the C:\WinGPrg\CH23 directory.

- Implement the frmAbout form with the Properties settings listed in Table 25.3. When you're finished, the form should look as shown in Figure 25.5.

TABLE 25.3: The Properties of the frmAbout Form

Object: Form	
Name: frmAbout	
Property	**Value**
BorderStyle	1 'Fixed Single
Caption	"About"
Height	5910
Left	1095
MaxButton	0 'False
MinButton	0 'False
Picture	C:\WinGPrg\CH23\About.BMP
Top	660
Width	5985

Object: CommandButton	
Name: cmdOK	
Property	**Value**
Caption	"&OK"
Height	495
Left	4320

TABLE 25.3: The Properties of the frmAbout Form (continued)

Object: CommandButton	
Name: cmdOK	
Top	4680
WIdth	735

FIGURE 25.5:

The frmAbout form in design mode

25

Attaching Code to the Click Event of the frmAbout Form

You'll now attach code to the Click event of the OK button of the frmAbout form.

- Enter the following code in the cmdOK_Click( ) procedure of the frmAbout form:

```
Private Sub cmdOK_Click( )
```

```
    Unload Me

  End Sub
```

This code unloads the frmAbout form whenever the user clicks the OK button of the frmAbout form.

Summary

In this chapter you completed writing the code of the frmMySprite form, and you implemented the frmControlPanel form.

Here is a short summary of how sprites operate: during design time, you set the SpriteFileName property of the Sprite control, drag and size this control, and examine the properties of the sprite. This enables you to determine the Top, Left, Sprite-Height, and SpriteWidth properties of the Sprite control (so that you'll be able to set the initial size and location of the sprite during runtime).

During runtime you perform the animation as follows:

- You draw the background picture (or a portion of the background picture) into the WinG window.

- You draw the animated sprite into the WinG window.

- You slam the contents of WinG into the window of your application.

Because the animated sprite "accepts" the background on which it is placed, you can perform some very powerful animation in your program with great ease.

CHAPTER

TWENTY-SIX

Adding Sound Effects to the Animation

26

In this chapter you'll add sound effects to the MySprite program. Recall that this program lets the user move a tank in various directions. But in the program's current form, no sound is played as the tank moves. In this chapter you'll add sound to the program.

Opening a Sound Session

Upon starting the MySprite program, the frmMySprite form is loaded, so the Form_Load() procedure is where we will put the code for opening a WAV session.

- Add code to open a WAV session in the Form_Load() procedure of the frmMySprite form, so that the procedure looks as follows:

```
Private Sub Form_Load()

Dim Path

Tegomm1.Visible = False

gDirection = "NoMotion"

' Extract the directory name from
' which this application is executed
Path = App.Path
If Right(Path, 1) <> "\" Then
   Path = Path + "\"
End If

Tegomm1.FileName = Path + "8Tank5.WAV"
Tegomm1.DeviceType = "WaveAudio"
Tegomm1.Command = "Open"
If Tegomm1.Error <> 0 Then
  MsgBox _
    "Can't open the " + Path + "8Tank5.WAV" + " file.", _
      vbCritical, _
      "Error"
End If

' Initialize the sprite controls.
sprBack.InitializeSprite Me.hWnd
sprTank.InitializeSprite Me.hWnd
```

```
' Open the sprites used in show.
gBkGnd0 = sprBack.OpenSprite(Path + "BkGnd0.bmp")
gTankF0 = sprBack.OpenSprite(Path + "TankF0.bmp")
gTankF1 = sprBack.OpenSprite(Path + "TankF1.bmp")
gTankR0 = sprBack.OpenSprite(Path + "TankR0.bmp")
gTankR1 = sprBack.OpenSprite(Path + "TankR1.bmp")
gTankL0 = sprBack.OpenSprite(Path + "TankL0.bmp")
gTankL1 = sprBack.OpenSprite(Path + "TankL1.bmp")
gTankB0 = sprBack.OpenSprite(Path + "TankB0.bmp")
gTankB1 = sprBack.OpenSprite(Path + "TankB1.bmp")

End Sub
```

In this code, we first extract the path from which the program is executed:

```
' Extract the directory name from
' which this application is executed
Path = App.Path
If Right(Path, 1) <> "\" Then
Path = Path + "\"
End If
```

This path, together with the WAV filename, is then assigned to the FileName property of the Multimedia control:

```
Tegomm1.FileName = Path + "8Tank5.WAV"
```

The 8Tank5.WAV file is assumed to reside in the same directory as the MySprite program.

The DeviceType property of the Multimedia control is set to WaveAudio:

```
Tegomm1.DeviceType = "WaveAudio"
```

And then the Open command is issued:

```
Tegomm1.Command = "Open"
```

An If statement verifies that the Open command was executed successfully:

```
If Tegomm1.Error <> 0 Then
   MsgBox _
   "Can't open the " + Path + "8Tank5.WAV" + " file.", _
   vbCritical, _
   "Error"
End If
```

26

477

Playing the File During the Forward Animation

When the user click the Forward option button, the Forward animation starts.

- Add code to the optForward_Click() procedure of the frmConrolPanel form, so that the procedure looks as follows:

```
Private Sub optForward_Click()

        frmMySprite.Tegomm1.Command = "Prev"
        frmMySprite.Tegomm1.Command = "Play"

        gDirection = "Forward"

        ' Draw the background
        frmMySprite.sprBack.SpriteHandle = gBkGndO
        frmMySprite.sprBack.DrawSprite

        ' Set initial size of sprite
        frmMySprite.sprTank.SpriteWidth = 81
        frmMySprite.sprTank.SpriteHeight = 81

        ' Place tank at initial point
        frmMySprite.sprTank.SpriteLeft = 40
        frmMySprite.sprTank.SpriteTop = 40

End Sub
```

The code that you added at the beginning of the procedure rewinds the WAV file:

```
frmMySprite.Tegomm1.Command = "Prev"
```

and then the Play command is issued:

```
frmMySprite.Tegomm1.Command = "Play"
```

Note that in these statements, the name of the form (frmMySprite) precedes the name of the Multimedia control (Tegomm1). This is necessary because you are accessing an object located in another form. That is, you access the Tegomm1 control from the frmControlPanel form, but this control resides in the frmMySprite form.

Playing the File During the Other Animation Shows

In a similar manner, you have to execute the Prev and Play commands whenever the user clicks the Backward, Left to Right, and Right to Left option buttons.

- Add the Prev and Play commands to the beginning of the cmdBackward_Click() procedure of the frmControlPanel form, so that the procedure looks as follows:

```
Private Sub optBackward_Click()

    frmMySprite.Tegomm1.Command = "Prev"
    frmMySprite.Tegomm1.Command = "Play"
.....
End Sub
```

26

- Add the Prev and Play commands to the beginning of the cmdRight_Click() procedure of the frmControlPanel form, so that the procedure looks as follows:

```
Private Sub optRight_Click()

    frmMySprite.Tegomm1.Command = "Prev"
    frmMySprite.Tegomm1.Command = "Play"

End Sub
```

- Add the Prev and Play commands to the beginning of the cmdLeft_Click() procedure of the frmControlPanel form, so that the procedure looks as follows:

```
Private Sub optLeft_Click()

    frmMySprite.Tegomm1.Command = "Prev"
    frmMySprite.Tegomm1.Command = "Play"

End Sub
```

Stopping the Playback

When the user clicks the No Tank Motion option button, the animation stops, and therefore the playback should also stop. You can issue the Stop command in the cmdNoMotion_Click() procedure of the frmControlPanel form, or you can issue this command in the Timer1_Timer() procedure of the frmMySprite form. We'll take the second alternative.

- Add the Stop command in the Timer1_Timer() procedure of the frmMySprite form, so that the procedure looks as follows:

```
Private Sub Timer1_Timer()

    Static TankFrame

    ' Don't perform animation when the
    ' program's window is minimized.
    If Me.WindowState = 1 Then
       Exit Sub
    End If

    ' Don't perform animation when the
    ' No Tank Motion option button is selected.
    If gDirection = "NoMotion" Then
          Tegomm1.Command = "Stop"
          Exit Sub
    End If
    ...
End Sub
```

As you can see from the preceding code, when gDirection is equal to NoMotion, the Stop command is issued:

```
If gDirection = "NoMotion" Then
      Tegomm1.Command = "Stop"
      Exit Sub
End If
```

Automatically Rewinding the WAV File

You'll now add code that rewinds the WAV file and starts playing it all over again whenever the file has been played in its entirety. So as long as a tank is shown moving, there will be a playback of sound in the background.

- Add the following code in the Tegomm1_Done() procedure of the frmMySprite form:

```
Private Sub Tegomm1_Done()

    If Tegomm1.Position = Tegomm1.Length Then

        Tegomm1.Command = "Prev"
        Tegomm1.Command = "Play"

    End If

End Sub
```

This code uses an If statement to examine why the Done event occurred. If the Position property of the Multimedia control is equal to the Length property, it means that the entire WAV file has been played. So the code under the If statement rewinds the WAV file and issues the Play command.

26

Summary

In this chapter you added sound effects to the MySprite program. As you saw, the Multimedia control is used for playing the WAV file. Because the buttons of the Multimedia control are not used during the execution of the program, in the Form_Load() procedure of the frmMySprite form you set the Visible property of the Multimedia control to False. So from the point of view of the user, the playback is accomplished automatically. Whenever the program displays the animation, the sound of a moving tank plays in the background.

PART V

Creating Windows 3D Virtual Reality Games

CHAPTER

TWENTY-SEVEN

3D Virtual Reality Programs

27

In the next chapter you'll start writing 3D virtual reality programs. As you'll see, writing programs of this type is actually very easy. And by using WinG technology and the multimedia tools on the accompanying CD-ROM, you'll be able to write powerful and fun Windows programs.

What Is a 3D Virtual Reality Program?

The term *virtual reality* has various meanings in the PC industry. For example, some software companies categorize their game programs as 3D virtual reality games.

Originally, the term *3D virtual reality program* meant a program that displays different 3D views according to the user's input. For example, a flight simulator program is a 3D virtual reality program. The user sees a display that looks exactly like the control panel in an airplane. The user activates the instruments of the control panel, and based on the particular switches and buttons pressed, the airplane takes off and flies. Another window displays the view that is seen from the cockpit of the aircraft—first the runway, then the view seen from the plane as it becomes airborne. How real is the view? That depends on the quality of the program. For example, a very expensive flight simulator may display the real view that is seen from the aircraft based on maps stored in the computer, the speed and direction at which the virtual aircraft is moving, wind conditions, and other factors.

As you can see, virtual reality programs have some serious applications. By using flight simulators, airline companies and the military can train pilots without the risk of an accident. Moreover, there is no need to spend money on fuel and maintenance, and the instructor can simulate a variety of weather conditions, instrument failures, and so on.

Other virtual reality applications include medicine, where complicated surgery is performed on virtual patients, and architecture, where a whole house or a building is constructed virtually. Potential investors and buyers can "travel" through the virtual house, test its conveniences, and "look" through the windows of the house to view the outside.

So we can define a 3D virtual reality application as a program that lets the user "walk" through a virtual environment and responds by displaying the various views according to the user input.

Arcade-Style Virtual Reality

Many amusement parks and arcades now include a virtual reality apparatus where for a small fee, you are attached to a set of goggles and participate in a virtual reality program. As shown in Figure 27.1, the goggles serve as a miniature screen. This gives the user a better sense of reality than a regular screen. Also, instead of using the keyboard or the mouse to move the player through the environment, these systems use a set of sensors connected to the user that transmit the user's movements to the program. If the game involves a gun it's also connected to a sensor, and depending on the direction of the gun, the program "knows" whether the user hits or misses the monsters that are displayed through the goggles.

27

FIGURE 27.1:

An arcade-style virtual reality apparatus

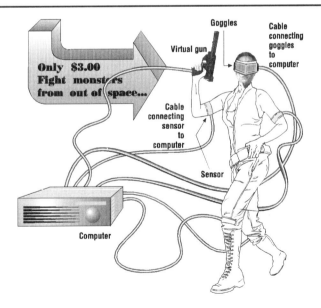

PC-Based 3D Virtual Reality Programs

A virtual reality system (hardware and software) can be very expensive (as is the case with a sophisticated flight simulator). Nowadays, 3D virtual reality programs are also implemented on multimedia personal computer systems. Because these applications require extensive use of the monitor, WinG technology is essential. During the operation of the 3D program, the computer is busy performing three major tasks:

1. Continuously displaying the current 3D view.

2. Taking user input.

3. Calculating the next 3D view to be displayed.

As you can see, the computer has a lot to do, and it must do all of these tasks in real time. For example, if the user moves to the right, the virtual reality program should immediately respond and display a different view.

What Is the Control Panel?

A 3D virtual reality program needs a way for the user to tell the program how he or she wants to move. We've seen that one way of accomplishing this is to use sensors, whose signals the program should interpret. A less expensive way to tell the program how to move is by using the mouse and keyboard, and by pushing various switches and buttons.

Typically, when implementing a 3D virtual reality program, you'll include a control panel window, which lets the user "move" in a 3D environment.

Generating 3D Views

Note that in previous chapters you implemented and executed a program that plays movie AVI files. As demonstrated, the movie AVI file is a video file that consists of a series of frames. So the AVI file is just a huge file composed of many BMP files (and a WAV file that serves as the sound track). By contrast, a 3D virtual reality program does not display the different views by extracting the views from BMP files. Instead, each view is generated from the previous view by performing complex mathematical calculations. In the following chapters, you'll create a sample program that does this.

Imagine a room with a square block in its center. One side of the block has the number 1 painted on it, another side has the number 2 painted on it, and so on. This block is shown in the middle of Figure 27.2.

FIGURE 27.2:

Rotating around a block

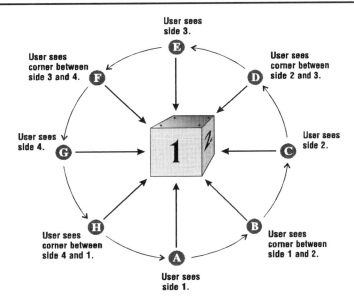

Your user will be able to move around this block. As the user moves around the block, different views of it are displayed. For example, at point A in Figure 27.2, the user will see the front of the block, with the number 1 painted on it. As the user moves counterclockwise around the block, he or she will see the corner of the block (between sides 1 and 2). View B in Figure 27.2 shows the block from this angle.

As you look at Figure 27.2, imagine yourself going through the sequence of points from A to H. You'll see a series of different sides and corners.

Of course, the 3D virtual reality program also needs to display the corresponding view from any point—for example, when the user is between points A and B.

But the angle of view is not the only consideration that has to be taken into account when displaying the objects. Figure 27.3 shows, for example, the view from point B of Figure 27.2. As the user gets closer to the object, it should appear larger. Figure 27.4 shows the result after getting closer to the object.

FIGURE 27.3:

The view from point B of Figure 27.2

FIGURE 27.4:

The view from point B of Figure 27.2 as the user approaches the object

The example we've considered so far is very simple. But what if we add another object in front of the block? Suppose that a monster is walking around. Your program will now have to show the monster in front of the block. The monster will only cover a portion of the block, and the remainder of the block has to be displayed at the proper angle and size.

These are just some of the tasks that have to be performed. As you can see, the computer has a lot to do while executing a 3D virtual reality program. Fortunately, thanks to some very useful and powerful software tools (which are included in the CD-ROM and which you'll use in subsequent chapters), writing the 3D virtual reality program is very easy, so that you can concentrate on the creativity and "game" aspect of your program, instead of writing code that has been written by others already.

27

Summary

In this chapter you learned that basically, a 3D virtual reality program lets the user "travel" in a 3D environment. The user uses the keyboard, mouse, pushbuttons, and switches, and the 3D program responds by displaying different 3D views based on the user actions.

WinG technology is required for the implementation of 3D based virtual reality programs, because the computer is involved in complex operations. It must take the user's input, interpret it, and display a different 3D view based on that input. And everything has to be done in real time.

In the next chapter you'll start implementing a 3D virtual reality program.

CHAPTER

TWENTY-EIGHT

Floor (FLR) Files for 3D Virtual Reality

As you saw in the last chapter, in a 3D virtual reality program the user is able to "move" in a 3D environment. The 3D program that you'll write in subsequent chapters will convert a two-dimensional (2D) drawing to a 3D picture, and then will let you "travel" inside the 3D space. So as you can see, the first thing that you have to do is prepare a 2D drawing.

Preparing Your 2D Drawings

As your first 2D drawing, you'll create a very simple drawing of one floor of a building. For simplicity, let's assume that the only building blocks you can use in your 3D pictures are cubes such as the one shown in Figure 28.1.

FIGURE 28.1:

The cube that serves as the building block of your 3D drawing

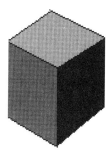

NOTE   The environment or space in which a 3D virtual reality game takes place is known as a *floor*, and the 2D drawings from which (as you'll see) these environments are generated are known as *floor files*. This usage refers to the floors of a building and dates back to the mainframe days, when 3D computer graphics were first developed for architectural modeling. In the context of games, you might think of a floor as a space station's deck or level.

A 3D picture of a simple floor is shown in Figure 28.2. As you can see, it is one big floor with no rooms or windows. Also, it has no pictures on the walls, tanks, people, or any other objects in it. The ceiling is not shown, so that you can see the inside of the floor.

FIGURE 28.2:

A very simple floor

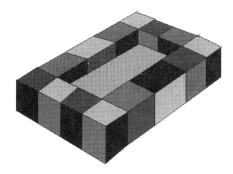

28

NOTE   Although the simple floor shown in Figure 28.2 has no objects or rooms in it, in subsequent chapters you'll learn how to make the floor as sophisticated as you want. That is, you'll be able to add pictures on the wall, people walking through the halls, tables and chairs, plants, and everything else that you may think is appropriate.

To begin creating this 2D drawing, we can represent the cubes as a series of ones like the following:

```
1111
1  1
1  1
1  1
1111
```

As you can see, each 1 represents a single cube.

Now let's suppose that you add dividers to the floor. Of course you can design the floor any way you like. One possible design is to add the dividers in the following manner:

```
1111
1   1
11  1
1   1
1111
```

The corresponding 3D version of this 2D drawing is shown in Figure 28.3.

FIGURE 28.3:

Adding a divider to the empty floor of Figure 28.1

As another example, the floor can be designed as follows:

```
1111
11  1
1   1
1  11
1111
```

This 2D drawing is shown as a 3D drawing in Figure 28.4.

FIGURE 28.4:

A different design for the empty
floor of Figure 28.2

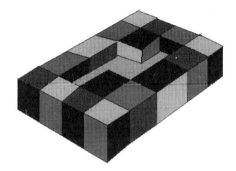

As you can see, by using these simple cubes, you can design the most complicated floor you can think of. The dimensions of the cube are not important. The drawings of Figures 28.2 through 28.4 are 4×5 drawings (4 columns and 5 rows). But you can use the cubes to build larger floors. For example, you can build a 50×50 floor (50 columns and 50 rows), or any other size that you want.

As an example, look at the following 10×10 2D drawing:

```
1111111111
1        1
1        1
11111111 1
1        1
111      1
1 1      1
1 11111  1
1        1
1111111111
```

This 2D drawing is translated to the 3D picture shown in Figure 28.5. (Notice that now the "cubes" have been made thinner and more realistic. Again, the point is that they are simply building blocks, whose dimensions don't matter in the initial design stage.)

28

FIGURE 28.5:

Dividing a floor

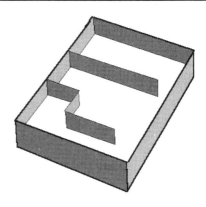

Creating a 2D Drawing with Your Text Editor

The easiest way to create a 2D drawing like those you've just seen is by using a simple text editor such as the Notepad program in Windows (or any other text editor).

In the \WinGPrg\Floors directory of the CD-ROM you'll see several files with the file extension FLR (e.g., MyFloor.FLR). These FLR files are regular text files that represent 2D drawings of floors.

For now, you should only use the numeral 1 as the building block of your 2D drawings. (In subsequent chapters you'll use additional "building blocks.")

- Use your text editor to create several 2D drawings. When creating these drawings, use only the 1 and space characters.

- Save your 2D drawings as files with the FLR file extension.

Creating 2D Drawings with Your Text Editor

When designing your 2D drawings, enclose the floor with 1's. For example, the following 2D drawing is a valid floor:

```
1111111111111111
1               1
1   1111111     1
1   1       1   1
1   1       1   1
1   11   111    1
1               1
1111111111111111
```

However, the following 2D drawing is invalid, because there is a missing 1 on the top row:

```
11111111111111  1
1               1
1   1111111     1
1   1       1   1
1   1       1   1
1   11   111    1
1               1
1111111111111111
```

28

Summary

In this chapter you learned about the building blocks of a 3D virtual reality application. As you saw, the "building material" consists of a simple cube. By putting the cubes together, you can generate a 3D floor with "rooms" in it.

Your job as the designer of the 3D virtual reality game program is to provide your user with the 2D drawing. Alternatively, you can create a program that lets your user design the 2D floor. In this chapter you learned how to use a simple text editor like Windows Notepad to generate 2D drawings in which the numeral 1 represents each block.

Traveling within a 3D Floor

In the previous chapter you learned how to generate 2D floor files (*.FLR files) with a text editor such a Notepad. In this chapter you'll execute the MyGame.EXE program, a program that loads a 2D floor file, converts it to a 3D picture, and then lets the user travel inside the 3D floor. In subsequent chapters you'll write the My-Game program yourself.

Executing the MyGame Program

Begin by running the MyGame.EXE program from the \WinGPrg\EXE directory. The window of the MyGame program appears as shown in Figure 29.1.

FIGURE 29.1:

The window of the MyGame program

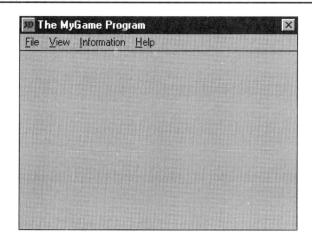

The MyGame window has the following menus: File, View, Information, and Help. These menus are shown in Figures 29.2 through 29.5.

FIGURE 29.2:

The File menu of the MyGame
program

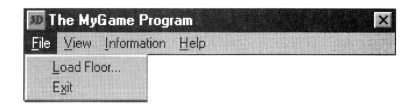

FIGURE 29.3:

The View menu of the MyGame
program

FIGURE 29.4:

The Information menu of the
MyGame program

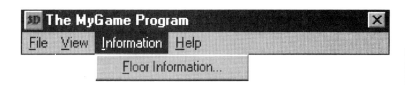

29

FIGURE 29.5:

The Help menu of the MyGame
program

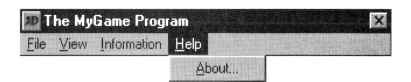

• Select About from the Help menu.

MyGame responds by displaying the About window (see Figure 29.6).

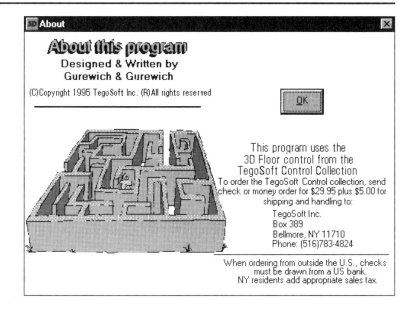

• Click the OK button to close the About window.

Loading a Floor File

You'll now load a floor file.

• Select Load Floor from the File menu of MyGame.

MyGame responds by displaying an Open dialog box that lets you select a file.

• Select the C:\WinGPrg\Floors\Floor01.FLR file.

MyGame responds by loading the Floor01.FLR file. As you can see in Figure 29.7, the caption of the window now indicates that the Floor01.FLR floor has been loaded.

FIGURE 29.7:

The window of the MyGame program after loading the Floor01.FLR floor

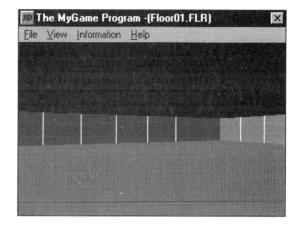

Before getting into the 3D aspect of the program, let's look at the 2D drawing of the Floor01.FLR floor:

- Select ASCII View from the View menu.

MyGame responds by displaying the 2D view of the Floor01.FLR floor, as shown in Figure 29.8.

FIGURE 29.8:

Displaying Floor01.FLR in ASCII format, with empty cells represented by spaces, and the user's current position indicated by the + character.

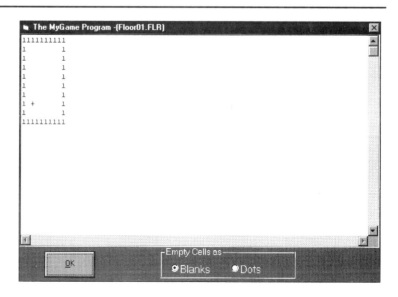

Note that in Figure 29.8, an empty cell is represented by a space. The "+" character represents the cell where the user is located. So as you can see, the user is currently located in the cell three rows from the bottom and three columns from the left.

- Click the Dots option button (at the bottom of the ASCII View window).

MyGame responds by displaying the 2D drawing of the Floor01.FLR floor, this time with each empty cell represented by a dot (see Figure 29.9).

FIGURE 29.9:

Displaying Floor01.FLR in ASCII format with empty cells represented by dots

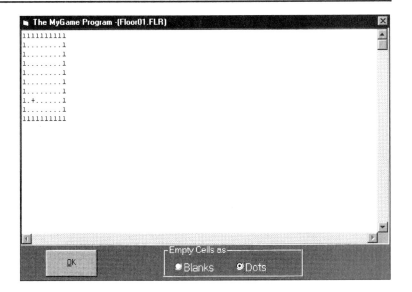

The MyGame program lets you display the 2D drawing with or without dots for the sake of flexibility. When you take a look at the 2D drawing, you probably want the empty cells to appear as blanks, to get a better understanding of the general structure of the floor. But when it is time to examine the 2D drawing in greater detail, it is convenient to display the dots so that you can count them to measure distances.

NOTE   The + character in the ASCII view represents the cell in which the user is located. However, it does not provide more precise information about the user's location within the cell.

- Click the OK button of the ASCII View window to return to the 3D view.

Traveling around the 3D Floor01.FLR Floor

You'll now travel around the Floor01.FLR floor. Figures 29.10 and 29.11 are examples of different views that you'll see along the way.

FIGURE 29.10:

Viewing the corner where two walls intersect

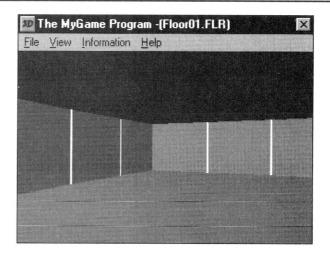

29

- Use the arrow keys on your keyboard to move in different directions around the floor.

FIGURE 29.11:

Getting closer to the corner where two walls intersect

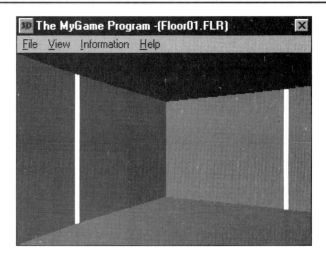

The MyGame program uses the following keys for moving on the floor:

- The up-arrow (↑) key is used to move forward.

- The down-arrow (↓) key is used to move backward.

- The left-arrow (←) key is used for rotating to the left (counterclockwise).

- The right-arrow (→) key is used to rotate to the right (clockwise).

Note that the user's position changes only when pressing the ↑ or ↓ key. That is, when pressing one of these two keys, the user moves closer toward or farther away from the walls. When pressing the → or ← key, only the direction of the user changes. This is illustrated in Figures 29.12 and 29.13. In Figure 29.12, the user sees a portion of the wall. After pressing the ← key, the user sees the corner shown in Figure 29.13. Figures 29.14 and 29.15 show what these views look like on the screen.

When you press the ↑ key, the direction remains the same. For example, if you are currently facing the wall, it is as if you are stepping toward the wall. The direction also remains the same when you press the ↓ key. If you are currently facing the wall, it is as if you are stepping backward away from the wall. The wall appears larger as you move forward and smaller as you move backward.

FIGURE 29.12:

The user's original view

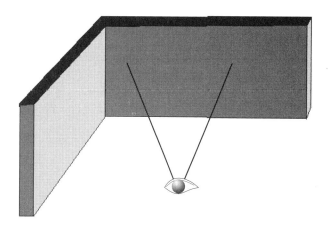

FIGURE 29.13:

The user's view after pressing the
left-arrow key

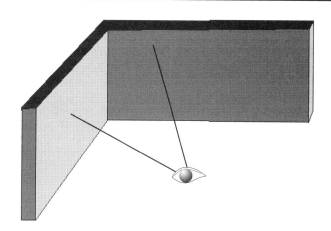

29

- Experiment with the MyGame program by going to all of its four corners, moving forward and backward, and rotating both counterclockwise and clockwise.

- Place yourself in the middle of the room, and then press the → key several times. In essence, it is as if you are standing on the same spot, and simply turning around. After pressing the right key several times, you'll see the same view that you started from.

FIGURE 29.14:

The screen corresponding to the user's view in Figure 29.12

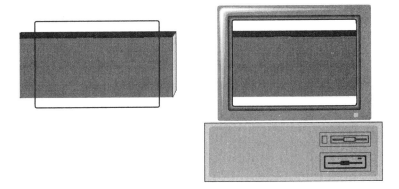

FIGURE 29.15:

The screen corresponding to the user's view in Figure 29.13

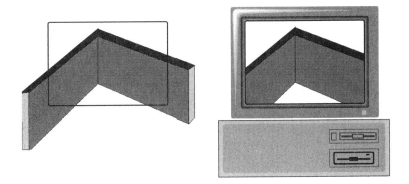

The MyGame program also includes the Information menu. We'll get back to this menu in the next chapter.

Displaying the Floor02.FLR Floor and Traveling around It

You'll now load and then travel around the Floor02.FLR floor. This file resides in the C:\WinGPrg\Floors directory. The drawing looks like this:

```
11111111111111111111
1                   1
1                   1
1       111111111   1
1               1   1
1       1       1   1
1       111111111   1
1                   1
1                   1
11111111111111111111
```

- Select Load Floor from the File menu of the MyGame program, and then select the \WinGPrg\Floors\Floor02.FLR file.

MyGame responds by loading the Floor02.FLR floor, and the 3D picture shown in the upper portion of Figure 29.16 is displayed. Note that the lower portion of Figure 29.16 shows the user's current view.

As you can see, once you load the floor, an initial coordinate position is set to determine the initial view. In the next chapter you'll write the code that sets the initial position and view angle.

- Select ASCII View from the View menu to display the ASCII view of the Floor02.FLR floor file.

MyGame responds by displaying the ASCII view of the Floor02.FLR file, as shown in Figure 29.17.

- Click the OK button of the ASCII view to close the window.

MyGame responds by returning to the main window, and the 3D picture is displayed again. As you can see in Figure 29.17, Floor02 contains an inner room. Let's get inside this room:

- Use the keyboard to move inside the inner room.

FIGURE 29.16:

The 3D picture displayed at the user's current view, along with the corresponding 2D drawing

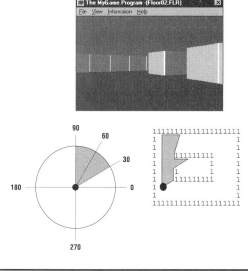

FIGURE 29.17:

The ASCII view of the Floor02.FLR file

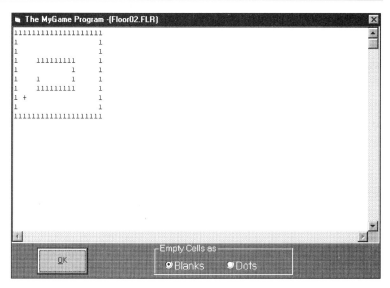

Figure 29.18 shows the 3D picture after getting closer to the entrance of the inner room. Figure 29.19 shows the 3D picture when you are at the entrance of the inner room. As you get inside the inner room, you'll see the view shown in Figure 29.20.

FIGURE 29.17:

Moving toward the entrance of the inner room

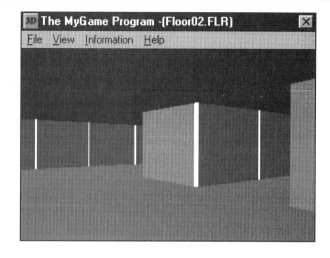

FIGURE 29.18:

At the entrance of the inner room

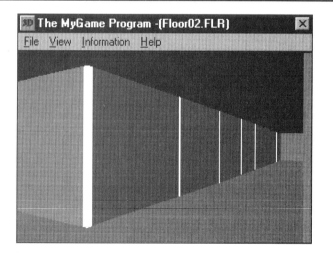

29

- Move forward inside the inner room, and then when you are just about in the middle of the room, press the right (or left) arrow key several times to rotate. Keep rotating until you see the entrance of the inner room (see Figure 29.21).

FIGURE 29.19:

Viewing the inner room

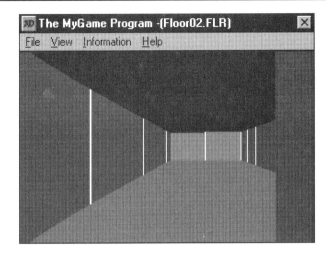

FIGURE 29.20:

Viewing the entrance of the inner room from inside

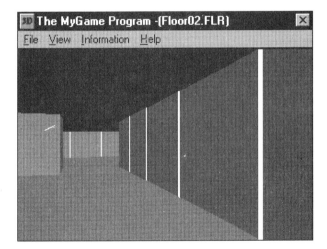

- Experiment with the Floor02 floor. For example, move out of the inner room, and then go around the inner room.

Now You Are on Your Own...

Use a text editor program such as Notepad to construct your own FLR files. Then, when you are ready, you can use them with the MyGame program:

- Select Load File from MyGame's File menu o, load the floor file that you prepared, and then travel through your floor.
- Select Exit from the File menu to terminate the MyGame program.

Summary

In this chapter you executed a very simple 3D virtual reality program. As you saw, the MyGame program lets you convert a 2D ASCII drawing to a 3D picture, and then lets you travel inside the 3D picture.

In the next chapter you'll implement the MyGame program. As you'll see, writing the MyGame program is very easy.

In subsequent chapters you'll add additional features to the floor. For example, as you'll see, it is actually very easy to show pictures of people walking inside the floor, pictures of still and moving objects, and so on.

29

CHAPTER

THIRTY

Implementing the 3D Virtual Reality MyGame Program

30

In the previous chapter you executed the MyGame program. In this chapter you'll implement the program. As you'll see, implementing a 3D virtual reality program is easy. Again, the MyGame program does not have sophisticated gadgets such as static and dynamic objects in it. You'll add these gadgets in subsequent chapters.

Creating the Project for the MyGame Program

First create the project of the MyGame program:

- Select New Project from the File menu of Visual Basic.

- Save the new form as MyGame.FRM and the new project file as MyGame.VBP, both in the C:\WinGPrg\CH27 directory.

- Implement the frmMyGame form with the Properties settings listed in Table 30.1. When you're finished, the form should look as shown in Figure 30.1.

TABLE 30.1: The Properties of the frmMyGame Form

Object: Form	
Name: frmMyGame	
Property	**Value**
BackColor	Light gray
BorderStyle	1 'Fixed Single
Caption	"The MyGame Program"
Height	3675
Icon	C:\WinGPrg\Icons\MyGame.ICO
Left	285
MaxButton	0 'False
MinButton	0 'False
ScaleMode	3 'Pixel
Top	1200
Width	4920

TABLE 30.1: The Properties of the frmMyGame Form(continued)

Object: Floor Control

Name: Floor1

Property	Value
Left	840
Top	1440

Object: Common Dialog box

Name: CommonDialog1

Property	Value
Left	240
Top	1440
Cancelerror	−1 'True

FIGURE 30.1:
The frmMyGame form in design mode

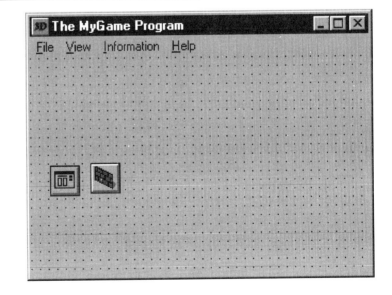

Note that you are placing the 3D Floor OCX control inside the frmMyGame form. The icon of the 3D Floor control inside the Tools window of Visual Basic is shown in Figure 30.2. The Floor control placed in the form appears in Figure 30.3. If your Tools window does not contain the Floor control, add it to the project by selecting Custom Controls from the Tools menu and then select the TegoSoft Floor Control. Note that the Floor control inside the form has a fixed size; you cannot enlarge it (just as you can't enlarge the size of the Timer and common dialog box controls).

FIGURE 30.2:

The icon of the Floor OCX control in the Tools window of Visual Basic

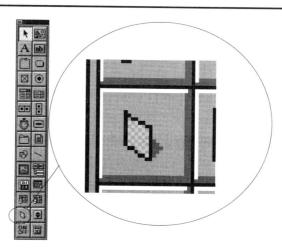

- Implement the menu of the frmMyGame form with the settings listed in Table 30.2.

FIGURE 30.3:
The Floor OCX control inside the form

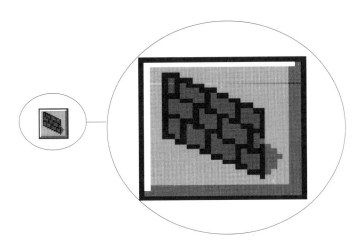

TABLE 30.2: The Menu of the MyGame Program

Caption	Name
&File	mnuFile
...&Load Floor...	mnuLoadFloor
...E&xit	mnuExit
&View	mnuView
...&ASCII View	mnuASCIIView
&Information	mnuInfo
...&Floor Information...	mnuFloorInfo
&Help	mnuHelp
...&About...	mnuAbout

30

The General Declarations Section of the frmMyGame Form

The next step is to write the code of the General Declarations section of the frmMy-Game form.

- Enter the following code in the General Declarations section of the frmMy-Game form:

```
' All variables must be declared
Option Explicit

' Variables used for saving the
' previous mouse cursor coordinates.
Dim gPrevX
Dim gPrevY
```

This code forces variable declarations. It also declares general variables that will be used to store mouse cursor coordinates. (The exact purpose of gPrevX and gPrevY will be discussed later in the development of the program.)

The Load Event of the frmMyGame Form

Upon starting the frmMyGame form, the Form_Load( ) procedure of the frmMy-Game form is executed.

- Enter the following code in the Form_Load( ) procedure of the frmMy-Game form:

```
Private Sub Form_Load( )

    gDistanceSpeed = 40

    Me.ScaleMode = 3 'Pixels
```

```
        mnuASCIIView.Enabled = False

    End Sub
```

This code sets the value of the gDistanceSpeed variable to 40. You'll declare the gDistanceSpeed variable later in the development of the program. For now, just note that gDistanceSpeed represents the speed at which the user can advance forward and backward when using the mouse.

The code then sets the ScaleMode property to pixels:

```
    Me.ScaleMode = 3 'Pixels
```

With the Floor OCX control, all dimensions are supplied in pixels, so this saves you the trouble of converting twips or other units to pixels.

The next statement disables the ASCII View menu (upon starting the program no floor file is loaded yet, so this menu item should be disabled):

```
    mnuASCIIView.Enabled = False
```

Later in the program, when you load a floor file, you'll make the ASCII View menu item enabled.

Attaching Code to the Click Event of the Exit Menu

You'll now attach code to the Click event of the Exit menu item.

- Enter the following code in the mnuExit_Click( ) procedure of the frmMyGame form:

```
Private Sub mnuExit_Click( )

    ' Unload the form
    Unload Me

End Sub
```

This code unloads the frmMyGame form, which terminates the MyGame program.

30

The Click Event of the Load Floor Menu Item

Whenever the user selects Load Floor from the File menu of the MyGame program, the mnuLoadFloor_Click( ) procedure is executed. You'll now write the code that loads a floor (FLR) file.

- Enter the following code in the mnuLoadFloor_Click( ) procedure of the frmMyGame form:

```
Private Sub mnuLoadFloor_Click( )

Dim OpenResult As Integer
Dim Message As String
Dim NumberOfRows, NumberOfCols
Dim CRLF


'''''''''''''''''''''''''''''''''''''''''''''''''''''
' DESCRIPTION:
' Selecting a *.FLR file (with the common dialog
' box control)
'''''''''''''''''''''''''''''''''''''''''''''''''''''

CRLF = Chr(13) + Chr(10)

' Set an error trap to detect whether the
' user clicked the Cancel button of the
' Open dialog box.
On Error GoTo OpenError

' Set the items of the File Type list box
CommonDialog1.Filter = _
    "All Files (*.*) ¦ *.* ¦Floor Files (*.flr)¦*.flr"

' Set the default File Type to *.flr
CommonDialog1.FilterIndex = 2

' Display the common dialog box as
' an Open File dialog box
CommonDialog1.Action = 1

' Remove the error trap
On Error GoTo 0
```

```
' Find number of rows in the
' selected floor file
NumberOfRows = FindNumOfRows

' Find number of columns in the
' selected floor file
NumberOfCols = FindNumOfCols

' Initialize and open the 3D Floor control
Floor1.FileName = CommonDialog1.FileName
Floor1.hWndDisplay = Me.hWnd
Floor1.NumOfRows = NumberOfRows
Floor1.NumOfCols = NumberOfCols

' Initial position
Floor1.X = STARTUP_X * Floor1.CellWidth + 25
Floor1.Y = STARTUP_Y * Floor1.CellWidth + 25

' Initial direction
Floor1.Angle = STARTUP_DIRECTION

' Open the FLR file
OpenResult = Floor1.Open

If OpenResult <> 0 Then
   Message = _
    "Unable to open file:" + Floor1.FileName + CRLF

   Message = _
       Message + _
      "Error Code: " + _
      Str(OpenResult)

   MsgBox Message, vbCritical, "Error"

   Me.Caption = _
      "The MyGame Program -(No file is loaded)"

   Exit Sub
End If

''''''''''''''''''''''''''''''''''''''''
' FLR file was successfully opened
''''''''''''''''''''''''''''''''''''''''
```

30

```
' Selected file name is:
' CommonDialog1.FileName (includes the path)
' CommonDialog1.FileTitle (includes only the filename)
Me.Caption = _
  "The MyGame Program -(" + CommonDialog1.FileTitle + ")"

' Enable the View menu
mnuASCIIView.Enabled = True

' Display the 3D view
Floor1.Display3D

' Exit this procedure
Exit Sub

OpenError:
    ' The user pressed the Cancel key
    ' of the common dialog
    ' Exit this procedure
    Exit Sub

End Sub
```

This code first declares several local variables:

```
Dim OpenResult As Integer
Dim Message As String
Dim NumberOfRows, NumberOfCols
Dim CRLF
```

The CRLF variable is then set as follows:

```
CRLF = Chr(13) + Chr(10)
```

Later in this procedure, you will write code that displays a message. The message is spread over more than one line by inserting the carriage return and line feed characters (Chr(13)+Chr(10)). So instead of entering **Chr(13)+Chr(10)**, you'll enter **CRLF**.

The CancelError property of the common dialog box was set to True during design time (see Table 30.1). This means that if the user clicks the Cancel button of the Open dialog box, an error will occur. So the next statement that you typed sets an error trap mechanism:

```
' Set an error trap to detect if the
' user clicked the Cancel button of the
' Open dialog box.
On Error GoTo OpenError
```

This causes the program to jump immediately to the OpenError label, located at the end of this procedure, if the user clicks the Cancel button of the common dialog box. The code that follows OpenError terminates the procedure.

Next, the Filter property of the common dialog box is set so that the user can easily select a file with the characters FLR as the file extension:

```
' Set the items of the File Type list box
CommonDialog1.Filter = _
    "All Files (*.*) ¦ *.* ¦Floor Files (*.flr)¦*.flr"

' Set the default File Type to *.flr
CommonDialog1.FilterIndex = 2
```

Now that the common dialog box is prepared, you can display it (as an Open dialog box):

```
' Display the common dialog box as
' an Open File dialog box
CommonDialog1.Action = 1
```

At this point in the program, the user has selected a floor file, so you can remove the error trapping mechanism:

```
' Remove the error trap
On Error GoTo 0
```

The next statement executes the FindNumOfRows function:

```
' Find number of rows in the
' selected floor file
NumberOfRows = FindNumOfRows
```

You'll write the code of the FindNumOfRows function later in this chapter. This function examines the floor file and extracts the number of rows. In the preceding statement, you assigned the returned value of the FindNumOfRows function to the NumberOfRows variable.

30

You then execute the FindNumOfCols function:

```
' Find number of columns in the
' selected floor file
NumberOfCols = FindNumOfCols
```

You'll write the code of the FindNumOfCols function later in this chapter. This function returns the number of columns in the selected floor file.

At this point, you've selected a floor file and extracted its number of rows and columns. So you can now set the properties of the Floor OCX control. The FileName property of the Floor control is set to the name of the selected file:

```
Floor1.FileName = CommonDialog1.FileName
```

Summary: The Floor OCX Control

The Floor OCX control displays the 3D picture of the floor whose 2D drawing is stored as a *.FLR text file. You provide the Floor control with the name of the *.FLR file as follows:

```
Floor1.FileName = CommonDialog1.FileName
```

This statement assumes that the name of the Floor OCX control is Floor1, and that the name of the floor file is stored as the FileName property of the common dialog box. That is, you have to supply the full name and path of the floor file.

Next, we set the hWndDisplay property of the Floor control as follows:

```
Floor1.hWndDisplay = Me.hWnd
```

We've set the hWndDisplay property of the Floor control to the hWnd property of the frmMyGame form. Why? Because the Floor control needs to know which window to display the 3D picture in. The preceding statement tells the Floor control to display the 3D picture in the window of the frmMyGame form.

Summary:The hWndDisplay Property of the Floor Control

The 3D picture will be displayed in the window whose handle is specified as the hWndDisplay property of the Floor control. For example, if you want to display the 3D picture inside a form called frmOurForm, use the following statement:

```
Floor1.hWndDisplay = frmOurForm.hWnd
```

The next statements set the NumOfRows and NumOfCols properties of the Floor control:

```
Floor1.NumOfRows = NumberOfRows
Floor1.NumOfCols = NumberOfCols
```

Recall that you extracted the number of rows and columns earlier in this procedure. So now you are telling the Floor control the number of rows and columns.

Summary: The NumOfRows and NumOfCols Properties of the Floor OCX Control

You tell the Floor control the number of rows and columns by setting the NumOfRows and NumOfCols properties of the Floor control. For example, you can set these properties as follows:

```
Floor1.NumOfRows = 50
Floor1.NumOfCols = 20
```

The X and Y properties of the Floor control are the coordinates of the user's current position. You set the current position of the user inside the 3D picture as follows:

```
' Initial position
Floor1.X = STARTUP_X * Floor1.CellWidth + 25
Floor1.Y = STARTUP_Y * Floor1.CellWidth + 25
```

STARTUP_X and STARTUP_Y are constants that are declared in a different BAS module. You'll add the BAS module later in this chapter. You'll declare the STARTUP_X and STARTUP_Y constants inside the separate BAS module as follows:

```
' Upon starting the program, the startup
' position is determined from the following
' constants:
Public Const STARTUP_X = 2
Public Const STARTUP_Y = 2
```

Each cell in the OCX Floor control has a default width and height of 65 pixels. As shown in Figure 30.4, by setting the X and Y properties of the Floor control to the values that you set in the preceding statements, you are placing the user in the third row from the bottom and third column from the left.

30

Summary: The X and Y Properties of the Floor OCX Control

The X and Y properties of the Floor control specify the user's current location in the 3D picture. You can read these properties to determine the user's current position.

You can also set these properties to place the user at a particular position, specifying the coordinates with the X and Y properties.

The bottom left point of the floor has the coordinates X=0, Y=0. So for example, the point shown in Figure 30.4 has the coordinates x=65×2+25, y=65×2+25. This means that this point is 65×2+25 pixels to the right of the left edge of the floor, and 65×2+25 pixels above the bottom of the floor.

FIGURE 30.4:

The user's initial location

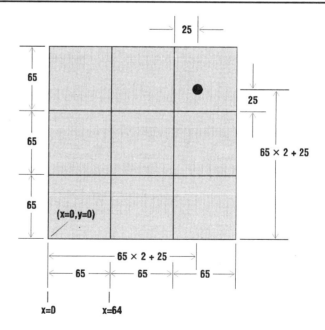

Similarly, you have to set the initial angle view of the user. You accomplish this by setting the Angle property of the Floor control as follows:

```
' Initial direction
Floor1.Angle = STARTUP_DIRECTION
```

Hitting the Wall

As you'll soon see, when you set the user's position with the arrow keys (or with the mouse), you execute code that causes the Floor control to update the X and Y properties automatically. The Floor control refuses to place the user inside a solid block. For example, when using the keyboard for moving the user, you cannot place the user inside a solid block.

You do have to be careful when you place the user by setting the X and Y coordinates of the floor. For example, the coordinate position X=32, Y=32 is occupied by a solid block. So naturally you don't want to place the user inside the solid block.

You also have to place the user a little bit away from a solid block. The Floor OCX control that you place the user at least 20 pixels from a solid block.

Figure 30.5 illustrates the view that the user sees when the Angle property is set to 60°. Again, later in this chapter you'll be instructed to write the separate BAS module that contains all the constant declarations. For now, note that the STARTUP_DIRECTION constant is declared as follows:

```
' Upon starting the program, the startup
' direction in degrees is:
Public Const STARTUP_DIRECTION = 60
```

The center angle of the view is set by the Angle property. Because you set the Angle property to 60, the user faces the 60° direction.

The Floor control supplied with this book lets the user view a total of 60°. Thus, the user can view the area shaded in Figure 30.5, which extends from the 30 degree direction to the 90 degree direction.

As another example, if you set the Angle property to 45°, then the user sees the view from 45–30=15° to 45+30=75°, as shown in Figure 30.6.

30

FIGURE 30.5:

The user's initial view angle

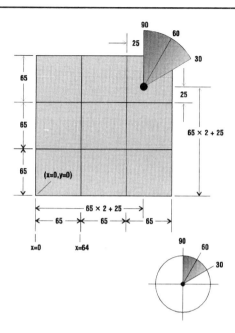

FIGURE 30.6:

The view seen by the user when the Angle property is set to 45°

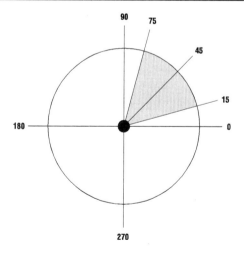

As our last example, if you set the Angle property to 270°, then the view that the user sees is the one shown in Figure 30.7. The user sees the view from 270–30=240° to 270+30=300°.

FIGURE 30.7:

The view seen by the user when the Angle property is set to 270°

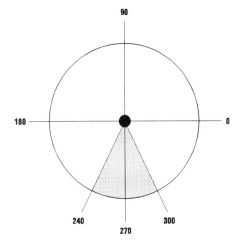

Summary: The Angle Property of the Floor OCX Control

The Floor OCX control lets the user view a range of 60 degrees. This means that if you set the Angle property of the Floor control to D, then the user sees the view seen from D–30 to D+30. For example, if the Angle property of the Floor control is set to 0 degrees, then the user sees the view from 0–30=–30 degrees (which is equivalent to 330 degrees) to 0+30–30 degrees. This is shown in Figure 30.8.

30

The next statement you entered opens the floor file:

```
' Open the FLR file
OpenResult = Floor1.Open
```

The Open method here assigns the result of the Open method to the OpenResult variable. An If statement is then executed to examine whether the floor file was opened successfully:

```
If OpenResult <> 0 Then
    Message = _
```

```
        "Unable to open file:" + Floor1.FileName + CRLF

    Message = _
        Message + _
        "Error Code: " + _
        Str(OpenResult)

    MsgBox Message, vbCritical, "Error"

    Me.Caption = _
        "The MyGame Program -(No file is loaded)"

    Exit Sub
End If
```

The Caption property of the frmMyGame form is then updated with the name of the floor file:

```
Me.Caption = _
    "The MyGame Program -(" + CommonDialog1.FileTitle + ")"
```

Recall that in the Form_Load( ) procedure you disabled the ASCII View menu item. Now that the floor file has been opened successfully, you can enable the ASCII View menu item:

```
' Enable the View menu
mnuASCIIView.Enabled = True
```

Finally, you display the 3D picture that corresponds to the loaded floor file and the view seen from the user's current position (indicated by the X, Y, and Angle properties of the Floor control).

Here is how you display the 3D picture:

```
' Display the 3D view
Floor1.Display3D
```

Summary: Executing the Open Method of the Floor OCX Control

Once you set the FileName property of the Floor control, and then set its X, Y, and Angle properties, you can execute the Open method as follows:

```
Floor1.Open
```

Once a floor file has been opened, you can display the 3D picture by executing the Display3D method:

```
Floor1.Display3D
```

Displaying the ASCII View of the Floor

Whenever the user selects the ASCII View menu item, the MyGame program displays the 2D drawing of the loaded file.

- Enter the following code in the mnuASCIIView_Click( ) procedure of the frmMyGame form:

```
Private Sub mnuASCIIView_Click( )

    frmASCIIView.Show 1

End Sub
```

This statement displays the frmASCIIView form as a modal window. You'll implement the frmASCIIView form in the next chapter.

Attaching Code to the Paint Event of the frmMyGame Form

The Paint event occurs whenever Windows senses that the window has to be redrawn. For example, if the user drags the frmMyGame form, the frmMyGame window has to be redrawn. Thus, you have to write redrawing code inside the Form_Paint( ) procedure of the frmMyGame form.

- Enter the following code in the Form_Paint( ) procedure of the form:

```
Private Sub Form_Paint( )

    ' Display the 3D view
    Floor1.Display3D

End Sub
```

This code executes the Display3D method. Thus, the 3D picture will be redrawn (with a view as seen from the point specified by the X,Y coordinates of the Floor control, and at an angle specified by its Angle property).

Attaching Code to the Information Menu

You'll now attach code to the Floor Information menu item. The purpose of this menu item is just to illustrate the code that is needed for extracting various information from the Floor control.

- Enter the following code in the mnuFloorInfo_Click( ) procedure of the frmMyGame form:

```
Private Sub mnuFloorInfo_Click( )

Dim Info As String
Dim CRLF

CRLF = Chr(13) + Chr(10)
```

```
Info = "File Name: " + Floor1.FileName + CRLF
Info = Info + CRLF

Info = Info + _
    "Number of Columns: " + _
    Str(Floor1.NumOfCols) + _
    CRLF

Info = Info + _
    "Number of Rows: " + _
    Str(Floor1.NumOfRows) + _
    CRLF

Info = Info + CRLF

Info = Info + _
    "Width of a cell in pixels: " + _
    Str(Floor1.CellWidth) + _
    CRLF

Info = Info + CRLF

MsgBox Info, vbInformation, "Information"

End Sub
```

This code displays a message box. For example, with the Floor01.FLR floor loaded, the Information message box looks as shown in Figure 30.8.

FIGURE 30.8:

The Floor Information message box for the Floor01.FLR floor file

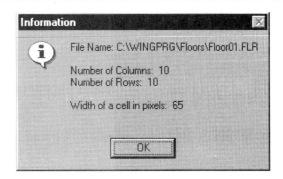

30

We use the FileName property of the Floor control to extract the name of the floor file:

```
Info = "File Name: " + Floor1.FileName + CRLF
```

The numbers of columns and rows are determined by examining the NumOfCols and NumOfRows properties of the Floor control:

```
Info = Info + _
       "Number of Columns: " + _
       Str(Floor1.NumOfCols) + _
       CRLF

Info = Info + _
       "Number of Rows: " + _
       Str(Floor1.NumOfRows) + _
       CRLF
```

The Floor control that is supplied with this book is 65 pixels wide. You extract the cell's width and height by using the CellWidth property of the Floor control:

```
Info = Info + _
       "Width of a cell in pixels: " + _
       Str(Floor1.CellWidth) + _
       CRLF
```

The cells are squares, so their height is the same as their width.

In the preceding code you constructed the Info string, and now you can display this string in a message box:

```
MsgBox Info, vbInformation, "Information"
```

Again, your user (who simply wants to play your game) does not need this type of information. We included this information for you, the programmer.

> **NOTE**
>
> The Floor OCX control supplied with this book always displays the 3D picture with a fixed width of 320 pixels. The default height of the 3D picture is 190 pixels. You can set the height of the floor by setting its Height3D property. (To read the value of the Height3D property use the GetHeight3D method, and to set the Height3D property use the SetHeight3D method.) You can set the Height3D property to an integer between 90 and 290. There are no restrictions on the number of rows and columns of the floor.

Attaching Code to the HitWall Event of the Floor Control

You'll now attach code to the HitWall event of the Floor control. Not surprisingly, this event occurs whenever the user hits the wall.

- Enter the following code in the Floor1_HitWall( ) procedure of the frmMy-Game form:

```
Private Sub Floor1_HitWall( )

    ''''Beep

End Sub
```

Whenever the user touches any of the walls, the PC beeps. We commented out the Beep statement, because just playing a beep may annoy the user. A refinement you might be able to add is to play a very small section of a WAV file that sounds like a man hitting a wall.

30

The HitWall Event of the Floor Control

When the user hits the wall, the HitWall events occurs. Use the Floor1_HitWall() procedure to write code that will be executed whenever the user hits the wall—playing WAV files, or any other special effects. The Floor OCX control generates the HitWall event whenever the user gets within 20 pixels of the wall.

The MouseMove Event of the frmMyGame Form

Although the MyGame program currently allows the user to move only by using the keyboard, you may also want to allow mouse movement. For that reason the frmMyGame form includes a MouseMove event and a Form_MouseMove() procedure:

```
Private Sub Form_MouseMove(Button As Integer, Shift As Integer, x As
    Single, y As Single)

''''''''''''''''''''''''''''''''
' Here you'll write code that
' will be executed whenever the
' user moves the mouse.
''''''''''''''''''''''''''''''''


End Sub
```

To move the user's position within the 3D picture by using the mouse, you need to compare the current position of the mouse with its previous position.

The current mouse position is given as the parameters of the Form_MouseMove() procedure. Figures 30.9 through 30.12 demonstrate how this is done.

In Figure 30.9, the mouse moves to the right, and its Y coordinate does not change. Only the X coordinate decreases. This means that you have to execute the same code that is executed whenever the user presses the ← key. In Figure 30.10, only the Y coordinate changes. Here you have to execute the same code that is executed whenever the user presses the ↑ key.

FIGURE 30.9:

Moving the mouse to the left
(equivalent to pressing the ← key)

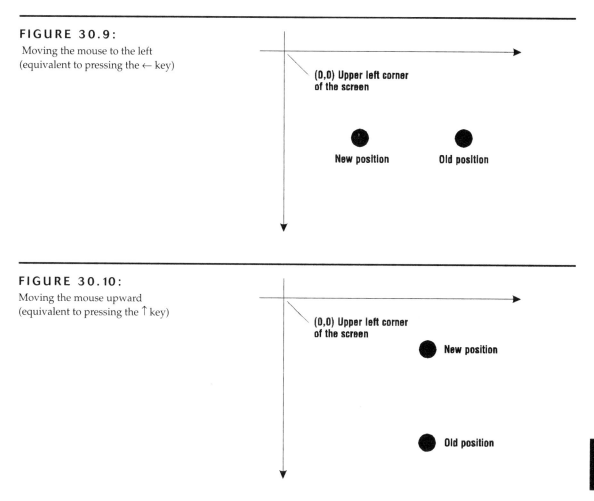

FIGURE 30.10:

Moving the mouse upward
(equivalent to pressing the ↑ key)

Similarly, Figure 30.11 shows that the new mouse position has an identical X coordinate, but a higher Y coordinate. This means that you have to execute the same code that is executed when the user presses the ↓ key.

As a last example, consider the situation shown in Figure 30.12. The new mouse position is above and to the left of the previous position. In this case, your code has to execute the same code that is executed when the user presses the ↑ key, and immediately executes the code of the ← key.

FIGURE 30.11:

Moving the mouse downward (equivalent to pressing the ↓ key)

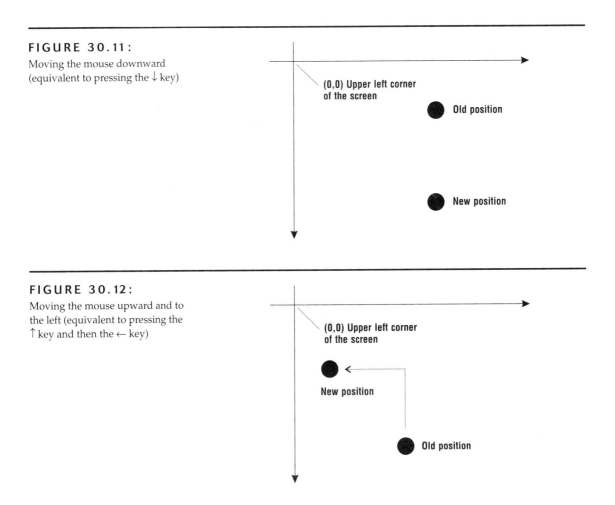

FIGURE 30.12:

Moving the mouse upward and to the left (equivalent to pressing the ↑ key and then the ← key)

Later in this chapter you'll write the code that is executed when the user presses the ↑, ↓, ←, and → keys. However, as you can see, moving the user inside the 3D picture with the mouse amounts to comparing the old mouse cursor position with the current mouse position, and then executing the code for the corresponding keystrokes.

As you'll soon see, whenever the user presses a key, the user changes position or angle inside the 3D picture. This change in position is expressed in a fixed number of degrees or pixels. For example, when the user presses the Up key, you can write code that moves the user 10 pixels forward.

So by what amount will you move the user when the mouse position is moved as shown in Figure 30.11? That is up to you! You can simply move the user forward by a fixed number of pixels regardless of the distance by which the mouse was moved. Alternatively, you can compare the current mouse position with the previous position, and execute the code of the ↑ key one or more times according to the distance (in pixels) by which the user moved the mouse.

> **TIP**
>
> You can use the other parameters of the Form_MouseMove( ) procedure for determining whether any of the mouse buttons were pressed during the mouse movements. For example, you may decide to implement the Form_Mouse( ) procedure in a way that changes the user's position only if the left button is pressed while the mouse moves.

Attaching Code to the KeyDown Event

You'll now attach code to the KeyDown event of the frmMyGame form. This event occurs whenever the user presses a key on the keyboard.

- Enter the following code in the Form_KeyDown( ) procedure of the frmMyGame form:

```
Private Sub Form_KeyDown(KeyCode As Integer, _
                  Shift As Integer)
```

30

```
Select Case KeyCode

        Case 37, 100
                ' Left key (37) or 4 key (100) was pressed
                ' to increase the direction angle.
                Floor1.Angle = Floor1.Angle + DIRECTION_CHANGE

        Case 39, 102
                ' Right key (39) or 6 key (102) was pressed
                ' to decrease the direction angle.
                Floor1.Angle = Floor1.Angle - DIRECTION_CHANGE

        Case 38, 104
                ' Up key (38) or 8 key (104) was pressed
                ' to advance forward.
                Floor1.Advance (DISTANCE_CHANGE)

        Case 40, 98 'Down or 2
                ' Down key (40) or 2 key (98) was pressed
                ' to advance backward.
                Floor1.Advance (-DISTANCE_CHANGE)

    End Select

    ''''''''''''''''''''''
    ' Display the 3D view
    ''''''''''''''''''''''
    Floor1.Display3D

End Sub
```

This code uses a Select Case statement to examine which key was pressed:

```
Select Case KeyCode

    Case 37, 100
.........................................
... Left arrow key or the 4 key was pressed.
        ...................................
    Case 39, 102
        ...................................
... Right arrow key or the 6 key was pressed.
        ...................................
```

```
Case 38, 104
........................................
... Up arrow key or the 8 key was pressed.
........................................

Case 40, 98 'Down or 2
.............................................
... Down arrow key or the 2 key was pressed.
.........................................
End Select
```

KeyCode is one of the parameters supplied to the Form_KeyDown( ) procedure, and it contains the code of the key that was pressed. (Why do we check for the 8 key as well as the ↑ key? Just in case your user has the Num Lock key in its ON state.)

TIP

We're letting the user move forward if the ↑ key is pressed, or the 8 key on the numeric pad is pressed. (Pressing the "regular" 8 key does not move the user forward.) It's a good idea to take the Num Lock key into consideration, because this makes your game programs easier to use. During the excitement of the game, your user's hand may stray and accidentally toggle the Num Lock key.

Let's look at the code that is executed when the user presses the ← key:

```
Case 37, 100
    ' Left key (37) or 4 key (100) was pressed
    ' to increase the direction angle.
    Floor1.Angle = Floor1.Angle + DIRECTION_CHANGE
```

Later in this chapter you'll declare the DIRECTION_CHANGE constant as follows:

```
' When the user presses the left/right arrow keys,
' the direction is changed by this number
' of degrees.
Public Const DIRECTION_CHANGE = 6
```

So if, for example, the Angle property is equal to 30, then after pressing the ← key, Angle is equal to 30+6=36. Similarly, the code executed when the user presses the → key decreases the Angle property by DIRECTION_CHANGE.

30

Summary: The Angle Property of the Floor Control

The Angle property can range in value from 0 to 360. So for example, if currently the Angle property is equal to 359 and you increase the Angle property by 6, then Angle is equal to:

359+6=365

But 365 degrees is the same as 5 degrees (365–360=5). So if you then examine the value of the Angle property, you'll discover that Angle is equal to 5. In other words, the Floor control automatically keeps the Angle property in the range between 0 and 360 degrees.

Here is the code that is executed whenever the user presses the → key:

```
Case 39, 102
     ' Right key (39) or 6 key (102) was pressed
     ' to decrease the direction angle.
     Floor1.Angle = Floor1.Angle – DIRECTION_CHANGE
```

This code is very similar to the code that is executed whenever the ← key is pressed. Of course, now the user is turning to the right (clockwise), so the Angle property is decreased.

When the ↑ key is pressed, the following code is executed:

```
Case 38, 104
     ' Up key (38) or 8 key (104) was pressed
     ' to advance forward.
     Floor1.Advance (DISTANCE_CHANGE)
```

You'll declare the DISTANCE_CHANGE constant later in this chapter as follows:

```
' When the user presses the up/down arrow keys,
' the distance is changed by this amount:
Public Const DISTANCE_CHANGE = 40
```

So the code executed whenever the user presses the ↑ key executes the Advance method with DISTANCE_CHANGE as its parameter. The Advance method advances the user by the number of pixels specified in its parameter. Thus, whenever the user presses the ↑ key, the user's position is changed in the forward direction by 40 pixels. Recall that the user advances in the direction set by the Angle property's current value. Figure 30.13 shows the result of pressing the ↑ key while the Angle property is approximately 135°.

FIGURE 30.13:
Advancing forward in the 135° direction

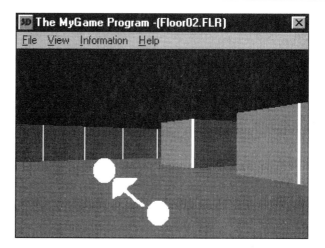

The last case under the Select Case statement specifies what happens when the user presses the ↓ key (or the 2 key on the numeric pad):

```
Case 40, 98 'Down or 2
    ' Down key (40) or 2 key (98) was pressed
    ' to advance backward.
    Floor1.Advance (-DISTANCE_CHANGE)
```

This code moves the user's point of view in the negative direction. As you can see, we do this by supplying a negative number for the parameter of the Advance method. Figure 30.14 shows the result after pressing the ↓ key when the Angle property is equal to 135°.

Finally, the 3D picture is displayed:

```
Floor1.Display3D
```

This statement displays the 3D picture from the current user position.

30

FIGURE 30.14:

Moving backward in the 135°
direction

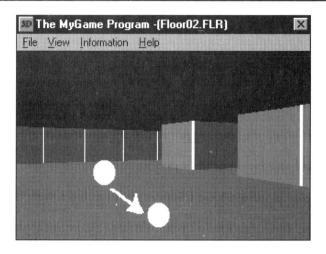

NOTE   After you execute the Advance method, the Floor control
automatically updates its X and Y properties.

Attaching Code to
the About Menu Item

You'll now attach code to the About menu item of the frmMyGame form.

- Enter the following code in the mnuAbout_Click( ) procedure of the frmMy-
Game form:

```
Private Sub mnuAbout_Click( )

    ' Display the About window
    ' as a modal window.
    frmAbout.Show 1

End Sub
```

This code displays the About window as a modal window.

Implementing the frmAbout Form

You'll now implement the frmAbout window.

- Select Form from the Insert menu.

Visual Basic responds by inserting a new form in the MyGame project.

- Save the new form as About.FRM in the C:\WinGPrg\CH27 directory.
- Implement the frmAbout form with the Properties settings listed in table 30.3. When you're finished, the form should look as shown in Figure 30.15.

TABLE 30.3: The Properties of the frmAbout Form

Object: Form
Name: frmAbout

Property	Value
BorderStyle	1 'Fixed Single
Caption	"About"
Height	5415
Icon	C:\WinGPrg\Icons\MyGame.ICO
Left	1095
MaxButton	0 'False
MinButton	0 'False
Picture	C:\WinGPrg\CH27\About.BMP
Top	660
Width	7410

Object: CommandButton
Name: cmdOK

Property	Value
Caption	"&OK"
Height	495
Left	5040
Top	1080
Width	855

30

FIGURE 30.15:

The frmAbout form in design mode

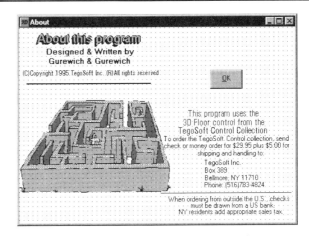

Attaching Code to the OK Button of the frmAbout Form

You'll now attach code to the Click event of the OK button of the frmAbout form.

- Enter the following code in the cmdOK_Click( ) procedure of the frmAbout form:

```
Private Sub cmdOK_Click( )

    ' Unload the form
    Unload Me

End Sub
```

This code closes the About window.

Implementing the MyGame.BAS Module

Throughout this chapter, you've used various constants. You'll now declare these constants.

- Select Module from the Insert menu.

Visual Basic responds by inserting a new BAS module into the MyGame project.

- Save the new module as MyGame.BAS in the C:\WinGPrg\Ch27 directory.

- Enter the following code in the General Declarations section of the My-Game.BAS module:

```
' All variables must be declared
Option Explicit

' Upon starting the program, the startup
' position is determined from the following
' constants:
Public Const STARTUP_X = 2
Public Const STARTUP_Y = 2

' Upon starting the program, the startup
' direction in degrees is:
Public Const STARTUP_DIRECTION = 60

' When the user presses the left/right arrow keys,
' the direction is changed by this number
' of degrees.
Public Const DIRECTION_CHANGE = 6

' When the user presses the up/down arrow keys,
' the distance is changed by this amount:
Public Const DISTANCE_CHANGE = 40

' A variable that represents the Value property of
' the Distance Speed scroll bar.
Public gDistanceSpeed As Integer
```

30

Implementing the FindNumOfRows( ) Function

In the mnuLoadFloor_Click( ) procedure of the frmMyGame form you used the FindNumOfRows( ) function to extract the number of rows in the loaded floor file. You'll now implement this function.

- Make sure MyGame.BAS is selected, and then select Procedure from the Insert menu.

- In the Insert Procedure dialog box, click the Function option button, set the name of the function to FindNumOfRows, and click OK.

- Once Visual Basic has inserted the FindNumOfRows function in the MyGame.BAS module, enter the following code in the function:

```
Public Function FindNumOfRows( )

''''''''''''''''''''''''''''''''''''
' This function finds the number of
' rows in the selected floor file.
''''''''''''''''''''''''''''''''''''

Dim FileNum
Dim Cell As String
Dim FloorFileLength
Dim I

FindNumOfRows = 0

' Get the next available file number
FileNum = FreeFile

' Open the floor file
Open frmMyGame.CommonDialog1.FileName For Binary As FileNum

' Extract the length of the floor file
FloorFileLength = FileLen(frmMyGame.CommonDialog1.FileName)

' Extract the number of rows in the floor file
For I = 1 To FloorFileLength
    Cell = " "
    Get #FileNum, I, Cell
    If Asc(Cell) = 13 Then
        FindNumOfRows = FindNumOfRows + 1
        If I + 1 > FloorFileLength Then Exit For
        Get #FileNum, I + 1, Cell
        If Asc(Cell) = 10 Then
            If I + 2 > FloorFileLength Then Exit For
            Get #FileNum, I + 2, Cell
            If Asc(Cell) = 13 Then
```

```
            Exit For
          End If
        End If
    End If
Next I

If Asc(Cell) <> 13 And _
   Asc(Cell) <> 10 And _
   Asc(Cell) <> 32 Then

   FindNumOfRows = FindNumOfRows + 1

End If

' Close the floor file
Close FileNum

End Function
```

This code first extracts the number of rows in the floor file. An available file number is extracted:

```
' Get the next available file number
FileNum = FreeFile
```

And then the selected floor file (which is stored as the FileName property of the common dialog box) is opened as binary file:

```
' Open the floor file
Open frmMyGame.CommonDialog1.FileName For Binary As FileNum
```

The length of the floor file is extracted:

```
' Extract the length of the floor file
FloorFileLength = FileLen(frmMyGame.CommonDialog1.FileName)
```

And then a For loop is executed to find the number of rows. The code within the For loop examines each character of the floor file, looking for a carriage return (Chr(13)) followed by a line-feed character (Chr(10)).

Because the name of the function is FindNumOfRows, you have to set the value of a variable called FindNumberOfRows. This variable holds the value returned by the FindNumOfRows function.

30

Finally, the floor file is closed:

```
' Close the floor file
Close FileNum
```

Implementing the FindNumOfCols Function

In the mnuLoadFloor_Click( ) procedure of the frmMyGame form you used the FindNumOfCols( ) function to extract the number of columns in the loaded floor file. You'll now implement this function.

- Make sure MyGame.BAS is selected, and then select Procedure from the Insert menu.

- In the Insert Procedure dialog box, click the Function option button, set the name of the function to FindNumOfCols, and finally click OK.

Visual Basic responds by inserting the FindNumOfCols function inside the MyGame.BAS module.

- Enter the following code in the FindNumOfCols function:

```
Public Function FindNumOfCols( )

''''''''''''''''''''''''''''''''''''''''''
' This function finds the number of
' columns in the selected floor file.
''''''''''''''''''''''''''''''''''''''''''

Dim FileNum
Dim Cell As String
Dim FloorFileLength
Dim I

FindNumOfCols = 0

' Get the next available file number
FileNum = FreeFile

' Open the file
```

```
Open frmMyGame.CommonDialog1.FileName For Binary As FileNum

' Extract the length of the floor file.
FloorFileLength = FileLen(frmMyGame.CommonDialog1.FileName)

' Extract the number of columns in the floor file.
For I = 1 To FloorFileLength
    Cell = " "
    Get #FileNum, I, Cell
    If Asc(Cell) = 13 Then Exit For
Next I
FindNumOfCols = I - 1

' Close the floor file.
Close FileNum

End Function
```

This code opens the floor file, examines the first row character-by-character, and updates the FindNumOfCols variable (which serves as the return value of the function) with the number of columns.

Summary

In this chapter you implemented a big portion of the MyGame program. (You'll implement this program's ASCII View feature in the next chapter.)

You began working with the Floor OCX control and saw that it lets you develop 3D virtual reality programs with great ease. In subsequent chapters you'll add additional features—static objects, moving objects, and so on—to the floor.

30

In the next chapter you'll implement the ASCII View feature of the MyGame program. If you wish to test the work that you have done during this chapter, comment out the code inside the mnuASCIIView_Click( ) procedure of the frmMyGame form, and execute the program.

THIRTY-ONE

Implementing the ASCII View Mechanism

In the previous chapter you started to implement the MyGame program. One of the features of the MyGame program is that it lets the user display the ASCII view of the floor.

Typically, if you are using the Floor OCX control for a game program, you'll want to keep the floor ASCII file a secret from the user. Part of the fun in playing 3D virtual reality games is finding your way around an unfamiliar environment. Naturally, if you supply your user with the ASCII view, you are taking away the mystery of the game. Nevertheless, for less experienced gamers who can't find their way around the room, you may consider implementing the ASCII View feature in your game programs.

Implementing the frmASCIIView Form

In the mnuASCIIView_Click( ) procedure of the frmMyGame program, you entered the following code:

```
Private Sub mnuASCIIView_Click( )

    frmASCIIView.Show 1

End Sub
```

That is, the frmASCIIView form is displayed when the user selects the ASCII View item from the View menu.

Also, recall that in the Form_Load( ) procedure of the frmMyGame form you disabled the ASCII View menu item. In the mnuLoadFloor_Click( ) procedure of the frmMyGame form, you enabled this menu item when a floor file has been opened successfully.

You'll now add the frmASCIIView form to the MyGame project.

- Select Form from the Insert menu of Visual Basic.

Visual Basic responds by inserting a new form into the MyGame project.

- Save the new form as ASCView.FRM in the C:\WinGPrg\CH27 directory.

- Implement the frmASCIIView form with the Properties settings listed in Table 31.1. When you're finished, the form should look as shown in Figure 31.1.

31

TABLE 31.1: The Properties of the frmASCIIView Form

Object: Form
Name: frmASCIIView

Property	Value
BackColor	Light gray
BorderStyle	1 'Fixed Single
Caption	"ASCII View ( )"
Height	6135
Left	435
MaxButton	0 'False
MinButton	0 'False
Top	195
Width	8790

Object: Text box
Name: txtASCIIView

Property	Value
Font Name	Courier New
Font size	8.25
Height	4935
Left	0
MultiLine	−1 'True
ScrollBars	3 'Both
Top	0
Width	8655

TABLE 31.1: The Properties of the frmASCIIView Form (continued)

Object: Frame
Name: Frame1

Property	Value
BackColor	Light gray
Caption	"Empty Cells as"
ForeColor	White
Height	735
Left	3360
Top	4920
Width	3255

Object: OptionButton
Name: optDots

Property	Value
BackColor	Light gray
Caption	"&Dots"
ForeColor	White
Height	300
Left	1680
Top	360
Width	975

Object: OptionButton
Name: OptBlanks

Property	Value
BackColor	Light gray
Caption	"&Blanks"
ForeColor	White
Height	300
Left	240
Top	360
Value	−1 'True
Width	1215

TABLE 31.1: The Properties of the frmASCIIView Form (continued)

Object: CommandButton

Name: cmdOK

Property	Value
Caption	"&OK"
Height	615
Left	600
Top	5040
Width	1215

FIGURE 31.1:

The frmASCIIView form in design mode

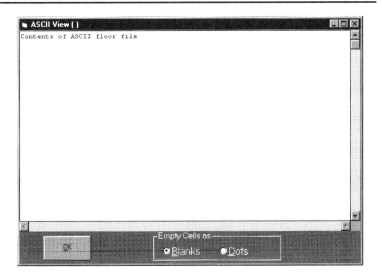

Attaching Code to the Click Event of the OK Button

You'll now attach code to the Click event of the OK button of the frmASCII-View form.

- Enter the following code in the cmdOK_Click( ) procedure of the frmASCII-View procedure:

```
Private Sub cmdOK_Click( )

    Unload Me

End Sub
```

This code closes the ASCII View window.

Attaching Code to the Paint Event of the frmASCIIView Form

The Paint event of the frmASCIIView form is executed whenever the frmASCII-View window needs to be redrawn. For example, when the user selects the ASCII View menu item, the frmASCIIView form is displayed, and this means that the Form_Paint( ) procedure is executed.

- Enter the following code in the Form_Paint( ) procedure of the frmASCII-View form:

```
Private Sub Form_Paint( )

    ' Update the caption of the window
    Me.Caption = frmMyGame.Caption

    ' Update the txtASCIIView label
    ' (To display the ASCII view of the floor)
    UpdateASCIILabel

End Sub
```

This code first sets the Caption property of the frmASCIIView form as follows:

```
' Update the caption of the window
Me.Caption = frmMyGame.Caption
```

31

It is a good idea to display the name of the floor file, so that the user can tell which floor file is being displayed.

Next, the UpdateASCIILabel procedure is executed:

```
' Update the txtASCIIView text box.
' (To display the ASCII view of the floor)
UpdateASCIILabel
```

The UpdateASCIILabel procedure updates the txtASCIIView text box with the contents of the floor file. You'll write the code of the UpdateASCIILabel procedure later in this chapter.

Attaching Code to the Click Event of the Blanks Option Button

The frmASCIIView form has two option buttons: Blanks and Dots. You'll now attach code to the Click event of the Blanks option button.

- Enter the following code in the optBlanks_Click( ) procedure of the frmASCIIView form:

```
Private Sub OptBlanks_Click( )

    UpdateASCIILabel

End Sub
```

This code executes the UpdateASCIILabel procedure. Again, you'll write the code of this procedure later in the chapter. The UpdateASCIILabel procedure fills the txtASCIIView text box with the 2D drawing of the floor, using either spaces or dots to represent empty cells.

Attaching Code to the Dots Option Button

You'll now attach code to the optDots_Click( ) procedure of the frmASCII-View form.

- Enter the following code in the optDots_Click( ) procedure of the frmASCII-View form:

```
Private Sub optDots_Click( )

    UpdateASCIILabel

End Sub
```

Again, the UpdateASCIILabel procedure is executed, so that the txtASCIIView text box will be filled with the contents of the floor file, showing each empty cell as a dot.

Filling the txtASCIIView Text Box with the Floor File

The UpdateASCIILabel procedure fills the txtASCIIView text box with the contents of the floor file. Each empty cell (a space in the FLR floor file) is either replaced by either a dot (if the Dots option button is selected) or displayed as a space (if the Blanks option button is selected).

- Make sure that the frmASCIIView form is selected, and then select Procedure from the Insert menu.

- In the Insert Procedure dialog box, set the name of the procedure to Update-ASCIILabel, make sure that the Procedure option button is selected, and then click OK.

Visual Basic responds by inserting the UpdateASCIILabel procedure in the General section of the frmASCIIView form.

- Enter the following code in the UpdateASCIILabel procedure:

```
Public Sub UpdateASCIILabel( )
```

```
''''''''''''''''''''''''''''''''''
' This procedure displays
' the floor in ASCII format.
''''''''''''''''''''''''''''''''''

Dim FileNum
Dim Contents As String
Dim CurrentCol
Dim CurrentRow
Dim ReplacePosition
Dim PositionCounter
Dim FileLength
Dim CurrentLocationInString

CurrentCol = _
    Int(frmMyGame.Floor1.X / frmMyGame.Floor1.CellWidth)

CurrentRow = _
    Int(frmMyGame.Floor1.Y / frmMyGame.Floor1.CellWidth)

CurrentLocationInString = _
(frmMyGame.Floor1.NumOfRows - CurrentRow - 1) * _
(frmMyGame.Floor1.NumOfCols + 2) + _
CurrentCol + 1

' Get a free file number
FileNum = FreeFile

' Open the file
Open frmMyGame.CommonDialog1.FileName For Input As FileNum

' Get the file length
FileLength = LOF(FileNum)

' Read the file contents
Contents = Input(FileLength, FileNum)

' Close the file
Close FileNum

' Place the "+" character at the user's current location
If CurrentLocationInString < Len(Contents) Then
   Mid(Contents, CurrentLocationInString, 1) = "+"
End If
```

```
If optDots.Value = True Then
   For PositionCounter = 1 To Len(Contents) Step 1

       ReplacePosition = InStr(1, Contents, " ", 1)
       If ReplacePosition <> 0 Then
           Mid(Contents, ReplacePosition, 1) = "."
       End If
   Next
End If


txtASCIIView.Text = Contents

End Sub
```

This code first declares several local variables:

```
Dim FileNum
Dim Contents As String
Dim CurrentCol
Dim CurrentRow
Dim ReplacePosition
Dim PositionCounter
Dim FileLength
Dim CurrentLocationInString
```

Then we calculate the CurrentCol and CurrentCell variables as follows:

```
CurrentCol = _
    Int(frmMyGame.Floor1.X / frmMyGame.Floor1.CellWidth)

CurrentRow = _
    Int(frmMyGame.Floor1.Y / frmMyGame.Floor1.CellWidth)
```

As you'll soon see, the FLR file will be loaded into a string called Contents, and the character in the Contents string that corresponds to the current position of the user will be replaced with the "+" character.

The character in the string that corresponds to the current position of the user is calculated as follows:

```
CurrentLocationInString = _
(frmMyGame.Floor1.NumOfRows - CurrentRow - 1) * _
(frmMyGame.Floor1.NumOfCols + 2) + _
CurrentCol + 1
```

To understand what this statement does, consider a FLR file that contains the following ASCII drawing:

```
11111
1   1
1   1
11111
```

As you'll soon see, you load the FLR file into the Contents string. The Contents string will therefore consist of the following characters:

```
"1"  "1"  "1"  "1"  "1"  13  10
"1"  " "  " "  " "  "1"  13  10
"1"  " "  " "  " "  "1"  13  10
"1"  "1"  "1"  "1"  "1"  13  10
```

That is, a carriage return (Chr(13)) and line feed (Chr(10)) are at the end of each line.

Further, assume that the current position of the user is at X=65×3+50 and Y=65×1+50. This means that in the ASCII view a "+" should be displayed as follows:

```
11111
1   1
1  +1
11111
```

Recall that the bottom left pixel of the floor is at x=0,y=0. So when the current user position is at x=65*3+50 and y=65*1+50, it means that the user is at the second row from the bottom and the 4th column from the left, as shown above.

Note that in this example, the number of columns is 5 and the number of rows is 4.

Thus, in the Contents string, you should replace the 18th character with the "+" character as follows:

```
"1"  "1"  "1"  "1"  "1"  13  10
"1"  " "  " "  " "  "1"  13  10
"1"  " "  " "  "+"  "1"  13  10
"1"  "1"  "1"  "1"  "1"  13  10
```

In this example, CurrentCol is calculated as follows:

```
CurrentCol = _
Int(frmMyGame.Floor1.X / frmMyGame.Floor1.CellWidth) =
Int( ( 65*3+50 ) / 65 ) = 3
```

And CurrentRow is calculated as follows:

```
CurrentRow = _
Int(frmMyGame.Floor1.Y / frmMyGame.Floor1.CellWidth) =
Int( ( 65*1+50 ) / 65 ) = 1
```

Now apply the statement that calculates the position in the string corresponding to the user's current position:

```
CurrentLocationInString = _
(frmMyGame.Floor1.NumOfRows - CurrentRow - 1) * _
(frmMyGame.Floor1.NumOfCols + 2) + _
CurrentCol + 1 =
( 4 - 1 - 1 ) * ( 5 + 2 ) + 3 + 1 = 18
```

So indeed, the 18th character in the Contents string is the character that represents the cell of the user's current position.

The next statement gets a file number:

```
' Get a free file number
FileNum = FreeFile
```

The FLR file is loaded:

```
' Open the file
Open frmMyGame.CommonDialog1.FileName For Input As FileNum
```

The length of the FLR file is extracted:

```
' Get the file length
FileLength = LOF(FileNum)
```

Then the Contents string is filled with the contents of the FLR file:

```
' Read the file contents
Contents = Input(FileLength, FileNum)
```

Again, if you examine the Contents string character-by-character, you'll see the Chr(13) and Chr(10) after each five characters (because there is a carriage-return/line-feed after each line in the FLR file).

You don't need the FLR File any more, so you can close it:

```
' Close the file
Close FileNum
```

You now replace the character in the Contents string that corresponds to the current user position with the "+" character:

```
' Place the "+" character at the user's current location
Mid(Contents, CurrentLocationInString, 1) = "+"
```

Now the Contents string is ready to display. The last thing to do is to examine whether the Dots option button is selected, and if so, replace each space with a dot:

```
If optDots.Value = True Then
    For PositionCounter = 1 To Len(Contents) Step 1

        ReplacePosition = InStr(1, Contents, " ", 1)
        If ReplacePosition <> 0 Then
            Mid(Contents, ReplacePosition, 1) = "."
        End If
    Next
End If
```

Finally, the textASCIIView text box is filled with the contents of the Contents string:

```
txtASCIIView.Text = Contents
```

NOTE
Many people use maps to travel from one place to another. Plumbers use floor maps to locate points in complex basements of large buildings, and so on. The ASCII View serves as the map of the floor. However, just as a traveler using a map may still get lost, your user may need more help than is provided by the ASCII View feature. To provide this further help, you implemented the current location feature, where the "+" character represents the cell where the user is currently located.

Letting the User Modify the ASCII Drawing

The text box that displays the ASCII 2D drawing of the floor lets the user type and modify the contents of the text box. However, if the user does this, the new contents of the text box are not saved as the new contents of the FLR file.

For completeness, you should write code that prevents the user from editing the text box.

Alternatively, you might let your user edit the text box, and then save the new contents of the text box into the floor file. Of course, if you let users write their own floor files, you have to write code that checks the validity of the FLR file. (For example, the floor area must be enclosed by blocks to prevent leakage.)

To use the new floor file, you must also open a new floor session with the new FLR file.

To see your code in action:

- Execute the MyGame program and verify that the code that you wrote produces the expected results.

Summary

In this chapter you implemented the ASCII View feature of the MyGame program. You also wrote the code that displays the current position of the user in the ASCII view. As you saw, this code works by performing string manipulation.

As a games programmer, you should always think about implementing features to make your games better and more enjoyable. For example, you could enhance the existing current-position feature so that the plus-sign marker is blinking; this will help the user to easily locate the current position cell. Remember that your floor can be very large with many halls and rooms. And as you'll see in subsequent chapters, the floor will also contain interesting static and dynamic objects. In such complex floors, the user will not be able to easily see the plus sign. So in this case, blinking is appropriate.

31

To implement the blinking plus sign you can use the Timer control, and in the Timer1_Timer( ) procedure alternate the character that represents the current cell. During one execution of the procedure place the space character in the current position cell, and the next execution use the plus sign character. This produces the blinking effect.

As you can see, there are practically no limits to the ingenuity that you can apply to such programs.

CHAPTER

THIRTY-TWO

Using the Mouse

In the previous chapter you implemented the MyGame program. The code you've written so far lets the user move around the floor using the keyboard. In this chapter you'll write code that enables the user to move using the mouse.

Operating the Mouse

Before implementing the mouse code, let's see the mouse in action:

- Execute the MyGame program. You'll see the window shown in Figure 32.1.

FIGURE 32.1:

The Window of the MyGame program.

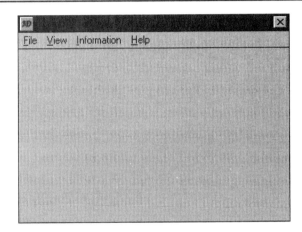

- Select Load Floor from the File menu of the MyGame program, and select the floor file \WinGPrg\Floors\Floor02.FLR.

MyGame loads the Floor02.FLR floor and displays the corresponding 3D picture, as shown in Figure 32.2.

In this chapter you'll also add the Help item to the Help menu (see Figure 32.3).

FIGURE 32.2:

The 3D picture of the
Floor02.FLR floor

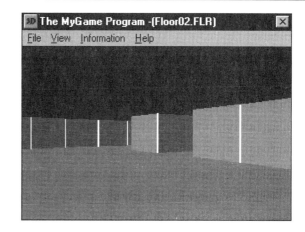

FIGURE 32.3:

The help item in the Help menu

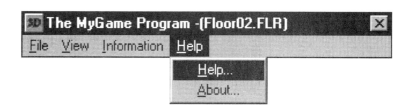

- Select the Help item from the Help menu. You'll see the Help window as shown in Figure 32.4.

As indicated in the Help window, to move within the floor, you place the mouse cursor inside the floor, hold down the left button, and move the mouse.

- Click the OK button to close the Help window.

- Use the mouse to move around the floor.

Moving the mouse upward has the same effect as pressing the ↑ key; moving it downward has the same effect as pressing ↓; moving it left has the same effect as pressing ←; and moving it right has the same effect as pressing →.

FIGURE 32.4:

The Help window

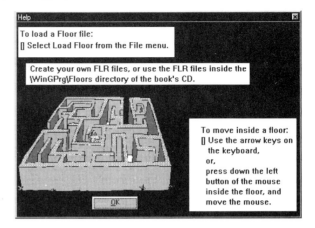

You can set the amount of displacement that will occur as a result of moving the mouse as follows:

- Place the mouse cursor inside the floor window, and click right. You'll see the Mouse Control Panel window (see Figure 32.5).

FIGURE 32.5:

The Mouse Control Panel window

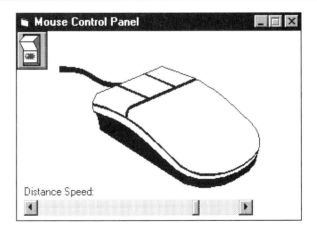

- Set the scroll bar to a new position and then click the Close switch (located in the upper-left corner of the Mouse Control Panel window). Setting the scroll bar to the leftmost position sets the distance speed to a minimum value.

- Use the mouse to move around the floor, and note that the speed at which you are now moving forward and backward corresponds to the setting of the scroll bar in the Mouse Control Panel window.

- Experiment with the MyGame program and then select Exit from the File menu to terminate the program.

32

Letting the User Work with the Mouse

Should you provide your user the ability to use the mouse in your games? Your users will expect this feature, so you might as well provide it.

With the keyboard, however, the user has better control over the operation of the program, because each movement corresponds to a single keystroke. With the mouse, it is difficult to control the operations, because the amount of movement depends how fast the user moved the mouse.

Using the mouse also makes it difficult to move only in the forward direction. That is, when moving the mouse upward, the user probably also moves the mouse slightly to the right or left. And this is equivalent to pressing first the ↑ key and then the ← or → key. So as you can see, using the keyboard gives the user more precise movement.

Generally speaking, you should let your user operate your games using both the mouse and the keyboard. In your documentation, however, point out that using the keyboard provides better control over the program. You might note that this is no different than using a program such as Paintbrush—you can draw lines and other shapes by using the mouse, but you can achieve better precision by using the keyboard.

Implementing the Mouse Panel Control Window

You'll now implement the frmMouseControl form.

- Select Form from the Insert menu.

Visual Basic responds by inserting a new form into the MyGame project.

- Implement the frmMouseControl form with the Properties settings listed in Table 32.1. When you're finished, the form should look as shown in Figure 32.5.

TABLE 32.1: The Properties of the frmMouseControl Form

Object: Form
Name: frmMouseControl

Property	Value
BorderStyle	1 'Fixed Single
Caption	"Mouse Control Panel"
Height	3495
Left	1080
MaxButton	0 'False
Picture	C:\WinGPrg\BMP\Mouse.BMP
Top	1170
Width	4905

Object: Horizontal ScrollBar
Name: hsbDistanceSpeed

Property	Value
Height	255
Left	120
Max	50
Min	10
Top	2760
Value	40
Width	3855

TABLE 32.1: The Properties of the frmMouseControl Form (continued)

Object: Label
Name: lblDistanceSpeed

Property	Value
Caption	"Distance Spccd:"
Height	255
Left	120
Top	2520
Width	1455

Object: Switch
Name: swClose

Property	Value
Height	630
Horizontal	False
Left	0
Top	0
Width	525
Value	−1 'True

The table instructs you to place the swClose switch in the frmMouseControl form. To add the Switch control to the MyGame project, select Custom Controls from the Tools menu and then select the TegoSoft Switch control. Visual Basic will respond by adding the Switch control to your Tools window. You then make the frmMouseControl form the active form, and double-click the Switch icon in the Tools window to place the Switch control inside the frmMouseControl panel.

32

The General Declarations Section of the frmMouseControl Form

- Enter the following code in the General Declarations section of the frmMouseControl form:

```
Option Explicit
```

This statement forces variable declarations.

Attaching Code to the Load Event of the frmMouseControl Form

Whenever the user presses the right mouse button, the frmMouseControl form is displayed. (You'll write the code that displays the frmMouseControl form later in this chapter.)

- Enter the following code in the Form_Load( ) procedure of the frmMouseControl form:

```
Private Sub Form_Load( )

    hsbDistanceSpeed.Value = gDistanceSpeed

End Sub
```

This code sets the Value property of the Distance Speed scroll bar to the value of the gDistanceSpeed variable. You declared the gDistanceSpeed variable in the General Declarations section of the MyGame.BAS module.

Attaching Code to the Click Event of the Close Switch

32

You'll now attach code to the Click event of the frmMouseControl form's Close switch.

- Enter the following code in the swClose_Click( ) procedure of the frmMouseControl form:

```
Private Sub swClose_Click( )

    Unload Me

End Sub
```

This statement closes the frmMouseControl form.

Closing the Mouse Control Panel

Typically, when you use the Switch control to terminate a program, you implement code that asks the user to confirm the request for termination. Your program displays a message box, and depending on whether the user clicks OK or Cancel, it either goes ahead and terminates the program or cancels the termination request.

When using the Switch control to close windows such as the Mouse Control Panel, typically you do not implement a confirmation mechanism, because you want the process of setting mouse operations to be quick and easy. Thus, the user clicks the right mouse button to display the Mouse Control Panel, sets a new value for the Distance Speed scroll bar, and clicks the Close switch to close the window.

Attaching Code to the Change Event of the Distance Speed Scroll Bar

You'll now attach code to the Change event of the Distance scroll bar. This event occurs whenever the user changes the Distance Speed scroll bar position.

- Enter the following code in the hsbDistanceSpeed_Change( ) procedure of the frmMouseControl form:

```
Private Sub hsbDistanceSpeed_Change( )

    gDistanceSpeed = hsbDistanceSpeed.Value

End Sub
```

This code sets the value of the gDistanceSpeed variable to the new Value property of the Distance Speed scroll bar.

Declaring Global Variables

As you saw in the preceding sections, the gDistanceSpeed variable represents the current Value property of the Distance Speed scroll bar. Make sure that this variable is declared in the General Declarations section of the MyGame.BAS module as follows:

```
' A variable that represents the Value property of
' the Distance Speed scroll bar.
Public gDistanceSpeed As Integer
```

This makes the gDistanceSpeed variable accessible from any procedure of any form of the MyGame.MAK project.

You'll now declare global variables in the General Declarations section of the frmMyGame form.

- Make sure that the following variable declarations appear in the General Declarations section of the frmMyGame form:

```
' Variables used for saving the
' previous mouse cursor coordinates.
Dim gPrevX
Dim gPrevY
```

You'll see the purpose of the gPrevX and gPrevY variables later in this chapter. For now, just note that they store the previous X and Y positions of the mouse cursor.

NOTE There's an important difference between the visibility of the general variables declared in the General Declarations section of the frmMyGame form, and that of the general variables declared in the General Declarations section of the MyGame.BAS module. While the variables declared in the MyGame.BAS module are accessible from any procedure of any form in the MyGame project, those declared in the frmMyGame form are accessible only from within procedures that reside in the frmMyGame form.

Adding Code to the Form_Load( ) Procedure of the frmMyGame Form

You'll now add code to the Form_Load( ) procedure of the frmMyGame form. Recall that in the Form_Load( ) procedure of the frmMouseControl form you wrote code that sets the Value property of the Distance Speed scroll bar to the value of the gDistanceSpeed variable:

```
hsbDistanceSpeed.Value = gDistanceSpeed
```

This means that you must initialize the gDistanceSpeed variable. In Visual Basic, when a variable is declared, Visual Basic sets its value to 0 or Null. If you don't set gDistanceSpeed to a certain value, then when the user displays the frmMouseSpeed form (by right-clicking the mouse), the Form_Load( ) procedure of frmMouseSpeed is executed, and the Value property of the Distance Speed scroll bar is assigned a value of 0. This will cause an error, because the Min property of the Distance Speed scroll bar is 10. So you must set the value of gDistanceSpeed to a value that is within the range of the Distance Speed scroll bar.

- Make sure that the gDistanceSpeed variable inside the Form_Load( ) procedure of the frmMyGame form is initialized as follows:

```
Private Sub Form_Load( )

    gDistanceSpeed = 40

    Me.ScaleMode = 3 'Pixels

    mnuASCIIView.Enabled = False

End Sub
```

This code sets the gDistanceSpeed variable to 40 (which is within the range of the Distance Speed scroll bar).

Attaching Code to the MouseDown Event of the frmMyGame Form

You'll now attach code to the MouseDown event of the frmMyGame form. This event occurs whenever the user presses one of the mouse buttons.

- Enter the following code in the Form_MouseDown( ) procedure of the frmMyGame form:

```
Private Sub Form_MouseDown(Button As Integer, _
                           Shift As Integer, _
                           X As Single, _
                           Y As Single)

        If Button And 2 Then
```

```
        frmMouseControl.Show 1

    End If

End Sub
```

The Button parameter of the procedure serves as an indication of which mouse button was pressed. An If statement is used to determine if the right button of the mouse was pressed:

```
If Button And 2 Then

    ...........................................
    ... The right button of the mouse was pressed
    ...........................................

End If
```

The code in the If statement is therefore executed if the user pressed the right mouse button. This code displays the frmMouseControl form as a modal window.

To understand how this If statement works, you need to be familiar with Boolean logical operations. The And operation here compares the value in the memory location represented by the Button variable with the binary number 2. We can paraphrase the statement as "If Button And 2 are equal, then…" In binary notation, 2 is 0000 0010. When the user presses the right mouse button, Visual Basic automatically sets the value of Button to 2. Thus, 0000 0010 And 2 is true, and therefore the If condition is satisfied. Similarly, the following If statement is used to determine whether the user pressed the left mouse button:

```
If Button And 1 Then
    ...........................................
    ... The left button of the mouse was pressed
    ...........................................
End If
```

Attaching Code to the MouseMove Event of the frmMyGame Form

You'll now attach code to the MouseMove event of the frmMyGame form. As you'll see, this code causes the user's position to change within the floor when the user moves the mouse (with the left mouse button pressed down).

- Enter the following code in the Form_MouseMove( ) procedure of the frmMyGame form:

```
Private Sub Form_MouseMove(Button As Integer, _
                           Shift As Integer, _
                           X As Single, _
                           Y As Single)

''''''''''''''''''''''''''''''''''
' Here you write code that
' will be executed whenever the
' user moves the mouse.
''''''''''''''''''''''''''''''''''

If Button And 1 Then

    If X < gPrevX Then
        ' Mouse was moved to the left
        Floor1.Angle = Floor1.Angle + DIRECTION_CHANGE

        '''''''''''''''''''''''
        ' Display the 3D view
        '''''''''''''''''''''''
        Floor1.Display3D
    End If

    If X > gPrevX Then
        ' Mouse was moved to the right
        Floor1.Angle = Floor1.Angle - DIRECTION_CHANGE
        '''''''''''''''''''''''
        ' Display the 3D view
        '''''''''''''''''''''''
        Floor1.Display3D
    End If
```

32

```
    If Y < gPrevY Then
       ' Mouse was moved upward
       Floor1.Advance gDistanceSpeed
       ''''''''''''''''''''''

       ' Display the 3D view
       ''''''''''''''''''''''

       Floor1.Display3D
    End If

    If Y > gPrevY Then
       ' Mouse was moved upward
       Floor1.Advance -gDistanceSpeed
       ''''''''''''''''''''''''

       ' Display the 3D view
       ''''''''''''''''''''''''

       Floor1.Display3D
    End If

 gPrevX = X
 gPrevY = Y

 End If

 End Sub
```

This code is enclosed within an If statement:

```
If Button And 1 Then
    .........................................
    ... This code is executed whenever the user
    ... moves the mouse in the frmMyGame form
    ... while the left mouse button is help down.
    .........................................
End If
```

The X and Y parameters of the Form_MouseMove( ) procedure indicate the X and Y coordinates of the mouse cursor at the time the mouse was moved. The code you entered compares the previous coordinates of the mouse cursor with the current coordinates; and based on the comparison, the user is moved forward or backward, or rotated clockwise or counterclockwise.

Let's look at the first inner If statement:

```
If X < gPrevX Then
```

```
' Mouse was moved to the left
Floor1.Angle = Floor1.Angle + DIRECTION_CHANGE
'''''''''''''''''''''''
' Display the 3D view
'''''''''''''''''''''''
Floor1.Display3D
End If
```

So when the current horizontal coordinate of the mouse cursor (X) is less than the value of gPrevX, the Angle is increased by DIRECTION_CHANGE. Note that this is the same code we used in the Form_KeyDown( ) procedure of the frmMyGame form when the user presses the ← key. So when the mouse is moved to the left, it is the same as if the user pressed the ← key.

The next inner If statement checks to see whether the user moved the mouse to the right:

```
If X > gPrevX Then
    ' Mouse was moved to the right
    Floor1.Angle = Floor1.Angle - DIRECTION_CHANGE
    '''''''''''''''''''''''
    ' Display the 3D view
    '''''''''''''''''''''''
    Floor1.Display3D
End If
```

Here we examine whether the mouse was moved to the right, and if so, you execute the same code as when the user presses the → key.

TIP

Currently the increment by which the angle changes is always the same. You can enhance the program by letting the user set this increment (just as you did with the Distance change in the frmMouseControl form). In other words, you would add a Direction Speed scroll bar, and let the user set the amount by which the Angle property will increase or decrease.

Helping the User Move Straight Ahead

When moving the mouse forward, the user will probably move forward and a little bit to the right or to the left. In other words, it is difficult to move the mouse forward in a perfectly straight line. The result will be that the user's position is moved forward and also rotated clockwise or counterclockwise a little.

You can easily negate the rotation by using the following code for the If statement that determines whether the user has moved the mouse to the left:

```
If X < gPrevX - 5 Then
    ' Mouse was moved to the left
    Floor1.Angle = Floor1.Angle + DIRECTION_CHANGE
    ''''''''''''''''''''''''

    ' Display the 3D view
    ''''''''''''''''''''''''

    Floor1.Display3D
End If
```

This code puts a stricter condition on the If statement. In order for the program to react to the left mouse movement, the user has to move the mouse at least 5 pixels to the left. So when the user moves the mouse forward, even if the user moved the mouse a little to the left, the left rotation will occur only if the mouse was moved at least 5 pixels to the left.

You can add a similar test for the right-rotation If statement. As you can see, the value 5 determines the sensitivity of the mouse. You can add another scroll bar to the Mouse Control Panel window that lets the user set the mouse sensitivity.

The If statements that check whether the mouse was moved to the left or to the right will then use the Value property of the sensitivity scroll bar (instead of using the constant 5).

32

The next inner If statement determines whether the user moved the mouse forward:

```
If Y < gPrevY Then
   ' Mouse was moved upward
   Floor1.Advance gDistanceSpeed
   ''''''''''''''''''''''

   ' Display the 3D view
   ''''''''''''''''''''''

   Floor1.Display3D
End If
```

Here we determine that the user has moved the mouse forward, and then execute the Advance method. Notice that the parameter of the Advance method determines how far the user's position is advanced—namely, by the amount specified by the Value property of the Distance Speed scroll bar.

In a similar manner, the last If inner statement detects that the user moved the mouse downward, and moves the user backward:

```
If Y > gPrevY Then
   ' Mouse was moved upward
   Floor1.Advance -gDistanceSpeed
   ''''''''''''''''''''''

   ' Display the 3D view
   ''''''''''''''''''''''

   Floor1.Display3D
End If
```

The last two statements in the Form_MouseMove( ) procedure set the value of the gPrevX and gPrevY variables with the current X and Y values:

```
gPrevX = X
gPrevY = Y
```

Again, X and Y are provided as the parameters of the Form_MouseMove( ) procedure. So the next time Form_MouseMove( )is executed, the previous mouse position is updated.

Restricting the User's Movement

It is important to understand that you must restrict the distance by which the user can advance forward or backward. In other words, you cannot supply a large number as the parameter of the Advance method. If the user is currently standing next to a solid cell and you advanced the user by an amount larger than the width of the solid cell, you are letting the user jump over the cell.

For example, in our Floor OCX control, the default dimensions of the solid cells are 65 pixels by 65 pixels. If you advance the user by 32 pixels, the Floor control will refuse to put the user inside the solid cell. But if you set the parameter of the Advance method to 100 pixels (and there is an empty cell beyond the solid cell), then you are jumping over the solid cell. This feature was implemented in the Floor OCX control so that you have the option of implementing "jumping" features. For example, you'll be able to display the solid cell as a pool of water with hungry alligators in it. Naturally, you want your user to jump over this obstacle. Similarly, you want your user to jump over fire, fences, and other dangerous objects.

Other Options for the Mouse Control Panel

So far, you've read about various options that you may implement inside the Mouse Control Panel window. For example, you can set the Distance Speed scroll bar, the Direction Speed scroll bar, and the Mouse Sensitivity scroll bar.

In addition, you can incorporate other important settings in the Mouse Control Panel window. In a "shoot-'em-up" game, for example, you might want to set the weapon type (machine gun, rockets), let the user view the current ammunition inventory (how many bullets are left), and so on.

Or, if you're concerned about the effects of violence in computer games on kids and adults, you might construct a more peaceful game where mouse operations correspond to the procedures involved in excavating an archaeological site, for example, or surveying wildlife in a given area, or…

Implementing the Help Window

You'll now implement the Help menu item.

- Make the frmMyGame form the active form.

- Select Menu Editor from the Tools menu of Visual Basic, and insert the Help menu item inside the Help menu. After inserting the menu item, the Help menu of the frmMyGame form should look as follows:

Caption	Name
&Help	mnuHelp
...&Help...	mnuHelpInstructions
...&About...	mnuAbout

- Enter the following code in the mnuHelpInstructions_Click( ) procedure of the frmMyGame form:

```
Private Sub mnuHelpInstructions_Click( )
    frmHelp.Show 1
End Sub
```

This code displays the frmHelp form as a modal dialog box. (You'll implement the frmHelp form in the following section.)

Implementing the frmHelp Form

You'll now implement the frmHelp form.

- Implement the frmHelp form with the Properties settings listed in Table 32.2. When you're finished, the form should look as shown Figure 32.6

Attaching Code to the OK Button of the frmHelp Form

You'll now attach code to the Click event of the OK button of the frmHelp form.

TABLE 32.2: The Properties of the frmHelp Form

Object: Form
Name: frmHelp

Property	Value
BorderStyle	4 'Fixcd ToolWindow
Caption	"Help"
Height	5250
Left	1080
MaxButton	0 'False
MinButton	0 'False
Picture	C:\WinGPrg\CH27\Help.BMP
Top	1170
Width	7380

Object: CommandButton
Name: cmdOK

Property	Value
Caption	"&OK"
Height	375
Left	1920
Top	4320
Width	1215

- Enter the following code in the cmdOK_Click( ) procedure of the frmHelp form:

```
Private Sub cmdOK_Click( )

    Unload Me

End Sub
```

This code closes the Help window.

FIGURE 32.6:

The frmHelp form in design mode

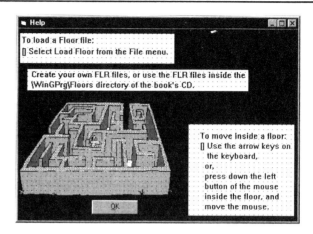

Summary

In this chapter you implemented the Mouse Control Panel window and the Help window.

You wrote code that lets the user use the mouse for moving the user's position inside the form. As discussed, you can enhance the program to adjust the sensitivity of the mouse in a variety of ways. In this chapter you let the user adjust the mouse operations by executing the Advance method and supplying the Value property of the Distance Speed scroll bar as the parameter of the Advance method.

An important thing to note when executing the Advance method is not to supply a large number as the parameter of the Advance method because if you do, the user's position will "jump" over the solid cell.

CHAPTER

THIRTY-THREE

33

Using Direction and Color
Control Panels

As you've seen, your user will use the keyboard (or the mouse) for movement. Sometimes, your user may want to be facing a certain precise direction. In this chapter you'll execute the MyWalls.EXE program, which implements a Direction Control Panel window where your user can view or set the direction in degrees.

The MyWalls.EXE program also implements the Select Color Control Panel window, where the user can change the colors of the walls, ceiling, floor, and partition stripes.

Executing the MyWalls.EXE Program

Start the MyWalls.EXE program, which is located in the \WinGPrg\EXE directory. You'll see the window shown in Figure 33.1.

FIGURE 33.1:
The MyWalls.EXE program

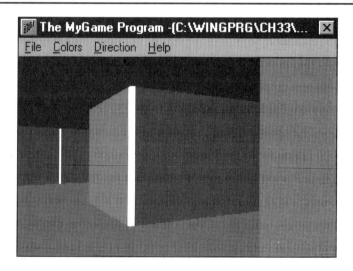

The MyWalls.EXE program uses the MyWalls.FLR file, which looks like this:

```
11111111111111111111
1                   1
1                   1
1    1111 1111       1
1                   1
1    1    1          1
1    1    1          1
1    1111 1111       1
1                   1
11111111111111111111
```

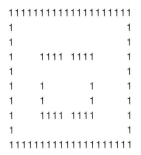

The MyWalls.EXE program includes the following menus: File, Colors, Direction, and Help. These menus are shown in Figures 33.2 through 33.5.

FIGURE 33.2:
The File menu

FIGURE 33.3:
The Colors menu

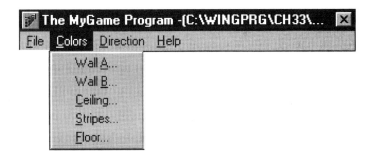

FIGURE 33.4:
The Direction menu

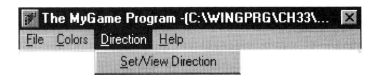

- Move around the floor using the arrow keys or the mouse.

FIGURE 33.5:

The Help menu

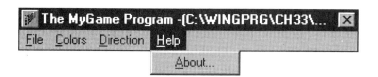

The MyWalls program lets the user display a Direction Control Panel window. To see the Direction Control Panel window in action:

- Select Set/View Direction from the Direction menu. You'll see the window shown in Figure 33.6.

FIGURE 33.6:

The Direction window

- Click the Show Direction button of the Direction window.

MyWalls responds by displaying a graph that represents the current direction; below the graph a label displays the direction in degrees (see Figure 33.7).

In Figure 33.7, the current direction is 60°. That is, as shown in Figure 33.8, the user faces the 60° direction, and the total view is 60° wide. So the user can see from the 30° line to the 90° line.

FIGURE 33.7:

Displaying the current direction

FIGURE 33.8:

The total view is 60°, ranging 30° below the 60° direction to 30° above the 60° direction.

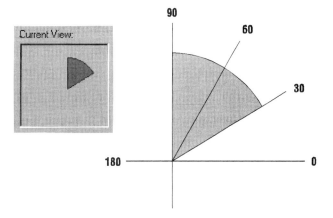

- Place the cursor on the arrow of the Spin control and hold down the left mouse button. While you do this, the direction changes. If you press the left arrow of the Spin control, the direction changes counterclockwise. If you press the right arrow, the direction changes clockwise. Figure 33.9 shows the Direction window after setting the direction to 210°.

FIGURE 33.9:

The Direction window after setting the direction to 210°

- Experiment with the Direction window and then click the Close switch to close the Direction window.

Changing the Colors of the Ceiling, Walls, Floor, and Stripes

The MyWalls program also lets the user change the colors of the walls, ceiling, floor, and stripes.

- Select Wall A from the Colors menu. You'll see the window shown in Figure 33.10.

The Floor control offers two types of walls, called Wall A and Wall B. This allows you to assign different colors to walls facing in different directions, for a better 3D effect. For example, Figure 33.11 shows the 3D picture of the wall after assigning both types of walls the light green color. It's hard to see what you are looking at on the left side of this 3D picture.

FIGURE 33.10:

The Select a Color window

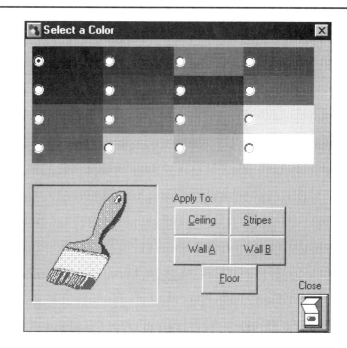

FIGURE 33.11:

The 3D picture of the floor when assigning both types of walls the light green color

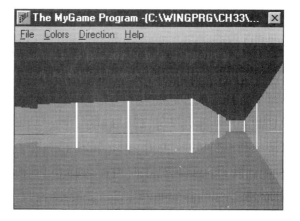

A better 3D picture is obtained by assigning different colors to the walls. For example, you can assign Wall A the light green color and Wall B the dark green color. The corresponding 3D picture is shown in Figure 3.12. As you can see, now the 3D picture is easier to understand.

FIGURE 33.12:

The 3D picture of the floor with one type of wall assigned the light green color, and the other type assigned dark green

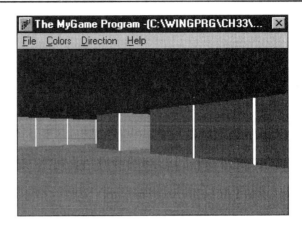

To change the color of the walls:

- Select the Black option button, and then select the Wall A button.

MyWalls responds by changing the colors of the walls of type A to black. (Drag the Select a Color window out of the way for a better view.)

In a similar way, you can set the color of the type B walls, the ceiling, the floor, and the stripes between wall segments. Select a color by clicking its option button, and then click the button for the object whose object you want to change.

- Experiment with the MyWalls program by setting different colors to the walls, ceiling, floor, and stripes.

- Click the Close switch to close the Select a Color window.

- Select Exit from the File menu of the MyWalls window to terminate the MyWalls program.

Summary

In this chapter you implemented the MyWalls program, in which users can set and view their current direction. The program also lets the user set the color of the walls, ceiling, floor, and stripes. In the next chapter you'll implement the MyWalls program yourself.

CHAPTER

THIRTY-FOUR

34

Implementing the MyWalls Application

In the previous chapter you executed the MyWalls program, which lets the user set and view the current direction. The MyWalls program also lets the user paint the walls, the ceiling, the stripes, and the floor. In this chapter you'll implement the My-Walls program.

Creating the Project of the MyWalls Program

The first step is to create the MyWalls project.

- Select New Project from the File menu of Visual Basic. Save the new form as MyGames.FRM and the new project file as MyWalls.VBP, both in the C:\WinGPrg\CH33 directory.

- Implement the frmMyWalls form with the Properties settings listed in Table 34.1. When you're finished, the form should look as shown in Figure 34.1.

TABLE 34.1: The Properties of the frmMyWalls Form

Object: Form	
Name: frmMyWalls	
Property	**Value**
BorderStyle	3 'Fixed Dialog
Caption	"The MyWalls Program"
Height	4095
Icon	C:\WinGPrg\Icons\MyWalls.ICO
Left	1440
MaxButton	0 'False
MinButton	0 'False
Top	1365
Width	3435

TABLE 34.1: The Properties of the frmMyWalls Form (continued)

Object: Floor

Name: Floor1

Property	Value
Left	480
Top	2400

34

FIGURE 34.1:

The frmMyGames form in design mode

Note that you're placing the Floor control in the frmMyWalls form. To add the Floor OCX control to your Visual Basic Tools window, select Custom Control from the Options menu, and select the Floor OCX control.

• Implement the menu of the frmMyWalls according to Table 34.2.

TABLE 34.2: The Menus of the frmMyWalls Form

Caption	Name
&File	mnuFile
...E&xit	mnuExit
&Colors	mnuWallColors
...Wall &A...	mnuWallA
...Wall &B...	mnuWallB
...&Ceiling...	mnuCeiling
...&Stripes...	mnuStripes
...&Floor...	mnuFloor
&Direction	mnuDirection
...&Set/View Direction...	mnuSetViewDirection
&Help	mnuHelp
...&About...	mnuAbout

The General Declarations Section of the frmMyWalls Form

- Enter the following code in the General Declarations section of the frmMy-Walls form:

```
Option Explicit
```

This code forces you to declare variables before using them.

Attaching Code to the Load Event of the frmMyWalls Form

You'll now attach code to the Load event of the frmMyWalls form.

- Enter the following code in the Form_Load( ) procedure of the frmMy-Walls form:

```
Private Sub Form_Load( )

Dim OpenResult As Integer
Dim Message As String
Dim NumberOfRows, NumberOfCols
Dim CRLF

gFloorFileName = App.Path + "\MyWalls.FLR"

CRLF = Chr(13) + Chr(10)

' Find number of rows in the floor file
NumberOfRows = FindNumOfRows

' Find number of columns in the floor file
NumberOfCols = FindNumOfCols

' Initialize and open the 3D floor control

Floor1.FileName = gFloorFileName

Floor1.hWndDisplay = Me.hWnd
Floor1.NumOfRows = NumberOfRows
Floor1.NumOfCols = NumberOfCols

' Initial position
Floor1.X = 4 * Floor1.CellWidth + 25
Floor1.Y = 4 * Floor1.CellWidth + 25

' Initial direction
Floor1.Angle = 60

' Open the FLR file
OpenResult = Floor1.Open

Me.Caption = Floor1.FileName

End Sub
```

34

This code is executed when the MyWalls program starts. You first declared several local variables:

```
Dim OpenResult As Integer
Dim Message As String
Dim NumberOfRows, NumberOfCols
Dim CRLF
```

The next statement assigns the path and name of a floor file to the gFloorFileName variable:

```
gFloorFileName = App.Path + "\MyWalls.FLR"
```

App.Path is the directory from which the program is executed. So for example, if the MyWalls program is executed from the C:\WinGPrg\CH33 directory, then App.Path is equal to C:\WinGPrg\CH33. You'll declare the gFloorFileName variable later in this chapter.

The CRLF variable is then assigned the carriage-return/line-feed characters:

```
CRLF = Chr(13) + Chr(10)
```

We then extract the number of rows in the floor file by executing the FindNumRows function:

```
' Find number of rows in the floor file
NumberOfRows = FindNumOfRows
```

You'll write the FindNumOfRows function later in this chapter. For now, just note that the FindNumOfRows function extracts the number of rows of the floor file indicated by the gFloorFileName variable.

The next statement extracts the number of columns from the floor file:

```
' Find number of columns in the floor file
NumberOfCols = FindNumOfCols
```

You'll write the FindNumOfCols function later in this chapter. For now, just note that the FindNumOfCols function extracts the number of columns of the floor file indicated by the gFloorFileName variable.

You can now initialize and open the floor file:

```
Floor1.FileName = gFloorFileName

Floor1.hWndDisplay = Me.hWnd
Floor1.NumOfRows = NumberOfRows
Floor1.NumOfCols = NumberOfCols
```

The user's initial position and direction are set:

```
' Initial position
Floor1.X = 4 * Floor1.CellWidth + 25
Floor1.Y = 4 * Floor1.CellWidth + 25

' Initial direction
Floor1.Angle = 60
```

You can now open the floor file:

```
' Open the FLR file
OpenResult = Floor1.Open
```

The Caption property of the floor is assigned the name of the floor file:

```
Me.Caption = Floor1.FileName
```

The 3D picture of the floor is ready to be displayed.

34

The Display3D Method of the Floor Control

When the 3D picture of the floor is ready to be displayed, you can issue the Display3D method as follows:

```
Floor1.Display3D
```

However, if you execute the Display3D method from within the Form_Load( ) procedure you will not see the 3D picture, because the Display3D method needs a window to draw the 3D picture into. You specified the frmMyWalls window for this purpose. But the frmMyWalls window will be ready to display the 3D picture of the floor only after the Form_Load( ) procedure is completed. This means that the Display3D method should be executed from another procedure. A good place to execute the Display3D method is from within the Form_Paint( ) procedure.

Attaching Code to the Form_Paint( ) Procedure of the frmMyWalls Form

You'll now attach code to the Form_Paint( ) procedure, executed whenever there is a need to paint the frmMyWalls window. For example, it's executed whenever the program starts and the frmMyWalls form needs to be displayed for the first time.

- Enter the following code in the Form_Paint( ) procedure:

```
Private Sub Form_Paint( )

    ' Display the 3D view
    Floor1.Display3D

End Sub
```

This code displays the 3D picture of the floor.

Attaching Code to the Unload Event of the frmMyWalls Form

Whenever the frmMyWalls form is closed, the Unload event occurs.

- Enter the following code in the Form_Unload( ) procedure of the frmMy-Walls form:

```
Private Sub Form_Unload(Cancel As Integer)

    Unload frmSelectColor

End Sub
```

This code unloads the frmSelectColor form. You'll implement the frmSelectColor later in this chapter. frmSelectColor is the form that lets the user select colors for the walls, ceiling, floor, and stripes.

Modal and Nonmodal Windows in the MyWalls Program

As you saw in the previous chapter, the MyWalls program lets the user display two additional forms: frmSelectColor (the window that lets the user select a color) and frmDirection (the window that lets the user select and view directions).

As you'll see later in this chapter, the frmSelectColor form is displayed as a nonmodal window. This means that the user can select a color from the Select a Color window, and then click inside the frmMyWalls form and move within the form. The Select a Color window is still displayed. So the user can display the frmSelectColor form, switch to the frmMyWalls form, and select Exit from the File menu of the frmMyWalls form.

But unless we close the frmSelectColor form, it will remain open. This is the reason for closing the frmSelectColor form from within the Form_Unload( ) procedure of the frmMyWalls form.

If the user does close the Select Color window before closing the MyWalls window, the Unload statement in the Form_Unload( ) procedure will attempt to unload a form that is closed already. Well, there is nothing wrong with that.

As stated, the MyWalls program also lets the user display the frmDirection form. However, as you'll see later in this chapter, the frmDirection form is displayed as modal window. This means that the user cannot switch back to the frmMyWalls form unless the frmDirection form is closed first. So there is no need to unload the frmDirection form from within the Form_Unload( ) procedure of the frmMyWalls form.

If in future projects you decide to display the frmDirection form as a nonmodal dialog box, don't forget to add the following statement to the Form_Unload( ) procedure:

```
Unload frmDirection
```

Attaching Code to the Exit Menu Item

You'll now attach code to the Click event of the File menu's Exit item.

- Enter the following code in the mnuExit_Click( ) procedure of the frmMy-Walls form:

```
Private Sub mnuExit_Click( )

    ' Unload the form
    Unload Me

End Sub
```

This code is executed whenever the user selects Exit from the File menu. It executes the Unload_Form( ) procedure of the frmMyWalls form.

Attaching Code to the Wall A Item of the Colors Menu

You'll now attach code to the Wall A item of the Colors menu of the frmMy-Wallsform.

- Enter the following code in the mnuWallA_Click( ) procedure of the frmMy-Walls form:

```
Private Sub mnuWallA_Click( )

    frmSelectColor.Show 0

End Sub
```

This code displays the frmSelectColor form as a nonmodal dialog box (because you supplied 0 as the parameter of the Show method). You'll implement the frmSelectColor form later in this chapter.

The Show Method of the Floor Control

To display a form, use the Show method. For example, to display the frmMy-Form form, use the following statement:

```
frmMyForm.Show X
```

where X is 0 when you display the form as a nonmodal (modeless) window, and X is 1 when you display the form as a modal window.

Again, a modal window is one that you must close before you can switch to another form in the program. A nonmodal window is one that lets you switch to another form of the project without first closing the nonmodal window.

34

Attaching Code to the Other Items of the Colors Menu

The Colors menu has the following items:

Wall A

Wall B

Ceiling

Floor

Stripes

Whenever the user selects any of these items, the frmSelectColors form is displayed. The user can then set the color for any item. So in essence, the Colors menu could have a single menu item, perhaps called Change Colors. However, having five items in the Colors menu makes the program easier to operate.

As stated, all the items in the Colors menu produce the same result. You'll now attach code to the mnuWallB_Click( ) procedure of the frmMyWalls form:

- Enter the following code in the mnuWallB_Click( ) procedure of the f2mMy-
  Walls form:

```
Private Sub mnuWallB_Click( )

    frmSelectColor.Show 0

End Sub
```

This displays the frmSelectColor form as a nonmodal window.

- Enter the following code in the mnuCeiling_Click( ) procedure of the frmMy-
  Walls form:

```
Private Sub mnuCeiling_Click( )

    frmSelectColor.Show 0

End Sub
```

- Enter the following code in the mnuFloor_Click( ) procedure of the frmMy-
  Walls form:

```
Private Sub mnuFloor_Click( )

    frmSelectColor.Show 0

End Sub
```

- Enter the following code in the mnuStripes_Click( ) procedure of the frmMy-
  Walls form:

```
Private Sub mnuStripes_Click( )

    frmSelectColor.Show 0

End Sub
```

Attaching Code to the Set/View Direction Item of the Direction Menu

- Enter the following code in the mnuSetViewDirection_Click( ) procedure of the frmMyWalls form:

```
Private Sub mnuSetViewDirection_Click( )

    frmDirection.Show 1

End Sub
```

34

This code displays the frmDirection form as a modal window. You'll implement the frmDirection form later in this chapter.

Attaching Code to the KeyDown Event of the frmMyWalls Form

The KeyDown event occurs whenever the user presses a key while the frmMyWalls form is active. The code that you'll enter in the Form_KeyDown( ) procedure of the frmMyWalls form is responsible for moving the user's current position within the 3D floor picture.

- Enter the following code in the Form_KeyDown( ) procedure of the frmMyWalls form:

```
Private Sub Form_KeyDown(KeyCode As Integer, _
                         Shift As Integer)

Select Case KeyCode

    Case 37, 100
        ' Left key (37) or 4 key (100) was pressed
        ' to increase the direction angle.
        Floor1.Angle = Floor1.Angle + 10
```

```
        Case 39, 102
                ' Right key (39) or 6 key (102) was pressed
                ' to decrease the direction angle.
                Floor1.Angle = Floor1.Angle - 10

        Case 38, 104
                ' Up key (38) or 8 key (104) was pressed
                ' to advance forward.
                Floor1.Advance (40)

Case 40, 98 'Down or 2
                ' Down key (40) or 2 key (98) was pressed
                ' to advance backward.
                Floor1.Advance (-40)


    End Select

    ''''''''''''''''''''''
    ' Display the 3D view
    ''''''''''''''''''''''
    Floor1.Display3D

    End Sub
```

This code uses a Select Case statement to determine which key was pressed. So depending on the keystroke, the user's current position is changed either by using the Advance method, or by changing the Angle property.

Finally, the 3D picture is displayed by executing the Display3D method:

```
    ''''''''''''''''''''''
    ' Display the 3D view
    ''''''''''''''''''''''
    Floor1.Display3D
```

Attaching Code to the MouseMove Event of the frmMyWalls Form

You'll now attach code to the MouseMove event of the frmMyWalls form. The MouseMove event occurs whenever the user moves the mouse in the frmMyWalls form.

- Enter the following code in the Form_MouseMove( ) procedure of the frmMyWalls form:

34

```
Private Sub Form_MouseMove(Button As Integer, _
                          Shift As Integer, _
                          X As Single, _
                          Y As Single)

''''''''''''''''''''''''''''''''
' Here you write code that
' will be executed whenever the
' user moves the mouse.
''''''''''''''''''''''''''''''''

Static PrevX, PrevY

If Button And 1 Then

    If X < PrevX Then
        ' Mouse was moved to the left
        Floor1.Angle = Floor1.Angle + 10

        '''''''''''''''''''''''''
        ' Display the 3D view
        '''''''''''''''''''''''''
        Floor1.Display3D
    End If

    If X > PrevX Then
        ' Mouse was moved to the right
        Floor1.Angle = Floor1.Angle - 10
        '''''''''''''''''''''''''
        ' Display the 3D view
        '''''''''''''''''''''''''
        Floor1.Display3D
```

```
        End If

        If Y < PrevY Then
            ' Mouse was moved upward
            Floor1.Advance 40
            ''''''''''''''''''''''

            ' Display the 3D view
            ''''''''''''''''''''''

            Floor1.Display3D
        End If

        If Y > PrevY Then
            ' Mouse was moved upward
            Floor1.Advance -40
            ''''''''''''''''''''''

            ' Display the 3D view
            ''''''''''''''''''''''

            Floor1.Display3D
        End If

    PrevX = X
    PrevY = Y

    End If

    End Sub
```

This code declares two static variables:

```
    Static PrevX, PrevY
```

As you'll soon see, PrevX and PrevY are used for storing the previous location of the mouse cursor. You declare the PrevX and PrevY variables as static variables, because you want these variables to maintain their values even after the Form_MouseMove( ) procedure is terminated.

An If statement is executed to determine whether the left button of the mouse is down:

```
    If Button And 1 Then
        ..............................................
        .... Yes, the left button of the mouse is down.
        ..............................................
    End If
```

Button is one of the parameters of the Form_MouseMove( ) procedure. It represents the status of the mouse button. So when the user moves the mouse while the left button of the mouse is down, the code under the If statement is executed.

The If statement contains several nested If statements. Each inner If statement examines and compares the previous coordinate of the mouse cursor with the current mouse coordinates. X and Y are the parameters of the Form_MouseMove( ) procedure. They represent the coordinates of the mouse at the time the mouse was moved and the Form_MouseMove( ) procedure was executed.

The first inner If statement compares the current X coordinate of the mouse cursor with the previous X coordinates of the mouse cursor:

```
If X < PrevX Then
    ' Mouse was moved to the left
    Floor1.Angle = Floor1.Angle + 10

    '''''''''''''''''''''''
    ' Display the 3D view
    '''''''''''''''''''''''
    Floor1.Display3D
End If
```

Because the current X coordinate of the mouse cursor is less than the previous X coordinate, it means that the mouse was moved to the left. Thus, the Angle property of the Floor control is increased.

Similarly, the next inner If statement tests whether the mouse cursor was moved to the right:

```
If X > PrevX Then
    ' Mouse was moved to the right
    Floor1.Angle = Floor1.Angle - 10
    '''''''''''''''''''''''
    ' Display the 3D view
    '''''''''''''''''''''''
    Floor1.Display3D
End If
```

In this code, the Angle property is decreased, because the mouse was moved to the right.

34

The next inner If statement examines whether the mouse was moved upward:

```
If Y < PrevY Then
        ' Mouse was moved upward
        Floor1.Advance 40
        '''''''''''''''''''''
        ' Display the 3D view
        '''''''''''''''''''''
        Floor1.Display3D
    End If
```

In this code, the Advance method is executed to advance the code 40 pixels forward.

The last inner If statement checks whether the user moved the mouse downward:

```
If Y > PrevY Then
        ' Mouse was moved upward
        Floor1.Advance -40
        '''''''''''''''''''''
        ' Display the 3D view
        '''''''''''''''''''''
        Floor1.Display3D
    End If
```

The last two statements update the PrevX and PrevY variables with the current coordinates of the mouse:

```
PrevX = X
PrevY = Y
```

The PrevX and PrevY variables are now ready for the next execution of the Form_MouseMove( ) procedure.

Attaching Code to the About Item of the Help Menu

You'll now attach code to the About menu item of the frmMyWalls form.

- Enter the following code in the mnuAbout_Click( ) procedure of the frmMy-Walls form:

```
Private Sub mnuAbout_Click( )

    frmAbout.Show 1

End Sub
```

This code displays the frmAbout form as a modal window. You'll implement the frmAbout form later in this chapter.

34

Declaring General Variables in a Separate Module

You'll now insert a new BAS module into the MyWalls project.

- Select Module from the Insert menu of Visual Basic.

Visual Basic responds by inserting a new BAS module into the MyWalls project.

- Save the new BAS module as MyWalls.BAS in the C:\WinFPrg\CH33 directory.

- Enter the following code in the General Declarations section of the My-Walls.BAS module:

```
' All variables must be declared
Option Explicit

Public gFloorFileName
Public gNewColor
Public gCeilingColor
```

The code that you typed forces variable declaration and declares several global variables. Because these variables are declared in the General Declarations section of a separate BAS module, they are accessible from any procedure of any form in the MyWalls project.

The FindNumOfRows( ) Function

Recall that in the Form_Load( ) procedure of the frmMyGames form you execute the FindNumOfRows( ) function. You'll now write the code of this function.

- Make sure that the MyWalls.BAS module is selected, select Procedure from the Insert menu of Visual Basic, and insert a new function. Set the name of the new function to FindNumOfRows.

- Enter the following code in the FindNumOfRows( ) function:

```
Public Function FindNumOfRows( )

''''''''''''''''''''''''''''''''''''''
' This function finds the number of
' rows in the selected floor file.
''''''''''''''''''''''''''''''''''''''

Dim FileNum
Dim Cell As String
Dim FloorFileLength
Dim I

FindNumOfRows = 0

' Get the next available file number
FileNum = FreeFile

' Open the floor file
Open gFloorFileName For Binary As FileNum

' Extract the length of the floor file
FloorFileLength = FileLen(gFloorFileName)

' Extract the number of rows in the floor file
For I = 1 To FloorFileLength
    Cell = " "
    Get #FileNum, I, Cell
    If Asc(Cell) = 13 Then
        FindNumOfRows = FindNumOfRows + 1
        If I + 1 > FloorFileLength Then Exit For
        Get #FileNum, I + 1, Cell
        If Asc(Cell) = 10 Then
```

```
            If I + 2 > FloorFileLength Then Exit For
            Get #FileNum, I + 2, Cell
            If Asc(Cell) = 13 Then
                Exit For
            End If
        End If
    End If
Next I

If Asc(Cell) <> 13 And _
   Asc(Cell) <> 10 And _
   Asc(Cell) <> 32 Then

    FindNumOfRows = FindNumOfRows + 1

End If

' Close the floor file
Close FileNum

End Function
```

This code extracts the number of rows in the floor file.

The FindNumOfCols( ) Function

Recall that in the Form_Load( ) procedure of the frmMyGames form you execute the FindNumOfCols( ) function. You'll now write the code of this function.

- Make sure that the MyWalls.BAS module is selected, select Procedure from the Insert menu of Visual Basic, and insert a new function. Set the name of the new function as FindNumOfCols.

- Enter the following code in the FindNumOfCols( ) function:

```
Public Function FindNumOfCols( )

'''''''''''''''''''''''''''''''''''''
' This function finds the number of
' columns in the selected floor file.
'''''''''''''''''''''''''''''''''''''
```

34

```
Dim FileNum
Dim Cell As String
Dim FloorFileLength
Dim I

FindNumOfCols = 0

' Get the next available file number
FileNum = FreeFile

' Open the file
Open gFloorFileName For Binary As FileNum

' Extract the length of the floor file.
FloorFileLength = FileLen(gFloorFileName)

' Extract the number of columns in the floor file.
For I = 1 To FloorFileLength
    Cell = " "
    Get #FileNum, I, Cell
    If Asc(Cell) = 13 Then Exit For
Next I
FindNumOfCols = I - 1

' Close the floor file.
Close FileNum

End Function
```

This code extracts the number of columns in the floor file.

Implementing the frmAbout Form

You'll now implement the frmAbout form.

- Implement the frmAbout form with the Properties settings listed in Table 34.3. When you're finished, the form should look as shown in Figure 34.2.

TABLE 34.3: The Properties of the frmAbout Form

Object: Form
Name: frmAbout

Property	Value
BorderStyle	1 'Fixed Single
Caption	"About"
Height	5415
Left	1095
MaxButton	0 'False
MinButton	0 'False
Picture	C:\WinGPrg\CH33\About.BMP
Top	660
Width	7410

Object: CommandButton
Name: cmdOK

Property	Value
Caption	"&OK"
Height	495
Left	5040
Top	1080
Width	855

34

Attaching Code to the OK Button

You'll now attach code to the Click event of the cmdOK button.

- Enter the following code in the cmdOK_Click( ) procedure of the frmAbout form:

```
Private Sub cmdOK_Click( )

    ' Unload the form
```

FIGURE 34.2:

The frmAbout form in design mode

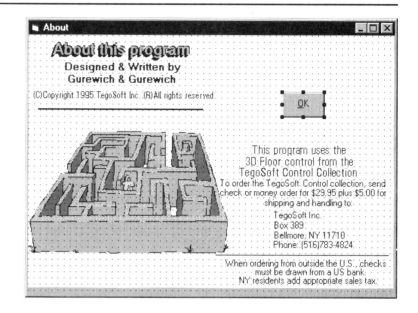

```
        Unload Me

    End Sub
```

This code closes the About window. So whenever the user clicks the OK button of the About window, the About window closes.

Implementing the frmSelectColor Form

The frmSelectColor form is used for selecting a color for the walls, ceiling, and other items. You'll now implement the frmSelectColor form.

- Implement the frmSelectColor form with the Properties settings listed in Table 34.4. When you're finished, the form should look as shown in Figure 34.3.

FIGURE 34.3:

The frmSelectColor form in
design mode

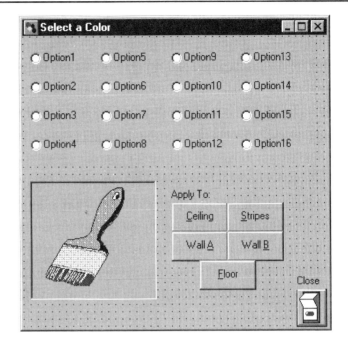

TABLE 34.4: The Properties of the frmSelectColor Form

Object: Form
Name: frmSelectColor

Property	Value
BorderStyle	1 'Fixed Single
Caption	"Select a Color"
Height	5235
Icon	C:\WinGPrg\Icons\SetColor.ICO
Left	4050
MaxButton	0 'False
MinButton	0 'False
Top	675
Width	5340

TABLE 34.4: The Properties of the frmSelectColor Form (continued)

Object: CommandButton

Name: cmdFloor

Property	Value
Caption	"&Floor"
Height	495
Left	3000
Top	3720
Width	975

Object: CommandButton

Name: cmdWallB

Property	Value
Caption	"Wall &B"
Height	495
Left	3480
Top	3240
Width	975

Object: CommandButton

Name: cmdWallA

Property	Value
Caption	"Wall &A"
Height	495
Left	2520
Top	3240
Width	975

TABLE 34.4: The Properties of the frmSelectColor Form (continued)

Object: CommandButton
Name: cmdStripes

Property	Value
Caption	"&Stripes"
Height	495
Left	3480
Top	2760
Width	975

Object: CommandButton
Name: cmdCeiling

Property	Value
Caption	"&Ceiling"
Height	495
Left	2520
Top	2760
Width	975

Object: OptionButton
Name: Option1

Property	Value
Caption	"Option1"
Height	495
Left	120
Top	120
Width	1215

Object: OptionButton
Name: Option2

Property	Value
Caption	"Option2"
Height	495

TABLE 34.4: The Properties of the frmSelectColor Form (continued)

Left	120
Top	600
Width	1215

Object: OptionButton
Name: Option3

Property	Value
Caption	"Option3"
Height	495
Left	120
Top	1080
Width	1215

Object: OptionButton
Name: Option4

Property	Value
Caption	"Option4"
Height	495
Left	120
Top	1560
Width	1215

Object: OptionButton
Name: Option5

Property	Value
Caption	"Option5"
Height	495
Left	1320
Top	120
Width	1215

TABLE 34.4: The Properties of the frmSelectColor Form (continued)

Object: OptionButton
Name: Option6

Property	Value
Caption	"Option6"
Height	495
Left	1320
Top	600
Width	1215

Object: OptionButton
Name: Option7

Property	Value
Caption	"Option7"
Height	495
Left	1320
Top	1080
Width	1215

Object: OptionButton
Name: Option8

Property	Value
Caption	"Option8"
Height	495
Left	1320
Top	1560
Width	1215

Object: OptionButton
Name: Option9

Property	Value
Caption	"Option9"
Height	495

TABLE 34.4: The Properties of the frmSelectColor Form (continued)

Left	2520
Top	120
Width	1215

Object: OptionButton
Name: Option10

Property	Value
Caption	"Option10"
Height	495
Left	2520
Top	600
Width	1215

Object: OptionButton
Name: Option11

Property	Value
Caption	"Option11"
Height	495
Left	2520
Top	1080
Width	1215

Object: OptionButton
Name: Option12

Property	Value
Caption	"Option12"
Height	495
Left	2520
Top	1560
Width	1215

TABLE 34.4: The Properties of the frmSelectColor Form (continued)

Object: OptionButton
Name: Option 13

Property	Value
Caption	"Option 13"
Height	495
Left	3720
Top	120
Width	1215

Object: OptionButton
Name: Option 14

Property	Value
Caption	"Option 14"
Height	495
Left	3720
Top	600
Width	1215

Object: OptionButton
Name: Option 15

Property	Value
Caption	"Option 15"
Height	495
Left	3720
Top	1080
Width	1215

Object: OptionButton
Name: Option 16

Property	Value
Caption	"Option 16"
Height	495

34

TABLE 34.4: The Properties of the frmSelectColor Form (continued)

Left	3720
Top	1560
Width	1215

Object: Label	
Name: Label1	
Property	**Value**
Caption	"Close"
Height	255
Left	4680
Top	3960
Width	495

Object: Label	
Name: Label2	
Property	**Value**
Caption	"Apply To:"
Height	255
Left	2520
Top	2520
Width	855

Object: Switch	
Name: swClose	
Property	**Value**
Height	630
Left	4680
Top	4200
Width	525
value	-1 'True

TABLE 34.4: The Properties of the frmSelectColor Form (continued)

Object: Image

Name: imgBrush

Property	Value
BorderStyle	1 'Fixed Single
Height	1965
Left	120
Picture	C:\WinGPrg\BMP\Brush.BMP
Top	2400
Width	214

34

The General Declarations Section of the frmSelectColor Form

- Enter the following code in the General Declarations section of the frmSe-lectColor form:

```
Option Explicit
```

This code forces variable declarations.

Attaching Code to the Load Event of the frmSelectColor Form

You'll now attach code to the Form_Load( ) procedure of the frmSelectColor form.

- Enter the following code in the Form_Load( ) procedure of the frmSelectColor( ) form:

```
Private Sub Form_Load( )

    Option1.Caption = ""
    Option1.BackColor = QBColor(0)

    Option2.Caption = ""
    Option2.BackColor = QBColor(1)

    Option3.Caption = ""
    Option3.BackColor = QBColor(2)

    Option4.Caption = ""
    Option4.BackColor = QBColor(3)

    Option5.Caption = ""
    Option5.BackColor = QBColor(4)

    Option6.Caption = ""
    Option6.BackColor = QBColor(5)

    Option7.Caption = ""
    Option7.BackColor = QBColor(6)

    Option8.Caption = ""
    Option8.BackColor = QBColor(7)

    Option9.Caption = ""
    Option9.BackColor = QBColor(8)

    Option10.Caption = ""
    Option10.BackColor = QBColor(9)

    Option11.Caption = ""
    Option11.BackColor = QBColor(10)

    Option12.Caption = ""
    Option12.BackColor = QBColor(11)

    Option13.Caption = ""
    Option13.BackColor = QBColor(12)
```

```
Option14.Caption = ""
Option14.BackColor = QBColor(13)

Option15.Caption = ""
Option15.BackColor = QBColor(14)

Option16.Caption - ""
Option16.BackColor = QBColor(15)
```

```
End Sub
```

This code sets the Caption properties of the option buttons for the 16 colors to null, and the BackColor properties to a color that corresponds to the name of the option button. For example, the BackColor property of option button Option16 is set to 15, the BackColor property of option button Option15 is set to 14, and so on.

34

Attaching Code to the Unload Event of the frmSelectColor Form

You'll now attach code to the Unload event of the frmSelectColor form.

- Enter the following code in the Form_Unload( ) procedure of the frmSelectColor form:

```
Private Sub Form_Unload(Cancel As Integer)

    Unload frmSelectColor

End Sub
```

This code unloads the frmSelectColor form.

Attaching Code to the Close Switch

You'll now attach code to the Click event of the swClose switch.

- Enter the following code in the swClose_Click( ) procedure of the frmSelectColors form:

```
Private Sub swClose_Click( )

    Unload Me

End Sub
```

This code unloads the frmSelectColor form.

Attaching Code to the Color Option Buttons

You'll now attach code to the Click events of the color option buttons.

- Enter the following code in the Option1_Click( ) procedure of the frmSelectColor form:

```
Private Sub Option1_Click( )

    gNewColor = 0

End Sub
```

This code sets the value of the general variable gNewColor to 0. In the Form_Load( ) procedure you entered code that sets the BackColor property of Option1 to the color QBColor(0), or black. So when the user clicks the black option button (Option1), gNewColor is set to 0.

Similarly, you'll now write code that sets gNewColor to 1 when the user clicks the Option2 button, to 2 when the user clicks the Option3 button, and so on.

- Enter the following code in the Option2_Click( ) procedure of the frmSelectColor form:

```
Private Sub Option2_Click( )

    gNewColor = 1

End Sub
```

- Enter the following code in the Option3_Click( ) procedure of the frmSelectColor form:

```
Private Sub Option3_Click( )

    gNewColor = 2

End Sub
```

34

- Enter the following code in the Option4_Click( ) procedure of the frmSelectColor form:

```
Private Sub Option4_Click( )

    gNewColor = 3

End Sub
```

- Enter the following code in the Option5_Click( ) procedure of the frmSelectColor form:

```
Private Sub Option5_Click( )

    gNewColor = 4

End Sub
```

- Enter the following code in the Option6_Click( ) procedure of the frmSelectColor form:

```
Private Sub Option6_Click( )

    gNewColor = 5

End Sub
```

- Enter the following code in the Option7_Click( ) procedure of the frmSelectColor form:

```
Private Sub Option7_Click( )

    gNewColor = 6

End Sub
```

- Enter the following code in the Option8_Click( ) procedure of the frmSelectColor form:

```
Private Sub Option8_Click( )

    gNewColor = 7

End Sub
```

- Enter the following code in the Option9_Click( ) procedure of the frmSelectColor form:

```
Private Sub Option9_Click( )

    gNewColor = 8

End Sub
```

- Enter the following code in the Option10_Click( ) procedure of the frmSelectColor form:

```
Private Sub Option10_Click( )

    gNewColor = 9

End Sub
```

- Enter the following code in the Option11_Click( ) procedure of the frmSelectColor form:

```
Private Sub Option11_Click( )

    gNewColor = 10

End Sub
```

- Enter the following code in the Option12_Click( ) procedure of the frmSelectColor form:

```
Private Sub Option12_Click( )

    gNewColor = 11

End Sub
```

- Enter the following code in the Option13_Click( ) procedure of the frmSelectColor form:

```
Private Sub Option13_Click( )

    gNewColor = 12

End Sub
```

- Enter the following code in the Option14_Click( ) procedure of the frmSelectColor form:

```
Private Sub Option14_Click( )

    gNewColor = 13

End Sub
```

- Enter the following code in the Option15Click( ) procedure of the frmSelectColor form:

```
Private Sub Option15_Click( )

        gNewColor = 14

End Sub
```

- Enter the following code in the Option16_Click( ) procedure of the frmSelectColor form:

```
Private Sub Option16_Click( )

    gNewColor = 15

End Sub
```

34

Attaching Code to the Ceiling Button

You'll now attach code to the Click event of the cmdCeiling button of the frmSelectColor form. When the user clicks the Ceiling button of the frmSelectColor form, the ceiling of the 3D pictures is painted with the color of the currently selected option button.

- Enter the following code in the cmdCeiling_Click( ) procedure of the frmSelectColor form:

```
Private Sub cmdCeiling_Click( )

    frmMyWalls.Floor1.CeilingColor = gNewColor

    frmMyWalls.Floor1.Display3D

End Sub
```

This code sets the CeilingColor property of the Floor control to the value of gNewColor:

```
frmMyWalls.Floor1.CeilingColor = gNewColor
```

Recall that gNewColor was set in the Option??_Click( ) procedure to a value that represents the color of the clicked option button.

The next statement displays the 3D pictures:

```
frmMyWalls.Floor1.Display3D
```

The CeilingColor Property of the Floor Control

To set the color of the ceiling in the 3D picture, set the CeilingColor property of the Floor control. For example, to set the color of the ceiling to black, use the following code:

```
frmMyWalls.Floor1.CeilingColor = QBColor(0)
```

Attaching Code to the Floor Button

You'll now attach code to the Click event of the cmdFloor button of the frmSelectColor form. When the user clicks the Floor button of the frmSelectColor form, the floor of the 3D picture is painted with the color of the currently selected option button.

- Enter the following code in the cmdFloor_Click( ) procedure of the frmSelectColor form:

```
Private Sub cmdFloor_Click( )

    frmMyWalls.Floor1.FloorColor = gNewColor

    frmMyWalls.Floor1.Display3D

End Sub
```

This code sets the FloorColor property of the Floor control to the value of gNewColor:

```
frmMyWalls.Floor1.FloorColor = gNewColor
```

And then the 3D picture of the floor is displayed:

```
frmMyWalls.Floor1.Display3D
```

The FloorColor Property of the Floor Control

To set the color of the floor in the 3D picture, use the FloorColor property of the Floor control. For example, to set the color of the floor to black, use the following code:

```
frmMyWalls.Floor1.FloorColor = QBColor(0)
```

34

Attaching Code to the Stripes Button

You'll now attach code to the Click event of the cmdStripes button of the frmSelectColor form. When the user clicks the Stripes button of the frmSelectColor form, the stripes on the walls of the 3D picture are painted with the color of the currently selected option button.

- Enter the following code in the cmdStripes_Click( ) procedure of the frmSelectColor form:

```
Private Sub cmdStripes_Click( )

    frmMyWalls.Floor1.StripeColor = gNewColor

    frmMyWalls.Floor1.Display3D

End Sub
```

This code sets the StripeColor property of the Floor control to the value of gNewColor:

```
frmMyWalls.Floor1.StripeColor = gNewColor
```

And then the 3D picture of the floor is displayed:

```
frmMyWalls.Floor1.Display3D
```

The StripeColor Property of the Floor Control

To set the color of the stripes in the 3D picture, use the StripeColor property of the Floor control. For example, to set the color of the stripes to black, use the following code:

```
frmMyWalls.Floor1.StripeColor = gNewColor
```

Attaching Code to the Wall A Button

You'll now attach code to the Click event of the cmdWallA button of the frmSelectColor form. When the user clicks the Wall A button of the frmSelectColor form, the type A walls of the 3D picture are painted with the color of the current selected option button.

34

- Enter the following code in the cmdWallA_Click( ) procedure of the frmSelectColor form:

```
Private Sub cmdWallA_Click( )

    frmMyWalls.Floor1.WallColorA = gNewColor

    frmMyWalls.Floor1.Display3D

End Sub
```

This code sets the WallColorA property of the Floor control to the value of gNewColor:

```
frmMyWalls.Floor1.WallColorA = gNewColor
```

The WallColorA Property of the Floor Control

To set the color of the walls of type A in the 3D picture, set the WallColorA property of the Floor control. For example, to set the color of walls of type A to black, use the following code:

```
frmMyWalls.Floor1.WallColorA = gNewColor
```

Attaching Code to the Wall B Button

You'll now attach code to the Click event of the cmdWallB button of the frmSelectColor form. When the user clicks the Wall B button of the frmSelectColor form, the walls of type B of the 3D pictures are painted with the color of the current selected option button.

- Enter the following code in the cmdWallB_Click( ) procedure of the frmSelectColor form:

```
Private Sub cmdWallB_Click( )

    frmMyWalls.Floor1.WallColorB = gNewColor

    frmMyWalls.Floor1.Display3D

End Sub
```

This code sets the WallColorB property of the Floor control to the value of gNewColor:

```
frmMyWalls.Floor1.WallColorB = gNewColor
```

The WallColorB Property of the Floor Control

To set the color of the walls of type B in the 3D picture, use the WallColorB property of the Floor control. For example, to set the color of walls of type B to black, use the following code:

```
frmMyWalls.Floor1.WallColorB = QBColor(0)
```

Attaching Code to the imgBrush Image

You'll now attach code to the Click event of the imgBrush image.

- Enter the following code in the imgBrush_Click( ) procedure of the frmSe-lectColor form:

```
Private Sub imgBrush_Click( )

    Dim Message
    Dim Result
    Dim CRLF

    CRLF = Chr(13) + Chr(13)

    Message = "Click the option button that has " + _
            CRLF

    Message = Message + _
            "the color of your choice" + _
            CRLF

    Message = Message + _
            "and then click the button that" + _
            CRLF

    Message = Message + _
            "corresponds to the object whose " + _
            CRLF

    Message = Message + _
            "color you want to change."

    MsgBox Message, vbInformation, "Select a Color"

End Sub
```

This code displays a message box whenever the user clicks the Image control. Figure 34.4 shows the message box.

Implementing the frmDirection Form

You'll now implement the frmDirection form.

FIGURE 34.4:

The message box that is displayed after clicking the imgBrush control

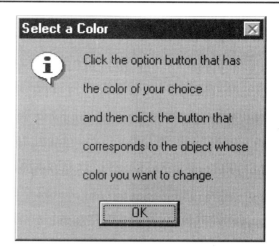

- Select Form from the Insert menu of Visual Basic.

Visual Basic responds by inserting a new form into the MyWalls project.

- Save the new form as Angle.FRM in the C:\WinGPrg\CH33 directory.

- Implement the Angle.FRM with the Properties settings listed in Table 34.5. When you're finished, the form should look as shown in Figure 34.5. Note that you're placing the Switch control in the frmDirection form. If your Visual Basic Tools window does not include the Switch OCX control, select Custom Controls from the Options menu, and add the TegoSoft Switch OCX control. The Switch OCX control was copied to your Windows\System directory by the CD-ROM's Install program.

FIGURE 34.5:

The frmDirection form (Angle.FRM) in design mode

TABLE 34.5: The Properties of the frmDirection Form

Object: Form

Name: frmDirection

Property	Value
BackColor	Light gray
BorderStyle	3 'Fixed Dialog
Caption	"Direction"
Height	4500
Icon	C:\WinGPrg\Icons\Angle.ICO
Left	5070
MaxButton	0 'False
MinButton	0 'False
Top	1785
Width	1965

TABLE 34.5: The Properties of the frmDirection Form (continued)

Object: CommandButton

Name: cmdShowDirection

Property	Value
Caption	"&Show Direction"
Height	495
Left	120
Top	600
Width	1575

Object: PictureBox

Name: picAngle

Property	Value
FillColor	Red
FillStyle	0 'Solid
Height	1455
Left	120
Top	2160
Width	1575

Object: Spin

Name: spnAngle

Property	Value
Height	615
Left	120
Top	1200
Width	1575
Bevelwidth	5
Horizontal	−1 'True
Interval	50

TABLE 34.5: The Properties of the frmDirection Form (continued)

Object: Label
Name: Label1

Property	Value
Caption	"Current View:"
Height	255
Left	120
Top	1920
Width	1095

Object: Switch
Name: swClose

Property	Value
Height	525
Left	0
Top	0
Width	630
Value	−1 'True
Horizontal	−1 'True

Object: Label
Name: lblAngle

Property	Value
Alignment	2 'Center
BorderStyle	1 'Fixed Single
Height	255
Left	120
Top	3720
Width	1575

The General Declarations Section of the frmDirection Form

- Enter the following code in the General Declarations section of the frmDirection form:

```
Option Explicit
```

This code forces variables declarations.

Attaching Code to the Close Switch

You'll now attach code to the Click event of the Close switch.

- Enter the following code in the swClose_Click( ) procedure of the frmDirection form:

```
Private Sub swClose_Click( )

    Unload Me

End Sub
```

This code unloads the frmDirection form.

Attaching Code to the ShowDirection Button

Whenever the user clicks the Show Direction button, the current direction is displayed.

- Enter the following code in the cmdShowDirection_Click( ) procedure of the frmDirection form:

```
Private Sub cmdShowDirection_Click( )

Dim PI
Dim X, Y
Dim Radius
Dim Color
Dim StartAngle
Dim EndAngle
Dim Aspect

PI = 3.14159265
X = picAngle.Width / 2
Y = picAngle.Height / 2
Radius = picAngle.Width / 3

picAngle.DrawWidth = 1

picAngle.Cls

StartAngle = frmMyWalls.Floor1.Angle - 30
If StartAngle < 0 Then
    StartAngle = 360 + StartAngle
End If

If StartAngle >= 360 Then
    StartAngle = StartAngle - 360
End If

EndAngle = frmMyWalls.Floor1.Angle + 30
If EndAngle < 0 Then
    EndAngle = 360 + EndAngle
End If

If EndAngle >= 360 Then
    EndAngle = EndAngle - 360
End If

Aspect = 1
```

34

```
lblAngle.Caption = "Direction: " + _
                   Str(frmMyWalls.Floor1.Angle) + _
                   " degrees"

' Draw the new arc
Color = QBColor(4)
picAngle.Circle (X, Y), _
                Radius, _
                Color, _
                -StartAngle * 2 * PI / 360, _
                -EndAngle * 2 * PI / 360, _
                Aspect

    End Sub
```

This code draws a filled arc that indicates the user's current direction. As you'll soon see, the arc is drawn by using the Circle method, and the Circle method needs to know where to draw the arc. The arc is drawn inside the picAngle picture control. So the location of the center of the arc is calculated based on the dimensions of the picAngle control:

```
X = picAngle.Width / 2
Y = picAngle.Height / 2
Radius = picAngle.Width / 3
```

The arc is a section of a circle whose center is at the middle of the picAngle picture control. The radius of the circle is one-third of the width of the picAngle picture control.

The arc is drawn with a pen that is 1 pixel wide:

```
picAngle.DrawWidth = 1
```

The previous arc is erased:

```
picAngle.Cls
```

Then the starting angle of the arc is calculated:

```
StartAngle = frmMyWalls.Floor1.Angle - 30
If StartAngle < 0 Then
   StartAngle = 360 + StartAngle
End If

If StartAngle >= 360 Then
   StartAngle = StartAngle - 360
End If
```

In these statements, the Angle property of the Floor control represents the user's current direction. Because the total view is 60 degrees, the starting angle is 30 degrees below the user's current direction.

Similarly, the ending angle of the arc is calculated as 30 degrees above the user's current direction:

```
EndAngle = frmMyWalls.Floor1.Angle + 30
If EndAngle < 0 Then
   EndAngle = 360 + EndAngle
End If

If EndAngle >= 360 Then
   EndAngle = EndAngle - 360
End If
```

Aspect is set to 1:

```
Aspect = 1
```

When you supply 1 as the Aspect parameter of the Circle method, a circle (or an arc of a circle) is drawn. If you supply a number other than 1 as the Aspect parameter of the Circle method, the resulting shape is an ellipse.

The Caption property of the lblAngle label is then set to display the user's current direction:

```
lblAngle.Caption = "Direction: " + _
                 Str(frmMyWalls.Floor1.Angle) + _
                 " degrees"
```

Finally, the arc is drawn:

```
' Draw the new arc
Color = QBColor(4)
picAngle.Circle (X, Y), _
               Radius, _
               Color, _
               -StartAngle * 2 * PI / 360, _
               -EndAngle * 2 * PI / 360, _
               Aspect
```

Because the Fill property of the picture control is set to red (see Table 34.5), the arc is filled with the red color. A negative sign is supplied to the starting and ending angles, because you want the arc to be drawn with straight lines connecting the endpoints of the arc to the center of the circle.

34

Degrees and Radians

The starting and ending angles of the arc are supplied to the Circle method in radians. If you are unfamiliar with representing angles in radians, use the following formula to convert degrees to radians:

```
[Number of radians] = [Number of degrees] * 2 * PI /360
```

where PI represents the number 3.14159265. For example, how many radians in 360 degrees?

```
[Number of radians]=360*2*3.14159265/360 = 6.28318
```

So 6.28318 radians is the same thing as 360 degrees.

Attaching Code to the SpinDown Event of the Spin Control

You'll now attach code to the SpinDown event of the spnAngle Spin control. When the user clicks the left arrow of the Spin control, it is equivalent to pressing the ← key of the keyboard.

- Enter the following code in the spnAngle_SpinDown( ) procedure of the frmDirection form:

```
Private Sub spnAngle_SpinDown( )

    frmMyWalls.Floor1.Angle = _
        frmMyWalls.Floor1.Angle + 10

    cmdShowDirection_Click
    frmMyWalls.Floor1.Display3D

End Sub
```

This code increases the Angle property of the floor:

```
frmMyWalls.Floor1.Angle = _
        frmMyWalls.Floor1.Angle + 10
```

Once the Angle property is increased, you display the arc that corresponds to the new direction as follows:

```
cmdShowDirection_Click
```

Finally, the 3D picture is displayed:

```
frmMyWalls.Floor1.Display3D
```

Attaching Code to the
SpinUp Event of the Spin Control

You'll now attach code to the SpinUp event of the spnAngle Spin control. Clicking the right arrow of the Spin control has the same effect as pressing the right arrow key on the keyboard.

- Enter the following code in the spnAngle_SpinUp( ) procedure of the frmDirection form:

```
Private Sub spnAngle_SpinUp( )

    frmMyWalls.Floor1.Angle = _
        frmMyWalls.Floor1.Angle - 10

    cmdShowDirection_Click
    frmMyWalls.Floor1.Display3D

End Sub
```

This code is very similar to the code you entered in the spnAngle_SpinDown( ) procedure. However, now you decrease the value of the Angle property:

```
frmMyWalls.Floor1.Angle = _
        frmMyWalls.Floor1.Angle - 10
```

Summary

In this chapter you implemented the MyWalls program. As you saw, the various objects of the floor (walls, ceiling, floor, stripes), can be painted with different colors.

Customizing the Spin Control

The Spin control has two pictures associated with it. One is used as the picture of the Down section of the Spin control, and the other as the Up section of the Spin control. Because you did not set the picture properties of the Spin control, the default pictures were used—one arrow pointing to the right, and another arrow pointing left.

If you wish, you can use your own pictures for the Spin control. For example, Figure 34.6 shows two possible pictures that are appropriate for the Spin control of the frmDirection form.

To create the customized picture, use Paintbrush to create the small BMP pictures that will be used as the pictures of the Spin control. Then, during design time (or during runtime), set the SpinPictureUp and SpinPictureDown properties of the Spin control.

FIGURE 34.6:

The frmDirection form (Angle.FRM) in design mode

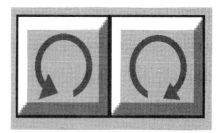

In this chapter you also implemented a Direction Control panel that lets users set and view their current direction.

CHAPTER

THIRTY-FIVE

Creating Your Own World

In this chapter you'll execute the MyWorld program. In subsequent chapters you'll implement this program yourself.

The MyWorld program demonstrates additional features and capabilities of the Floor OCX control. As you'll see, the Floor OCX control enables you to create your own world! You can place static and dynamic (moving) objects in the halls and rooms of the floor, you can dynamically change characteristics of the floor such as the dimensions of the rooms, you can move people across the halls and from one room to another, and in short, you can have a lot of fun. But more importantly, you can design your 3D floor with a practically unlimited number of objects and possibilities to make your 3D virtual reality games fun and easy to use.

Executing the MyWorld Program

As shown in Figure 35.1, there is a lamp in the room! As you'll see when you implement the program, the lamp is what's called a "soft sprite." That is, the user is able to walk under the lamp. You can place soft sprites just like any other regular sprite. For example, Figure 35.2 shows the ASCII view of the floor. As usual, the + character represents the user's current position. You can display the ASCII view as follows:

Execute the MyWorld program; you'll find it in the \WinGPrg\EXE directory of the book's CD.

- Select ASCII View from the Option menu.
- Scroll down the resulting ASCII view by clicking the down arrow of the vertical scroll bar.

As shown in Figure 35.2, the user's current position is in the lower-left room. In this room, the D character represents the Lamp sprite. You'll set the D sprite as a soft sprite in the Form_Load( ) procedure of the form.

- Click the OK button of the ASCII View window.

MyWorld returns to the 3D view.

FIGURE 35.1:

Placing a lamp inside the room. The user is able to pass under the lamp.

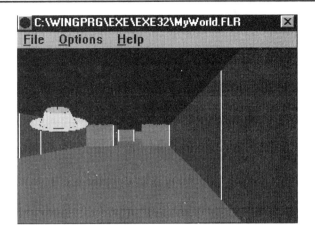

35

FIGURE 35.2:

The ASCII view of the floor. The + character represents the user's current position, and the D character represents the lamp.

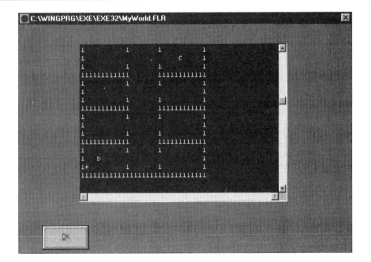

A Crazy Man with a Sword in His Hand...

Don't move outside the room yet. Why? Because there is a crazy man with a sharp sword in his hand running in the hall!

- Click the right mouse button inside the room.

MyWorld responds by displaying the Control Panel.

- Check the Running Man check box, and then click the Back to 3D World button.

- Move closer to the door of the room, as shown in Figure 35.3 (but do not leave the room yet).

FIGURE 35.3:

Getting closer to the door of the lower-left room

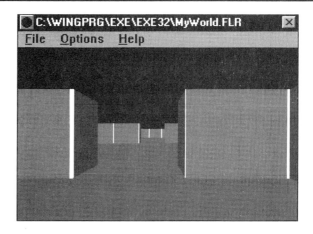

The man is running from one end of the long hall to the other end. So it may take 10 or 20 seconds for you to see him. If you're patient, eventually you'll see him as shown in Figure 35.4.

FIGURE 35.4:

Viewing the man with his sword from the lower-left room

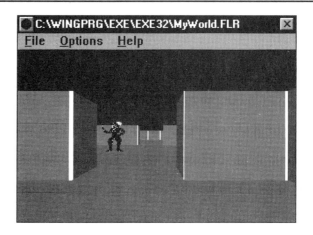

- Move outside the room into the hall to see the view shown in Figure 35.5. Note that in the hall, the man with the sword is running in an endless loop. When the man reaches his destination (the end of the hall), he starts the trip all over again.

FIGURE 35.5:

Getting closer to the man with the sword in the hall

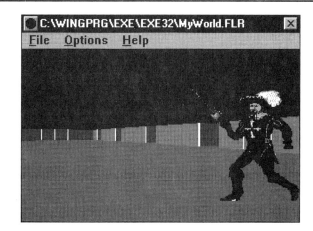

C:\WINGPRG\EXE\EXE32\MyWorld.FLR

File   Options   Help

TIP

As we said at the beginning of this chapter, it is your world, and you can put as many things in it as you wish. But you should be aware that as you add dynamic objects such as the running man with the sword, the program needs more resources from the PC, and this means that on slow computers, the program will run slower. Naturally, when you execute the program as a 32-bit application on a 32-bit Windows, it runs much faster. If you plan to write programs to run on slow PCs, place dynamic sprites inside the rooms (not inside the halls). This way, the program will slow down only while the user is inside the room that contains the dynamic sprite.

- If you are currently executing the MyWorld program on a slow PC, click the right mouse button inside the room, and clear the Running Man check box. Then click the Back to 3D View button.

Meet President Lincoln...

Look at the ASCII view shown in Figure 35.6. The A character in the upper-left room represents the sprite of President Lincoln.

FIGURE 35.6:

The ASCII view showing the room at the top of the 2D floor diagram

FIGURE 35.6:

The ASCII view showing the room at the top of the 2D floor diagram

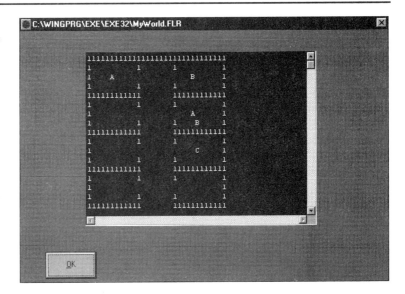

- Move to the upper-left room.

As shown in Figure 35.7, President Lincoln stands inside the upper-left room.

Meet (and Hear) President Kennedy...

Look again at Figure 35.6. In the upper-right room of the 2D view you see the letter B, representing the sprite of President Kennedy.

- Move into the upper-right room.

FIGURE 35.7:
President Lincoln stands in the upper-left room.

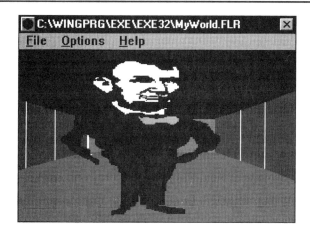

If you have a sound card in your system, as soon as you enter the room, you'll hear a famous speech by President Kennedy. And as shown in Figure 35.8, you'll see him in the room.

FIGURE 35.8:
President Kennedy stands in the upper-right room.

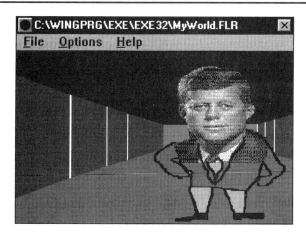

Take a third look at Figure 35.6. The room located on the second row from the top in the right column contains the A and B characters. This means that inside the room you'll see Lincoln and Kennedy.

- Move into the room on the second row from the top and in the right column.

As you can see (Figure 35.9), the room contains Lincoln and Kennedy.

FIGURE 35.9:

Presidents Lincoln and Kennedy in
the room located second row from
the top on the right

Placing Other People in a Room

Again take a look at Figure 35.6. Inside the room located in the right column, third row from the top you see the C character. This character represents a sprite of a woman.

- Move into the room located on the right column, third row from the top.

As you can see (Figure 35.10), a woman is sitting in the room.

Animated Sprites

The Lincoln sprite, the Kennedy sprite, and the woman sprite are examples of *static sprites*. The lamp in the lower-left room is an example of a static sprite (and also a soft sprite, meaning that the user: can pass through the sprite). The running man with the sword is an example of a *dynamic sprite* (or an animated sprite). You'll now view two additional animated sprites.

- Move into the room on the left column, and second row from the top.

FIGURE 35.10:

A woman sitting in the room located on the right column, third row from the top

As you can see (Figure 35.11), in this room two friends of the running man are practicing fencing.

FIGURE 35.11:

In the room on the left column and the second row from the top you see two men practicing fencing

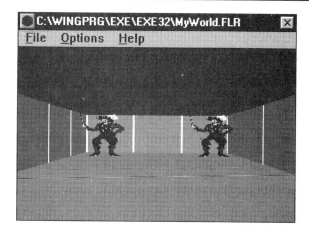

Of course, you can make the two men surrender to you!

- While inside the room where the two men appear, press the space bar.

The moment you press the space bar, the two men surrender to you as shown in Figure 35.12.

The two fencing men surrender

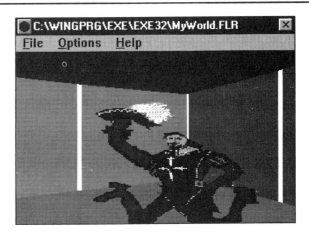

- Press the space bar again.

The moment you press the space bar, the animated icons start the animation again.

The Snake Charmer

You can view another animated sprite inside the room located on the left column, third row from the top.

- Move inside the room located on the left column, third row from the top.

As you can see (Figure 35.13), inside the room there is a man playing a flute and manipulating a snake out of a basket.

The Control Panel Feature

The MyWorld program has a Control Panel feature (you already used the Control Panel to enable and disable the running man). To see the Control Panel in action, follow the following steps.

- Right click the form.

FIGURE 35.13:

The snake charmer (an animated sprite)

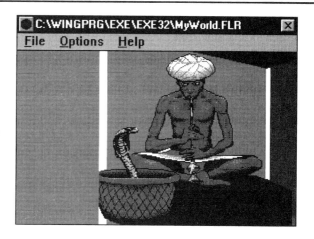

35

MyWorld responds by displaying the Control Panel window, as shown in Figure 35.14.

FIGURE 35.14:

The Control Panel window that MyWorld program displays when you right click the form.

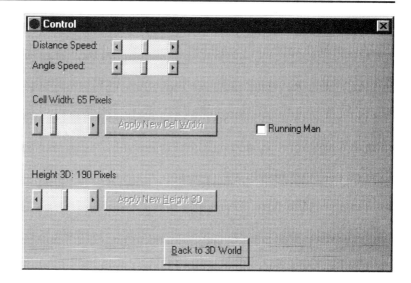

Changing the Characteristics of the 3D Floor

The Control Panel window lets you change various characteristics of the 3D room.

The **Distance Speed** scroll bar lets the user change the speed of his or her movement in the 3D room.

The **Angle Speed** scroll bar lets the user change the speed at which to rotate in the 3D room.

• The **Cell Width** scroll bar lets the user change the width of the rooms. Once you change the Cell Width scroll bar, you have to click the Apply New Cell Width button to make the change take effect.

• The **Height 3D** scroll bar lets the user change the height of the rooms. Once you change the Height 3D scroll bar, you have to click the Apply New Height 3D button to make the change take effect.

• Experiment with the Control Panel window and then terminate the My-World program.

Summary

In this chapter you executed the MyWorld program. As you saw, the Floor OCX control lets you perform various powerful operations such as placing static sprites, animated sprites, dynamic sprites (where a sprite can go from room to room or across the hall), and activating sound in response to the user's activity. In this chapter you also learned how a soft sprite behaves. A soft sprite is one that the user can pass through. Thus, you use a soft sprite for implementing a ceiling lamp, for example. Another use is in 3D virtual reality games where the user must fight off bad creatures. Once an opponent has been killed, your program would display it as a soft sprite, so that the user can then step over the dead body.

CHAPTER

THIRTY-SIX

Modifying the 3D Floor during Runtime

In this chapter you'll start implementing the MyWorld program that you executed in the previous chapter. In particular, you'll implement that part of the MyWorld program that lets the user change the characteristics of the floor.

Creating the MyWorld Project

As always, start by creating the project of the MyWorld program.

- Start Visual Basic.

- Select New Project from the File menu; save the new form as MyWorld.FRM and the new project file as MyWorld.VBP, both in the C:\WinGPrg\CH35 directory.

- Implement the frmMyWorld form with the Properties settings listed in Table 36.1. When you're finished, the form should look as shown in Figure 36.1.

TABLE 36.1: The Properties of the frmMyWorld Form

Object: Form
Name: frmMyWorld

Property	Value
BorderStyle	3 'Fixed Dialog
Caption	"The MyWorld Program"
Height	4830
Icon	C:\WinGPrg\Icons\MyWorld.ICO
Left	1080
MaxButton	0 'False
MinButton	0 'False
Top	1170
Width	2895

Object: Floor OCX control
Name: Floor1

Property	Value
Left	480
Top	1440

FIGURE 36.1:
The frmMyWorld Form in design mode

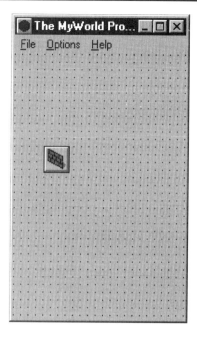

• Implement the menu of the frmMyWorld form with the settings listed in Table 36.2.

TABLE 36.2: The Menu of the frmMyWorld Form

Caption	Name
&File	mnuFile
...E&xit	mnuExit
&Options	mnuOptions
...&Select Options...	mnuSelectOptions
...&ASCII View...	mnuASCIIView
&Help	mnuHelp
...&Help...	mnuHelpHelp
...&About...	mnuAbout

36

The General Declarations Section of the frmMyWorld Form

- Enter the following code in the General Declarations section of the frmMy-World form:

```
Option Explicit
```

As usual, this statement forces variable declarations.

Attaching Code to the Load Event of the frmMyWorld Form

You'll now attach code to the Load event of the frmMyWorld form. This procedure is executed whenever the MyWorld program starts.

- Place the following code in the Form_Load( ) procedure of the frmMyWorld:

```
Private Sub Form_Load( )

Dim OpenResult As Integer
Dim NumberOfRows, NumberOfCols

' Update the variable with the name of the floor file.
If Right(App.Path, 1) <> "\" Then
    gFloorFileName = App.Path + "\" + FLOOR_FILE_NAME
Else
    gFloorFileName = App.Path + FLOOR_FILE_NAME
End If

''' MsgBox gFloorFileName

' Set units to pixels
Me.ScaleMode = 3 'Pixels

' Find number of rows in the floor file
```

```
NumberOfRows = FindNumOfRows

' Find number of columns in the floor file
NumberOfCols = FindNumOfCols

' Initialize and open the 3D Floor control

Floor1.FileName = gFloorFileName

Floor1.hWndDisplay = Me.hWnd
Floor1.NumOfRows = NumberOfRows
Floor1.NumOfCols = NumberOfCols

gCellWidth = 65
Floor1.CellWidth = gCellWidth

' Initial position
Floor1.X = 1 * Floor1.CellWidth + 25
Floor1.Y = 1 * Floor1.CellWidth + 25

' Initial direction
Floor1.Angle = 0

' Open the FLR file
OpenResult = Floor1.Open

Me.Caption = Floor1.FileName

gAngleSpeed = DELTA_ANGLE
gDistanceSpeed = DELTA_DISTANCE
gHeight3D = 190

End Sub
```

36

This code updates the gFloorFileName variable with the path and filename of a
Floor file:

```
' Update the variable with the name of the floor file.
If Right(App.Path, 1) <> "\" Then
   gFloorFileName = App.Path + "\" + FLOOR_FILE_NAME
Else
   gFloorFileName = App.Path + FLOOR_FILE_NAME
End If
```

Here you set the value of a global variable called gFloorFileName. You'll declare this variable in a separate BAS module later in this chapter. Also, you'll declare the value of the constant FLOOR_FILE_NAME. As you'll see, FLOOR_FILE_NAME is declared as MyWorld.FLR. So you can see that the MyWorld program uses the MyWorld.FLR file, which is assumed to reside in the same directory as the MyWorld program.

The ScaleMode property of the frmMyWorld form is set to 3:

```
' Set units to pixels
Me.ScaleMode = 3 'Pixels
```

It is a good idea to set the ScaleMode to 3 (Pixels), because the Floor control accepts dimensions in pixels. So if, for example, you want to set a certain property of the Floor control based on the dimension of the frmMyWorld form, you will not have to convert the dimension to pixels.

We extract the number of rows in the MyWorld.FLR file by executing the FindNumOfRows function:

```
' Find number of rows in the floor file
NumberOfRows = FindNumOfRows
```

And we extract the number of columns in the MyWorld.FLR file by executing the FindNumOfCols function:

```
' Find number of columns in the floor file
NumberOfCols = FindNumOfCols
```

You'll write the code of the FindNumOfRows and FindNumOfCols functions later in this chapter.

The FileName property of the Floor control is set:

```
Floor1.FileName = gFloorFileName
```

The window in which the 3D floor picture will be displayed is set to the window of the frmMyWorld form:

```
Floor1.hWndDisplay = Me.hWnd
```

And the NumOfRows and NumOfCols properties of the Floor control are set:

```
Floor1.NumOfRows = NumberOfRows
Floor1.NumOfCols = NumberOfCols
```

The gCellWidth property is set to 65:

```
gCellWidth = 65
```

You'll declare the gCellWidth variable later in this chapter. The gCellWidth variable is maintained throughout the MyWorld program to hold the width of the cells.

The CellWidth property of the Floor control is then set:

```
Floor1.CellWidth = gCellWidth
```

NOTE In previous chapters when you implemented programs with the Floor control, you did not set its CellWidth property. Why? Because if you do not set the CellWidth property, the Floor control uses the default value of 65 pixels for the CellWidth property. In the MyWorld program, the CellWidth property is changed during runtime. Thus, as you'll see, there is a need to maintain the gCellWidth variable that always stores the current value of the CellWidth property.

36

The user's initial position is set as follows:

```
' Initial position
Floor1.X = 1 * Floor1.CellWidth + 25
Floor1.Y = 1 * Floor1.CellWidth + 25
```

This means that the initial position is in the cell located at the second column from the left and the second row from the bottom.

The initial angle of the user's view is set to 0:

```
' Initial direction
Floor1.Angle = 0
```

The user's initial view is from 330° to 30° (because the total view is 60 degrees).

OK, you are now ready to open the MyWorld.FLR file:

```
' Open the FLR file
OpenResult = Floor1.Open
```

The Caption property of the frmMyWorld form is set to indicate the name of the Floor file:

```
Me.Caption = Floor1.FileName
```

The MyWorld program lets the user change the speed at which the view angle is changed when the user rotates, the speed at which the distance is changed when the user moves forward and backward, and the height of the 3D picture. Thus, throughout the MyWorld program, the following general variables are maintained:

```
gAngleSpeed = DELTA_ANGLE
gDistanceSpeed = DELTA_DISTANCE
gHeight3D = 190
```

You'll declare these general variables and constants later in this chapter.

Attaching Code to the Paint Event of the frmMyWorld Form

You'll now attach code to the Form_Paint( ) procedure of the frmMyWorld form. This procedure is executed whenever there is a need to paint the form. After the Form_Load( ) procedure is executed, there is a need to paint the frmMyWorld form, and the Form_Paint( ) procedure is executed.

- Enter the following code in the Form_Paint( ) procedure of the frmMyWorld form:

```
Private Sub Form_Paint( )

''''''''''''''''''''''''''
' Display the 3D view
''''''''''''''''''''''''''
Floor1.Display3D

End Sub
```

This code displays the 3D picture of the floor.

Attaching Code to the Unload Event of the frmMyWorld Form

You'll now attach code to the Unload event of the frmMyWorld form, which occurs whenever the user closes the form.

- Enter the following code in the Form_Unload( ) procedure of the frmMyWorld form:

```
Private Sub Form_Unload(Cancel As Integer)

    Unload frmControl

End Sub
```

36

This code unloads the frmControl form. You'll implement the frmControl form later in this chapter. As you'll soon see, you'll display the frmControl form as a nonmodal (modeless) window. This means that the user could display the frmControl form and then, without closing the frmControl form, switch back to the frmMyWorld form and close it. The frmControl form would remain open after the frmMyWorld form is closed! To prevent this from happening, we unload the frmControl form at the time the frmMyWorld form is closed.

Attaching Code to the Form_KeyDown( ) Procedure of the frmMyWorld Form

You'll now attach code to the Form_KeyDown( ) procedure of the frmMyWorld form. This procedure is executed whenever the user presses a key while frmMyWorld is the active form. The code you'll attach moves the user's position according to the key that was pressed.

- Enter the following code in the Form_KeyDown( ) procedure of the frmMyWorld form:

```
Private Sub Form_KeyDown(KeyCode As Integer, _
```

```
                          Shift As Integer)

     Select Case KeyCode

          Case 37, 100
               ' Left key (37) or 4 key (100) was pressed
               ' to increase the direction angle.
               Floor1.Angle = Floor1.Angle + gAngleSpeed

          Case 39, 102
               ' Right key (39) or 6 key (102) was pressed
               ' to decrease the direction angle.
               Floor1.Angle = Floor1.Angle - gAngleSpeed

          Case 38, 104
               ' Up key (38) or 8 key (104) was pressed
               ' to advance forward.
               Floor1.Advance (gDistanceSpeed)

          Case 40, 98 'Down or 2
               ' Down key (40) or 2 key (98) was pressed
               ' to advance backward.
               Floor1.Advance (-gDistanceSpeed)
     End Select

     ''''''''''''''''''''''''
     ' Display the 3D view
     ''''''''''''''''''''''''
     Floor1.Display3D

     End Sub
```

This code sets a new value for the Angle property of the floor whenever the user presses the ← or → keys. Also, when the user presses the ↑ or ↓ keys, the Advance method is executed.

The amounts of angle change and distance change are represented by gSpeedAngle and gDistanceSpeed, respectively. You'll learn more about these global variables later in this chapter.

Attaching Code to the MouseMove Event of the frmMyWorld Form

You'll now attach code to the MouseMove event of the frmMyWorld form, which occurs whenever the user moves the mouse.

- Enter the following code in the Form_MouseMove( ) procedure of the frmMyWorld form:

```
Private Sub Form_MouseMove(Button As Integer, _
                           Shift As Integer, _
                           X As Single, _
                           Y As Single)

''''''''''''''''''''''''''''''''
' Here you write code that
' will be executed whenever the
' user moves the mouse.
''''''''''''''''''''''''''''''''


Static PrevX, PrevY

If Button And 1 Then

    If X < PrevX Then
        ' Mouse was moved to the left
        Floor1.Angle = Floor1.Angle + gAngleSpeed

        ''''''''''''''''''''''''
        ' Display the 3D view
        ''''''''''''''''''''''''

        Floor1.Display3D
    End If

    If X > PrevX Then
        ' Mouse was moved to the right
        Floor1.Angle = Floor1.Angle - gAngleSpeed
        ''''''''''''''''''''''''
        ' Display the 3D view
        ''''''''''''''''''''''''

        Floor1.Display3D
```

36

```
        End If

        If Y < PrevY Then
            ' Mouse was moved upward
            Floor1.Advance gDistanceSpeed
            '''''''''''''''''''''''

            ' Display the 3D view
            '''''''''''''''''''''''

            Floor1.Display3D
        End If

        If Y > PrevY Then
            ' Mouse was moved upward
            Floor1.Advance -gDistanceSpeed
            '''''''''''''''''''''''

            ' Display the 3D view
            '''''''''''''''''''''''

            Floor1.Display3D
        End If

    PrevX = X
    PrevY = Y

    End If

End Sub
```

This code uses an If statement to examine whether the left button of the mouse was
down at the time the mouse was moved. If so, the various inner If statements are
executed. Each of these statements compares the current coordinates of the mouse
with the previous coordinates, and accordingly increases or decreases the Angle
property or executes the Advance method.

The last two statements in the Form_MouseMove( ) procedure set the values of
PrevX and PrevY to the current mouse coordinates:

```
    PrevX = X
    PrevY = Y
```

X and Y are the parameters of the Form_MouseMove( ) procedure. They hold
the mouse coordinates at the time the Form_MouseMove( ) procedure is executed.

So the next time the Form_MouseMove( ) procedure is executed, the PrevX and
PrevY variables are updated with the previous mouse coordinates. Note that PrevX

and PrevY are declared as static variables at the beginning of the Form_MouseMove( ) procedure. Hence, the PrevX and PrevY variables maintain their values even after the termination of the Form_MouseMove( ) procedure.

Attaching Code to the MouseDown Event of the frmMyWorld Form

You'll now attach code to the MouseDown event of the frmMyWorld form. The MouseDown event occurs whenever the user presses any of the mouse button inside the frmMyWorld form.

- Enter the following code in the Form_MouseDown( ) procedure of the frmMyWorld form:

36

```
Private Sub Form_MouseDown(Button As Integer, _
                           Shift As Integer, _
                           X As Single, _
                           Y As Single)

If Button And 2 Then
    mnuSelectOptions_Click
End If

End Sub
```

This code uses an If statement to examine the value of the Button parameter:

```
If Button And 2 Then
    ........................................
    ... The right button of the mouse was pressed
    ........................................
End If
```

The If condition is satisfied if the user pressed the right button of the mouse.

The code under the If statement executes the mnuSelectOptions_Click( ) procedure:

```
mnuSelectOptions_Click
```

So selecting the Select Options item from the Options menu has the same effect as clicking the right mouse button in the frmMyWorld form. You'll write the code of the mnuSelectOptions_Click( ) procedure in the next section.

TIP

When designing your programs, always provide your user with an easy way of doing things. For example, to display the Control window, the user can use Select Options from the Option menu. Doing this while playing requires the user to open the Option menu, and then select the Select Option item. However, the MyWorld program offers an easier way for the user to display the Control window—by using the mouse. That is, the user's hand is constantly operating the mouse. So from the user's point of view, it is an easy one-step operation to press the right mouse button for the purpose of displaying the Control window.

Attaching Code to the Select Options Menu Item

Whenever the user chooses the Select Options item from the Option menu (or right-clicks the mouse), the mnuSelectOptions_Click( ) procedure is executed and the Control window is displayed.

- Enter the following code in the mnuSelectOptions_Click( ) procedure of the frmMyWorld form:

```
Private Sub mnuSelectOptions_Click( )

    ' Display the control panel
    frmControl.Show 0

End Sub
```

This code displays the frmControl form as a nonmodal window. You'll implement the frmControl form later in this chapter.

Attaching Code to the Exit Item of the frmMyWorld Form

You'll now attach code to the Click event of the Exit menu item of the frmMy-World form.

- Enter the following code in the mnuExit_Click( ) procedure of the frmMy-World form:

```
Private Sub mnuExit_Click( )

    Unload Me

End Sub
```

This code unloads the frmMyWorld form. So whenever the user selects the Exit menu item, the Unload event is generated and the Form_Unload( ) procedure of the frmMyWorld form is executed.

36

Attaching Code to the ASCII View Menu Item

You'll now attach code to the Click event of the ASCII View menu item of the frmMyWorld form.

- Enter the following code in the mnuASCIIView_Click( ) procedure of the frmMyWorld form:

```
Private Sub mnuASCIIView_Click( )

    frmASCIIView.Show 1

End Sub
```

This code displays the frmASCIIView form as a modal window. You'll implement the frmASCIIView form later in this chapter.

Attaching Code to the About Menu Item

You'll now attach code to the Click event of the About menu item of the frmMy-World form.

- Enter the following code in the mnuAbout_Click( ) procedure of the frmMy-World form:

```
Private Sub mnuAbout_Click( )

    ' Display the About window
    frmAbout.Show 1

End Sub
```

This code displays the frmAbout form as a modal window. You'll implement the frmAbout form later in this chapter.

Attaching Code to the Help Menu Item

You'll now attach code to the Click event of the Help menu item.

- Enter the following code in the mnuHelpHelp_Click( ) procedure of the frmMyWorld form:

```
Private Sub mnuHelpHelp_Click( )

    ' Display the Help window
    frmHelp.Show 1

End Sub
```

This code displays the frmHelp form as a modal window. You'll implement the frmHelp form later in this chapter.

Adding the MyWorld.BAS Module to the MyWorld Project

You'll now add the MyWorld.BAS module to the MyWorld project.

- Select Module from the Insert menu of Visual Basic.

Visual Basic responds by inserting a new BAS module into the MyWorld project.

- Save the new BAS module as MyWorld.BAS in the C:\WinGPrg\CH35 directory.

- Add the following code in the General Declarations section of the My-World.BAS module:

```
Option Explicit

Public Const FLOOR_FILE_NAME = "MyWorld.FLR"
Public gFloorFileName

Public Const DELTA_ANGLE = 10
Public Const DELTA_DISTANCE = 30

Public gAngleSpeed
Public gDistanceSpeed
Public gCellWidth
Public gHeight3D
```

This code declares various constants and global variables that are used throughout the forms of the MyWorld project. Because these constants and variables are declared in a separate BAS module, they are accessible from within any procedure of any form in the project.

The FindNumOfRows( ) Function

In the Form_Load( ) procedure of the frmMyWorld form you executed the FindNumOfRows( ) function to extract the number of rows in the MyWorld.FLR file. You'll now enter the code of this function.

36

- Make sure that the MyWorld.BAS module is highlighted in the Project window, click the View Code button of the Project window, and finally select Procedure from the Insert menu of Visual Basic.

Visual Basic responds by displaying the Insert Procedure dialog box.

- Select the Function option button in the Insert Procedure dialog box (to indicate that you are inserting a new function), and set the name of the function to FindNumOfRows.

- Click the OK button of the Insert Procedure dialog box.

Visual Basic responds by inserting the FindNumOfRows function in the MyWorld.BAS module.

- Enter the following code in the FindNumOfRows function:

```
Public Function FindNumOfRows( )

'''''''''''''''''''''''''''''''''''''
' This function finds the number of
' rows in the selected floor file.
'''''''''''''''''''''''''''''''''''''

Dim FileNum
Dim Cell As String
Dim FloorFileLength
Dim I

FindNumOfRows = 0

' Get the next available file number
FileNum = FreeFile

' Open the floor file
Open gFloorFileName For Binary As FileNum

' Extract the length of the floor file
FloorFileLength = FileLen(gFloorFileName)

' Extract the number of rows in the floor file
For I = 1 To FloorFileLength
    Cell = " "
    Get #FileNum, I, Cell
```

```
      If Asc(Cell) = 13 Then
         FindNumOfRows = FindNumOfRows + 1
         If I + 1 > FloorFileLength Then Exit For
         Get #FileNum, I + 1, Cell
         If Asc(Cell) = 10 Then
            If I + 2 > FloorFileLength Then Exit For
            Get #FileNum, I + 2, Cell
            If Asc(Cell) = 13 Then
               Exit For
            End If
         End If
      End If
Next I

If Asc(Cell) <> 13 And _
   Asc(Cell) <> 10 And _
   Asc(Cell) <> 32 Then

   FindNumOfRows = FindNumOfRows + 1

End If

' Close the floor file
Close FileNum

   End Function
```

This code extracts the number of rows in the MyWorld.FLR floor file.

The FindNumOfCols( ) Function

In the Form_Load( ) procedure of the frmMyWorld form you executed the FindNumOfCols( ) function to extract the number of columns in the MyWorld.FLR file. You'll now enter the code of this function.

- Make sure the MyWorld.BAS module is highlighted in the Project window, click the View Code button, and finally select Procedure from the Insert menu of Visual Basic.

Visual Basic responds by displaying the Insert Procedure dialog box.

- Select the Function option button in the Insert Procedure dialog box (to indicate that you are inserting a new function), and set the name of the function to FindNumOfCols.

- Click the OK button of the Insert Procedure dialog box.

Visual Basic responds by inserting the FindNumOfCols function into the My-World.BAS module.

- Enter the following code in the FindNumOfCols function:

```
Public Function FindNumOfCols( )

''''''''''''''''''''''''''''''''''
' This function finds the number of
' columns in the selected floor file.
''''''''''''''''''''''''''''''''''

Dim FileNum
Dim Cell As String
Dim FloorFileLength
Dim I

FindNumOfCols = 0

' Get the next available file number
FileNum = FreeFile

' Open the file
Open gFloorFileName For Binary As FileNum

' Extract the length of the floor file.
FloorFileLength = FileLen(gFloorFileName)

' Extract the number of columns in the floor file.
For I = 1 To FloorFileLength
    Cell = " "
    Get #FileNum, I, Cell
    If Asc(Cell) = 13 Then Exit For
Next I
FindNumOfCols = I - 1

' Close the floor file.
Close FileNum

End Function
```

This code extracts the number of columns in the MyWorld.FLR floor file.

Implementing the frmControl Form

As stated, whenever the user presses the right mouse button or chooses Select Options from the Options menu of the frmMyWorld form, the frmControl window is displayed. The frmControl form lets the user sets various options that are related to the characteristics of the 3D floor. You'll now implement the frmControl form.

- Select Form from the Insert menu of Visual Basic.

Visual Basic responds by inserting a new form into the MyWorld project.

- Save the new form as Control.FRM inside the C:\WinGPrg\CH35 directory.

- Implement the frmControl form with the Properties settings listed in Table 36.3. When you're finished, the form should look as shown in Figure 36.2.

36

TABLE 36.3: The Properties of the frmControl Form

Object: Form

Name: frmControl

Property	Value
BorderStyle	3 'Fixed Dialog
Caption	"Control"
Height	4545
Icon	C:\WinGPrg\Icons\MyIcon
Left	1080
MaxButton	0 'False
MinButton	0 'False
Top	1170
Width	6810

TABLE 36.3: The Properties of the frmControl Form (continued)

Object: CommandButton

Name: cmdApplyNewHeight3D

Property	Value
Caption	"Apply New &Height 3D"
Enabled	0 'False
Height	375
Left	1440
Top	2760
Width	2055

Object: Horizontal scroll bar

Name: hsbHeight3D

Property	Value
Height	375
LargeChange	10
Left	120
Max	290
Min	90
Top	2760
Value	190
Width	1215

Object: CommandButton

Name: cmdApplyNewCellWidth

Property	Value
Caption	"Apply New Cell &Width"
Enabled	0 'False
Height	375
Left	1440
Top	1440
Width	2055

TABLE 36.3: The Properties of the frmControl Form (continued)

Object: Horizontal scroll bar
Name: hsbCellWidth

Property	Value
Height	375
LargeChange	10
Left	120
Max	125
Min	50
Top	1440
Value	65
Width	1215

Object: CommandButton
Name: cmdBackTo3DWorld

Property	Value
Caption	"&Back to 3D World"
Height	495
Left	2520
Top	3600
Width	1575

Object: Horizontal scroll bar
Name: hsbAngleSpeed

Property	Value
Height	255
Left	1560
Max	20
Min	1
Top	480
Value	10
Width	1215

36

TABLE 36.3: The Properties of the frmControl Form (continued)

Object: Horizontal scroll bar

Name: hsbDistanceSpeed

Property	Value
Height	255
Left	1560
Max	50
Min	10
Top	120
Value	30
Width	1215

Object: Label

Name: lblHeight3D

Property	Value
Caption	"Height 3D: 190 Pixels"
Height	255
Left	120
Top	2400
Width	1695

Object: Label

Name: lblCellWidth

Property	Value
Caption	"Cell Width: 65 Pixels"
Height	255
Left	120
Top	1080
Width	1575

TABLE 36.3: The Properties of the frmControl Form (continued)

Object: Label
Name: Label1

Property	Value
Caption	"Distance Speed:"
Height	255
Left	120
Top	120
Width	1335

Object: Label
Name: Label2

Property	Value
Caption	"Angle Speed:"
Height	255
Left	120
Top	480
Width	1335

36

FIGURE 36.2:

The frmControl form in design mode

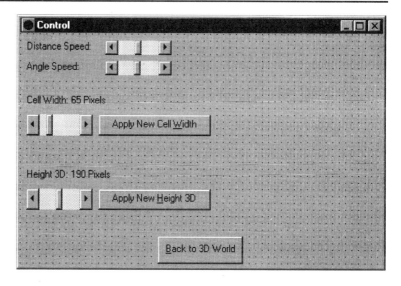

The General Declarations
Section of the frmControl Form

- Enter the following code in the General Declarations section of the frmControl form:

```
Option Explicit
```

This code forces variables declarations.

Attaching Code to the Load
Event of the frmControl Form

Whenever the user displays the frmControl form, the Form_Load( ) procedure of the frmControl form is executed.

- Enter the following code in the Form_Load( ) form of the frmControl form:

```
Private Sub Form_Load( )

hsbAngleSpeed.Value = gAngleSpeed
hsbDistanceSpeed.Value = gDistanceSpeed
hsbCellWidth.Value = gCellWidth
hsbHeight3D.Value = gHeight3D

End Sub
```

This code performs various initializations. You'll learn more about the purpose of these initializations later in this chapter. For now, note that the code you entered here sets the Value properties of various scroll bars according to the values of the global variables. When you load a frmControl form, the Value properties of the scroll bars are as set during the visual implementation of the form. During the execution of the program, the user may change the value of the scroll bars of the frmControl form, and then close the form. Later, the user may open the frmControl form again. But what will be the setting of the scroll bars? As you'll see, the global variables are updated after the user changes the scroll bar positions. So the next time the frmControl form is loaded, the scroll bar positions are set as they were the last time the frmControl form was opened.

Attaching Code to the Back To 3D World Button of the frmControl Form

The frmControl form includes the Back To 3D World command button. The user can change the setting of the 3D floor (by changing the scroll bar positions), and then click the Back To 3D World button to return to the 3D picture of the form.

- Enter the following code in the cmdBackTo3DWorld_Click( ) procedure of the frmControl form:

```
Private Sub cmdBackTo3DWorld_Click( )

    frmMyWorld.Show

End Sub
```

36

This code executes the Show method on the frmMyWorld form, which makes the frmMyWorld form to be the active window.

NOTE Recall that you displayed the frmControl form as a nonmodal window. This means that the user does not have to close the frmControl form before returning to the frmMyWorld form. So for example, if a portion of the frmMyWorld form is exposed on the monitor, the user can click inside the frmMyWorld form to make the frmMyWorld window active. Nevertheless, an easier way to return to the frmMyWorld form is to click the Back To 3D World button.

Attaching Code to the Change Event of the Distance Speed Horizontal Scroll Bar

The Distance Speed scroll bar of the frmControl from lets the user set the speed at which to move forward or backward around the 3D floor.

- Enter the following code in the hsbDistanceSpeed_Change( ) procedure of the frmControl form:

```
Private Sub hsbDistanceSpeed_Change( )

    gDistanceSpeed = hsbDistanceSpeed.Value

End Sub
```

The hsbDistanceSpeed_Change( ) procedure is executed whenever the user changes the Distance Speed scroll bar position of the frmControl form. This code sets the gDistanceSpeed global variable to the Value property of the Distance Speed Scroll bar.

Recall that in the Form_KeyDown( ) and Form_MouseMove( ) procedures of the frmMyWorld form you execute the Advance method with gDistanceSpeed as its parameter. So putting it all together, the user sets the position of the Distance Speed scroll bar, and the new position of the scroll bar will determine the amount by which the user will advance forward or backward in the 3D picture.

Attaching Code to the Change Event of the Angle Speed Scroll Bar

You'll now attach code to the Change event of the Angle Speed scroll bar of the frmControl form.

- Enter the following code in the hsbAngleSpeed_Change( ) procedure of the frmControl form:

```
Private Sub hsbAngleSpeed_Change( )

    gAngleSpeed = hsbAngleSpeed.Value

End Sub
```

This code sets the value of the gAngleSpeed variable to the Value property of the Angle Speed scroll bar.

The hsbAngleSpeed_Change( ) procedure is executed whenever the user changes the Angle Speed scroll bar position. This code sets the gAngleSpeed global variable to the Value property of the Angle Speed Scroll bar.

Recall that in the Form_KeyDown( ) and Form_MouseMove( ) procedures of the frmMyWorld form you increase or decrease the Angle property of the Floor control by gAngleSpeed. So putting it all together, the user sets the position of the Angle Speed scroll bar, and this new position will determine the amount by which the user will rotate clockwise or counterclockwise in the 3D picture.

36

Setting New Room Sizes at Runtime

It is interesting to note that you can change the cell width of the floor at runtime. Why is this feature important? Because the 3D picture looks different when the cell width is different. So during runtime, you can determine the cell where the user is currently located, and when the user is within a certain range of cells, your code will change the cell width. This way, you'll be able to create different rooms on the same 3D floor.

Attaching Code to the Change Event of the Cell Width Scroll Bar

You'll now attach code to the Change event of the hsbCellWidth scroll bar.

Determining the Current Cell

When determining the current cell (the cell where the user is currently located), remember that the X and Y properties of the Floor control always indicate the current pixel location of the user.

Furthermore, remember that the (0,0) point of the floor is the lower-left corner of 2D floor. This means that the cell on the leftmost column on the lower row of the 2D floor is cell (0,0). To determine the current cell, you can use the following statements:

```
CurrentCol = _
    Int(frmMyWorld.Floor1.X / frmMyWorld.Floor1.
    CellWidth)

CurrentRow = _
    Int(frmMyWorld.Floor1.Y / frmMyWorld.Floor1.
    CellWidth)
```

For example, if X is equal to 70 and Y is equal to 150, and the cell width is equal to 60 pixels, then:

```
CurrentCol = Int(70/60) = 1
CurrentRow = Int(150/60) = 2
```

The preceding calculations mean that if you look at the 2D ASCII view of the floor, the user's current cell location is on the second column from the left and the third row from the button.

When you know how to calculate the user's current cell, you can perform various interesting effects.

To begin with, in the Form_KeyDown() and Form_MouseMove() procedures of the frmMyWorld form you can determine the user's new cell position. And *before* displaying the new 3D view, you can determine based on the user's new cell position whether to change the characteristics of the rooms. For example, you can change the colors of the floors, stripes, ceiling or floors, and you can change the width of the rooms (as we will discuss next).

- Enter the following code in the hsbCellWidth_Change( ) procedure of the frmControl form:

```
Private Sub hsbCellWidth_Change( )

    cmdApplyNewCellWidth.Enabled = True

    gCellWidth = hsbCellWidth.Value

    lblCellWidth.Caption = _
        "Cell Width: " + Str(gCellWidth) + " Pixels"

End Sub
```

This code enables the Apply New Cell Width button:

```
cmdApplyNewCellWidth.Enabled = True
```

36

Normally, the Apply New Cell Width button is disabled. However, now that the user changed the Cell Width scroll bar, it makes sense to enable the Apply Cell Width button. (Once the user clicks the Apply New Cell Width button, the new cell width will take effect.)

NOTE   As previously stated, you'll change the cell width of the rooms during runtime whenever the user enters a room that you want to display as a larger or smaller room. The only reason we implement the mechanism for changing cell width inside the frmControl form is to make it easier to follow the code that is required for changing the cell width. But again, notice how powerful this feature is; it lets you change the sizes of the rooms at runtime!

The gCellWidth global variable is set to the new Value property of the Cell Width scroll bar:

```
gCellWidth = hsbCellWidth.Value
```

Finally, the lblCellWidth label is updated to display the new setting of the Cell Width scroll bar:

```
lblCellWidth.Caption = _
        "Cell Width: " + Str(gCellWidth) + " Pixels"
```

Again, to a person who is playing your game, the actual number of the cell width is not important. What is important to your users is the appearance of entering smaller or larger rooms as they travel around the 3D floor.

Applying the New Cell Width

In the MyWorld program, the user clicks the Apply New Cell Width button to make the change of the cell width effective. Here is how you apply the new cell width:

- Enter the following code in the cmdApplyNewCellWidth_Click( ) procedure of the frmControl form:

```
Private Sub cmdApplyNewCellWidth_Click( )

Dim OpenResult
Dim NumberOfRows, NumberOfCols

cmdApplyNewCellWidth.Enabled = False

' Set the new Cell Width
frmMyWorld.Floor1.CellWidth = gCellWidth

' Find number of rows in the floor file
NumberOfRows = FindNumOfRows

' Find number of columns in the floor file
NumberOfCols = FindNumOfCols

' Initialize and open the 3D Floor control

frmMyWorld.Floor1.FileName = gFloorFileName

frmMyWorld.Floor1.hWndDisplay = frmMyWorld.hWnd
frmMyWorld.Floor1.NumOfRows = NumberOfRows
frmMyWorld.Floor1.NumOfCols = NumberOfCols
```

```
' Initial position
frmMyWorld.Floor1.X = 1 * frmMyWorld.Floor1.CellWidth + 25
frmMyWorld.Floor1.Y = 1 * frmMyWorld.Floor1.CellWidth + 25

' Initial direction
frmMyWorld.Floor1.Angle = 0

' Open the FLR file
OpenResult = frmMyWorld.Floor1.Open

cmdBackTo3DWorld_Click

End Sub
```

Basically, this code is very similar to the code you entered in the Form_Load( ) procedure of the frmMyWorld form. That is, you load the floor file. This process of opening the floor file is performed so fast that the user will not notice that the floor file is being loaded all over again. Of course, before applying the Open method, you set the CellWidth property of the floor.

The Apply New Cell Width button is disabled:

```
cmdApplyNewCellWidth.Enabled = False
```

It makes sense to disable this button because this procedure applies the new cell width, so there is no need to have the Apply New Cell Width button enabled anymore.

The CellWidth property of the Floor control is set to the new cell width:

```
' Set the new Cell Width
frmMyWorld.Floor1.CellWidth = gCellWidth
```

The default cell width that the Floor control uses is 65 pixels. The minimum cell width is 30 pixels, and the maximum cell width is 200 pixels.

At this point, make sure not to display the 3D picture of the floor. That is, the Floor control is currently loaded, all of its parameters are calculated, and the 3D picture of the floor is displayed inside the frmMyWorld form. In the preceding statement, you changed the CellWidth property of the floor. This naturally confuses the Floor control. In fact, the rest of the statements that you entered complete the process of opening the floor file.

36

The number of rows and columns are calculated:

```
' Find number of rows in the floor file
NumberOfRows = FindNumOfRows

' Find number of columns in the floor file
NumberOfCols = FindNumOfCols
```

The FileName property is set:

```
frmMyWorld.Floor1.FileName = gFloorFileName
```

Other properties that require initialization prior to opening the floor file are set:

```
frmMyWorld.Floor1.hWndDisplay = frmMyWorld.hWnd
frmMyWorld.Floor1.NumOfRows = NumberOfRows
frmMyWorld.Floor1.NumOfCols = NumberOfCols
```

The user's initial position is set:

```
' Initial position
frmMyWorld.Floor1.X = 1 * frmMyWorld.Floor1.CellWidth + 25
frmMyWorld.Floor1.Y = 1 * frmMyWorld.Floor1.CellWidth + 25

' Initial direction
frmMyWorld.Floor1.Angle = 0
```

Here you set the user's current position to a new initial position. You can leave the current cell unchanged; however, because the cell width changed, you need to include code that ensure that the user's current position is not inside a solid cell.

And finally, the floor file is opened:

```
' Open the FLR file
OpenResult = frmMyWorld.Floor1.Open
```

The last statement in the procedure executes the cmdBackTo3DWorld_Click( ) procedure:

```
cmdBackTo3DWorld_Click
```

This causes the 3D picture to be displayed. It will be displayed with the new properties that you set, including the new cell width.

Setting the Height of the 3D Picture

So far in this book, the 3D floor pictures that you displayed have always had the same height. You'll now learn how to set a new height for the 3D picture.

Why will you need to set a new height for the 3D picture? Suppose that you are implementing a very complex 3D virtual reality game that lets the user view more than one floor on the screen simultaneously. In such cases, you may want to display the 3D floors with a smaller height so that you can fit as many 3D floor pictures on the user's monitor as possible. Similarly, you may want to display the currently active floor with a greater height (for emphasis).

In the MyWorld program the mechanism that enables the user to increase or decrease the floor height is implemented in the frmControl form simply to make the code that implements the mechanism easier to understand.

36

NOTE As stated, you can place more than one 3D picture on the screen. For example, if your "world" consists of five floors, then you can either place five Floor controls in the form that displays your 3D pictures, or create five different forms, each containing one Floor control. In the following chapters you'll learn how to display moving objects in the floors. The beauty of displaying several floors simultaneously on the monitor is that the user can move around one floor and still see the objects on the other floors moving. Depending on the objective of the game and the moving object seen, the user may decide to switch to another floor.

Attaching Code to the Change Event of the Height 3D Scroll Bar

You'll now attach code to the Change event of the Height 3D scroll bar. The hsbHeight3D_Change( ) procedure of the frmControl floor is executed whenever the user changes the Height 3D scroll bar.

- Enter the following code in the hsbHeight3D_Change( ) procedure of the frmControl form:

```
Private Sub hsbHeight3D_Change( )

    cmdApplyNewHeight3D.Enabled = True

    gHeight3D = hsbHeight3D.Value

    lblHeight3D.Caption = _
            "Height 3D: " + _
            Str(gHeight3D) + _
            " Pixels"

End Sub
```

This code enables the Apply New Height 3D button:

```
cmdApplyNewHeight3D.Enabled = True
```

It makes sense to enable the Apply New Height 3D button at this point because the user has changed the Height 3D scroll bar.

The new position of the Height 3D scroll bar is assigned to the gHeight3D global variable:

```
gHeight3D = hsbHeight3D.Value
```

Finally, the lblHeight3D label is updated:

```
lblHeight3D.Caption = _
            "Height 3D: " + _
            Str(gHeight3D) + _
            " Pixels"
```

Applying the New Height to the 3D Picture

Once the user changes the position of the Height 3D scroll bar, the Apply New Height 3D button is enabled. You'll now write the code that applies the new height to the 3D picture.

- Enter the following code in the cmdApplyNewHeight3D_Click( ) procedure of the frmControl form:

```
Private Sub cmdApplyNewHeight3D_Click( )
```

```
Dim OpenResult
Dim NumberOfRows, NumberOfCols

cmdApplyNewHeight3D.Enabled = False

' Set the new Height 3D
frmMyWorld.Floor1.Height3D = gHeight3D

' Find number of rows in the floor file
NumberOfRows = FindNumOfRows

' Find number of columns in the floor file
NumberOfCols = FindNumOfCols

' Initialize and open the 3D Floor control

frmMyWorld.Floor1.FileName = gFloorFileName

frmMyWorld.Floor1.hWndDisplay = frmMyWorld.hWnd
frmMyWorld.Floor1.NumOfRows = NumberOfRows
frmMyWorld.Floor1.NumOfCols = NumberOfCols

' Initial position
frmMyWorld.Floor1.X = 1 * frmMyWorld.Floor1.CellWidth + 25
frmMyWorld.Floor1.Y = 1 * frmMyWorld.Floor1.CellWidth + 25

' Initial direction
frmMyWorld.Floor1.Angle = 0

' Open the FLR file
OpenResult = frmMyWorld.Floor1.Open

cmdBackTo3DWorld_Click

End Sub
```

This code displays the 3D picture with a new height. Basically, you are simply changing the Height3D property of the Floor control:

```
' Set the new Height 3D
frmMyWorld.Floor1.Height3D = gHeight3D
```

However, just as you did when you set a new value for the CellWidth property of the Floor control, you have to open the Floor file all over again. The code that opens the Floor control is similar to the code that you wrote in the Form_Load( ) procedure of the frmMyWorld form.

The default value used for the Height3D property of the Floor control that is supplied with this book is 90 pixels. The minimum value that you can assign to this property is 90 pixels, and the maximum value is 290 pixels.

Implementing the frmASCIIView Form

Whenever the user selects ASCII View from the Options menu the ASCII View window is displayed. You'll now implement the frmASCIIView form.

- Select Form from the Insert menu of Visual Basic.

Visual Basic responds by inserting a new form into the MyWorld project.

- Save the new form as AscView.FRM in the C:\WinGPrg\CH35 directory.

- Implement the frmASCIIView form with the Properties settings listed in Table 36.4. When you're finished, the frmASCIIView form should look as shown in Figure 36.3.

FIGURE 36.3:

The frmASCIIView form in design mode

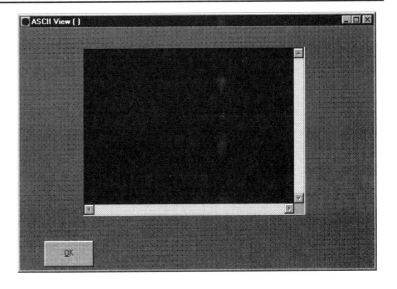

TABLE 36.4: The Properties of the frmASCIIView Form

Object: Form

Name: frmASCIIView

Property	Value
BackColor	Light gray
BorderStyle	1 'Fixed Single
Caption	"ASCII View ( )"
Height	6135
Icon	C:\WinGPrg\CH35\MyWOrld.ICO
Left	435
MaxButton	0 'False
MinButton	0 'False
Top	195
Width	8790

36

Object: TextBox

Name: txtASCIIView

Comment: The Locked property is set to True. This means that the user cannot change the contents of the text box.

Property	Value
BackColor	Black
Font Name	"Courier New"
Font Size	8.25
ForeColor	White
Height	3975
Left	1560
Locked	−1 'True
MultiLine	−1 'True
ScrollBars	3 'Both
Top	480
Width	5415

TABLE 36.4: The Properties of the frmASCIIView Form (continued)

Object: CommandButton

Name: cmdOK

Property	Value
Caption	"&OK"
Height	615
Left	600
Top	5040
Width	1215

The General Declarations Section of the frmASCIIView Form

- Enter the following code in the General Declarations section of the frmASCII-View form:

```
Option Explicit
```

This statement forces variable declarations.

Attaching Code to the OK button of the frmASCIIView Form

You'll now attach code to the Click event of the OK button of the frmASCII-View form.

- Enter the following code in the cmdOK_Click( ) procedure of the frmASCII-View form:

```
Private Sub cmdOK_Click( )
```

```
    Unload Me

End Sub
```

This code unloads the frmASCIIView form. So whenever the user clicks the OK button of the ASCII View window, the ASCII View window is closed.

Attaching Code to the Paint Event of the frmASCIIView Form

36

You'll now attach code to the Paint event of the frmASCIIView form.

- Enter the following code in the Form_Paint( ) procedure of the frmASCIIView form:

```
Private Sub Form_Paint( )

    ' Update the caption of the window
    Me.Caption = frmMyWorld.Caption

    ' Update the txtASCIIView text box.
    ' (To display the ASCII view of the floor)
    UpdateASCIILabel

End Sub
```

This code updates the caption of the form:

```
    Me.Caption = frmMyWorld.Caption
```

and then the text box is filled with the 2D map of the floor:

```
    UpdateASCIILabel
```

You'll write the code of the UpdateASCIILabel procedure in the next section.

Filling the Text Box with the 2D Map of the floor

You'll now write the code of the UpdateASCIILabel procedure. This procedure (which you executed from the Form_Paint( ) procedure of the frmASCIIView form) fills the text box with the contents of the 2D map.

- Make sure that the frmASCIIView item is highlighted inside the Project window, click the View Code button inside the Project window, and finally select Procedure from the Insert menu of Visual Basic.

Visual Basic responds by displaying the Insert Procedure dialog box.

- Make sure the Procedure option button is selected, set the name of the procedure to UpdateASCIILabel, and then click the OK button of the Insert Procedure dialog box.

Visual Basic responds by inserting the UpdateASCIILabel procedure in the general section of the frmASCIIView form.

- Enter the following code in the UpdateASCIILabel procedure of the frmASCII-View form:

```
Public Sub UpdateASCIILabel( )

''''''''''''''''''''''''''''''''
' This procedure displays
' the floor in ASCII format.
''''''''''''''''''''''''''''''''

Dim FileNum
Dim Contents As String
Dim CurrentCol
Dim CurrentRow
Dim ReplacePosition
Dim PositionCounter
Dim FileLength
Dim CurrentLocationInString

CurrentCol = _
Int(frmMyWorld.Floor1.X / frmMyWorld.Floor1.CellWidth)
```

```
CurrentRow = _
Int(frmMyWorld.Floor1.Y / frmMyWorld.Floor1.CellWidth)

CurrentLocationInString = _
(frmMyWorld.Floor1.NumOfRows - CurrentRow - 1) * _
(frmMyWorld.Floor1.NumOfCols + 2) + _
CurrentCol + 1

' Get a free file number
FileNum = FreeFile

'''MsgBox gFloorFileName

' Open the file
Open gFloorFileName For Input As FileNum

' Get the file length
FileLength = LOF(FileNum)

' Read the file contents
Contents = Input(FileLength, FileNum)

' Close the file
Close FileNum

' Place the "+" character at the user's current location
If CurrentLocationInString < Len(Contents) Then
    Mid(Contents, CurrentLocationInString, 1) = "+"
End If

txtASCIIView.Text = Contents

End Sub
```

This code fills the text box with the contents of the 3D map of the floor.

Implementing the About Window

You'll now implement the frmAbout form.

- Select Form from the Insert menu of Visual Basic.

Visual Basic responds by inserting a new form into the MyWorld project.

- Save the new form as About.FRM in the C:\WinGPrg\CH35 directory.

- Implement the frmAbout form with the Properties settings listed in Table 36.5. When you're finished, the form should look as shown in Figure 36.4.

TABLE 36.5: The Properties of the frmAbout Form

Object: Form
Name: frmAbout

Property	Value
BorderStyle	1 'Fixed Single
Caption	"About"
Height	5415
Icon	C:\WinGPrg\Icons\MyWorld.ICO
Left	1095
MaxButton	0 'False
MinButton	0 'False
Picture	C:\WinGPrg\CH35\About.BMP
Top	660
Width	7410

Object: CommandButton
Name: cmdOK

Property	Value
Caption	"&OK"
Height	495
Left	5040
Top	1080
Width	855

FIGURE 36.4:

The frmAbout form in design mode

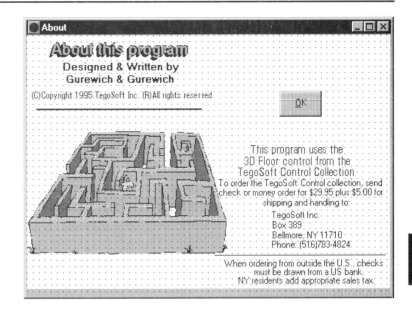

Attaching Code to the OK Button of the About Window

You'll now attach code to the Click event of the OK button of the About window.

- Enter the following code in the cmdOK_Click( ) procedure of the frmAbout form:

```
Private Sub cmdOK_Click( )

    ' Unload the form
    Unload Me

End Sub
```

This code unloads the frmAbout form.

Implementing the Help Window

You'll now implement the frmHelp form.

- Select Form from the Insert menu of Visual Basic.

Visual Basic responds by inserting a new form into the MyWorld project.

- Save the new form as Help.FRM in the C:\WinGPrg\CH35 directory.
- Implement the frmHelp form with the Properties settings listed in Table 36.6. When you're finished, the form should look as shown in Figure 36.5.

FIGURE 36.5:

The frmHelp form in design mode

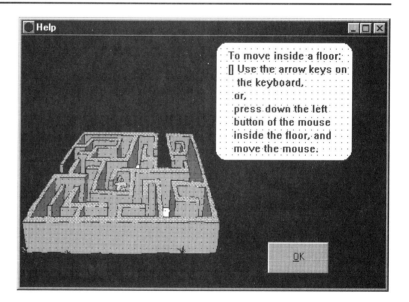

Attaching Code to the OK Button of the Help Window

You'll now attach code to the Click event of the OK button of the frmHelp form.

TABLE 36.6: The Properties of the frmHelp Form

Object: Form

Name: frmHelp

Property	Value
BorderStyle	3 'Fixed Dialog
Caption	"Help"
Height	5250
Icon	C:\WinGPrg\Icons\MyWorld.ICO
Left	1080
MaxButton	0 'False
MinButton	0 'False
Picture	C:\WinGPrg\CH35\Help.BMP
Top	1170
Width	7380

Object: CommandButton

Name: cmdOK

Property	Value
Caption	"&OK"
Height	615
Left	4920
Top	3960
Width	1215

36

- Enter the following code in the cmdOK_Click( ) procedure of the frmHelp form:

```
Private Sub cmdOK_Click( )

    Unload Me

End Sub
```

This code unloads the frmHelp form.

Summary

In this chapter you started to implement the MyWorld program. As you saw, the Control window includes code that lets the user change the characteristics of the 3D rooms and halls. Typically, you'll implement the mechanism that changes these characteristics from within the procedures that move the user's current position. That is, your code will examine the user's new cell position, and based on the new cell's position your code will display the rooms and halls with different colors, different cell width, different ceiling, and so on.

In the next chapter you'll continue to implement the MyWorld program. In particular, you'll learn how to move objects within the 3D floor.

CHAPTER

THIRTY-SEVEN

Adding Static Objects to the 3D Floor

In this chapter you'll learn how to add static objects to the 3D floor of the MyWorld program. As you'll soon see, adding static objects is very easy with the Floor OCX control.

Creating the Static Object

Your first step is to create the BMP file of the static object. You can use Paintbrush to create this BMP file. In particular, your objective is to place the President Lincoln object in one of the rooms. This means that you have to draw a picture of President Lincoln.

Figure 37.1 shows the Linc00.BMP picture and its mask, the MLinc00.BMP picture. Recall that BMP files have to be saved as 256-color BMP files. The Linc00.BMP and MLinc00.BMP files reside in the C:\WinGPrg\CH35 directory.

FIGURE 37.1:

The Linc00.BMP picture (a picture of president Lincoln) and its mask, the MLinc00.BMP picture

Placing Objects in the 3D Picture

You can place objects in the 3D picture during design time, or you can place them during runtime. Let's start by placing an object in the 3D picture during design time. (In the next chapter we'll place animated objects in the picture during runtime.)

- Use a text editor program such as Notepad to load the MyWorld.FLR file, which resides in the C:\WinGPrg\CH35 directory.

- Type the character A in the middle of the upper-left room.

The MyWorld.FLR file should now look as shown in Figure 37.2.

FIGURE 37.2:
Typing the character A in the upper-left room of the MyWorld.FLR file

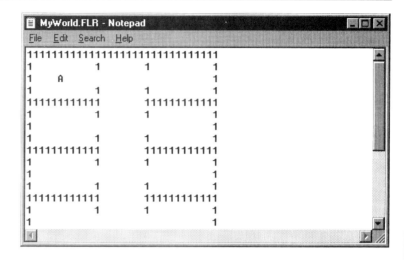

Loading the Lincoln Sprite

You'll now add code to tell the Floor control that the A character is the Lincoln object.

- Add code to the beginning of the Form_Load( ) procedure of the frmMy-World form, so that it looks as follows:

```
Private Sub Form_Load( )

Dim OpenResult As Integer
Dim NumberOfRows, NumberOfCols

''''''''''''''''''''
' Load the sprites.
''''''''''''''''''''
' Set the path for the BMP files of the sprites

If Right(App.Path, 1) <> "\" Then
   Floor1.SpritePath = App.Path + "\"
Else
```

```
      Floor1.SpritePath = App.Path + "\"
   End If

   ' Assign BMP files.
   Floor1.Sprite(65) = "Linc00.bmp"
   ...
   ...
   ...
End Sub
```

This code sets the SpritePath property of the Floor control:

```
' Set the path for the BMP files of the sprites

If Right(App.Path, 1) <> "\" Then
   Floor1.SpritePath = App.Path + "\"
Else
   Floor1.SpritePath = App.Path + "\"
End If
```

For example, if the MyWorld program resides in the C:\WinGPrg\CH35 directory, then the SpritePath property of the Floor control is set to C:\WinGPrg\CH35\.

Summary: The SpritePath Property of the Floor Control

During the execution of the program, your code will load many sprite files. Every time your code loads a BMP file, the path and filename must be specified. The SpritePath property allows you to specify only one path for all the sprite BMP files. Then, each time the Floor control needs to load a file, it will search in the directory named in the SpritePath property.

The next statement correlates the A character with the Linc00.BMP file:

```
' Assign BMP files.
Floor1.Sprite(65) = "Linc00.bmp"
```

Note that the ASCII value of the character A is 65.

That's it! The Lincoln object is now inside the upper-left room of the floor.

NOTE The code you added to the Form_Load( ) procedure assumes that the Linc00.BMP file and its mask file MLinc00.BMP reside in the directory from which the MyWorld program was executed.

To see the Lincoln object in action, take the following steps:

• Save your work and then execute the MyWorld program.

Windows responds by executing the MyWorld program, and the 3D picture shown in Figure 37.3 is displayed. Figure 37.4 shows the corresponding 2D ASCII view, where you can see that the user's current position (the + character) is in the lower-left room. (You'll need to scroll down to see this part of the FLR file on your screen.)

FIGURE 37.3:
The initial 3D view displayed upon starting the MyWorld program

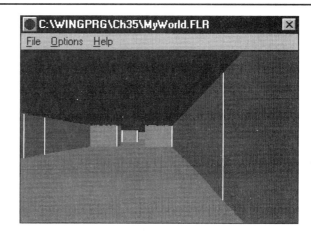

C:\WINGPRG\Ch35\MyWorld.FLR

File   Options   Help

37

Recall that you typed the code that sets the user's initial position in the Form_Load( ) procedure of the frmMyWorld form.

• Select ASCII View from the Options menu.

MyWorld responds by displaying the ASCII View of the floor. As shown in Figure 37.5, the A character appears in the upper-left room of the floor.

• Scroll down the contents of the text box in the ASCII View window.

FIGURE 37.4:

The initial user position in the 2D view

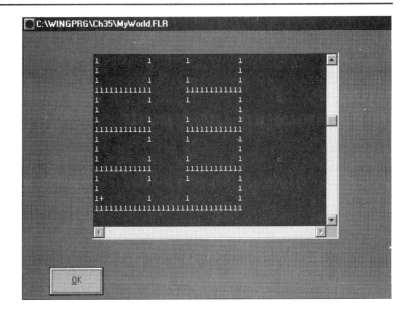

FIGURE 37.5:

The A character appears in the upper-left room of the floor.

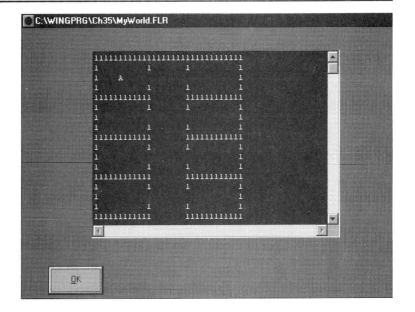

The + character (the user's current position) appears in the lower-left room of the 2D drawing shown in Figure 37.6. (You have to scroll down the drawing to see the lower-left room.)

FIGURE 37.6:

The view as seen from the entrance of the upper left room of the floor

- Use the keyboard keys (or the mouse) to go into the upper-left room where President Lincoln is located.

Figure 37.6 shows the view seen from the entrance of the upper-left room. As shown, the user can see Lincoln standing in the middle of the room.

FIGURE 37.7:

As you get closer to the Lincoln image, it appears larger.

- Use the keyboard keys (or the mouse) to move toward and away from Lincoln.

Figure 37.7 shows that as you get closer, Lincoln appears larger.

Experiment with the program by going around President Lincoln. In particular, note that the Lincoln sprite has the interesting feature of "looking" at you directly, no matter how you rotate around the object. For example, go into the upper-left room and position yourself so that you see the entrance of the room. As shown in Figure 37.8, you do not see the back of President Lincoln. No matter where you are in the room, you always see his face.

FIGURE 37.8:

Looking at the entrance of the upper-left room from inside the room

This feature is useful in games where the object automatically rotates so it always faces the user. If you don't want this effect, you'll have to implement code that displays different BMP files according to the user's movement. For example, when the user is located so that the back of President Lincoln should be shown, your code would replace the sprite with a BMP picture showing that view. In the next chapter you'll learn how to replace sprite BMP files during runtime.

Placing Other Static Objects in the Rooms

For practice, let's place another static object in another room of the 3D floor. You've already placed President Lincoln in the upper-left room, so now let's place President Kennedy in the upper-right room.

- Use a text editor such as Notepad to load the MyWorld.FLR file from the C:\WinGPrg\CH35 directory.

- Add the character B in the upper-right room of the floor.

- Add code to the beginning of the Form_Load( ) procedure of the frmMy-World form, so that it looks as follows:

```
Private Sub Form_Load( )

Dim OpenResult As Integer
Dim NumberOfRows, NumberOfCols

''''''''''''''''''''
' Load the sprites.
''''''''''''''''''''
' Set the path for the BMP files of the sprites

If Right(App.Path, 1) <> "\" Then
   Floor1.SpritePath = App.Path + "\"
Else
   Floor1.SpritePath = App.Path + "\"
End If

' Assign BMP files.
Floor1.Sprite(65) = "Linc00.bmp" 'The A character
Floor1.Sprite(66) = "Ken00.bmp" ' The B character
...
...
...
End Sub
```

37

This code correlates the Ken00.BMP picture with the character B in the My-World.FLR ASCII file:

```
Floor1.Sprite(66) = "Ken00.bmp"
```

Note that the ASCII value of the B character is 66.

The Ken00.BMP picture and its mask, MKen00.BMP, are shown in Figure 37.9. The Ken00.BMP and MKen00.BMP files reside in the C:\WinGPrg\CH35 directory.

FIGURE 37.9:

The Ken00.BMP picture and its mask, MKen00.BMP

- Execute the MyWorld program.
- Select ASCII View from the Options menu of the MyWorld program.

MyWorld responds by displaying the ASCII View window as shown in Figure 37.10.

- Use the keyboard keys (or the mouse) to travel to the upper-left room.

As you can see, the Lincoln object is still in this room.

- Now travel across the hall to where the Kennedy object resides.

Figure 37.11 shows that indeed the Kennedy object is in the upper-right room of the floor.

FIGURE 37.10:

The ASCII View window with the B character (which represents the President Kennedy object) in the upper-right room. The A character in the upper-left room represents the Lincoln object.

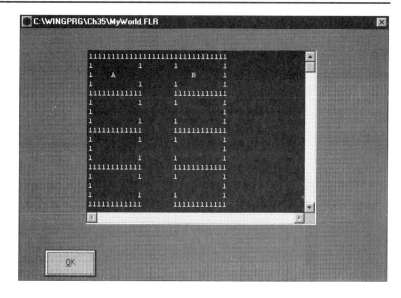

FIGURE 37.11:

The Kennedy object is in the upper-right room of the floor.

Placing Additional Objects of the Same Type

So far, you've placed the Lincoln object in the upper-left room and the Kennedy object in the upper right room. You'll now place additional Lincoln and Kennedy objects inside the 3D floor. As it turns out, once you've correlated BMP files with characters in the FLR file, you do not have to write any additional code to display additional copies of those objects inside the 3D floor. Simply add A characters and B characters to the MyWorld.FLR file. To see this in action:

- Use a text editor program such as Notepad to load the MyWorld.FLR file from the C:\WinGPrg\CH35 directory.

- Add the characters A and B inside the room on the second row from the top and in the right column (see Figure 37.12).

- Execute the MyWorld program, and select ASCII View from the Options menu.

FIGURE 37.12:

Placing Lincoln (A) and Kennedy (B) in the same room (2D View)

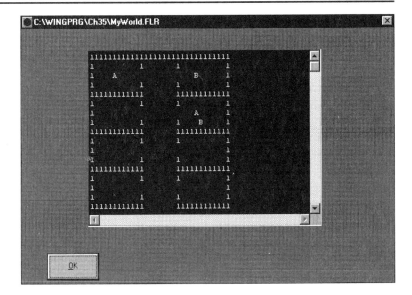

MyWorld responds by displaying the 2D floor as shown in Figure 37.12.

- Click the OK button to close the ASCII View window.

- Travel into the various rooms and verify that each room contains the appropriate object(s) as specified in the FLR file.

As shown in Figures 37.13 and 37.14, the object that is closer to the user's current location appears larger.

FIGURE 37.13:

Inside the room that contains both Lincoln and Kennedy. The user is currently closer to the Lincoln object.

FIGURE 37.14:

Inside the room that contains both Lincoln and Kennedy. The user is currently closer to the Kennedy object.

NOTE To see the view shown in Figure 3.14, you need to move around the Lincoln object and rotate to face the Kennedy object.

Placing Large Objects in the 3D Picture

You may have noticed that we've said nothing so far about the size of the Lincoln and Kennedy objects! This is because the Floor control sizes the objects according to the Floor dimensions and of course according to the distance from the user's current position to the object. Nevertheless, you should always try to make the sprites smaller, so that the Floor control can process their BMP files faster.

As an example, consider the BMP picture Woman.BMP and its mask file MWoman.BMP, which reside in the C:\WinGPrg\CH35 directory. These BMP pictures are shown in Figure 37.15.

- Use a text editor such as Notepad to add the character C inside the room on the left column and the third row from the top (see Figure 37.16).
- Add code, at the beginning of the Form_Load( ) procedure of the frmMy-World form, that correlates the C character with the Woman.BMP picture. The resulting procedure should look as follows:

```
Private Sub Form_Load( )

Dim OpenResult As Integer
Dim NumberOfRows, NumberOfCols
```

FIGURE 37.16:

Adding the C object to the room located in the right column, on the third row from the top (2D view)

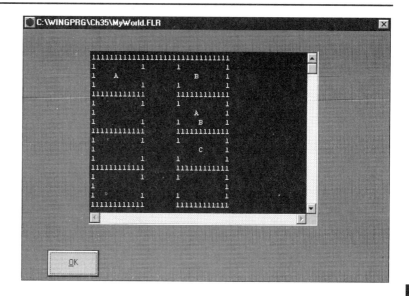

```
' ' ' ' ' ' ' ' ' ' ' ' ' ' ' ' ' '
' Load the sprites.
' ' ' ' ' ' ' ' ' ' ' ' ' ' ' ' ' '
' Set the path for the BMP files of the sprites

If Right(App.Path, 1) <> "\" Then
   Floor1.SpritePath = App.Path + "\"
Eise
   Floor1.SpritePath = App.Path + "\"
End If

' Assign BMP files.
Floor1.Sprite(65) = "Linc00.bmp" 'The A character
Floor1.Sprite(66) = "Ken00.bmp" 'The B character
Floor1.Sprite(67) = "Woman.bmp" 'The C character
...
...
...
End Sub
```

This code correlates the C character (whose ASCII value is 67) with the Woman.BMP file:

```
Floor1.Sprite(67) = "Woman.bmp" 'The C character
```

37

- Execute the MyWorld program and travel to the rooms that have objects in them.

As you can see in Figure 37.17, the room located in the right column and the third row from the top contains the Woman picture.

FIGURE 37.17:

The Woman.BMP sprite resides in the room located in the right column and the third row from the top.

Experimenting on Your Own

As an experiment, try creating your own BMP sprites and placing them in the MyWorld program:

- Use Paintbrush to draw your own BMP pictures (that will serve as sprites), and save them as 256-color BMP files.

- Create mask files for your new BMP pictures and save them as 256-color BMP files. Recall that the filename of a mask file must start with the character M, and the remaining characters must be the same as the original BMP file. Chapter 22 of this book includes a detailed discussion of creating mask files.

- Add objects to the rooms of the MyWorld.FLR file. Name the objects D, E, F, G, and so on.

- Add code to the Form_Load( ) procedure of the frmMyWorld form that correlates the characters that you added to the 2D ASCII floor file with the names of the BMP files. For example, if you create a Cat.BMP file (and its mask file MCat.BMP) and add the character D inside the MyWorld.FLR file, you would add this statement to the Form_Load( ) procedure:

```
Floor1.Sprite(68) = "Cat.bmp"  'The D character
```

Note that 68 is the ASCII value of the D character.

- Execute the MyWorld program and verify that your objects appear in the rooms where you placed them.

Summary

In this chapter you learned how to place static objects in the rooms of the 3D floor. As you saw, it takes only one line of code (in the Form_Load( ) procedure) to correlate the BMP of a sprite with the character that represents the sprite in the 2D FLR file.

In the next chapter you'll learn how to animate the sprites that you place in the rooms.

37

CHAPTER
THIRTY-EIGHT

Animating the Sprites in the 3D Pictures

In the previous chapter you learned how to place static sprites in a 3D picture during design time (by using a text editor to modify the 2D floor file). In this chapter you'll learn how to animate sprites inside the rooms of the 3D pictures. As you'll see, this requires placing the sprites in the 3D pictures during runtime.

The BMP Pictures of the Animation

Animation is created by displaying a sequence of frames. As usual, you can create the frames of the animation by using Paintbrush. Figure 38.1 shows three frames that are used for creating an animation that shows men fencing. Figure 38.2 shows the corresponding mask BMP files.

FIGURE 38.1:

The three frames of the fencing animation (Fence01.BMP, Fence02.BMP, and Fence03.BMP)

Loading the Sprites

You'll now write the code that loads the Fence??.BMP file.

FIGURE 38.2:

The mask files for the fencing animation (MFence01.BMP, MFence02.BMP, and MFence03.BMP)

- Enter the following code in the Form_Load( ) procedure of the frmMy-World form:

```
Private Sub Form_Load( )

Dim OpenResult As Integer
Dim NumberOfRows, NumberOfCols

''''''''''''''''''''
' Load the sprites.
''''''''''''''''''''
' Set the path for the BMP files of the sprites

If Right(App.Path, 1) <> "\" Then
   Floor1.SpritePath = App.Path + "\"
Else
   Floor1.SpritePath = App.Path + "\"
End If

' Assign BMP files.
Floor1.Sprite(65) = "Linc00.bmp" 'The A character
Floor1.Sprite(66) = "Ken00.bmp" 'The B character
Floor1.Sprite(67) = "Woman.bmp" 'The C character

Floor1.Sprite(11) = "Fence01.BMP"
Floor1.Sprite(12) = "Fence02.BMP"
Floor1.Sprite(13) = "Fence03.BMP"
```

38

```
   ...
   ...
   ...
   End Sub
```

The code you added correlates the Fence??.BMP pictures with the numbers 11, 12, and 13 as follows:

```
Floor1.Sprite(11) = "Fence01.BMP"
Floor1.Sprite(12) = "Fence02.BMP"
Floor1.Sprite(13) = "Fence03.BMP"
```

Here you correlated Fence01.BMP with sprite number 11. Why 11? You can have a total of 256 different sprites inside the 3D picture. So in essence, you can choose any integer number from 0 to 255. However, certain integers are taken already. For example, 1 is used for the walls. Similarly, 65, 66, and 67 are used for the Lincoln, Kennedy, and Woman sprites. So to summarize, you can select any integer number between 0 and 255, but do not use the same integer twice.

Using the Timer Control for the Animation

In displaying a series of frames for animation, your program needs to determine how long to display each frame before moving on to the next. The MyWorld program uses Visual Basic's Timer control for implementing the delay between frames.

- Place the Timer control inside the frmMyWorld form.

- Set the Name property of the Timer control to Timer1 (the default name that Visual Basic assigns to the Timer control).

- Set the Interval property of the Timer1 control to 250 milliseconds.

- Enter the following code in the Timer1_Timer( ) procedure of the frmMyWorld form:

```
Private Sub Timer1_Timer( )

Static FencingFrame

If FencingFrame = 0 Then FencingFrame = 10
```

```
FencingFrame = FencingFrame + 1
If FencingFrame = 14 Then
   FencingFrame = 11
End If

Floor1.SetCell 1, 5, FencingFrame

Floor1.Display3D

End Sub
```

This code declares a static variable:

```
Static FencingFrame
```

This means that the FencingFrame variable maintains its value even after the Timer1_Timer( ) procedure is terminated.

Next, an If statement determines whether this is the first time the Timer1_Timer( ) procedure has been executed:

```
If FencingFrame = 0 Then FencingFrame = 10
```

When the Timer1_Timer( ) procedure is executed for the first time, Visual Basic sets the values of the FencingFrame static variable to 0. Thus, the preceding If statement is satisfied when Timer1_Timer( ) is executed for the first time.

38

The FencingFrame variable is increased by 1, and an If statement is executed to make sure that FencingFrame does not exceed 13:

```
FencingFrame = FencingFrame + 1
If FencingFrame = 14 Then
   FencingFrame = 11
End If
```

So if you looked at the values of FencingFrame after executing the preceding If statement, you would see the following values:

10, 11, 12, 13, 10, 11, 12, 13, …

Recall that in the Form_Load( ) procedure you correlated the Fence??.BMP pictures as follows:

Fence00.BMP with 10

Fence01.BMP with 11

Fence02.BMP with 12

The following statement places a sprite inside a cell:

```
Floor1.SetCell 1, 5, FencingFrame
```

The first two parameters of the SetCell method are the cell coordinates. For example, cell (0,0) is the upper-left cell. As you know, this cell is occupied by a wall. So the SetCell method that you executed places a sprite in the cell at the second column from the left and the sixth row from the top.

The third parameter of the SetCell method indicates which sprite to place. So when FencingFrame is equal to 10, the SetCell method places the Fenc00.BMP sprite inside the cell. Then, the next time the Timer1_Timer( ) procedure is executed, FencingFrame is equal to 11, so Fence01.BMP is placed inside the cell. This process continues, and the sequence of sprites that the user sees is therefore Fence00.BMP, Fence01.BMP, Fence02.BMP, Fence00.BMP, Fence01.BMP, and so on.

Floor Coordinates and the SetCell Method

Recall that the Floor control has the properties X and Y, which indicate the pixel coordinates of the user's current location. These coordinates assume that (0,0) is the pixel at the lower-left corner of the floor.

With the SetCell method, however, the cell coordinates represented by the X and Y coordinates refer to the *upper*-left cell. That is, the leftmost cell on the top row is cell (0,0). For example, in the following 2D floor:

```
11111111
1.A....1
1......1
11111111
```

The A sprite is located on the third column from the left and second row from the top. Its cell coordinates are (X=2,Y=1).

The last statement in the Timer1_Timer( ) procedure displays the 3D picture:

```
Floor1.Display3D
```

To see your code in action:

- Execute the MyWorld program.

- Use the keyboard (or the mouse) to travel to the room located on the left column, and the second row from the top.

As you get into the room, you see a man fencing. Figure 38.3 shows one of the frames of the animation.

- Experiment with the MyWorld program and then select Exit to terminate the program.

FIGURE 38.3:

An animation of a man fencing is performed in the room on the left column, and the second room from the top (frame 1 of 3).

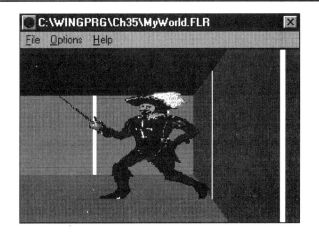

38

Placing Additional Animated Sprites in the 3D Picture

As practice, let's place additional animated sprites inside the 3D picture. In particular, let's place another fencing man in the room on the left column and the second row from the top.

- In the Timer1_Timer( ) procedure of the frmMyWorld form add another SetCell statement, placing another man in the other corner of the room. The resulting procedure should look as follows:

```
Private Sub Timer1_Timer( )

Static FencingFrame

If FencingFrame = 0 Then FencingFrame = 10

FencingFrame = FencingFrame + 1
If FencingFrame = 14 Then
   FencingFrame = 11
End If

Floor1.SetCell 1, 5, FencingFrame
Floor1.SetCell 1, 7, FencingFrame

Floor1.Display3D

End Sub
```

Here you added the following SetCell statement:

```
Floor1.SetCell 1, 7, FencingFrame
```

As you can see, the sprite is placed inside the cell located on the second column from the left and the eighth row from the top.

- Execute the MyWorld program.

- Use the keyboard (or the mouse) to travel to the room where you added the sprite. As you can see in Figure 38.4, now the room contains two men fencing.

In your own programs, concentrate your efforts on the cosmetic aspects. For example, instead of using only three frames for the animation, use additional frames to make the animation more realistic.

Another way to improve the animation is to display the animated sprites out of synchronization. That is, currently, the two fencers go through the same sequence of frames. A better way to implement this double animation is to display different sequences.

- Modify the Timer1_Timer( ) procedure( ) so that it looks as follows:

```
Private Sub Timer1_Timer( )
```

FIGURE 38.4:

The room contains two animated fencing men.

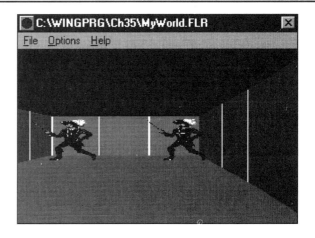

```
Static FencingFrame
Static FencingFrame2

If FencingFrame = 0 Then FencingFrame = 10
If FencingFrame2 = 0 Then FencingFrame = 12

FencingFrame = FencingFrame + 1
If FencingFrame = 14 Then
   FencingFrame = 11
End If

FencingFrame2 = FencingFrame2 + 1
If FencingFrame2 = 14 Then
   FencingFrame2 = 11
End If

Floor1.SetCell 1, 5, FencingFrame
Floor1.SetCell 1, 7, FencingFrame2

Floor1.Display3D

End Sub
```

Here you declared another static variable, named FencingFrame2. You've seen that the FencingFrame variable takes the following series of values:

10, 11, 12, 10, 11, 12 …

The FencingFrame2 variables takes the following series of values:

12, 13, 11, 12, 13, 11…

So now, as you enter the room, the two men are not synchronized as they perform the fencing animation.

Killing Your Enemies

Of course, no action game is complete without code that kills your enemies. Rather than get too realistic about this, we'll implement code that simply causes the fencing men to surrender whenever the user presses the space bar. Figure 38.5 shows the BMP picture of the fencing man surrendering and its mask file.

FIGURE 38.5:
Fence04.BMP (the fencing man surrendering) and its mask (MFence04.BMP)

Determining the User's Current Position

First we need to determine the user's current position. As you know, this position is indicated by the X and Y properties of the Floor control. Figure 38.6 shows the 2D MyWorld.FLR floor. The lower-left pixel of the floor has the coordinates (0,0). The coordinates of the room where the two men are fencing are calculated based on the CellWidth property of the Floor control. You can see that whenever the user's current position is within the range:

FIGURE 38.6:

Calculating the range of coordinates of the room where the two men are fencing

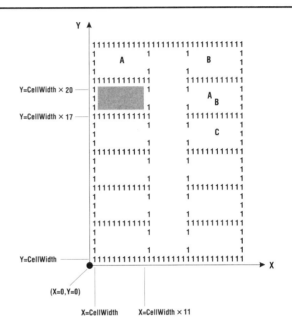

```
Floor1.X > Floor1.CellWidth _
   And _
Floor1.X < Floor1.CellWidth*11
   And _
Floor1.Y > Floor1.CellWidth*17
And _
Floor1.Y < Floor1.CellWidth*20
```

the user is inside the room where the two men are fencing.

- Enter the following code in the General Declarations section of the frmMy-World form:

```
Option Explicit
Dim gNoFencing
```

This code declares the general variable gNoFencing. As you might have guessed, this variable serves as a flag that indicates whether the two men should perform the fencing animation or should surrender. When gNoFencing is equal to 0, the fencing animation is performed. When gNoFencing is equal to 1, the two men surrender to the user. Note that upon starting the MyWorld program, Visual Basic sets the value of gNoFencing to 0. So this means that when the user enters the fencing room, the fencing animation is performed.

- Enclose the statements that show the fencing animation (in the Timer1_Timer( ) procedure of the frmMyWorld form) with an If statement that prevents the fencing animation whenever the gNoFencing variable is equal to 1. After you add this code, the Timer1_Timer( ) procedure should look as follows:

```
Private Sub Timer1_Timer( )
...
...
...
If gNoFencing = 0 Then
   Floor1.SetCell 1, 5, FencingFrame
   Floor1.SetCell 1, 7, FencingFrame2
End If

Floor1.Display3D

End Sub
```

That is, as long as gNoFencing is equal to 0, the fencing animation is performed. But if gNoFencing is equal to a number other than 0, no fencing animation will be performed.

- Add code to the Form_Load( ) procedure of the frmMyWorld form that correlates the number 14 with the Fence04.BMP file. After you add the code, the beginning of the Form_Load( ) procedure should look as follows:

```
Private Sub Form_Load( )

Dim OpenResult As Integer
Dim NumberOfRows, NumberOfCols
```

```
''''''''''''''''''''
' Load the sprites.
''''''''''''''''''''
' Set the path for the BMP files of the sprites

If Right(App.Path, 1) <> "\" Then
   Floor1.SpritePath = App.Path + "\"
Else
   Floor1.SpritePath = App.Path + "\"
End If

' Assign BMP files.
Floor1.Sprite(65) = "Linc00.bmp" 'The A character
Floor1.Sprite(66) = "Ken00.bmp"  'The B character
Floor1.Sprite(67) = "Woman.bmp"  'The C character

Floor1.Sprite(11) = "Fence01.BMP"
Floor1.Sprite(12) = "Fence02.BMP"
Floor1.Sprite(13) = "Fence03.BMP"

Floor1.Sprite(14) = "Fence04.BMP"
...
...
...
End Sub
```

This code correlates the number 14 with the Fence04.BMP file:

```
Floor1.Sprite(14) = "Fence04.BMP"
```

At this point, everything is ready to detect the user's current position and to make the two men surrender when the user is inside the room.

- Enter the following code at the end of the Form_KeyDown( ) procedure of the frmMyWorld form:

```
Private Sub Form_KeyDown(KeyCode As Integer, _
                         Shift As Integer)

Select Case KeyCode
    ....
    ....
    ....
End Select
```

```
If KeyCode = 32 Then
   If Floor1.X > Floor1.CellWidth And _
      Floor1.X < Floor1.CellWidth * 11 Then
         If Floor1.Y > Floor1.CellWidth * 17 And _
            Floor1.Y < Floor1.CellWidth * 20 Then

            Floor1.SetCell 1, 5, 14
            Floor1.SetCell 1, 7, 14

            If gNoFencing = 1 Then
               gNoFencing = 0
            Else
               gNoFencing = 1
            End If

         End If
   End If
End If

'''''''''''''''''''''''
' Display the 3D view
'''''''''''''''''''''''
Floor1.Display3D

End Sub
```

An If statement is used to determine whether the user has pressed the space bar:

```
If KeyCode = 32 Then
   ....
   ....
   ....
End If
```

The ASCII value of the space bar key is 32. So if the user pressed the space bar, the rest of the inner If statements are executed.

The code you entered detects that the user is in the fencing room, and then the men are shown in a surrendering position:

```
Floor1.SetCell 1, 5, 14
Floor1.SetCell 1, 7, 14
```

Another If statement is then executed:

```
If gNoFencing = 1 Then
    gNoFencing = 0
Else
    gNoFencing = 1
End If
```

This If...Else statement toggles the value of gNoFencing. So if the user enters the fencing room and presses the space bar, the men surrender. If the user presses the space bar again, the men start fencing again.

- Experiment with the MyWorld program. Use the keyboard or the mouse to get inside the fencing room, and then press the space bar.

As you can see, every time you press the space bar, the men either start fencing or they surrender to the user. The men in a surrendering position are shown in Figure 38.7.

FIGURE 38.7:
The two men surrender after the user presses the space bar.

38

It's Your World...

Its your world! You can create whatever you want in it! So do you like snakes? Why not place a snake inside one of the rooms?

The Snake01.BMP, Snake02.BMP, and Snake03.BMP pictures and their corresponding mask BMP files are shown in Figures 38.8, 38.9, and 38.10.

FIGURE 38.8:

The Snake01.BMP picture and its mask, MSnake01.BMP

FIGURE 38.9:

The Snake02.BMP picture and its mask, MSnake02.BMP

FIGURE 38.10:

The Snake03.BMP picture and its mask, MSnake03.BMP

Correlating the Snake BMP Pictures with Sprites

You'll now correlate the Snake??.BMP pictures with sprites.

- Add code to the Form_Load( ) procedure of the frmMyWorld form so that it looks as follows:

```
Private Sub Form_Load( )

Dim OpenResult As Integer
Dim NumberOfRows, NumberOfCols

''''''''''''''''''''
' Load the sprites.
''''''''''''''''''''
' Set the path for the BMP files of the sprites

If Right(App.Path, 1) <> "\" Then
   Floor1.SpritePath = App.Path + "\"
Else
   Floor1.SpritePath = App.Path + "\"
End If

' Assign BMP files.
Floor1.Sprite(65) = "Linc00.bmp" 'The A character
```

38

```
Floor1.Sprite(66) = "Ken00.bmp" 'The B character
Floor1.Sprite(67) = "Woman.bmp" 'The C character

Floor1.Sprite(11) = "Fence01.BMP"
Floor1.Sprite(12) = "Fence02.BMP"
Floor1.Sprite(13) = "Fence03.BMP"

Floor1.Sprite(14) = "Fence04.BMP"

Floor1.Sprite(20) = "Snake01.BMP"
Floor1.Sprite(21) = "Snake02.BMP"
Floor1.Sprite(22) = "Snake03.BMP"

....
....
....
End Sub
```

The code you added assigns the following sprites:

```
Floor1.Sprite(20) = "Snake01.BMP"
Floor1.Sprite(21) = "Snake02.BMP"
Floor1.Sprite(22) = "Snake03.BMP"
```

To perform the Snake animation, add code to the Timer1_Timer( ) procedure of the frmMyWorld form.

- Add the Snake animation code in the Timer1_Timer( ) procedure of the frmMyWorld form. After you add the code, procedure should look as follows:

```
Private Sub Timer1_Timer( )

Static FencingFrame
Static FencingFrame2
Static SnakeFrame

If FencingFrame = 0 Then FencingFrame = 10
If FencingFrame2 = 0 Then FencingFrame = 12
If SnakeFrame = 0 Then SnakeFrame = 20

FencingFrame = FencingFrame + 1
If FencingFrame = 14 Then
   FencingFrame = 11
End If
```

```
FencingFrame2 = FencingFrame2 + 1
If FencingFrame2 = 14 Then
   FencingFrame2 = 11
End If

SnakeFrame = SnakeFrame + 1
If SnakeFrame = 23 Then
   SnakeFrame = 20
End If

If gNoFencing = 0 Then
   Floor1.SetCell 1, 5, FencingFrame
   Floor1.SetCell 1, 7, FencingFrame2
End If

Floor1.SetCell 1, 9, SnakeFrame

Floor1.Display3D

End Sub
```

As you can see, the code that implements the Snake animation is basically the same as the code for the Fencing animation.

- Execute the MyWorld program.

- Use the keyboard (or the mouse) to go inside the room on the left column and the third row from the top.

Inside the room you can see the Snake animation. Figure 38.11 shows a frame from the Snake animation.

Enhancing the MyWorld Program

You'll now enhance the MyWorld program by implementing a dynamic (animated) sprite of a man running across the hall with a sword in his hand. The man waves his sword as he runs. You'll also implement a lamp as a soft sprite, and you'll play a famous Kennedy speech whenever the user enters the Kennedy room.

FIGURE 38.11:

Viewing the Snake animation

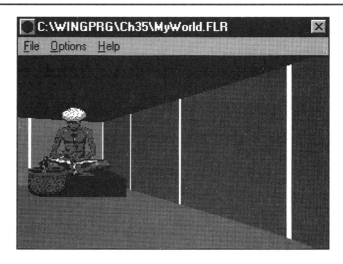

- Place a check box in the frmControl form. Set the Name property of the check box to chkRunningMan.

- Enter the following code in the chkRunningMan_Click( ) procedure of the frmControl form:

```
Private Sub chkRunningMan_Click( )

    If gRunningMan = 1 Then
        gRunningMan = 0
    Else
        gRunningMan = 1
    End If

End Sub
```

This code toggles the value of the global variable gRunningMan between 0 and 1. You'll declare the gRunningMan variable, a flag that determines whether to animate the running man, in the following section.

- In the General Declarations section of the frmMyWorld.BAS module declare the following two global variables:

```
Public gRunningMan
Public gKennedyVoice
```

As stated in the previous section, the gRunningMan variable enables or disables the running man from running.

You'll use the gKennedyVoice variable to play back the Kennedy speech whenever the user enters the Kennedy room.

- Place the TegoSoft Multimedia control in the frmMyWorld form. Make sure that the Name property of the Multimedia control is Tegomm1.

- Use a text editor such as Notepad to load the MyWorld.FLR file, and add the D character inside the lower-left room. The D character represents the lamp (which you'll later set as a soft sprite).

- Add code in the Form_Load( ) procedure of the frmMyWorld form so that it looks as follows:

```
Private Sub Form_Load( )

Dim OpenResult As Integer
Dim NumberOfRows, NumberOfCols

Tegomm1.Visible = False
Tegomm1.DeviceType = "WaveAudio"
If Right(App.Path, 1) <> "\" Then
   Tegomm1.FileName = App.Path + "\"
Else
   Tegomm1.FileName = App.Path + "\"
End If
Tegomm1.FileName = Tegomm1.FileName + "8Kenned3.WAV"
Tegomm1.Command = "Open"


''''''''''''''''''''''
' Load the sprites.
''''''''''''''''''''''
' Set the path for the BMP files of the sprites

If Right(App.Path, 1) <> "\" Then
   Floor1.SpritePath = App.Path + "\"
Else
   Floor1.SpritePath = App.Path + "\"
End If
```

```
' Assign BMP files.
Floor1.Sprite(65) = "Linc00.bmp" 'The A character
Floor1.Sprite(66) = "Ken00.bmp" 'The B character
Floor1.Sprite(67) = "Woman.bmp" 'The C character

Floor1.Sprite(11) = "Fence01.BMP"
Floor1.Sprite(12) = "Fence02.BMP"
Floor1.Sprite(13) = "Fence03.BMP"

Floor1.Sprite(14) = "Fence04.BMP"

Floor1.Sprite(20) = "Snake01.BMP"
Floor1.Sprite(21) = "Snake02.BMP"
Floor1.Sprite(22) = "Snake03.BMP"

Floor1.Sprite(25) = "Fence01.BMP"
Floor1.Sprite(26) = "Fence02.BMP"
Floor1.Sprite(27) = "Fence03.BMP"

Floor1.Sprite(68) = "Lamp.BMP"
' Set sprite number 68 as a soft sprite.
' (i.e. the user can walk through this sprite).
' e.g. Light.BMP
Floor1.SetSpriteSoft (68)

' Update the variable with the name of the floor file.
If Right(App.Path, 1) <> "\" Then
   gFloorFileName = App.Path + "\" + FLOOR_FILE_NAME
Else
   gFloorFileName = App.Path + FLOOR_FILE_NAME
End If

''' MsgBox gFloorFileName

' Set units to pixels
Me.ScaleMode = 3 'Pixels

' Find number of rows in the floor file
NumberOfRows = FindNumOfRows

' Find number of columns in the floor file
NumberOfCols = FindNumOfCols

' Initialize and open the 3D floor control
```

```
Floor1.FileName = gFloorFileName

Floor1.hWndDisplay = Me.hWnd
Floor1.NumOfRows = NumberOfRows
Floor1.NumOfCols = NumberOfCols

gCellWidth = 65
Floor1.CellWidth = gCellWidth

' Initial position
Floor1.X = 1 * Floor1.CellWidth + 25
Floor1.Y = 1 * Floor1.CellWidth + 25

' Initial direction
Floor1.Angle = 0

' Open the FLR file
OpenResult = Floor1.Open

Me.Caption = Floor1.FileName

gAngleSpeed = DELTA_ANGLE
gDistanceSpeed = DELTA_DISTANCE
gHeight3D = 190

End Sub
```

38

The code that you added sets the Visible property of the Multimedia control to False, and the DeviceType is set so that the Multimedia control will play through the sound card:

```
Tegomm1.Visible = False
Tegomm1.DeviceType = "WaveAudio"
```

You set the Visible property of the Multimedia control to False because there is no need to see the Multimedia control at runtime.

The FileName property of the Multimedia control is set to the 8Kenned3.WAV file, which is assumed to reside in the directory from which the program is executed:

```
If Right(App.Path, 1) <> "\" Then
   Tegomm1.FileName = App.Path + "\"
Else
   Tegomm1.FileName = App.Path + "\"
End If
```

```
Tegomm1.FileName = Tegomm1.FileName + "8Kenned3.WAV"
```

Finally, the Open command is issued:

```
Tegomm1.Command = "Open"
```

The sprites that hold the BMP pictures of the running man are declared as 25, 26, and 27 as follows:

```
Floor1.Sprite(25) = "Fence01.BMP"
Floor1.Sprite(26) = "Fence02.BMP"
Floor1.Sprite(27) = "Fence03.BMP"
```

The Lamp.BMP picture is declared as the D character:

```
Floor1.Sprite(68) = "Lamp.BMP"
```

(The ASCII value of D is 68). The Lamp.BMP file was generated as 256-color BMP file with Paintbrush.

Next, you set the Lamp sprite to be a soft sprite:

```
' Set sprite number 68 as a soft sprite.
' (i.e. the user can walk through this sprite).
' e.g. Light.BMP
Floor1.SetSpriteSoft (68)
```

- Add the following code to the Timer1_Timer( ) procedure of the frmMy-World form:

```
Private Sub Timer1_Timer( )

Static FencingFrame
Static FencingFrame2
Static SnakeFrame

Static YInHall
Static HallFrame

If FencingFrame = 0 Then FencingFrame = 10
If FencingFrame2 = 0 Then FencingFrame = 12
If SnakeFrame = 0 Then SnakeFrame = 20

FencingFrame = FencingFrame + 1
If FencingFrame = 14 Then
    FencingFrame = 11
End If
```

```
FencingFrame2 = FencingFrame2 + 1
If FencingFrame2 = 14 Then
   FencingFrame2 = 11
End If


SnakeFrame = SnakeFrame + 1
If SnakeFrame = 23 Then
   SnakeFrame = 20
End If


If gNoFencing = 0 Then
   Floor1.SetCell 1, 5, FencingFrame
   Floor1.SetCell 1, 7, FencingFrame2
End If
Floor1.SetCell 1, 9, SnakeFrame

If gRunningMan = 1 Then
   If YInHall > 0 Then
      Floor1.SetCell 15, YInHall, 0
   End If

   If HallFrame = 0 Then
      YInHall = YInHall + 1
   End If

   If YInHall >= 22 Then
      YInHall = 1
   End If
   HallFrame = HallFrame + 1
   If HallFrame > 2 Then
      HallFrame = 0
   End If
   Floor1.SetCell 15, YInHall, 25 + HallFrame

End If

If Floor1.X > Floor1.CellWidth * 19 And _
   Floor1.Y > Floor1.CellWidth * 21 Then
      If gKennedyVoice = 0 Then
         gKennedyVoice = 1
         Tegomm1.Command = "Prev"
         Tegomm1.Command = "Play"
      End If
```

```
    Else
        gKennedyVoice = 0
        Tegomm1.Command = "Stop"
    End If


    Floor1.Display3D

 End Sub
```

The code that you added declares two static variables:

```
    Static YInHall
    Static HallFrame
```

An If statement is then executed to determine whether to display the running man across the hall:

```
 If gRunningMan = 1 Then
     If YInHall > 0 Then
         Floor1.SetCell 15, YInHall, 0
     End If

     If HallFrame = 0 Then
         YInHall = YInHall + 1
     End If

     If YInHall >= 22 Then
         YInHall = 1
     End If
     HallFrame = HallFrame + 1
     If HallFrame > 2 Then
         HallFrame = 0
     End If
     Floor1.SetCell 15, YInHall, 25 + HallFrame

 End If
```

If gRunningMan is equal to 1, the animation is performed.

Next, an inner If statement is executed to examine the value of YInHall:

```
 If YInHall > 0 Then
     Floor1.SetCell 15, YInHall, 0
 End If
```

The last parameter of the SetCell method is 0. This means that the sprite located at X=15 and Y=YInHall is erased. YInHall represents the current Y cell coordinate of the running man. When displaying the running man, the previous running man sprite is erased. But you want to make sure that YInHall is greater than 0.

The animation of the running man consists of three BMP pictures. During the animation, the running man is displayed in the current cell as Fence01.BMP. The next time the Timer1_Timer( ) procedure is executed, the running man is displayed in the same cell location, but as the Fence02.BMP picture. The third time the Timer1_Timer( ) procedure is executed, the running man is displayed as Fence03.BMP. The fourth time the Timer1_Timer( ) procedure is executed, however, the running man is displayed as Fence01.BMP but in the next Y cell location. The static variable HallFrame serves as a counter that determines the current BMP picture of the running man. Thus, Hall-Frame takes the following values:

0, 1, 2, 0, 1, 2, …

Every time HallFrame returns to 0, the Y cell coordinate (YInCell) is increased by 1. This is implemented as follows:

```
If HallFrame = 0 Then
    YInHall = YInHall + 1
End If
```

Another If statement makes sure that YInHall does not exceed 22:

```
If YInHall >= 22 Then
        YInHall = 1
End If
```

HallFrame is increased by 1, and an If statement is executed to make sure that Hall-Frame does not exceed 2:

```
HallFrame = HallFrame + 1
If HallFrame > 2 Then
    HallFrame = 0
End If
```

We declare the BMP files that represent the running man as sprites 25, 26, and 27 (or 25+0, 25+1, and 25+2). So SetCell displays the running man as follows:

```
Floor1.SetCell 15, YInHall, 25 + HallFrame
```

Now let's look at the code that starts the playback of the 8Kenned3.WAV file whenever the user enters the Kennedy room.

38

An If statement is executed to determine whether the user is in the Kennedy room:

```
If Floor1.X > Floor1.CellWidth * 19 And _
    Floor1.Y > Floor1.CellWidth * 21 Then
      If gKennedyVoice = 0 Then
          gKennedyVoice = 1
          Tegomm1.Command = "Prev"
          Tegomm1.Command = "Play"
      End If
Else
      gKennedyVoice = 0
      Tegomm1.Command = "Stop"
End If
```

This code plays the WAV file whenever the user is inside the Kennedy room.

Further Enhancements

In the Timer1_Timer( ) procedure you wrote code that moves the running man from one side of the hall to the other side. When the man reaches the end of the hall, you display the running man as starting to run from the YInHall=1 cell all over again.

Of course, you can make the animation more interesting by writing code that displays the running man going back across the hall. That is, once the man reaches the end of the hall, your code can start decreasing the value of YInHall. Thus, the running man will be shown as running across the hall, back and fourth.

You can also write code that changes the X cell coordinates of the running man. This way, you can design the running man as running into rooms, exiting rooms, and running across the halls.

You can also set the X and Y cell coordinates of the running man so that they are based on the coordinates of the user's current position. That is, the X and Y cell coordinates of the running man can be calculated to approach the user's position, so that the running man appears to chase the user. If the user stands in one place for too long, the running man will catch the user. (Every time the Timer1_Timer( ) procedure is executed, the running man gets closer to the user's current position.)

Summary

In this chapter you added some significant enhancements to the MyWorld program. You learned how to animate sprites inside the 3D picture. As you saw, typically you'll use a Timer control that displays the frames of the animation one after the other.

You also learned to detect the user's current location and change the animation based on that location. When the user is in the Fencing room, the fencing animation stops, and the fencing men surrender to the user.

You also implemented code that plays a WAV file when the user enters the Kennedy room, and you added a lamp, implemented as a soft sprite (an object the user can pass through).

38

INDEX

Note to the Reader: First-level entries are in **bold.** Boldfaced numbers indicate pages where you will find the principal discussion of a topic or the definition of a term. *Italic* page numbers indicate pages where topics are illustrated in figures.

Numbers

C

D

N

O

T

u

in RECORD.EXE, 298, 304, 307–308

in WAVInfo.EXE, 246, 261–265

V

Value property, in WAVInfo.EXE, 245, 262–264

variables. *See* **BAS modules; General Declarations section**

VBBMP.EXE program, 20, **92–107, 110–139**

BMP files, **94–106**

determining number of colors in, 138–139

opening and displaying, 94–99, *96*

procedures for opening and displaying BMP files, 117–122, *120*

saving as 16-color or 256-color files, 99–101, *100, 101*

sizing pictures with composite colors, 103–106, *105, 106*

sizing windows and pictures proportionally, 100

solid versus composite colors in, 101–103, *102, 103*

creating project file, **110**

executing, **92–94**, 139

frmVBBMP form, **110–130**

Caption property, 121

closing WinG session, 116–117

creating, 110–111, *112, 113*

creating menu bar of, 111–113, *114*

DisplayBM( ) function, 126–130, *126, 129*

error traps, 119, 120

File menu Exit command code, 117

Filter property, 119

Form_Load( ) procedure, 115–116

Form_Paint( ) procedure, 122–124, *122, 123*

Form_Resize( ) procedure, 124–125

Form_Unload( ) procedure, 116–117

General Declarations section, 114–115

hWndDisplay property, 116

mnuExit_Click procedure, 117

procedures for opening and displaying BMP files, 117–122, *120*

properties of, 111

ScaleMode property, 115

Help menu, **131–135**

creating About option, 131

creating About window, 132, *133*

creating About window OK button, 133

creating Help option, 131

creating Help window, 133–134, *135*

creating Help window OK button, 135

If statements, 124, 125

Information menu, **136–139**

creating, 136–138

determining number of colors in BMP files, 138–139

mnuExit_Click( ) procedure, 117

W

X

y

FOR EVERY COMPUTER QUESTION,
THERE IS A SYBEX BOOK THAT HAS THE ANSWER

Each computer user learns in a different way. Some need thorough, methodical explanations, while others are too busy for details. At Sybex we bring nearly 20 years of experience to developing the book that's right for you. Whatever your needs, we can help you get the most from your software and hardware, at a pace that's comfortable for you.

We start beginners out right. You will learn by seeing and doing with our **Quick & Easy** series: friendly, colorful guidebooks with screen-by-screen illustrations. For hardware novices, the **Your First** series offers valuable purchasing advice and installation support.

Often recognized for excellence in national book reviews, our **Mastering** titles are designed for the intermediate to advanced user, without leaving the beginner behind. A **Mastering** book provides the most detailed reference available. Add our pocket-sized **Instant Reference** titles for a complete guidance system. Programmers will find that the new **Developer's Handbook** series provides a more advanced perspective on developing innovative and original code.

With the breathtaking advances common in computing today comes an ever increasing demand to remain technologically up-to-date. In many of our books, we provide the added value of software, on disks or CDs. Sybex remains your source for information on software development, operating systems, networking, and every kind of desktop application. We even have books for kids. Sybex can help smooth your travels on the **Internet** and provide **Strategies and Secrets** to your favorite computer games.

As you read this book, take note of its quality. Sybex publishes books written by experts—authors chosen for their extensive topical knowledge. In fact, many are professionals working in the computer software field. In addition, each manuscript is thoroughly reviewed by our technical, editorial, and production personnel for accuracy and ease-of-use before you ever see it—our guarantee that you'll buy a quality Sybex book every time.

To manage your hardware headaches and optimize your software potential, ask for a Sybex book.

FOR MORE INFORMATION, PLEASE CONTACT:

Sybex Inc.
2021 Challenger Drive
Alameda, CA 94501
Tel: (510) 523-8233 • (800) 227-2346
Fax: (510) 523-2373

Sybex is committed to using natural resources wisely to preserve and improve our environment. As a leader in the computer books publishing industry, we are aware that over 40% of America's solid waste is paper. This is why we have been printing our books on recycled paper since 1982.

This year our use of recycled paper will result in the saving of more than 153,000 trees. We will lower air pollution effluents by 54,000 pounds, save 6,300,000 gallons of water, and reduce landfill by 27,000 cubic yards.

In choosing a Sybex book you are not only making a choice for the best in skills and information, you are also choosing to enhance the quality of life for all of us.

[1727-9] The WinG Bible: For Visual Basic 4 Programmers

GET A FREE CATALOG JUST FOR EXPRESSING YOUR OPINION.

Help us improve our books and get a **FREE** full-color catalog in the bargain. Please complete this form, pull out this page and send it in today. The address is on the reverse side.

Name _____ Company _____

Address _____ City _____ State ____ Zip _____

Phone (   ) _____

1. How would you rate the overall quality of this book?

❑ Excellent
❑ Very Good
❑ Good
❑ Fair
❑ Below Average
❑ Poor

2. What were the things you liked most about the book? (Check all that apply)

❑ Pace
❑ Format
❑ Writing Style
❑ Examples
❑ Table of Contents
❑ Index
❑ Price
❑ Illustrations
❑ Type Style
❑ Cover
❑ Depth of Coverage
❑ Fast Track Notes

3. What were the things you liked *least* about the book? (Check all that apply)

❑ Pace
❑ Format
❑ Writing Style
❑ Examples
❑ Table of Contents
❑ Index
❑ Price
❑ Illustrations
❑ Type Style
❑ Cover
❑ Depth of Coverage
❑ Fast Track Notes

4. Where did you buy this book?

❑ Bookstore chain
❑ Small independent bookstore
❑ Computer store
❑ Wholesale club
❑ College bookstore
❑ Technical bookstore
❑ Other _____

5. How did you decide to buy this particular book?

❑ Recommended by friend
❑ Recommended by store personnel
❑ Author's reputation
❑ Sybex's reputation
❑ Read book review in _____
❑ Other _____

6. How did you pay for this book?

❑ Used own funds
❑ Reimbursed by company
❑ Received book as a gift

7. What is your level of experience with the subject covered in this book?

❑ Beginner
❑ Intermediate
❑ Advanced

8. How long have you been using a computer?

years _____

months _____

9. Where do you most often use your computer?

❑ Home
❑ Work

❑ Both
❑ Other _____

10. What kind of computer equipment do you have? (Check all that apply)

❑ PC Compatible Desktop Computer
❑ PC Compatible Laptop Computer
❑ Apple/Mac Computer
❑ Apple/Mac Laptop Computer
❑ CD ROM
❑ Fax Modem
❑ Data Modem
❑ Scanner
❑ Sound Card
❑ Other _____

11. What other kinds of software packages do you ordinarily use?

❑ Accounting
❑ Databases
❑ Networks
❑ Apple/Mac
❑ Desktop Publishing
❑ Spreadsheets
❑ CAD
❑ Games
❑ Word Processing
❑ Communications
❑ Money Management
❑ Other _____

12. What operating systems do you ordinarily use?

❑ DOS
❑ OS/2
❑ Windows
❑ Apple/Mac
❑ Windows NT
❑ Other _____

13. On what computer-related subject(s) would you like to see more books?

_____

_____

_____

_____

14. Do you have any other comments about this book? (Please feel free to use a separate piece of paper if you need more room)

_____

_____

_____

_____

PLEASE FOLD, SEAL, AND MAIL TO SYBEX

SYBEX INC.
Department M
2021 Challenger Drive
Alameda, CA
94501

Let us hear from you.

alk to SYBEX authors, editors and fellow forum members.

et tips, hints and advice online.

ownload magazine articles, book art, and shareware.

Join the SYBEX Forum on **CompuServe**®

If you're already a CompuServe user, just type GO SYBEX to join the SYBEX Forum. If not, try CompuServe for free by calling 1-800-848-8199 and ask for Representative 560. You'll get one free month of basic service and a $15 credit for CompuServe extended services—a $23.95 value. Your personal ID number and password will be activated when you sign up.

Join us online today. Type GO SYBEX on CompuServe. If you're not a CompuServe member, call Representative 560 at 1-800-848-8199 .

SYBEX

(outside U.S./Canada call 614-457-0802)

What's on the CD-ROM?

Everything you'll need for this book is included on the CD-ROM. All you need is a PC with Windows installed (Windows 3.1x, Windows 95 or Windows NT), and Visual Basic for Windows version 4.0 or above. If you have a sound card, you'll also be able to hear the programs.

The CD-ROM includes all the files required for implementing the book's projects—all the WAV, MIDI, BMP, Movie AVI files, as well as various software such as OCX files, WinG files, and others. The OCX files are supplied in both 16-bit and 32-bit versions, so that you can implement both 16-bit and 32-bit programs.

The CD-ROM includes the book's EXE programs, so that you can immediately execute the programs and gain a better understanding of what they are supposed to do. It also includes the program source code, so that you can compare your work with the finished programs.

Installing the CD-ROM

To install the CD-ROM, read the ReadMe.TXT file, located on its root directory. Also, make sure to read the software license agreement, which you'll find in the CD's LICENSE directory.